# FORMS OF PLURALISM AND DEMOCRATIC CONSTITUTIONALISM

# FORMS OF PLURALISM AND DEMOCRATIC CONSTITUTIONALISM

EDITED BY
ANDREW ARATO,
JEAN L. COHEN, AND
ASTRID VON BUSEKIST

Columbia University Press
*New York*

Columbia University Press
*Publishers Since 1893*
New York    Chichester, West Sussex
cup.columbia.edu

Columbia University Press wishes to express its appreciation for assistance given
by the Columbia Alliance Program in the publication of this book.

Library of Congress Cataloging-in-Publication Data
Names: Arato, Andrew, editor. | Cohen, Jean L., 1946– editor. | Busekist,
    Astrid von, editor.
Title: Forms of pluralism and democratic constitutionalism / edited by
    Andrew Arato, Jean L. Cohen, Astrid von Busekist.
Description: New York : Columbia University Press, 2018. | Includes
    bibliographical references and index.
Identifiers: LCCN 2018022949 | ISBN 9780231187022 (cloth : alk. paper) |
    ISBN 9780231187039 (pbk : alk. paper) | ISBN 9780231546959 (e-book)
Subjects: LCSH: Cultural pluralism—Political aspects—Case studies. |
    Multiculturalism—Political aspects—Case studies. | State, The.
Classification: LCC HM1271 .F685 2018 | DDC 305.8—dc23
LC record available at https://lccn.loc.gov/2018022949

Columbia University Press books are printed on permanent
and durable acid-free paper.
Printed in the United States of America

Cover design: Lisa Hamm
Cover image: Copyright © Successió Miró Archive / Artists Rights Society (ARS),
New York / ADAGP, Paris 2018.

# CONTENTS

# ACKNOWLEDGMENTS

We would like to thank the Columbia University Alliance Program for their generous grant that sponsored our conference on Forms of Pluralism and Democratic Constitutionalism, which took place in Paris in 2016 at Columbia's Reid Hall and led to the publication of this volume. We would also like to thank the Department of Political Science and Sciences Po for their generous support.

# FORMS OF PLURALISM AND DEMOCRATIC CONSTITUTIONALISM

# INTRODUCTION

*Forms of Pluralism and Democratic Constitutionalism*

ANDREW ARATO AND JEAN L. COHEN

I ssues of political form and jurisdiction are once again on the international intellectual agenda. This is so in part due to the increase and politicization of plurality within societies, and even more to the challenges posed by political and legal globalization, the proliferation of transnational legal regimes, and the increased mobility of persons, legal and artificial, across borders. Two questions animate this volume: "What political form is best suited to preserving and expanding the achievements of democratic constitutionalism in our globalizing and pluralistic twenty-first-century world?" and "What principles should structure the allocation of jurisdiction and representation in a democratic polity?" We use the term *political form* to refer to the type of polity operating in the international order: that is, whether it is a sovereign state, a nation-state, an empire, an international organization, a confederation, a federation of states, or a federal state. This dimension is distinct from regime type and multicultural policy.[1] Indeed, the very way we pose the question entails that the political regime we are presupposing/advocating is a democratic constitutionalist one. The volume's consideration of what forms of organized pluralism are compatible with it focuses less on multicultural policies or the specifics of democratic regime type and more on jurisdictional pluralism, political forms of the polity, and their effects. We thus take up the pressing question of how to deal with societal pluralism, and deep divisions over values and ways of life, from a distinct political theoretical perspective.

It is our thesis that questions of political form and jurisdiction have again become highly salient thanks to the current, albeit hardly the first, crisis of the modern sovereign nation-state. Historians are right to describe the nineteenth century as the age of nationalism. Although many also depict the twentieth century as the triumph of the nation-state, with more justice it could be called the century of its failure, given the disastrous wars engaged in by and over nation-states despite the vast proliferation of the form.[2] In our current century, there are countless examples of the failure of the nation-state to solve the problem that brought it into being—the management of plurality and the self-determination of different political identities. Historically, it was assumed that the sovereign state was the requisite political form and that some variant of nationalism—the most important ideology of nation-states—was the best response to the question of how to attain political autonomy and to integrate and govern diversity. Civic-republican and ethno-nationalist conceptions of the nation, whatever their fundamental differences, were both based on the assumption that a people wishing to exist politically could and should have its own state, with the relevant collective identity (nationality) defined on ethnic, linguistic, racial, religious, or purely political grounds. In the dismantling of multinational and colonial empires, it was assumed by many that the liberation of the numerous minorities, and at times the majority, also depended on each "people" achieving its own sovereign state. Self-determination of peoples was the slogan: the representative, sovereign nation-state was the supposed solution to the problem of social plurality and democratic equality, domestically and internationally. For those nation-states that are, perforce, multinational, minority rights, guaranteed by treaty or by domestic constitutions, seemed to be the way to manage politically salient diversity.

This assumption—the inevitability and superiority of the nation-state form—turned out to be fundamentally misleading given the heterogeneity and multiple natures of societal forms of difference in all modern societies and the changing realities of size, power, and market forces in the aftermath of WWII. With astonishing regularity, the various secessions, partitions, and processes of decolonization tended to produce or reproduce the same minority problems within the nation-state that the latter was expected to avoid. International laws designed to protect minorities in the generalized system of sovereign states were more often than not unenforceable moral desiderata and, at times, exacerbated or politicized otherwise relatively benign social divisions within the national citizenry, inviting discrimination or worse. The same is true of the so-called multicultural jurisdictions granted to internal minorities over family law and education.

For a long time, nevertheless, the achievements of democratic constitutionalism seemed to be closely linked to the modern sovereign nation-state with its claims to internal jurisdictional supremacy, external autonomy, monopoly over the legitimate use of force and coercive law, and priority regarding its citizens' loyalty. Social solidarity among the citizenry and its allegiance to the republic was assumed, at least under civic-nationalist assumptions, to be compatible with social plurality—of opinions, ethnicities, races, and religion—provided that equal individual rights, social justice, and a voice for all were ensured by the liberal democratic sovereign national welfare state.

This apparent consensus is gone today. One important intellectual and political tendency now links the modern democratic nation-state not with freedom but with "statism," entailing hierarchy and domination, and ties national identity not to civic solidarity but to the dominance of substantive domestic majorities along ethnic, racial, or religious lines and the exclusion of racialized others; it also associates the very idea of the supremacy and comprehensive domestic jurisdiction of public civil law (internal sovereignty) not with justice but with homogenization, leveling, antipluralism, and repression. Similarly, on the international level, external state sovereignty is linked to imperialist strivings, war, global inequality, and injustice. Indeed, what is striking today is the proliferation of challenges to the sovereign national state on the supra- and subnational levels in the name of autonomy, pluralism, and corporate self-governance. To many critics, not only is the nation-state a dismal failure when it comes to coping with diversity, but state sovereignty itself seems to be an anachronistic and dangerous myth antithetical to democracy, plurality, and justice. Today neither individual nor minority rights are deemed sufficient to mitigate the harms and inequalities entailed by the allocation of sovereignty to nation-states by the international legal and political system.[3]

Moreover, the monopoly over lawmaking, the supremacy and comprehensive scope of the sovereign state's internal jurisdiction and regulatory reach is being eviscerated by the increasing autonomy of multinational business corporations (wed to a particular form of legal pluralism and economic liberalism), the domestic and even transnational political reemergence of the corporate religious, and the expanding role of both public and private trans- and supranational governance institutions. In our view, the greatest challenges in the twenty-first century come from these sources—all of which undermine the sovereign state as fact and norm without providing functional equivalents that preserve or expand the achievements of democratic constitutionalism. However, we do not view the recent revival of nationalist-statist particularism by populists and power hungry political entrepreneurs (secular or religious) to be a normatively attractive alternative. Indeed, this, too, poses a serious threat to constitutional democracy. Although pretending to revive and protect the "real" sovereignty of peoples organized into states, the neopopulist nationalist, once in power, typically pushes for an exclusionary ethnic, racial, or religious conception of the people or nation while revealing a marked predilection for executive power and dictatorial methods at the expense of constitutionalism and basic rights. The rise of neopopulism, however, must be taken seriously: analysts should not throw out the baby—self-governing autonomous political communities oriented to freedom and social justice—with the bathwater of exclusionary nationalism, monistic absolute sovereignty, and protectionist particularism. In short, it is important to be cautious and clear regarding the particular features of the modern sovereign state that render it normatively objectionable or anachronistic and those that are normatively defensible, and to reflect carefully on the appropriate political forms and legal jurisdictions that might suitably transform, supplement, or replace it. Put a different way, before jettisoning the sovereign state, it would be wise to reflect on which political and legal formations can serve as normatively desirable functional equivalents in ways that expand rather than limit achievements in freedom and equality entailed in democratic constitutionalism that have so long been associated with that political form. Let us insist that the sovereign state is not necessarily a nation-state and that constitutionally democratic multinational and federal states can be sovereign without unfairly privileging a particular ethnos or substantive group of citizens and without being monist in political structure, imperialist, or exclusive regarding the jurisdiction of supranational governance institutions.

If the nation-state has failed as an answer to problems of diversity and political autonomy, what other options are available for managing pluralism, fostering self-government, and providing equal freedom in a normatively acceptable way? Few wish to restore or defend undemocratic multinational empires, even in the modern versions characteristic of the Soviet Union and China. Although forms of neocolonialism are still practiced, these no longer permit normative justification. Indeed, as part I of this volume shows, during the collapse of imperial structures, alongside questions of political regime (liberal democratic, communist, socialist, presidential, or parliamentary), the debate concerning their replacement was between advocates of the nation-state and those who sought alternatives to it due to its already anticipated difficulties and normative problems. The latter aspect has been largely forgotten. But it was and is profoundly misleading to assume the inevitability of the sovereign nation-state form at any point in the history of modernity because alternatives were proposed at the beginning, middle, late (the period of decolonization), and now again in our postmodern epoch. Yet, as indicated, it is also too soon to relegate the state form to the dustbin of history. Sovereignty regimes change over time, and a new one appropriate to new political and legal forms could be in the making. Today, however, an emergent antistate neo-medievalism seems to be on the agenda—one that resurrects corporate forms of sovereignty, transnational governance, and jurisdictional pluralism for economic, religious, or other groupings in the stead of the state, with no ordering principle nor public instance that can settle the inevitable conflicts or secure democracy, justice, and equal individual rights within or between the relevant domains.[4] Our interest is in those alternatives that promise to be more democratic, more inclusive, and more just than existing political forms and even many of the replacements that have been proposed. Just what alternatives are democratic, and which ones are suitable to twenty-first-century realities and well worth our inquiry?

This volume considers four principles of organization deemed alternatives to the sovereign nation-state: federation, subsidiarity, status group legal pluralism, and transnational corporate autonomy. None of these are new. Federation, religious status group jurisdictional autonomy, and corporate autonomy of socioeconomic groups have been important alternatives to the ideology and project of absolute royal sovereignty, and subsidiarity seemed to provide a substitute for the centralizing project of modern "monistic" state sovereignty at the beginning of the state-building process in Europe. Moreover, in the past and again today, they have been—in our view erroneously—equated with one another. For the most part, the sovereign state won out over its competitors; this history is being recovered in our postmodern epoch by theorists disillusioned with the limits of nation-states and interested in different pluralistic political and jurisdictional forms both within and above the state.[5] The recovery is made more plausible by the fact that, on their own and occasionally in combination, federal polities, status group legal pluralism, the subsidiarity principle, and corporate autonomy of socioeconomic groups have had some success in providing arrangements apparently more friendly to plurality and difference than supposedly homogeneous unitary and centralized nation-states, while also being associated with democratic constitutionalism.

The United States is the first large, modern federal republic, and the principle of federation was, from the beginning, considered an alternative to the nation-state form domestically and internationally.[6] Canada and Australia, too, have successfully experimented with different forms of federalism, the former with an asymmetric version. India has combined a fairly centralized federal state with status group legal pluralism and elements of asymmetric federalism, and in Israel religiously based legal pluralism is set up within a multinational society coexisting, however tenuously, in an ethno-national formally democratic unitary state. South Africa has a quasi-federal state with constitutional supremacy in an uneasy combination with elements of status group legal pluralism ("traditional" tribal jurisdictions). There and elsewhere, the corporate form has been a way for groups to attain immunities and jurisdictional and governance prerogatives over members and others in their control. All of these polities have democratic constitutionalist political regimes, however inadequately they function. The European Union (EU), alternatively, has been characterized as a new supranational political formation based on the principle of subsidiarity.

Nevertheless, as these examples show, each of these forms has normative (and empirical) problems from the standpoint of democracy and justice. As U.S. history shows, federal organization renders units autonomous but not necessarily democratic or rights respecting on the local level. It has often been linked to the domination of local elites, whereas the federal center has been criticized for homogenizing tendencies in the decentralized units. Moreover, federalism has been associated with socioeconomic inequality given the greater difficulties it has in effecting redistributive justice within and among the units than does a centralized state. Asymmetric federalism seems contrary to egalitarian principles and tends to trigger resentment and demands for more autonomy and powers on the part of privileged and nonprivileged groups. Status group legal pluralism and corporate autonomy of functional groups have often been established in terms of elite rule, nondemocratic internal hierarchy, and violation of especially women's but also workers and children's rights within the groups. Similar to the contemporary contractual self-understanding of incorporated membership groups and business entities, "jurisdictional political pluralism" privatizes public power, creating unaccountable and often undemocratic public-private governance hybrids.[7] In democratic republics, all power supposedly stems from the political community, and the individual is the carrier of citizenship and basic rights. Status group pluralism typically derives power and authority from traditional group and transcendent sources, and in either case it is largely unaccountable to the full membership and to the larger polity. Federal arrangements distribute powers between *public* governmental bodies at the center and among the units, guarding the sovereignty of the whole and of civil law, whereas religious status group legal pluralism establishes *private* particular jurisdictional governance entities within the state, sometimes with external political allegiances and in competition with public regulatory power. Contemporary corporate business entities also sever themselves from dependence on and regulation by the national state in which they are originally incorporated by becoming multi- or transnational entities. Moreover, they seek and seem able to escape regulation or accountability to public power on the transnational or "global" level by co-opting the plurality of legal regimes to serve their interests, rendering them normatively ambivalent from the perspective of liberal justice and democratic or constitutionalist principles.[8]

Finally, there is the ambivalence of the principle of subsidiarity, defended by some as a superior alternative to federalism because it is neither restricted to two levels of governance nor presupposes the sovereign state as its institutional embodiment (as do most existing political forms of federation today). But the principle of subsidiarity also can undermine democratic will formation and its efficacy. Some analysts of the European Union, global governance, and global constitutionalism, with an eye to plurality within and across existing states and regions, deem subsidiarity to be the best principle to guide the allocation of decision making and jurisdiction among organizational groups and levels of government. But insofar as it is associated with governance, rather than government, subsidiarity is also invoked by transnational corporate powers, economic or religious. Indeed, the term hails from Catholic theology when the Church competed with emerging modern states, and many today seek to resurrect the idea of "sphere sovereignty" linked to principles of subsidiarity as a better way to reflect and organize diversity and community than state sovereignty.[9] Others present subsidiarity as an efficient and benign administrative organizational principle that unburdens political bodies of technical decision making beyond their expertise. Still other critics view it as an antidemocratic mode of technocratic governance that establishes new elites, inequalities, and powers. Instead of openly, inclusively, and democratically debating and resolving political issues that arise over governance levels and policies, the latter occlude them and decide them arbitrarily.

Which of these forms and principles is a superior answer to the problems of difference and demands of group autonomy from the perspective of democracy and liberal or social democratic constitutionalism? Can their drawbacks be managed or minimized? Is their combination the best way to imagine institutional design, and if so, under the overarching framework of which political form? Indeed, when a political form "fails" from the perspective of democratic constitutionalism and individual equality, what are the reasons for this failure? Are there certain preconditions for its success? This volume engages in an interdisciplinary dialogue on the best match between the core principles of democratic constitutionalism (equal liberty, voice, status, and justice for all individuals, and accountable public decision making) and the various strategies and legal and political forms for constructing, integrating, and managing pluralism that have become salient in the twenty-first century.

The authors of this introduction do have a clear preference for federal political forms among the various alternatives discussed here. Given contemporary imperatives of size and coordination necessary to cope with globalization and the problems states face regarding migration, ecology, corporate economic power, and so forth, it seems to us that democratic constitutionalism and public regulation to prevent injustice and provide public goods can survive only if existing on multiple coordinated levels of political association The federal principle excels in this regard. As indicated previously, most polities today are already multinational and multireligious, and democratic constitutionalism and political autonomy seem at risk in most states absent membership in a regional association enabling coordination and requiring democratic republican political regimes as a condition of membership. Certainly the issue of size is pertinent again in the context of contemporary modes of economic globalization and corporate economic power. We see federating and constitutional pluralism as a way to grow larger that has an elective affinity with republican representative political regimes and democratic constitutionalism.[10] We believe the same cannot be said for status group legal pluralism, the principle of subsidiarity on its own, or transnational corporate autonomy coupled with legal particularism.[11] The dangers of illiberal or undemocratic unit autonomy under federalism can be mitigated by the supremacy of a federal constitution with a well-developed structure of rights. The opposite dangers of federal supremacy can be mitigated by a constitutional amendment rule requiring high-level participation on both union and unit levels, or more generally by a principle of shared jurisdiction over jurisdiction (Kompetenz-Kompetenz). Within a federal frame, the principle of subsidiary can indeed foster efficiency without replacing voice, and the drawbacks of existing forms of status group pluralism could be mitigated and ultimately turned into more benign modes of multicultural policy by being subject to the regulation of self-regulation by the federal republic and its civil rights requirements. Federation acknowledges the plurality of ways of life without reifying it, and unlike status group legal pluralism, federation has a flexible linkage between substantive identity and political form. Likewise with the forms of legal pluralism currently associated with multinational corporate business enterprise. Only regional federal power and, ultimately, legal and perhaps confederal political coordination on the global level could hope to regulate the self-regulation of corporate economic power and mitigate its negative side effects on states and peoples worldwide without purporting to erect a homogenizing world state, an unfeasible and questionable utopia at any rate. Federations tend to be less socioeconomically egalitarian compared with centralized states, but gross discrepancies across the units could be alleviated with redistributive policies and mechanisms established by the center.

To be sure, history has taught us that there are preconditions for the success of federation, and we wish to mention some of these because they are not addressed in the contributions to this volume. It is clear that ethnic, linguistic, religious, and racial heterogeneity can lead to conflicts in federations as in any other political formation. But so does the attempt to establish homogeneity by relying on any of these factors. As one of us argued in a previous book, the requisite homogeneity for the success of federation as a political form is homogeneity of political regime—ideally the construction of the same republican, democratic constitutionalist structure of government and fundamental rights throughout the federation, entrenched preferably in both state and union constitutions.[12] We assumed that a civic notion of citizenship would follow from this institutional framework, if supported in the public sphere and the educational system. But this minimal condition of homogeneity—a civic notion of citizenship and inclusion—can degenerate into a religious or ethnic one on the level of member states, and even though such a deformation is less likely on the federal level, it is possible because resources for solidarity and identification are thin in multiethnic, multireligious federations. Ethnic, racial, religious, and linguistic divides are always available for mobilization by political entrepreneurs who can make them politically salient under the right conditions, fomenting resentment, fostering conflict and violence, and ultimately undermining the achievements of democratic constitutionalism even of well-consolidated federal republics. Political homogeneity is not enough to ward this off. But we suggest that controlling for the effects of socioeconomic inequality in federal unions would help to minimize the likelihood of successful political mobilization of other social differences if these are prevented from mapping onto one another. Put a different way, greater economic homogeneity among the federal units and across social categories would help block the emergence of the political salience of difference in antiprogressive ways. Indeed, as the American Civil War shows, the heterogeneity of economic structures and related modes of life, even in a context of homogeneity of language and religion, can lead to the violent breakdown of a federal union. Precisely because federations do not entail homogeneity of size of the component units, and because these units may or may not track other forms of difference, it is imperative that redistributive politics at the center foster socioeconomic justice and distribute the benefits and burdens of the polity fairly across social identities and regions. In short, the institutional capacity of the center to control for gross inequalities and engage in basic redistributive justice and protective social policy across the units is crucial for the success of federal polities coupled with democratic constitutionalism. What policies this might entail is not our concern here; rather, we want to argue that on the level of the federal constitution provision for the institutional mechanisms empowered to accomplish it be put in place.

From the historical example of the first and best known modern federation project, the United States, we have learned two of the minimal preconditions for successful federal union: the importance of homogeneity of the basic political and economic regimes and the capacity of the center to engage in redistributive social policy. These two desiderata can be satisfied even when a third is absent. This third precondition, already noticed by Hannah Arendt, can be gleaned from the more recent twentieth-century context of decolonization: namely, the importance of experience of quasi-self-government on the part of the colonized prior to emancipation.[13] Even under terms of subjection and foreign control, the mode of control and especially whether or not it facilitated participation in local legislative governmental bodies apparently matters a great deal for the success and durability of a democratic constitutionalist federal project after liberation. Where this condition is relatively absent, because of colonial neglect or postcolonial authoritarianism, political (i.e., democratic) and economic (i.e., welfare state) homogeneity become even more important to establish and should be the key targets for international soft intervention and especially assistance.

Notwithstanding our predilection for the federal political form as a way to dedramatize state sovereignty and acknowledge internal plurality while extending and enriching democratic constitutionalism, there is much room for debate and much to be learned from alternative approaches. History has a great deal to teach us regarding the four alternative political forms discussed here. Contemporary innovations also are well worth our attention and analysis. We turn to these now.

## After Empire, Historical Alternatives

The book is divided into four parts. Part I, "After Empire: Historical Alternatives," discusses historical roads not taken and the changing meaning of forms of political and legal pluralism in the context and aftermath of empire. The first two chapters reflect on a variety of federal projects after WWII proposed by protagonists among the colonized who were involved in the actual events of liberation and polity construction in French former colonies. The third chapter reflects on earlier postimperial projects of federation in the Americas, and the final chapter in this section takes us back to the beginnings in colonized Algeria to reveal the multiplicity of valences and implications of status group jurisdictional pluralism under imperial rule and its aftermath.

Fred Cooper and Gary Wilder both try to restore in historical memory the recognition that the sovereign nation-state was neither seen as inevitable nor as the most desirable political form that postcolonial polities should take after liberation. Unfortunately, the protagonists who advocated union with the former colonial power and even larger regional federations were castigated by their competitors and by later historians as "co-opted natives" and "imperial apologists." Because they did not embrace revolutionary nationalism, or due to the near total hegemony of the nation-state form in the aftermath of decolonization, the alternatives they advocated have been forgotten and the sovereign nation-state presented as the only viable outcome.

As both Cooper and Wilder demonstrate, the discussion concerning postimperial futures in French West Africa, the French Caribbean, and Indian Ocean colonies were focused on political form. They both tell the story of the debates in the 1945–46 French Constituent Assemblies (and afterward) that included delegates from the colonies, the most famous being Leopold Senghor of Senegal and Aimé Césaire from Martinique. Cooper rightly insists that we should not read history backward and assume that the failure of the various federal alternatives to the nation-state form are proof that they are only irrelevant historical artifacts today. At the time, the protagonists had before their eyes the dismal example of independent Haiti, and they drew the appropriate conclusions regarding the risks of balkanization and penury. Instead of trying to build homogeneous nation-states, the point was to think about union, federation, and confederation as alternatives that could deal with the legacies of empire: socioeconomic disadvantage due to decades of exploitation, cultural diversity, and compound identities inevitable within any viable future unit. Instead of independence in the form of separation, they advocated various forms of union with the former mother country. Césaire, as Wilder shows, first sponsored a 1946 law transforming the former island colonies into equal departments in the French state. He later joined with Senghor in 1956 to sponsor a postnational federal democratic union. As Cooper shows, the federalist projects of the colonials differed from de Gaulle's neo-imperial conception of the French Union that was to (and briefly did) follow decolonization. He also traces the evolution and varieties of the federal project in French West Africa, including a fascinating discussion of Senghor's three tiered approach: an imagined African federation of member polities (open to all who wanted to join including Morocco and Algeria) that would then confederate with France.

Although Cooper and Wilder agree on the importance of the historical alternatives to the nation-state form, their papers analyze the developments from different perspectives. Cooper's focus is on West Africa and varieties of federal union proposals, analyzed from the internal perspective of a postsovereign political form of political association and belonging in which "sovereignty" would not describe the internal relations of the member "states" toward one another or toward the federal center. Wilder's focus is on the new international sovereignty regime of sovereign equality established with the UN Charter system and policed by the great powers in the Security Council, based on the principles of territorial integrity, national independence, and state sovereignty, and less prominently, human rights, versus the postnational alternative to external state sovereignty and international relations predicated on it and embodied in the federal vision. In light of simultaneous projects for a European Union, Wilder finds the "timely untimeliness" of federal thinking as an alternative to an international order predicated on the sovereign state relevant both in the postwar epoch and for us today.

We all know the ultimate outcome: decolonization, separation, and in some cases (Algeria) bloody war, and now strife and conflict within and among the new "nation-states" formed in Africa. So even if the federal project failed, we might well ask with Cooper whether the idea of a multinational federation in which plurality and difference go together with equality, multilayered political autonomy, self-government, and democracy instead of monistic centralized sovereignty would have been and still may be a preferable alternative. And we might question with Wilder whether the existing *nomos* of international relations based on the sovereign nation-state isn't entering a moment of crisis and whether we should think seriously again about novel forms of political consociation that might be adequate to the plural, translocal, interdependent demands of our historical present.

Joshua Simon's chapter, "From the American System to Anglo-Saxon Union," reminds us that a century earlier, in the Americas, projects of federal union were also conceived as the best way to exit empire and to ensure independence, well-being, and political freedom for former colonies. But what is less well known is that federal union there too was seen as an alternative to the international system of sovereign states developed in Europe, based at the time on the premise that equal sovereignty, trade, diplomacy, and balance of power would civilize international relations. In an important reversal, the American Federalists argued that political union—that is, a constitutionalized, republican federal union of states—is the sine qua non for civilizing relations between states and the precondition for preserving representative republican government on the state level. Indeed republican polities could avoid the wars, intrigue, and despotisms of European states only if states gave up claims to be absolutely sovereign, renounced the balance of power version of interstate competition, and joined together in a new polity—a constitutionalized federal union—that protected local interests and secured political autonomy while being equipped with the institutional and decisional power to foster the common good by ensuring mobility of persons and goods and political voice for individuals and member states at the center. By replacing state with popular sovereignty and by rendering the external internal, federal union was construed as the anti-type of the European system of international relations. It was the better way to grow larger compared with empires or unitary sovereign states, and together with the principle of representation federal union, it came to be construed as the sine qua non for the security and survival of republican forms of government in the member states. In a fascinating rereading of the Unionist project, Simon describes federation as a means of extension of the polity through the voluntary inclusion of new members that entailed from the start a supranationalist imaginary transcending political borders and cultural and linguistic differences. Its advocates did not only see federal union as the best route out of empire; initially its continuities with as well as its differences from empire were reflected upon. There, too, various conceptions of unity with the former imperial power under the King were imagined, akin to a commonwealth but without subjection to the "despotism" of the British Parliament. But this path was not taken. Indeed, Simon argues that during the first fifty years after independence, influential American statesmen envisioned a hemisphere-spanning unionist "American system" that would encompass all of the independent republics of the New World, including those that emerged in what is now called Latin America. Indeed, there is no structural limit to federation with respect to size, and as the Federalists argued, if coupled with a republican form of representative government on both member state and federal levels, and if based on the principle of popular sovereignty, Federal Union could combine the advantages of monarchy and empire (greater size of the polity) with the advantages of freedom once deemed the preserve of small republics. No one knew the shape that the union would take in advance, and nothing prevented the inclusion of parts of what are now Canada, Mexico, and central or Latin America.

Simon also traces the demise of the hemispheric unionist project and its replacement by a different supranationalism—a version based on racist rhetoric, on the insistence on racial and linguistic homogeneity, and white Anglo-Saxon supremacy internally, and on imperialist intervention into and conquest of different (allegedly inferior) peoples and regions in Spanish America and later the Philippines. Simon reflects on the political theoretical implications of this history by asking whether there are particular circumstances that permit or encourage the construction of supranational institutions despite substantive heterogeneity among member states. Are there particular arguments or ideologies that can inspire populations to set aside their cultural differences? Conversely, what processes are likely to raise latent divisions to political salience and forestall or undo federative projects?

Perhaps the specific nature of types of imperial rule has something to do with the success or failure of postimperial projects of reconciling deep plurality, equal citizenship, freedom, and political autonomy. History can be instructive in this regard as well. Certainly the experience of local self-government by the colonized, however restricted, matters, as we argued previously, but so does the particular mode of organizing pluralism in the colonized territory by the imperial power. Emmanuelle Saada's chapter, "Constitutions and Forms of Pluralism in the Time of Conquest," takes us back to the beginnings of the French Empire and its colonial project, highlighting the shifting nature of the forms of pluralism it established in its prize colony, Algeria, over the course of the nineteenth century. Her goal is twofold: to relativize the stark dichotomy introduced by Mamdani between "civil society" (i.e., the part of colonial society enjoying the protection of French civil law as citizens) and "indigenous society" (i.e., "natives" living under customary religious law and as mere subjects of the imperial French state), and to blur another stark dichotomy, that between empire and federation.[14] She reminds us that in its older colonies (Martinique, Guadeloupe, French Guiana, and Réunion), all inhabitants were made full citizens when the Second French Republic abolished slavery in 1848. She also notes that a unitary conception of citizenship prevailed alongside, to be sure, institutionalized racism that did not, however, take the form of the recognition of customary power or law. Meanwhile she observes that the colonized on the coast of India and in Senegal were given voting rights in the French Parliament without having to renounce their customary personal status law or to become subject to the French civil code. Her point is that the citizen-subject dichotomy does not capture the complexity of the forms of pluralism and recognition of difference in French colonies.

Moreover, as the Algerian case reveals, although the form of religious group-based legal pluralism that predominated after the 1880s was indeed hierarchical and based on invidious status distinctions, this was the result of the emergence of an extremely repressive mode of settler colonialism. Consequently, the legal discrimination between "citizen" and "subject" ultimately tainted all aspects of relations between colonizers and colonized. The same, however, was not true of earlier versions of legal pluralism and colonial relations in Algeria. Indeed, Saada argues that the later, destructive form of status group legal pluralism was not inevitable and should not be deemed the paradigm of legal pluralism everywhere in the past or in the future.

Saada's aim goes beyond correcting the historical record and enriching our understanding of status group legal pluralism. Her exploration of the early versions of legal pluralism and of the heated debates among the French political elite at the time over how to organize relations among groups and legal systems within an emerging French empire can, she thinks, shed light on continued tensions and fissures in France regarding its "politics of difference." That the conception of a larger polity inclusive of "different civilizations" in an *associational* rather than an *assimilationist* model was debated, if not enacted in the long term, strongly resonates with contemporary debates on pluralism and republicanism in France today. She is well aware that the connection between religion and law apparently inherent in Islam did indeed ultimately serve to exclude Muslim Algerians and other colonial populations from civil and political rights based on their presumed inability to follow both the Shari'a and French civil law. Legal pluralism, in turn, ultimately justified the invidious distinction between citizen and subject. But in the early period it apparently was the vehicle for including local Muslim elites in government and for showing respect to plurality and local practices. The tolerance of social, religious, and legal pluralism of that period is overlooked and has lessons for contemporary assimilationist French republicans. Just what these lessons are, however, is open to contestation.

## New Federal Formations and Subsidiarity

Part II turns to contemporary proposals for new federal formations, their relation to societal plurality, and debates over subsidiarity. In chapter 5, "The Constitutional Identity of Indigenous Peoples in Canada: Status Groups or Federal Actors?," Patrick Macklem brings us back to the Americas, this time focusing on the issue of the political and legal relationship of European colonists to Native American indigenous peoples. His focus is the history of these relationships as they evolved in Canada and on future possibilities. He poses the question quite clearly as to the respective normative and empirical gains and losses of coordinating the plurality of indigenous legal orders with the Canadian legal order through status group legal pluralism via the mechanism of treaties or via federation—that is, the inclusion of indigenous peoples in the Canadian Federation—through the mechanism of constitutional pluralism. To be sure, constitutional pluralism is a variant of legal pluralism insofar as it also entails a multiplicity of legal orders within the same territorial space of a polity. A federal constitution vests lawmaking authority in at least two levels of government, each relatively autonomous from the other in the production of legal norms that pertain to the construction and exercise of public power. Status group legal pluralism, religious, tribal, or ethno-linguistic, vests minorities with a measure of lawmaking authority relatively shielded from the legislative power of the broader political community in which it is located. This can take the form of private power, which is often the case with religious status group legal pluralism, or it can overlap with federal principles as in the case of the asymmetric federalism practiced with respect to the province of Quebec in Canada. There the centrifugal special guarantees regarding language and local majority status for francophones are counterbalanced by a voice in national institutions and the overall Canadian commitment to fundamental rights, bilingualism, guaranteed seats on the Supreme Court, and other measures. Whatever one thinks of asymmetrical federalism of this sort, it is clearly a hybrid between federal principles meant to ensure the continued political existence and autonomy of a territorial unit and status group legal pluralism aimed at securing the autonomy and survival of particular substantive minorities. What is innovative about this chapter is, in part, the way in which it traces the evolution of the constitutional relationship between indigenous peoples and the Canadian federal republic as entailing the rise, demise, and now the resurgence of constitutional pluralism. But the piece is also important insofar as it applies the distinction between status group legal pluralism and constitutional pluralism/federation to the issue of indigenous legal and political autonomy. Macklem identifies the specific institutional and normative challenges each pose in the context of constitutional recognition of indigenous governing authority.

By taking us through the legal cases, Macklem shows how the nascent constitutional pluralism regulating the colonial encounter with indigenous legal and political orders in Canada changed. It came to be replaced by a singular, hierarchical conception of sovereignty incapable of comprehending multiple sovereign actors on a given territory. This informed the Crown's negotiation of treaties that ultimately served as a legal technology of indigenous dispossession and blocked any chance of mutual recognition. Not unlike Saada, Macklem argues that this shift was not inevitable. Also like her, he acknowledges that the apparent reciprocity involved in the early recognition of the autonomous sources of native law and indigenous self-government was probably due to the relative weakness and lack of organization of the burgeoning colonial state at a moment of intense hesitation regarding the form of rule. Today, Macklem notes, an opening exists once again regarding the possibility of a reciprocal relationship between indigenous legal norms and Canadian constitutional law. The choice, apparently, is between a backward looking status group legal pluralist approach (multicultural jurisdiction) based on the original claims of indigenous populations, which would have the drawback of separating out, freezing, and essentializing indigenous cultural and legal norms, and a future-oriented flexible federal conception that construes indigenous legal orders as federal actors in the Canadian federation. This mode of constitutional pluralism would have to entail institutions of self-rule and of shared rule, perhaps instituting another distinct segment of asymmetrical federalism within the overarching federal polity. Just how individual rights would be secured within and across this innovative federal conception would, of course, have to be clarified.

Chapter 6 turns to another innovative conception of federation devised to cope with plurality in ways that comport with democratic constitutionalism. Alfred Stepan and Jeff Miley argue for recuperating and improving on a little known version of federation—federacy—as a feasible way to help resolve violent conflict over the inclusion of a territorially discrete minority within an already existing sovereign nation-state. In "Federacy and the Kurds: Might This New Political Form Help Mitigate Hobbesian Conflicts in Turkey, Iraq, and Syria?," they develop an ideal type of "federacy" and propose this as a solution to the seemingly intractable problem of Kurdish autonomy in the context of the nation-states in which they form a linguistic and ethnic minority. Indeed, what is distinctive about federacy is that it involves the creation of a political, legal, and administrative unit within an otherwise unitary state such that the federated unit has constitutionally or quasi-constitutionally embedded exclusive power in certain areas, some legislative power, and rights (e.g., to language and culture) that cannot be changed unilaterally, and the inhabitants have full citizenship rights in the larger polity.[15] This could be considered a version of asymmetric federalism but is distinct in that unlike the contexts in which that version typically occurs, a federacy is a member unit not of a federal polity but in an otherwise unitary state.

Stepan and Miley trace the history of federacy as a political form and the role it has played in resolving seemingly intractable conflicts over plurality, belonging, and territory. The claim is that if the appropriate form of constitutionalized autonomy—voice in the center and minority guarantees—is put in place for the special unit, pressures toward secession from below and homogenization from above are minimized, thus enhancing the chances of peaceful democratic consolidation. Federacy, as a solution to international and domestic conflict over disputed territory and rights of a local or transnational but territorially located minority group, has historically emerged through elaborate negotiations and compromises, both international and domestic. Indeed Stepan and Miley argue that if one drops the dogma of indivisible sovereignty, federacy can help resolve a range of potential conflicts by constitutionally embedding "divided" sovereignty between a unitary nation-state and one part of its territory that is culturally, linguistically, and historically radically "other." Thus, as a political form, federacy is a version of constitutional pluralism designed to accommodate social plurality, but because it entails inclusion in a state and because its members have national citizenship, vote, and send representatives to the central parliament, it is distinct both from a confederation or treaty organization and from status group legal pluralism that typically lacks a territorial component. Stepan and Miley argue that federacy arrangements can help resolve domestic and international conflicts over the control of certain territorially situated minority groups such as the Kurds in the Middle East and the Tibetans in China. It is the only feasible way out of the current Hobbesian situation in which they now exist, one that is compatible with democratic constitutionalism.

But what Macklem and Stepan and Miley leave unclear is the question of the rights of individual members within the federated unit, be it of the indigenous in a new version of constitutional pluralism or of the group members in federacies. Federation is a way to make the external internal that downplays separatism and seeks to avoid secession through compromises and reciprocity. But how can conflicts be handled over local cultural norms and individual fundamental rights guaranteed under democratic constitutionalism for the polity as a whole? This problem plagues all versions of religious status group legal pluralism, as the next section makes clear, and the overlaps between that version of legal pluralism and the federal forms imagined for special national minorities are obvious. Theories of federations today can hardly ignore this issue.

Indeed, devising protections for individual rights has been front and center in the European Union (EU), the most integrated regional form of non-state unionism in existence today, and where the role of the European Court of Justice (ECJ) as the protector of individual rights on the domestic and transnational levels is deemed crucial. The EU is also the locus classicus of the discourse of constitutional pluralism: it has been construed as a hybrid supranational constitutional treaty organization whose courts and policies may not violate (or fall behind) the level of rights protections extant in its member states.[16] The EU has a democracy clause not dissimilar to the republican clause in the American federation for member states and has been construed, ideally at least, as a political association with its own autonomous law of constitutional quality that aims to secure peace, prosperity, and welfare and to manage pluralism in ways compatible with democracy and human rights.

But the EU as we know it is flawed in many respects and seems to have entered into a crisis indicated by the escalating debate over its democratic deficit, its failure to respond adequately to migration, its seemingly unfair austerity policies imposed on weaker members, its apparent inability to protect social rights of EU citizens against the neoliberal onslaught, and, of course, Brexit. The rise of right-wing populist movements that reject the EU, and the entry into power of populist parties in some member states (Hungary, Poland) that challenge the EU's and the ECJ's regulatory reach and strain its democratic proviso for membership, have given many analysts pause. Indeed, much ink already has been spilled over the nature of the European Union—it is not a federal state nor federation of states based on a clear constitutional commitment to federation, but it is a union of states of "constitutional quality" that is more integrated than a set of alliances or an international organization. Nevertheless, the word *confederation* is as uninformative as is the term *supranational polity*. Indeed, as chapter 7 by Robert Howse indicates, much blame for the current crisis has been placed on the inadequate architecture of this mule animal that is the EU. That is why many on the left and the right argue for an overhaul of the flawed architecture, whether it be a democratic constitutional reconstruction along the lines of a federal union/state or in the form of a retreat from Europe back to the nation-state and a set of alliances but little more—a position long advocated by Euroskeptics on the left (and now by right-wing nationalists). Howse's piece is clearly situated on the left, but he insists that it is time to move beyond the abstract conceptual debate *and* to realize that, however imperfect, the EU's architecture does not preclude progressive reforms even if in the long run a more radical transformation may be required. It is his thesis, in short, that the EU's law and overall architecture provide ample room for the development of an effective social Europe. What is needed is the political will to enter into the ideological and political struggle over the direction, rather than the architecture, of the EU. Put a different way, it is time to confront head on the political disagreements around genuine sociological differences across vast territories, comprising many peoples, different levels of economic development, and connected to general conflicts over neoliberalism, neonationalism, and globalization that are at the heart of the EU's problems today. Thus, in "Europe—What's Left? Toward a Progressive Pluralist Program for EU Reform," Howse argues that the goal is to construct a progressive political agenda for the EU—one that is based on political imagination, cooperation, and concerted action by progressive left parties, movements, and governments. A concrete progressive politics is needed to safeguard and expand the social democratic achievements of member states and to ensure that the EU continues in ways that protect plurality and autonomy and foster the solidaristic integration needed for social justice on all levels. Howse shows that within the flawed architecture of the EU are possibilities for a progressive version of "social Europe" that does not require fundamental legal change or deep fundamental constitutional reconstitution. No need to wait for that. In particular, Howse stresses the framework outside of the monetary union dubbed "Social Europe," which includes the Charter of Fundamental Rights; the directives on minimum standards for workers rights, collective bargaining, and social protection; and the Social Chapter annexed to the Treaty of Maastricht as well as some ILO conventions incorporated into EU or member state law. Howse's thesis, in short, is that Social Europe, as it already exists, provides a diffuse normative framework that could, given the appropriate political will, be transformed into a European pillar of social rights and, together with democratizing initiatives involving various modes of codetermination among the demoi of Europe, turn a technocratic neoliberal Europe into a social and democratic one. Thinking along these lines has already begun on the part of European intellectuals (Balibar, Nicolaidis) and political actors (Varoufakis, Macron) and could end the paralysis of political initiatives due in part to the fruitless wait for a fundamental overhaul of the basic architecture. Whether this will happen, of course, remains to be seen.

With Nadia Urbinati's contribution we turn to the discourse, ideology, and practice of subsidiarity, one of the foundational organizing principles of the EU. Subsidiarity entails that social and political issues should be dealt with at the most immediate level consistent with their most adequate resolution. It seems focused on efficiency insofar as only those tasks and decisions that cannot, or for some reason should not, be handled at the local level should be ascribed to the central authority to decide and administer. It is thus touted as a way to accommodate plurality and liberty (local autonomy) and is a viable alternative to "monistic" sovereignty and statism. Indeed, subsidiarity is a way to govern a large, multilayered formation without the latter having to take the form of a federation or an empire.

Urbinati's piece shows the ambivalence of the subsidiarity principle with respect to liberal republican and democratic principles. Although it has an affinity with a conception of freedom as noninterference, it can easily come into tension with liberal principles of justice to persons and individual equality, democratic principles of a voice for everyone, and the republican principle of freedom as nondomination. This is so because the principle of subsidiarity applies liberty not to individuals but to groups, and it does not come with any requirement of equal voice or democratic procedures for local or other levels of decision making.

Urbinati notes that the concept has historical religious roots in the Catholic Church and then in reformed Christianity (with its related idea of sphere sovereignty), and it was generated in the context of the battles over the formation of territorial states in the postmedieval age. Hence its conflict-laden relation to the two main constructions of modernity: the modern state and the individual. Hence, also, the tension of the subsidiarity principle with, and explicit opposition to, the principles of state or popular sovereignty. The discourse of subsidiarity was and is still used by some to challenge the priority of public, secular, governmental power over religious and other corporate organizations. Equating the state, regardless of its political regime (republican or a constitutional democracy) or form (centralized or federal), with absolutist and monist sovereignty, advocates of subsidiarity, like some advocates of federation, challenge the very principle of unitary sovereignty in the name of the autonomy of a plurality of corporate associations. Unlike republican and democratic federalists, they do not seek to bring politics to the people or to enhance democratic participation and individual liberties. Rather, they want to bypass politics altogether in favor of administrative rationality.

Urbinati argues that this legacy is evident in the EU. The principle of subsidiarity appears in its constitutive treaties and is presented by advocates as an alternative to both the sovereign state and to a constitutionalized political federation. Its core principles—proximity (of agents to needs, interests, problems, and issues), self-responsibility (and responsibility toward one's primary community), and efficiency of scale—are used to substitute administrative and judicial power for politics in Urbinati's view. Accordingly, in the absence of a real political federation to which member states constitutionally commit, subsidiarity has exacerbated instead of mitigated the democratic deficit in the EU, fostering technocratic regulation and the depoliticization of citizenship. Whether the principle could be freed from the trajectory of its historical genesis and be rendered benign and useful in a reformed federalized EU remains an open question.

## Status Group Legal Pluralism

Part III turns to reflection on deeply divided societies and asks what form of institutional recognition, especially of religious difference, is compatible with constitutional democracy and justice toward minorities. The chapters in this section discuss countries with a colonial legacy of religious status group pluralism that have, upon liberation, reinstituted revised versions of it for religious minorities and, in some cases, majorities. Whether this fully mitigates the dichotomy between citizen and subject, however, remains to be seen because the rights of individual members of the respective religious groups are subject to the dictates of religious law and authorities even when these conflict with their individual human rights and equality provisions under the constitution of their respective polities. We now turn to this conundrum as it exists in postcolonial contemporary contexts.

The chapter by Christophe Jaffrelot discusses one of the most diverse constitutional democracies in the world—India—and the distinctive form of political secularism and recognition of religious pluralism it institutionalized in the aftermath of decolonization, upon independence. India is a federal republic that created an innovative form of political secularism that permits intrusive regulation of those religious practices of various groups, including the majority Hindus, that conflict with constitutional principles of individual equality and social justice, while recognizing religious groups and channeling state funds to their schools and various religious projects. The model of political secularism R. Bhargava calls "principled distance" differs from the liberal model of strict separation allegedly characteristic of the U.S. version of political secularism and from the French republican approach, which banishes religion from the public sphere entirely. Indian political secularism entails constitutional guarantees for freedom of conscience, speech, and worship; an antidiscrimination principle; and religious groups' rights to establish religious and charitable institutions, manage their own affairs, and create schools. The model permits differential treatment of religious groups as long as privileges and disabilities are not distributed to them unfairly. According to Jaffrelot, the distinctive "principled distance" model of Indian secularism includes the institutionalization of religious status group jurisdictional pluralism regarding personal law. The Indian legal system treats the particularistic religious personal family law of the various religious communities as enforceable private law, and their religious authorities and courts as legally authoritative. India never established a uniform civil code of personal law even though the Constitution's "directive principles" call for the state to do so.

Jaffrelot's essay traces the trajectory of the current crisis of Indian secularism, documenting the demise of principled distance and impartiality toward religious minorities and majorities in the relevant court decisions from the mid-1980s onward. The equation of Hinduism with Hinduvta, Hindu nationalist ideology, began to penetrate those decisions and to undermine Indian secularism by entrenching an ethno-religious, exclusionary version of national identity and of the Indian "cultural" way of life at the expense of religious minorities' equal citizenship and equal standing in the polity. He considers two competing explanatory approaches to the crisis of Indian secularism: one culturalist, the other political, and clearly favors the latter. His analysis focuses on the role of Hindu nationalist political entrepreneurs who politicize and ethnicize religion and invoke democratic principles to insist on the prerogatives of the majority to make policy conforming to their interests without concessions to minorities. The rise of political religion cum populist nationalism and its challenges to political secularism are, to be sure, hardly unique to India. Indeed, Jaffrelot ends his piece wondering whether the transformation of India's multicultural democracy is not transitioning to an "ethnic democracy" along Israeli lines.

However, it is unclear what relation these challenges to political secularism in India and elsewhere have to the institutionalization of religious status group legal pluralism. Does religious status group legal pluralism exacerbate or mitigate religious divisions? Does it invite politicization of religious communal attachments? Is it really intrinsic to the ideals of principled distance if the religious law it empowers discriminates gravely against women and if the religious authorities are by no means democratic in their procedures or outlook? Is there not a conflict between religious status group legal pluralism that hives off personal law from a general civil code and from liberal constitutional democracy?

Both Michael Karayanni and Yüksel Sezgin think there certainly is. They have each analyzed the negative effects on human rights of individual members of these jurisdictions in other works, showing how they undermine equal citizenship and other principals of constitutional democracy. Both stress the special vulnerability of weaker members of the religious communities—women and children—when subject to the jurisdiction of patriarchal religious law and authorities.

In chapter 10, "Tainted Liberalism: Israel's Millets," Karayanni shows how jurisdictional religious pluralism in Israel conflicts with liberalism even as it uses multiculturalism as a cover. Karayanni's study of religious millets in Israel challenges the claim that the jurisdictional authority granted to the Palestinian-Arab religious communities is a form of minority accommodation that is tolerant, pluralistic, liberal, and multicultural in nature. Israel is a nation-state, and it privileges the religious majority regarding national identity and in other respects while claiming nonetheless to be a secular democracy and to accord liberal principles of religious freedom, freedom of conscience, and group rights of self-government over personal family law to religious minorities by giving decisions of their religious courts legal effect. It grants all citizens the right to vote and thus does not officially link religious jurisdictional pluralism to subject status. This permits Israel to claim to be a liberal multicultural democracy that accommodates instead of assimilating group difference through its particular form of jurisdictional pluralism while guaranteeing equal citizenship.

Karayanni pushes back against this claim in two ways: by going back to the genesis of these millets at the founding of the Israeli state and by making a conceptual argument regarding the incompatibility of religious millets—status group jurisdictional pluralism—with the individualist and egalitarian premises of political liberalism. As is well known, the millet system was inherited from the Ottoman Empire and, later, British imperial rule. By researching newly available archival materials, Karayanni shows that the recognition accorded to the Palestinian-Arab religious communities and the construction of other minority millets by the newly independent Israeli state was primarily driven by institutional interests of control and nation-building desiderata rather than by a concern for the well-being of the minorities. A divide and rule strategy more typical of empires than of democratic nation-states meshed with a nation-building project focused on Jewishness and ensuring a Jewish majority: hence, the importance of endogamy and strategies of blocking intermarriage all around. But genesis isn't validity, and it could be that whatever the original reasons for it jurisdictional pluralism for religious status groups over personal law might comport with liberal principles. Karayanni refutes this idea, arguing that liberalism is predicated on the equal standing, moral worth, and basic human rights of every individual and that religious status group jurisdictional pluralism conflicts with this core principle insofar as it ascribes rights to the group and to its religious authorities without conditioning these rights on liberal principles of equality for group members. Jurisdictional pluralism without provision for individual rights and voice for group members, especially in patriarchal religious communities, conflicts with rather than instantiates liberal principles, the possibility of forum shopping and the multicultural label notwithstanding. Accordingly, it essentializes difference, freezes unequal rights and privileges within the group, and turns the minorities it reifies into unequal members of the political association.

Sezgin apparently agrees. His concern in "Jurisdictional Competition and Internal Reform in Muslim Family Law in Israel and Greece" is how to generate progressive reform in countries that already have religious status group legal pluralism and mitigate the rights violations and inequities it clearly fosters. His essay puts to the test a proposal for fostering internal reform in contexts in which religious status group jurisdictional pluralism has been entrenched. Sezgin's piece engages in a comparative analysis of the outcomes of reform attempts along these lines in Israel and Greece in relation to Muslim communities' family law in each country. His concern is "the paradox of multicultural vulnerability" that ensues when group-based jurisdictional rights accorded to religious communities as collectives clash with individual rights and liberties accorded to their members under constitutional and international law.[17] Here, too, the focus is on women's rights.

Sezgin discusses Shachar's "joint governance" model, in which neither civil nor religious courts have monopolistic control over personal law. Each would have specific subject-matter jurisdiction over distinct but complementary matters and concurrent jurisdiction as well. For instance, if marriage and divorce are placed under the purview of religious courts, related family matters such as custody and alimony would be placed under the jurisdiction of civil courts. Concurrent jurisdiction would enable individuals to transfer disputes between courts if one jurisdiction does not, in their view, adequately address their concerns. The idea is that forum shopping among courts with concurrent jurisdictions promotes jurisdictional competition and could exert pressure toward internal liberal reform if religious courts are faced with the prospect of massive exit regarding adjudication of family law matters. Ex ante review by superior courts, mandatory secular training for religious judges, mandatory legal counsel for those appearing before religious courts, permission for third parties to appear, and a prior review of religious court decisions could foster the internalization by religious authorities of civil secular norms of equality.

Focusing on Muslim family law in Greece and Israel, Sezgin notes that both jurisdictions incorporated some reforms along these lines and employed some ex ante oversight techniques. Although there has been no major "transformative" change in Muslim law or patriarchal structures in either religious community, there has nonetheless been some progress in Israel but not in Greece. The analysis tries to account for this variation. Although jurisdictional competition, oversight, and other regulatory civil controls are certainly preferable to none, his ultimate conclusion is that the meager results regarding gender equality in Muslim personal law in each country reveal that they are insufficient.

Sezgin suggests that there is a need for legal aid, a vibrant civil society and NGO sector, and especially women's rights organizations to pressure for internal reform. Simply abolishing these special jurisdictions seems to be politically impossible. Accordingly, making them comport with human rights and gender equality norms requires cautious legal measures, societal resistance, and pressure. Given the dismal outcomes for women in countries that institutionalize jurisdictional pluralism for religious authorities over family law, and the difficulty of progressive reform, it would seem to be unwise to institutionalize such systems where they do not exist. As a solution to deep societal division, it may seem that such a mechanism to "accommodate" plurality can ward off violent conflict in time 1, but given the patriarchal structure and assumptions undergirding most traditional and orthodox versions of religious family law, it is women and children who will invariably pay the price at time 2, as will the social integration of the larger political community and the generality and efficacy of the civil law. This seems to be the case now in India. Thus status group legal pluralism as an alternative to "monistic" state sovereignty, or the federal approach in short, has been an ambivalent alternative and remains a highly contentious issue.

## The Challenge of Corporate Power

Federalism and religious status group jurisdictional pluralism are not the only versions of legal pluralism presented as an alternative to the monopolistic legal stance of sovereign nation-states. Part IV shifts to the international perspective and considers another challenge to the system of sovereign states, that posed by transnational business corporations and the distinctive form of global legal pluralism they are empowered by and foster. Indeed, economic power and competition over it are never far from the conflicts over political and legal forms of pluralism, domestic and transnational.

As is fairly well known, by the end of the nineteenth century, business corporations were no longer construed as state-chartered bodies accountable to civil polity with duties to the public. Instead, they came to be seen as private contractual entities, incorporated in a state via its law but having minimal duties to outsiders and rarely constrained to serve the public interest directly. In the twenty-first century, transnational business enterprises have now emancipated themselves even from the law of the state in which they are incorporated, and now appear independent of and unaccountable to public power on the national as well as the transnational level. Katharina Pistor and Tsilly Dagan address the new forms of legal particularism this entails and the challenges transnational corporate economic powers pose, not just to the sovereign state and its ability serve the public interest but to civil regulation in the public interest on any level of the global political and legal system. Moreover, corporations are claiming the same rights as natural persons, even invoking international human rights law to protect their autonomy and interests against state regulation.[18] Here, too, liberalism is invoked as justification against the "overextension" of regulatory public power. We thus face a new version of corporatism and a new form of legal pluralism tied to neoliberal economic ideology and at times allied with resurgent religious corporatist claims. They are strange bedfellows in the legal pluralist universe, but the emergence of religious "neoliberalism" coupled with claims of pluralist corporatism has been quite successful in challenging the regulatory policies even of powerful states such as the United States.[19] This form of managing pluralism is thus well worth looking into.

As Katharina Pistor notes in "Corporate Legal Particularism," business corporations are creatures of law, and contemporary state law confers on them full legal personality, enabling them to contract, sue, and own assets. But corporations have morphed, like the sorcerer's apprentice, into masters of the emergent particular transnational legal order that serves their interests. Sovereign states have facilitated and accommodated the rise of such corporate power by recognizing entities created by foreign law and allowing them to penetrate their borders and by delegating lawmaking and enforcement powers to business corporations, enabling them to set standards not only for their contractual counterparts but even for states. Via these means, in an effort to gain competitive advantage, states have, in effect, transferred a key part of their public sovereign prerogatives of rule and regulation to private powers—corporate business entities. Transnational legal pluralism plays a key role in this.

Pistor introduces an important distinction between legal particularism and legal pluralism to explain what is at issue. Legal particularism is a legal order that is controlled by and primarily serves particular interests. Legal pluralism, at least normatively defensible versions of it, ideally connects actors and bridges differences because it operates in a background context of shared norms on domestic or global levels. In her words, both involve "multi-juralism," but they stand for radically different ways of ordering the relation of legal orders to one another. Globally, legal particularism owes it rise to legal pluralism insofar as it entails the ability to pick and choose among multiple legal orders that allow business corporations to play different lawmakers against one another and thereby gain influence over lawmaking. It also enables global corporate actors to elude oversight by a shared common overarching legal order because it undermines the regulatory reach of existing public political forms while distorting new ones on regional or global levels. Pistor notes that a normatively defensible legal pluralist order requires some common principles, but it also involves mutual accommodation and tolerance for differences. In a federal political formation, for example, the federal unit can develop a jurisdictional constitutional anchor to mitigate the free choice of law by corporations among member states and preclude opting out of general legal oversight. But carve-outs from general law to favor particular interests segregated from regulatory oversight by a shared common legal order do not serve the common interest. We have seen this in the case of religious status group legal pluralism.

Focusing on the world of transnational trade and investment law where the source of corporate power is international treaty law, Pistor analyzes the rise of transnational corporate economic power and how it turns global legal pluralism into legal particularism and triggers a competitive race to the bottom regarding regulatory control by states, undermining their sovereignty. If corporations can freely choose the law that suits their interests, states lose the ability to govern them in ways that comport with the public interest. By invoking pluralist and liberal rhetoric of the contract, business corporations have become adept at fostering their own particular interests at the expense of those of the people in the states in which they operate. Pistor argues that the current legal pluralism and free choice of law empowers some but at the expense of collective self-governance in the public interest by states, absent a functional equivalent to a federal legal order on regional and global levels. The principle of free incorporation set the stage for a struggle over domination between states and corporations. Corporations cannot win without the help of states, but all they need is one willing state in order to play their game of legal particularism.

Tsilly Dagan's analysis in "The Marketing of Tax Sovereignty" makes a similar and related point. Focusing on the all-important sovereign power to tax to fund programs and set redistributive policies that serve the public, Dagan demonstrates that multinational enterprises use their competitive advantage under the rules of global legal pluralism to undermine this power. They shop around for sovereign goods and make use of state competition for investment to pay as little tax as possible. Because residents (and particularly incorporated residents), their businesses, capital, resources, and profits are highly mobile across national borders under current rules, they put sovereign states under competitive pressure to attract them. Hence, in terms of taxation, sovereigns no longer hold the monopolistic power to govern. Instead, they themselves become similar to market actors competing for resources (IP, capital, jobs, and innovation), tax revenues, and residents.

From the traditional perspective of civil power and civil law, a democratic sovereign polity is entrusted—through a political process—with legislative tax powers, aiming ideally to maximize welfare (efficiency) and justly (re) distribute while reinforcing the underlying normative values shared by its constituents. Such a sovereign has the power and—assuming it treats its constituents justly—legitimacy to so govern. But the competition unleashed by unbridled transnational corporate business enterprises seems to permeate into the very nature of tax sovereignty, altering the traditional role played by the sovereign. It affects the kinds and quantities of public goods and privileges offered by the state to its constituents; it affects the underlying meanings and values of the sovereign-subject interaction; and it transforms modes of political participation and schemes of distribution. As Dagan shows, this entails a serious distortion: the reduction of political for economic power, favoring business and eviscerating the core public purposes of constitutional democracies. Although touted as yet another efficient and productive example of legal pluralism, Pistor's concept of legal particularism applies quite well to this use of the rules by business enterprises to escape taxation and political oversight by the democratic sovereign.

The appropriate solution to this conundrum is unclear. Absent cooperation, states cannot preserve their tax rates (and their levels of redistribution) without sacrificing the collective welfare of their constituents. But cooperation carries the risk—particularly for developing countries—of being subject to the cartelistic powers of a dominant group of countries that might undermine not only states' independence in shaping their tax policies but also global justice.

The final chapter of this volume illustrates this conundrum perfectly. In "The Politics of Horizontal Inequality: Indigenous Opposition to Wind Energy Development in Mexico," Courtney Jung explores the tensions and the opportunities generated by the various forms of legal pluralism in Mexico regarding indigenous peoples' voice and rights in domestic conflicts over development. Her focus is the clash over "energy development" via the erection of wind turbines in the Isthmus of Tehuantepec, home to more than a thousand indigenous communities. Mexico is a federal republic in which, as Jung notes, the states exercise significant powers, enabling them to allow municipalities to be governed by *usos y costumbres*—a range of indigenous customs and practices, including jurisdiction over family law, inheritance, land allocation, and criminal punishment. Accordingly, the state of Oaxaca, in response to indigenous demands for more autonomy, allows municipalities to choose whether to be governed by party politics or traditional practices, and now almost all municipalities in the isthmus are governed by usos y costumbres. This is an example of a federal power exercised by a state invoking the principle of subsidiarity to change its municipal governing structures and institute status group political and legal pluralism for a local indigenous population in order to accommodate diversity.

Mexico is also embedded in a supranational network of organizations, treaties, agreements, and courts that further multiply the legal fora, spaces, and frameworks that govern politics. Moreover, Mexico depends on foreign direct investment to fulfill many of its development goals. In making the switch to clean renewable energies, Mexico has relied on investment from multinational corporations and consortiums of corporations that exercise considerable polit-ical and economic power but are also partly governed by various trade agree-ments and loan conditions.

Jung's piece shows how the complexity of forms of legal pluralism have shaped the political process and indigenous protests by providing a variety of frames for articulating grievances, at times facilitating, at times blocking, democratic self-government. Indeed, the complexity of the situation and the ambivalence of the effects of the various plural legal fora is a theme of the chapter. As Jung notes, some of the legal and political spaces and frames accommo-date difference and autonomy, some are easy to access, and some enhance and protect the principles of equality, voice, individual, and collective rights, but others violate rights and shut down democratic voice and representation. For example, she cites research showing that usos y costumbres systems of status group pluralism discriminate against women in terms of office holding and other rights. She also notes that it tends to obscure differences of opinion and interests within the indigenous communities, reifying and essentializing them, just what Macklem indicated is a flaw of this form of institutionalizing pluralism. Instead of diminishing conflict, it has exacerbated it among the various indig-enous communities and groups, leading to violence between inhabitants of central villages where municipal authority is concentrated and those in rural areas. Moreover, rights to individual freedom, due process, and a fair trial tend to be systematically violated by communities governed by usos y costumbres systems, although they also foster greater trust of officials than communities governed by political parties and the civil law.

Jung shows how some of this plurality of legal forms leaves the outcomes open by multiplying avenues and ways of framing protest and contestation. Jung seems to conclude that enabling migration among political and legal ven-ues secures the contingency that undergirds constitutional democracy. But the complexity and fragmentation of levels of governance also could be a way to disempower certain populations and undermine basic individual rights. More-over, it creates coordination problems among the various legal instances, and it is unclear whose autonomy is enhanced by the fragmentation of the civil law or who is ultimately responsible and accountable to whom. How do the various legal orders relate, and how should they be coordinated ideally to comport with democratic constitutionalism? Who ensures that the particular form of status group legal pluralism practiced in Mexico comports with the principles of democratic constitutionalism and basic rights, and who has the competence to determine these questions? It could be that this complexity raises more prob-lems than it resolves, giving the illusion of consent and autonomy regarding development and other issues at the price of individual rights. All of this merits further study there and regarding forms of pluralism elsewhere, and it is the aim of this volume to trigger just that.

# Notes

1. Jean L. Cohen, *Globalization and Sovereignty: Rethinking Legality, Legitimacy and Constitutionalism* (Cambridge: Cambridge University Press, 2012), 80–87 for a discussion of the concept of political form. See also chapter 6 by Alfred Stepan and Jeff Miley in this volume.
2. Andrew Arato, "The Promise and Logic of Federations and the Problem of Their Stability" (lecture, The Public Seminar, New York, N.Y., June 22, 2016).
3. Patrick Macklem, *The Sovereignty of Human Rights* (Oxford: Oxford University Press, 2015).
4. For a sophisticated justification of domestic jurisdictional political pluralism, see Victor M. Muniz-Fraticelli, *The Structure of Pluralism* (Oxford: Oxford University Press, 2014). For a critique, see Jean L. Cohen, "Sovereignty, the Corporate Religious, and Jurisdictional/Political Pluralism," *Theoretical Inquiries in Law* 18, no. 2 (July 2017): 547–75. For the problem of the fragmentation plaguing global legal pluralism, see International Law Commission, *Fragmentation of International Law: Difficulties Arising from the Diversification and Expansion of International Law*, Report of the Study Group of the International Law Commission (finalized by Martti Koskenniemi), UN Doc. A/CN4/L.682 (April 13, 2006).
5. Hendrik Spruyt, *The Sovereign State and Its Competitors* (Princeton, N.J.: Princeton University Press, 1994).
6. David C. Hendrickson, *Peace Pact: The Lost World of the American Founding* (Lawrence: University Press of Kansas, 2003); and Peter Onuf and Nicholas Onuf, *Federal Union, Modern World: The Law of Nations in an Age of Revolutions 1776–1814* (Indianapolis, Ind.: Madison House Publishers, 1993). Both argue that the constitutional project of federal union was deemed an alternative to international relations of sovereign states based on the European balance of power model (Vattel) and to the danger of universal monarchy and despotic empire in which central control obliterated the autonomy of member units. Federal union was seen as a way to make the external internal and to render sovereignty irrelevant to the internal relations among the member states of the federation.
7. See Jean L. Cohen, "The Politics and Risks of the New Legal Pluralism in the Domain of Intimacy," *International Journal of Constitutional Law* 10, no. 2 (March 2012): 380–97.
8. See chapter 12 by Katharina Pistor and chapter 13 by Tsilly Dagan in this volume. See also Julian Arato, "Corporations as Lawmakers," *Harvard International Law Journal* 56, no. 2 (2015): 229–95.
9. See chapter 8 by Nadia Urbinati in this volume.
10. See Cohen, "Constitutionalism and Political Form: Rethinking Federation," in *Globalization and Sovereignty*, 80–158.
11. See chapter 12 by Katharina Pistor in this volume.
12. Cohen, *Globalization and Sovereignty*, 80–158.
13. Hanna Arendt, *On Revolution* (New York: Penguin Books,1963).
14. Mahmood Mamdani, *Citizen and Subject: Contemporary Africa and the Legacy of Late Colonialism* (Princeton, N.J.: Princeton University Press, 1996).
15. See Chapter 6 by Alfred Stepan and Jeff Miley in this volume.
16. See Neil Walker, "The Idea of Constitutional Pluralism," *Modern Law Review* 65, no. 3 (2002): 317–59. For a critique of the EU's brand of constitutionalism, see Turkuler Isiksel, *Europe's Functional Constitutionalism* (Oxford: Oxford University Press, 2016).

17. Szegin borrows the term "the paradox of multicultural vulnerability" from Ayelet Shachar, *Multicultural Jurisdictions* (Cambridge: Cambridge University Press, 2005). For a critique of Shachar's argument see Cohen, "Politics and Risks of the New Legal Pluralism," 380–97.
18. Cristina Lafont, "Should We Take the 'Human' Out of Human Rights? Human Dignity in a Corporate World," *Ethics and International Affairs* 30, no. 2 (2016): 233–52.
19. See Jason Hackworth, *Faith Based: Religious Neoliberalism and the Politics of Welfare in the United States* (Athens: University of Georgia Press, 2012); and Nancy J. Davis and Robert V. Robinson, *Claiming Society for God: Religious Movements and Social Welfare* (Bloomington: Indiana University Press, 2012).

# Bibliography

Arendt, Hannah. *On Revolution*. New York, N.Y.: Penguin Books, 1963.

Arato, Andrew. *Post Sovereign Constitution Making: Learning and Legitimacy*. Oxford: Oxford University Press, 2017.

——. "The Promise and Logic of Federations and the Problem of Their Stability." Lecture, The Public Seminar, New York, N.Y., June 22, 2016.

Arato, Julian. "Corporations as Lawmakers." *Harvard International Law Journal* 56, no.2 (2015): 229–95.

Cohen, Jean L. *Globalization and Sovereignty: Rethinking Legality, Legitimacy and Constitutionalism*. Cambridge: Cambridge University Press, 2012.

——. "The Politics and Risks of the New Legal Pluralism in the Domain of Intimacy." *International Journal of Constitutional Law* 10, no. 2 (2012): 380–97.

——. "Sovereignty, the Corporate Religious, and Jurisdictional/Political Pluralism." *Theoretical Inquiries in Law* 18, no. 2 (July 2017): 547–75.

Davis, Nancy J., and Robert V. Robinson. *Claiming Society for God: Religious Movements and Social Welfare*. Bloomington: Indiana University Press, 2012.

Hackworth, Jason. *Faith Based: Religious Neoliberalism and the Politics of Welfare in the United States*. Athens: University of Georgia Press, 2012.

Hendrickson, David C. *Peace Pact: The Lost World of the American Founding*. Lawrence: University Press of Kansas, 2003.

International Law Commission. *Fragmentation of International Law: Difficulties Arising from the Diversification and Expansion of International Law*. Report of the Study Group of the International Law Commission. Finalized by Martti Koskenniemi. UN Doc A/CN.4/L.682 and Add. 1 and Corr. 1. New York: International Law Commission, 2006.

Isiksel, Turkuler. *Europe's Functional Constitutionalism*. Oxford: Oxford University Press, 2016.

Lafont, Cristina. "Should We Take the 'Human' Out of Human Rights? Human Dignity in a Corporate World." *Ethics and International Affairs* 30, no. 2 (2016): 233–52.

Macklem, Patrick. *The Sovereignty of Human Rights*. Oxford: Oxford University Press, 2015.

Mamdani, Mahmood. *Citizen and Subject: Contemporary Africa and the Legacy of Late Colonialism*. Princeton, N.J.: Princeton University Press, 1996.

Muniz-Fraticelli, Victor M. *The Structure of Pluralism*. Oxford: Oxford University Press, 2014.

Onuf, Peter, and Nicholas Onuf. *Federal Union, Modern World: The Law of Nations in an Age of Revolutions 1776–1814*. Indianapolis, Ind.: Madison House Publishers, 1993.

Shachar, Ayelet. *Multicultural Jurisdictions*. Cambridge: Cambridge University Press, 2005.

Spruyt, Henrik. *The Sovereign State and Its Competitors*. Princeton, N.J.: Princeton University Press, 1994.

Walker, Neil. "The Idea of Constitutional Pluralism." *Modern Law Review* 65, no. 3 (2002): 317–59.

# PART I

## AFTER EMPIRE

*Historical Alternatives*

# 1

# FEDERATION, CONFEDERATION, TERRITORIAL STATE

*Debating a Postimperial Future in French West Africa, 1945–1960*

FREDERICK COOPER

In French Africa in the 1950s, federalism was not a utopian nor a theoretical option. Most political actors thought some combination of political union of African territories with each other and with France was preferable to what they considered the "nominal" independence of the territorial nation-state. They thought about the institutions that could make federalism a practical proposition; they wrote a constitution for a francophone West African federation, and for a brief period an African federation held power, first within the French Community, then as an independent entity with two member states. The Mali Federation, as it was called, broke up. Since then, its failure has been taken as inevitable in the face of the supposedly inexorable drive of people to have their own nation-states, and it is easily forgotten that the nation-state was a fallback option for the leaders most involved at the time.

The starting point for the political inventiveness of French Africans in the 1950s—also easily ignored—was not an abstract idea or the existence of nations that might agree to unify in a federal form but rather empire, specifically, colonial empire. African political leaders had grown up with this reality, and they understood very well the racial denigration and economic exploitation that existing empires entailed. But they also understood that empires were linguistically and culturally heterogeneous. The question they posed as they confronted a France trying to reimagine itself after its defeat in World War II was how to transform a structure of unequal connections into one that respected diversity, acknowledged the economic and social inequality colonization had produced, and was capable of transforming society toward substantive as well as formal equality.

They confronted influential elements of a colonial empire who thought Africans were inferior and whose role in a French polity could only be to serve French economic and political interests. But the self-evident quality of such thinking was much diminished after the debacle of world war, and an alternative viewpoint within part of the French political establishment overlapped with the perspective of African politicians. One of the more thoughtful members of that establishment, Robert Delavignette, argued in 1945 that France did not *have* an empire, it *was* an empire.[1] What constituted France as a state, he meant, was the totality of its parts, however unequal they were; a French state independent of its overseas territories did not exist. For all the prejudices of the French elite, that conception offered a way out of the problem they faced in 1945. Rather than having to think about giving up something France claimed to possess, the relationship of parts of the empire could be rearranged to preserve the whole.

## Postimperial Federalism?

Although Jean Cohen persuasively emphasizes the distinction between empire and federation,[2] the two share an important dimension: both notions acknowledge the heterogeneity of the political unit. By granting limited political autonomy to overseas territories while keeping overall direction in Paris, France could respond to newly invigorated critics of colonial domination while retaining a sense of belonging to a "grand ensemble," crossing seas and continents and governing themselves on their own territory. French Africans would not have to think they would cease to be Africans if they entered a federation, although they would remain, in another sense, French.

An influential colonial governor positioned the alternative this way in 1943: "France brings the colonies into a French federal system, following in this respect the international movement toward federation that is particularly well illustrated by the British Empire, Soviet Russia, and, in one form or another, by North America and China." Postimperial federalism did not, for the time being at least, imply equality. European France would retain a tutelary role, supervising the evolution of institutions for each territory.[3] A federation with a strong central authority appealed to Charles de Gaulle as he moved from leader of resistance to Vichy rule to the authority governing France's postwar transition: "I believe that each territory over which floats the French flag should be represented within a system of federal form in which the Metropole will be one part and in which the interests of everyone can be heard."[4] Federalist ideas were also being bandied about in the Dutch and British empires in anticipation of a changing postwar political environment.[5]

In 1945, the man who was to become one of French West Africa's most influential politicians, Léopold Sédar Senghor, was also thinking along federalist lines. Senghor often cited Delavignette, and Delavignette cited him. Senghor wanted a degree of autonomy for France's African territories sufficient for them to develop their own political personality, but he wanted all to share a common citizenship, turning all of France's people into "citizens of empire." Heretofore, the empire's population had been divided into rights-bearing citizens, mostly of European origin, and the large majority of the indigenous population of overseas territories, who were considered subjects—French but without the rights of the citizen. Postimperial federalism would give an institutional framework to the way Senghor viewed the relationship of world civilizations: different but equivalent and connected.[6]

But as soon as French and Africa leaders thought more specifically about institutions, they confronted a dual problem. In its classic formulations, federalism presumes equality among its components, but a colonial situation is fundamentally unequal. At the same time, as a committee of jurists looking into the problem stated, "One can only federate that which exists."[7] Colonies had no juridical standing as political entities, no institutions as yet to govern themselves or to act in relation to the federal governing apparatus.

Whatever the jurists said, French politicians were intent on inventing something new. The government was serious enough about demonstrating an inclusive vision of a postimperial polity to give a place to representatives of different categories of people from overseas France in the National Constituent Assembly that was to write a new constitution. Colonial subjects would be among them, but not in proportion to population. Subjects would vote in a separate electoral college, with a limited franchise. There were 6 African deputies from French West Africa (settlers had their own representatives) in an assembly of 586, and 64 from overseas France as a whole.

I have discussed the deliberations over what became the Constitution elsewhere, so I will be brief.[8] The word "federal" and possible federal institutions were debated at length at the Assembly, but federalism was in the end neither accepted nor rejected. Instead, everyone agreed that the empire should be renamed (as had been suggested earlier) the French Union, embodying another category of political theory and echoing the Union of Soviet Socialist Republics, whose structure around national republics was cited as a precedent even by anticommunist deputies.[9] The Preamble to the Constitution referred to the French Union as "composed of nations and peoples," in the plural. The Constitution did not confer significant power on any legislative body in the territories, although it did not prohibit the National Assembly from doing so via subsequent legislation. Sovereignty and legislative authority remained in Paris, in the hands of the National Assembly, in which overseas territories were represented but not in proportion to population. The federal idea was expressed in the Assembly of the French Union, half of whose members were from the overseas territories. This assembly had to be consulted on matters relevant to Overseas France—and it proved to be an important forum for debate—but it had no actual legislative power. From then on, two of the most important demands of African politicians were to give territorial legislatures real power over internal affairs and to give the Assembly of the French Union real power over the Union as a whole.

After intense debates and a brief but dramatic walkout, the overseas deputies had won their bottom-line demand: the demeaning status of "subject" was abolished first by a law proposed by an African deputy, then by the Constitution of October 1946. All inhabitants of the territories of overseas France were now citizens. Moreover, they had a right that citizens of European France did not: their personal affairs did not have to come under the French Civil Code. Marriage, inheritance, and filiation could be regulated under Islamic or "customary" law unless the overseas citizen chose to renounce his or her "personal status." The Constitution (Article 82) specified that keeping one's personal status "can in no case constitute a motive to refuse or limit the rights and liberties attached to the quality of French citizen." In that sense, the Constitution recognized that people could be citizens in more than one way.

The Ministry of Overseas France could assert, in effect, that postwar France was now both egalitarian and multicultural.[10] It was in fact neither. With power concentrated in an assembly dominated by metropolitan deputies and interests, with racial prejudice still prevalent, a franchise that was only slowly moving toward universality (it took ten years to get there), with colonial governors still in place and territorial legislatures unorganized, and with economic power and access to education and health facilities unevenly distributed over the French Union, many elements of the colonial situation remained in place.

## Alternative Federalisms

Citizenship is a claim-making construct, a right to claim rights. The claim to rights lies in the same framework as the state's claim to obligations and authority. Senghor was not entirely displeased with the National Constituent Assembly's ambiguous position on federalism because it allowed the African territories two possible futures: toward full integration into the French Republic (a path followed by the Caribbean colonies) or toward a looser form of federalism, in which the territories would be largely self-governing within a larger French ensemble.[11]

For Africans in French West Africa and French Equatorial Africa, up to 1957 or 1958, the *least* sought after option was independence as a territorially defined nation-state. Senghor referred to nationalism as "an old hunting rifle." His close collaborator in Senegalese politics, Mamadou Dia, stated, "It is necessary that the imperialist concept of the nation-state give way definitively to the modern concept of the multi-national state."[12] The only major political party that advocated independence before 1957 was the Union des Populations du Cameroon, which was marginalized and eventually driven underground by the administration.[13] Senghor's campaign to balance the political expression of Africans with the benefits of belonging to a "grand ensemble" was shared by the other most influential political movement in French Africa, the Rassemblement Démocratique Africain (RDA) founded in the fall of 1946, an organization that was attempting to unite political parties in all the French territories. Its manifesto stated, "We have taken care to avoid equivocation and not to confuse PROGRESSIVE BUT RAPID AUTONOMY within the framework of the French Union with separatism, that is immediate, brutal, total independence. Doing politics, do not forget, is above all to reject chimeras, however seductive they may be and to have the courage to affront hard realities." The manifesto concluded, "Vive l'Afrique Noire, Vive l'Union Française des Peuples Démocratiques."[14]

There were as many routes out of empire as there were different ways of governing people within empire. The federalist alternative was attractive in sub-Saharan Africa, not least because its leaders were conscious of how impoverished and ill-educated their peoples were and hence how great their needs. The Caribbean colonies—where slaves had been freed and made into citizens in 1848—generally supported full integration into the French Republic, although some later had doubts about how much they benefited from their successful effort. Indochina, meanwhile, was spinning out of control. Having been chased out by the Japanese, the French left a vacuum quickly filled by the forces of Ho Chi Minh. In September 1945, Ho proclaimed the Republic of Vietnam, leaving open its relationship to France. Whether or not an accommodation between the avowed Communist movement and the French government was ever plausible, the French military preempted the possibility and began an eight-year-long war that ended in France's defeat.

Algeria had since 1848 been considered an integral part of the French Republic, but most of its Muslim majority was excluded from citizenship. Assertions of an Algerian nation had come to the fore before the war, but French leaders hoped that at least one major leader, Ferhat Abbas, had federalist leanings.[15] But the insistence of much of the French political establishment—not just the die-hard colonialists—that Algeria must remain in the Republic and not just in the Union made such a position virtually untenable. After 1946, the French settlers in Algeria used their own citizenship and their connections to ensure that Muslim Algerians would not be able to exercise theirs. Whatever opportunities there were in 1945 or 1946 to balance Muslim Algerians' national aspirations and participation in a federal system were lost, and Algeria was on a path to a bitter war of liberation.

The split between settlers and indigenous people in Morocco and Tunisia was comparable, if not so acute, to that in Algeria, but the political structure was different. Tunisia and Morocco were protectorates, and they had never lost their sovereignty or their nationality even when France took over de facto governance (in 1881 and 1911, respectively). They were supposed to participate in the French Union as Associated States. Their rulers refused to send representatives to Union institutions, and there was nothing the French government could do except to pretend it was ruling in the name of the noncooperating sovereigns. France faced nationalist mobilization in both states, and there was considerable violence and repression. When things came to a boil, France had an easier exit option than it did in Algeria; the government could not be accused of surrendering territory that was integral to France.[16] In 1956, Morocco and Tunisia became independent; Algeria was at war; Vietnam was lost; and sub-Saharan Africa was in the midst of political mobilization (with little violence) to reform the French Union to strengthen Africans' claims to both political voice and social and economic equality with fellow French citizens.

Different federalisms were in play throughout the late 1940s and 1950s. In 1947, de Gaulle set out his version of the French Union's diverse components:

> Each, in the framework of French sovereignty, must receive its own statute, governing, according to the very variable degree of its development, very variable ways and means by which the representatives of the inhabitants, French or native, would be able to deliberate locally internal affairs and take part in their management. . . . We will not be able to bring the French Union to life without institutions of a federative character.

There was no question about the place of France in de Gaulle's federal scheme: "The French Union must be French, which implies that the authority, and I mean the authority of France, will be clearly exercised on the ground, and that her duties, rights, and responsibilities remain beyond question in the domains of public order, national defense, foreign policy, and the common economy."[17]

Meanwhile Senghor and his allies were calling for "an active federalism."[18] They wanted to amend the Constitution to give real power to the territories and to the federal assembly, but in this regard they were getting nowhere. They had more success on the social front, particularly because trade unions were joining the politicians in demanding equal pay and benefits for equal work for all French citizens. The unions were strong enough to stage some monumental strikes in the late 1940s and early 1950s. They could pick up allies in the center-right in France, mainly from a group of "social Catholics" concerned with giving workers a secure place in the social order to encourage family formation and to counter Communists' efforts to woo the working class. The high point of social citizenship came with the labor code of 1952, following much effort by African deputies in Paris and a one-day general strike across all of French West Africa. The code put African workers on the same plane as workers from Europe and extended such fruits of social democracy as the forty-hour week, paid vacations, and union recognition to African wage workers.[19]

The social gains and political stalemate led the government, under constant pressure from Africans to improve social conditions and for more territorial autonomy and an equitable voting system, to move toward a fuller form of federalism. In 1956, the National Assembly passed a law that enabled each territory (Senegal, Dahomey, Côte d'Ivoire, and others) to elect a legislature by universal suffrage, which in turn would choose a "conseil de gouvernment," a cabinet that would function as an executive with regard to internal matters.

## Territorial Self-Government as Opportunity and as Trap

That meant that an African political party would be governing each territory. Sovereignty would still rest with the French Republic, and sovereign functions such as defense and foreign affairs would remain in French hands. A French-appointed governor would have authority in each territory and would be given the title of Président du Conseil, and the elected leader would be called Vice-Président du Conseil. The civil service would now be under the control of the territorial legislature and the executive. If African politicians wanted to give civil servants better benefits, they would have to convince the taxpayers who elected them of the merit of their proposition. For the government, the only way to convince African political leaders to lower their social claims was to give them real power. This was still short of a true federalism, for the constitution was unchanged and the powers devolved could presumably be taken back by the National Assembly that had conferred them; in addition, the presence of a French governor was a reminder that the colonial situation had not entirely been transcended. The law also represented an attempt to separate the future of sub-Saharan Africa from that of Algeria. It did not restructure the French Union as a whole.[20]

For Senghor, the new law was a victory with regard to key demands but a threat to his ultimate goal. Power was being conferred to each territory, and that, he realized, would create vested interests on the part of political actors in power in the territory. He repeatedly referred to the "Balkanization" of Africa. The law intervened in a debate that was going on among Africans about the kind of federalism they desired, a debate he was determined to continue. This became known in African circles as the battle of federation and confederation.[21]

Senghor was both a consummate politician, whose understanding of relations in different corners of Senegalese society enabled him to put together a powerful movement, and a thinker who dealt in political concepts with clarity.[22] Two lines of thought are important to understanding his evolving position on federation and confederation. First was a distinction he made beginning in 1948 between horizontal and vertical solidarity. Vertical solidarity grew out of Africa's connection to France, a past of exploitation, but also the source of education and technique, of a heritage of rights and democracy, and of needed material resources. He was acknowledging inequality in order to transcend it. The vertical relationship was still a relationship, a useful one but only if combined with something else.

There was "another solidarity, more real because based on ethnology and geography, that is 'horizontal solidarity' that ties together people of the same continent or the same condition." Horizontal solidarity needed to be organized "on the basis of equality among all peoples, whatever their race or religion."[23] Africans across all French territories needed to work together to reinforce their sense of self and to make claims on the resources of the French Union. Vertical solidarity without the horizontal would be the old colonialism restored, but horizontal solidarity without the vertical would be unity in poverty, a failure to understand interdependence in an unequal world.

The second distinction he elaborated was among *patrie*, nation, and state. His notion of the "petite patrie" had both African and French roots— his own origins in the Serer ethnic group and resentment against the larger and more domineering Wolof of Senegal melded with the romance of the "terroir-province" dear to politicians and intellectuals in France.[24] Nation, in contrast, was constructed:

The Nation, if it brings together, the *patries*, it is to transcend them. It is not, like the patrie, a natural determination, an expression of its milieu, but rather the will to construct, or better to reconstruct. In terms of its realization, the Nation builds out of its provinces a harmonious ensemble.

The state helps to build the nation:

The state is to the nation what the entrepreneur is to the architect. It incarnates itself in institutions: government, parliament, public services. The civil servants are the workers. It is that state that accomplishes the will of the nation and assures its permanence. Inside, it mixes together the *patries*, it kneads together individuals in the mold of the "archetype"; toward the exterior it defends the integrity of the nation, which it guards against foreign intrigue.[25]

Senghor's relational view of politics—as the conjugation of vertical and horizontal solidarities—dates to at least the late 1940s, and over the 1950s he became increasingly concerned with the project of constructing a nation: an African nation that is. In the 1940s, he had advocated an open-ended form of federalism, capable of evolving toward further or lesser integration into France, but with a claim on the resources of the French Union as a whole. By the mid-1950s, Senghor had seen little sign that French leaders were willing to consider African territories as full partners in a federation, and he was also seeing Morocco and Tunisia (and colonial territories elsewhere) move toward independence. He was now thinking about federation and confederation in relation to each other.

Senghor's ideas crystalized around a three-layered approach to political structure. Each French African territory would have an elected legislature and executive. Together, the territories would constitute a federation—what he sometimes called a primary federation—with its own legislature and executive. This would be the state that constructed the African nation. The primary federation, not the individual territory, would join metropolitan France in a confederation, which would be open to Morocco, Tunisia, and any other state that wanted to join.[26]

Although political theorists see federation and confederation as variations on a theme,[27] the distinction was important to Senghor above all because he saw confederation as recognizing the distinct national personality of its component parts, whereas federation was for him the level at which he wanted to construct the African nation. In simultaneously constructing the nation and looking beyond it, he was going against views of sovereignty as indivisible. His African federation might claim sovereignty, but only to give some of it up:

> A nation in formation promoted to autonomy must move past it and insert itself, at the last stage, in a larger ensemble: a confederation. "She consents freely to abandonments of sovereignty; she dies at the absolute fiction of independence in order to enjoy real independence. And the more the confederated states are diverse in race and culture, the stronger the confederation is because its members are complementary."[28]

In practical terms, Senghor had a place from which to depart. The French government, not long after it began to rule eight territories in west Africa and four in central Africa, grouped them into two administrative entities, which it sometimes misleadingly labeled federations: French West Africa (AOF) and French Equatorial Africa (AEF). In each, a governor general presided over the governors of the respective territories and over common services. From 1947, African politicians from the major parties of West Africa (chosen by the territorial assemblies) sat in the Grand Conseil of AOF. The Grand Conseil had limited powers, including review of the budget, but it was at least an indirectly elected body with some appearance of a legislature. Senegalese politician

Lamine Guèye could assert, prematurely, that its opening heralded the "establishment of a federal system thanks to which the different territories of AOF and AEF now enjoy a large economic and financial autonomy."[29] He was right to the extent that the Grand Conseil became the focus of claims to turn it into a true legislature, which in turn could appoint an executive, who could administer AOF alongside or instead of the governor general. To do so would turn AOF from an administrative into a political unit and thus constitute the basis of a federation.

That was exactly what a considerable range of African politicians, including members of the Grand Conseil, were demanding. From the late 1940s, the call to rewrite the sections of the Constitution on the French Union were frequently heard in newspapers such as *L'Afrique Nouvelle*, in party reports and statements, and in resolutions introduced in the National Assembly or the Assembly of the French Union.[30] The proposals got buried in the controversies over Algeria and the ineptitude of the institutions of the Fourth Republic, but they were manifestations of African politicians' quest for a middle layer in the structure of the French Union.

One of the most radical of African politicians, Sékou Touré, head of the RDA branch in Guinea, differed with Senghor in many respects, but not on the twin points of advocating an African federation and, until his conflict with de Gaulle of August 1958, participating in a political union with France: "We are decided to build the Franco-African Community, while maintaining the unity of Africa which is dear to it."[31]

The sentiment, however, was not unanimous. It had two well-placed opponents, Sourou Migan Apithy of Dahomey and Félix Houphouët-Boigny of the Côte d'Ivoire. During the debates over the 1956 legislation to devolve powers to the territories, Apithy made an argument that was both political and cultural:

> Africans, like all populations of the overseas territories, have the strongest sentiment of belonging to a collectivity, a country, a "patrie locale" (Senegal, Sudan, Dahomey, Chad, Gabon, and so on) that forms part of the French Republic but distinguishes itself from the other members of the French community by its geographic, historical, and human originality, by the conditions of its economic, psychological, and religious life.[32]

He feared that federal institutions in Africa would diminish the effectiveness of the new territorial governments. In contrast to Senghor, Apithy's patrie was a territory delimited by colonization, not an African cultural or linguistic grouping.

Houphouët-Boigny, president of the RDA, differed with RDA member Sékou Touré in defending a two-layer approach to postimperial federalism. Houphouët-Boigny wanted African territories to adhere directly to a federation in which metropolitan France and its former colonies would be equals. "Federal executive?" he asked, "Yes, but in Paris, not in Dakar."[33] Houphouët-Boigny differed with Senghor in that he wanted the highest level of union to be a federation, not a confederation, but he agreed that this unit should cross lines of difference: "Many of us want to reconcile the life of our states and their personalities with those of the Community itself. It is at the same time a marriage of reason and of love. I believe in it, that is why we remain to the limit partisans of the multinational state."[34]

With the RDA split over the African federation, Senghor tried to put together his own version of a party that would cover all of French West Africa. The Parti du Regroupement Africain (PRA, later reconstituted as the Parti de la Fédération Africaine) carried on the push for the federal executive and parliament for French Africa and a confederal relationship with France. But even within these organizations there was disagreement over whether to push first for independence and then unite, or to unite first and then push for independence.[35]

## Africa and the French Community

In the summer of 1958, the crisis in Algeria brought Charles de Gaulle back to power. A new constitution had to be written for what would become the Fifth Republic.[36] The constitution redefined overseas territories as Member States of the Community, the new name of the French Union, and gave them what the 1946 Constitution had denied—the right to independence if they so chose. Africans were no longer represented in the National Assembly in Paris, but the heads of Member States joined an Executive Council that met with the president of France regularly to decide matters common to the Community. It did not repair one of the fundamental anomalies of the earlier constitution: the Community had a president (none other than the president of the French Republic), but there was no federal cabinet and no federal bureaucracy, military, and treasury to implement the Executive Council's decisions.

African territories had a choice of whether to accept this constitutional proposal or to become independent. Senghor and others saw this text as a compromise, but one they could live with. In the end, only Guinea voted against the constitution and only after de Gaulle refused to modify it according to Sékou Touré's wishes. Guinea immediately became independent, and the rest of French Africa became Member States of the Community.[37] Guinea's go-it-alone independence made Sékou Touré's deep desire to promote African unity all the harder to achieve. Meanwhile, the Côte d'Ivoire continued to oppose a West African federation.

In late 1958 and 1959, leaders from Senegal, the Soudan, Upper Volta, and Dahomey attempted to put together a federation among themselves. To make a long story short, only two territories, Senegal and Sudan, agreed to unite, founding the Mali Federation in January 1959. The other leaders feared that larger or wealthier units might overwhelm them or that poorer units would claim a share of their resources, and they feared going against the will of the Côte d'Ivoire, the region's richest territory. Mali made a serious attempt to make federation work. Malian leaders, notably Senghor and Dia from Senegal and Modibo Keita from Soudan, worked out an arrangement for sharing "competences" between Mali and its two member states. They wrote a constitution for Mali.[38]

Although Senegal and Sudan were represented in the Executive Council as Member States of the Community, its leaders persuaded the French government to accept that Mali would be its interlocutor in negotiating a future status. Mamadou Dia made clear that the Mali Federation was the focus of political imagination: "that is how Mali will build itself, and how we can best demonstrate our consciousness, our Malian national will; I do not say Senegalese or Sudanese, because there cannot be a nation at the level of our states—I say our Malian will, and we have the steady conviction that the cause which we serve is the Malian cause, and through it the cause of Africa."[39]

As African leaders failed to reach agreement with each other, the French government saw the danger heightened that each territory would go its separate way. In a remarkable admission, the French High Commissioner in French West Africa told his bosses in Paris that Dia, with his staunch support of confederation, was the best hope to save the Community.[40]

The French government's acute desire to keep the Community alive led it to yield to an African conception on an important matter. The 1958 Constitution stated explicitly that there was only one citizenship and that was "of the French Republic and of the Community." But the Constitution said nothing about nationality. Initially, the French government insisted that there could be only one nationality, the French one. But African leaders realized that such a position diminished their own standing. In fact, two conceptions of nationality were in play. French leaders saw nationality as a quality of a political entity recognized by the community of already existing nations; overseas territories had no such status except through the French state. African leaders thought of nationality as coming not from without but from within, as a sense of collective purpose and action.

French leaders eventually realized how much it meant for African states to have their own nationalities. A committee of "experts" advanced the idea of a "superposed" nationality. Each Member State would have its own nationality; it would write its own nationality legislation and decide whom to consider a national. The nationality conferred by an individual state would automatically confer the nationality of "The French Republic and of the Community." The committee's version of superposed nationality was accepted by the Executive

Council in December 1959.[41] Here we see how far the French government would go to preserve some kind of supranational entity.

But the discussion of superposed nationality, so heated in 1959, was over by the spring of 1960. The Mali Federation, unable to capture aspirations to African unity beyond its two member states, began to negotiate with France over independence. France not only accepted the Mali Federation as its negotiating partner but agreed to modify its definition of the Community to allow Mali to remain in the Community even when it became independent. It would guarantee Malians coming to European France the rights of the French citizen, and Mali would reciprocate. Senghor still wanted to retain Community citizenship, but the Soudanese leader Modibo Keita did not, apparently because he sought a less layered notion of sovereignty and a more unitary state.[42] As negotiations went on, they focused less on the Community as a political entity and more on the bilateral relationship between France and Mali.[43]

The attraction of the Community had been, for many African leaders, linked to the possibility of an African federation within it; French-speaking Africans could work with each other as fellow citizens.[44] Once the possibilities of wider African union faded, the suprasovereignty of Community offered less than the reciprocal rights (and the possibilities of aid) that could be negotiated as a sovereign state with France and the possibilities of direct connections to other states and to international organizations.[45] At the same time, the move toward independence was softened by agreements that kept in place some of the rights, but not the name, associated with common citizenship.

The Mali Federation soon fell victim to the same kinds of tensions that had made a wider African federation unattainable. Senghor and Dia, on one hand, and Keita, on the other, were both colleagues in government and political rivals, both fearing that having built up political bases in their territories they were at risk in a federation of having their rival undermine the political base.[46] When Keita attempted to take power into his own hands in August 1960, two months after independence, Senghor and Dia mobilized police units and supporters to block him and took Senegal out of the Federation.

## From Community to Nation-States

After rejecting the notion of "Senegality," Senghor, Dia, and other leaders from Senegal ended up with just that. Within days of the collapse of the Mali Federation, they were advocating the building of a Senegalese nation.[47] The former Soudan kept the name of Mali for itself, but it was now the Republic of Mali, not the Federation. Once the nation-state became the reality with which African elites had to work, most of them turned to a strong and exclusive notion of the nation.

European France also became more national. Africans coming to European France had, in the 1950s, been exercising the right of citizens to come, go, and seek jobs and residence as they chose, extended by treaties for some years after independence. But in 1974 their rights of entry were severely restricted by a unilateral decision of the French government. From an empire-state trying to keep diverse people within a political unit, France became a nation-state worried about keeping people out, including the descendants of the same people it had tried to keep in.

The story of federation in French West Africa is usually told backward, as if its failure is the point. Told forward, the story underscores the importance to political leaders of the time to find an exit from empire that did not lead to the territorial nation-state. Federation and confederation allowed them to think specifically about building political institutions that confronted the reality of social and economic inequality and cultural difference. They confronted disagreements among themselves and with the rulers of France. The vested interests in territorial political bases that thwarted the efforts of Senghor, Sékou Touré, and others to create an African federation were not givens but developed as France tried to regain control over its overseas territories. The territorial units that eventually became nation-states were not the "petites patries" that Senghor distinguished from the nation. Senghor's federation and the territorial states that eventually came into being were both works of political construction, but they were built on different structures and imaginaries.

The territorially bounded state was not what most political leaders in French Africa in the 1940s and 1950s most wanted, but it was what they could get. The consequence, in these resource-poor states, has been that sovereignty became the ruling elite's principal asset, and protecting it became a zero-sum game. Senghor himself was no exception to the tendency that he warned against in the 1950s for elites to cling to territorial power.

If France did not make good on the possibility of turning empire into confederation, it eventually decided that it liked the idea of confederation for itself. The European Union is a confederation of sovereign states, in which each cedes some of its sovereign functions to the collective body. In 2017, it faces a problem of political imagination—whether people believe in a European project—and the problem of actual inequality among Member States that are supposed to be equivalent. Meanwhile the possibility of reviving the quest for African unity shows some glimmers in the Economic Community of West African States (ECOWAS), which attempts to act collectively in some practical matters and has set forth a project of creating a West African citizenship, superposed on national citizenships somewhat in the manner of the superposed nationality proposed for the French Community in 1959 or the citizenship of the European Union created in 1993.[48]

Federation and confederation offered postimperial possibilities to both African and European states. Decolonization allowed European states both to consolidate themselves as national polities and, when freed of the inter-empire rivalries that had led to two world wars, to find new bases for cooperation with each other. For fifteen years after World War II, political leaders in French Africa explored variants on federation and confederation that offered opportunities to reconcile two forms of political connection: horizontal (among African territories) and vertical (between Africans and their former colonizers). Now, in the early twenty-first century, the European Union appears both innovative and fragile, and African unity remains a distant possibility. The relationship of European and African states is characterized by their separate sovereignties and formal equality, and by extreme inequality in practice. It is still worth contemplating how seriously political leaders in the 1950s took the possibility of alternative ways of organizing politics and how far they got in thinking through the practicalities such an effort entailed. In the end, these efforts did not succeed, but the problem they addressed has yet to be solved: how to live in a world that is both unequal and connected.

# Notes

1. Delavignette was invoked in subsequent debates, for example, Débats, March 20, 1945, Assemblée Consultative Provisoire, Bibliothèque Nationale de France 591 (hereafter cited as ACP). His thinking is developed in Robert Delavignette, "L'Union Française à l'échelle du monde, à la mesure de l'homme," *Esprit* 112 (July 1945): 214–36.

2. Jean L. Cohen, *Globalization and Sovereignty: Rethinking Legality, Legitimacy, and Constitutionalism* (Cambridge: Cambridge University Press, 2012), 94.

3. Gouverneur P.-O. Lapie, "Pour une politique coloniale nouvelle," *Renaissances* (November 1943): 29–34, and (October 1944): 16–20. The Brazzaville Conference of 1944 also referred to federal institutions, but in a vague way. La Conférence Africaine Française, 30 Janvier-8 Février 1944, Brazzaville, Bibliothèque Nationale de France.

4. Extract from press conference given by Charles de Gaulle, July 10, 1944, Washington, D.C., AP 214, Archives d'Outre-Mer, Aix-en-Provence, Bibliothèque Nationale de France (hereafter cited as AOM).

5. Michael Collins, "Decolonisation and the 'Federal Moment,'" *Diplomacy and Statecraft* 24, no. 1 (2013): 21–40; Jennifer Foray, *Visions of Empire in the Nazi-Occupied Netherlands* (Cambridge: Cambridge University Press, 2012).

6. Léopold Sédar Senghor, "Vues sur l'Afrique noire, ou assimiler non être assimilé," in *La communauté impériale française*, ed. Robert Lemaignen, Léopold Sédar Senghor, and Prince Sisonath Youtévong (Paris: Alsatia, 1945), 57–98, at 58.

7. Report of commission of experts, including circular letter of Secretary General of Ministère des Colonies, April 4, 1945, AE 38, Archives Nationales de France, Bibliothèque Nationale de France (hereafter cited as ANF).

8. Frederick Cooper, *Citizenship between Empire and Nation: Remaking France and French Africa 1945–1960* (Princeton, N.J.: Princeton University Press, 2014), chap. 2.

9. The term was first proposed in March 1945 when France was considering how to remake the territories that made up Indochina, which officials considered in itself to constitute a federation.: "The Indochinese Federation forms with France and other parts of the community a 'French Union' whose external interests will be represented by France. Indochina will enjoy, within this union, a liberty of its own. The inhabitants of this Indochinese Federation will be Indochinese citizens and citizens of the French Union. In these terms, without discrimination of race, religion, or origin and given equality of merit, they will have access to all federal positions and employment in Indochina and in the Union." Declaration of French Government, March 25, 1945, 17 G 176, Archives du Sénégal, Dakar (hereafter cited as AS).

10. The Ministry claimed during the constitutional debates that "the legislature wanted to mark the perfect equality of all in public life, but not the perfect identity of the French of the metropole and the overseas French." Directeur Général des Affaires Politiques, Administratives et Sociales, AOF; note, July 1946, 17G 152, AS.

11. Gary Wilder, *Freedom Time: Negritude, Decolonization, and the Future of the World* (Durham, N.C.: Duke University Press, 2015).

12. Léopold Sédar Senghor, "Rapport sur la méthode du Parti," Congress of Bloc Démocratique Sénégalais, April 15–17, 1949; *La Condition Humaine*, April 26, 1949; Mamadou Dia, *La Condition Humaine*, August 29, 1955.

13. Meredith Terretta, *Nation of Outlaws, State of Violence: Nationalism, Grassfields Tradition, and Statebuilding in Cameroon* (Athens: Ohio University Press, 2013). The Parti Africain de l'Indépendance was only founded in 1957, although student organizations had earlier advocated independence.

14. RDA Manifesto, reproduced in Joseph Roger de Benoist, *L'Afrique occidentale française, de la conférence de Brazzaville (1944) à l'indépendance (1960)* (Dakar: Nouvelles Editions Africaines, 1982), 559–61; *Réveil*, September 30, 1946.

15. James McDougall, *History and the Culture of Nationalism in Algeria* (Cambridge: Cambridge University Press, 2006).

16. Adria Lawrence, *Imperial Rule and the Politics of Nationalism: Anti-Colonial Protest in the French Empire* (Cambridge: Cambridge University Press, 2013).

17. Charles de Gaulle, speech in Bordeaux, reported in *Le Monde*, May 17, 1947. De Gaulle was not in government at the time, but his pronouncements carried weight with those who were.

18. Déclaration du groupe interparlementaire des Indépendants d'Outre-Mer, Décembre 24, 1948, and Situation des Indépendants d'outre-mer en 1950, AP 2257/3, AOM; Statement of political parties, Débats, July 6, 1951, 5909, Assemblée Nationale; *La Condition Humaine*, February 25, 1953, April 2, 1953, December 21, 1954.

19. Frederick Cooper, *Decolonization and African Society: The Labor Question in French and British Africa* (Cambridge: Cambridge University Press, 1996).

20. Cooper, *Decolonization*, chaps. 7 and 11; Cooper, *Citizenship*, chap. 5.

21. Cooper, *Citizenship*, chaps. 4 and 5.

22. Wilder, *Freedom Time*.

23. *La Condition Humaine*, July 11, 1948.

24. Etienne Smith, " 'Senghor voulait qu'on soit tous des Senghor': Parcours nostalgiques d'une génération," *Vingtième Siècle Revue d'Histoire* 118 (2013): 97–100.

25. Report to congrès constitutif of Parti de la Fédération Africaine, reprinted in *L'Afrique Nouvelle*, July 3, 1959.

26. Since France, beginning in the late 1940s, had broached the possibility of some sort of confederal relationship with other European states, both French and African leaders had to consider the possibility of an inclusive "Eurafrica." African leaders insisted on having full voice in such a structure. By 1957 it became clear that France's European partners did not want Eurafrica. This saga is discussed in Cooper, *Citizenship*.

27. Cohen, *Globalization and Sovereignty*, 143.

28. Léopold Sédar Senghor, "Pour une République Fédérale dans une Union Confédérale," *Union Française et Parlement* 97 (1958): 5–11, at 9. On the divisibility of sovereignty, see James Sheehan, "The Problem of Sovereignty in European History," *American Historical Review* 111 (2006): 1–15.

29. *Paris-Dakar*, October 4, 1947.

30. Cooper, *Citizenship*, chap. 6.

31. *L'Afrique Nouvelle*, October 1, 1957.

32. Apithy, Débats, March 21, 1956, 1119–23, Assemblée Nationale.

33. *L'Afrique Nouvelle*, April 18, 1958.

34. *Abidjan-Matin*, September 17, 1959.

35. See reports on the debates at the party congress on July 25–27, 1958; *L'Afrique Nouvelle*, August 1, 1958; and de Benoist, *L'Afrique occidentale française*, 404–08.

36. On the constitutional debates, see Cooper, *Citizenship*, chap. 6.

37. Elizabeth Schmidt, *Cold War and Decolonization in Guinea, 1946–1958* (Athens: Ohio University Press, 2007), esp. chap. 6.

38. William Foltz, *From French West Africa to the Mali Federation* (New Haven, Conn.: Yale University Press, 1965).

39. Opening and closing speeches of Mamadou Dia to first national study seminar for political, parliamentary, and government leaders, "on national construction," October 26, 1959, VP 93, AS.

40. High Commissioner to Secretary General of the Community, August 20, 1959, AP 221/3, AOM.

41. The story is told in Cooper, *Citizenship*, chap. 7.

42. Note d'information concernant les institutions de la Communauté, n.d. [December 1959?], FPU 198; Haut Commissaire, Bamako, telegram to Secretariat General of Community, April 14, 1960, May 5, 1960, FPU 1677; "note à l'attention de M. le Président de la Communauté," March 21, 1960, FPR 106, all in ANF.

43. See the papers in the file "citoyenneté: négociations Mali 10–15 Mars 1960," FPU 201, ANF.

44. Boissier Palun, report on "Condition des personnes dans la perspective de l'indépendance du Mali," enclosed in Haut Commissaire, Dakar, to President of Community, December 8, 1959, FPU 198, ANF. On the slow and controversial move to claim independence, see Cooper, *Citizenship*, chap. 8.

45. Madeira Keita, Address to meeting of Union Soudanaise, May 28–31, 1960, FPU 1677, ANF.

46. Foltz, *From French West Africa to the Mali Federation*.

47. *L'Afrique Nouvelle*, September 14, 1960.

48. Michael P. Okom and J. A. Dada, "ECOWAS Citizenship: A Critical Review," *American Journal of Social Issues and Humanities* 2, no. 3 (2012): 100–16.

## Bibliography

Archives d'Outre-Mer, Aix-en-Provence.

Archives Nationales, Bibliothèque Nationale de France.

Archives du Sénégal, Dakar.

Assemblée Consultative Provisoire. Débats, 1945. Bibliothèque Nationale de France, Paris.

Assemblée Nationale. Débats, 1945–58. Bibliotheque Nationale de France, Paris.

Césaire, Aimé. *Discours sur le colonialisme.* Paris: Editions Réclame, 1950.

Cohen, Jean L. *Globalization and Sovereignty: Rethinking Legality, Legitimacy, and Constitutionalism.* Cambridge: Cambridge University Press, 2012.

Collins, Michael. "Decolonisation and the 'Federal Moment.'" *Diplomacy and Statecraft* 24, no. 1 (2013): 21–40.

Cooper, Frederick. *Citizenship between Empire and Nation: Remaking France and French Africa 1945–1960.* Princeton, N.J.: Princeton University Press, 2014.

——. *Decolonization and African Society: The Labor Question in French and British Africa.* Cambridge: Cambridge University Press, 1996.

de Benoist, Joseph Roger. *L'Afrique occidentale française, de la conférence de Brazzaville (1944) à l'indépendance (1960).* Dakar: Nouvelles Editions Africaines, 1982.

de Gaulle, Charles. Extract from press conference. Washington, D.C., July 10, 1944. AP 214, Archives d'Outre-Mer, Aix-en-Provence.

Delavignette, Robert. "L'Union Française à l'échelle du monde, à la mesure de l'homme." *Esprit* 112 (July 1945): 214–36.

Foltz, William. *From French West Africa to the Mali Federation.* New Haven, Conn.: Yale University Press, 1965.

Foray, Jennifer. *Visions of Empire in the Nazi-Occupied Netherlands.* Cambridge: Cambridge University Press, 2012.

Lapie, P. O. "Pour une politique coloniale nouvelle." *Renaissances* (1943): 29–34 and (1944): 16–20.

Lawrence, Adria. *Imperial Rule and the Politics of Nationalism: Anti-Colonial Protest in the French Empire.* Cambridge: Cambridge University Press, 2013.

Marr, David. *Vietnam 1945: The Quest for Power.* Berkeley: University of California Press, 1995.

McDougall, James. *History and the Culture of Nationalism in Algeria.* Cambridge: Cambridge University Press, 2006.

Okom, Michael P., and J. A. Dada. "ECOWAS Citizenship: A Critical Review." *American Journal of Social Issues and Humanities* 2, no. 3 (2012): 100–16.

*Report of commission of experts, including circular letter of Secretary General of Ministère des Colonies.* Archives Nationales de France, April 4, 1945: AE 38.

Schmidt, Elizabeth. *Cold War and Decolonization in Guinea, 1946–1958.* Athens: Ohio University Press, 2007.

Senghor, Léopold Sédar. "Pour une République Fédérale dans une Union Confédérale. *Union Française et Parlement* 97 (1958): 5–11.

——. "Rapport sur la méthode du Parti." Congress of Bloc Démocratique Sénégalais. April 15–17, 1949.

——. "Vues sur l'Afrique noire, ou assimiler non être assimilé." In *La communauté impériale française,* ed. Robert Lemaignen, Léopold Sédar Senghor, and Prince Sisonath Youtévong, 57–98. Paris: Alsatia, 1945.

Sheehan, James. "The Problem of Sovereignty in European History." *American Historical Review* 111, no. 1 (2006): 1–15.

Smith, Etienne. "'Senghor voulait qu'on soit tous des Senghor': Parcours nostalgiques d'une génération." *Vingtième Siècle Revue d'Histoire* 118, no. 2 (2013): 97–100.

Terretta, Meredith. *Nation of Outlaws, State of Violence: Nationalism, Grassfields Tradition, and Statebuilding in Cameroon.* Athens: Ohio University Press, 2013.

Wilder, Gary. *Freedom Time: Negritude, Decolonization, and the Future of the World.* Durham, N.C.: Duke University Press, 2015.

2

# DECOLONIZATION AND POSTNATIONAL DEMOCRACY

GARY WILDER

The United Nations began its official existence in October 1945 when the five permanent members of the new Security Council and a majority of other signatories ratified the Charter.[1] That same month, Aimé Césaire, from colonial Martinique, and Léopold Sédar Senghor, from colonial Senegal, were elected as deputies to a new Constitutive Assembly in Paris. Following France's wartime occupation by Germany and the Vichy state's collaboration with the Nazi regime, this body was charged with drafting the constitution for a Fourth Republic.

In January 1946, the first session of the UN General Assembly convened in New York. Among the issues it addressed that year were the discovery of atomic energy, the extradition and punishment of war criminals, the problem of refugees and displaced peoples, the crime of genocide, the establishment of an International Court of Justice, economic reconstruction projects for member countries devastated by the war, rules governing admission to membership, world armament regulation, a commission for writing an international Declaration on Fundamental Human Rights and Freedom, and the creation of a World Health Organization (WHO). Here were the general outlines of the new postwar order.[2]

The first General Assembly (GA) also responded to more immediate challenges, including a world food shortage, the need for an international children's emergency fund, the political rights of women, the treatment of Indians in South Africa, the future status of South West Africa, and the situation in Palestine. Clearly the question of decolonization would have to be engaged directly.

The GA created a Trusteeship Council to oversee the administration of colonized, or "non-self-governing," peoples in accordance with the Charter, which had pledged to promote their "well-being" and "to develop self-government" for them "according to the particular circumstances of each territory . . . and their varying stages of advancement."[3]

Over the next ten years, a growing number of colonized peoples in Asia, Africa, and the Middle East obtained political independence. For most anticolonial movements (whether moderate or revolutionary, liberal or socialist) throughout the world, the national state became the unquestioned framework through which self-determination should be secured. Curiously, this preference for a national form of decolonization was shared by the existing world powers. When France and Britain recognized that they could no longer remain imperial states, they negotiated bilateral agreements with moderate nationalist allies, thereby creating spheres of neocolonial influence. The United States pursued a similar strategy toward new Third World nations, cultivating blocs of noncommunist allies, exploitable resources, and potential consumers within a system of "free trade" among nominally sovereign national states.[4]

These powerful international actors were equally invested in a UN world order committed to a stable interstate system.[5] It was to be organized around the already existing principles of territorial integrity, national independence, and state sovereignty. It would be policed and protected through a directorate of great powers (the Security Council) and administered through a series of international agencies staffed by bureaucratic and technocratic experts. Of course, it would also have the ability to override the national sovereignty of member states when it was determined that they violated their own population's human rights. But this ad hoc ability to elevate abstract humanity over state sovereignty did not fundamentally challenge the principles of territoriality, nationality, or sovereignty; it was meant, rather, to protect the interstate system that the UN supervised.[6]

Geopolitically and economically, the postwar world would be framed by this structure linking great powers, nominally sovereign states, abstract individuals (now possessing human rights), and international agencies and experts. Despite appearances, nationalism, human rights, international law, and global governance composed a single order (*nomos*) that presupposed the norm of territorial sovereignty and would create conditions favorable for new types of neocolonial capitalism and legalized imperialism.

Yet during this very time Césaire and Senghor pursued *non-national* approaches to decolonization for African and Caribbean peoples. In March 1946, Césaire sponsored the historic law that would officially transform France's so-called old Caribbean and Indian Ocean colonies (Martinique, Guadeloupe, Guyane, and Réunion) into full departments of the French nation-state. That same month, Senghor led a vigorous debate in the Paris Assembly on a constitution that would transform the unitary French republic into a postimperial and postnational federation. This new polity would include former colonies as freely associated members and would reconstitute the former metropole as a federated territory within a new type of decentralized polity and plural democracy. When Césaire in 1956 concluded that departmentalization had become an obstacle to, rather than a vehicle for, Antillean self-determination, he resigned from the French Communist Party, founded an autonomous political party in Martinique, and joined forces with Senghor's movement in the National Assembly to create a postnational federal democracy.[7]

Their aim was not only to abolish colonialism and establish conditions for genuine African and Caribbean self-determination but, at the same time, to overcome the traditional notion of a sovereign and unitary national state, thereby inventing a new political form for a different world order. Their "untimely" belief that decolonization might *not* require national independence, that self-determination might *not* require state sovereignty, helps to account for why their interventions have been consistently misunderstood by subsequent generations of critics and scholars who often dismiss Césaire and Senghor as imperial apologists simply because they were not revolutionary nationalists (as if these were the only two possible alternatives). From our current vantage, we can see how the futures they envisioned were based on timely readings of the emergent postwar order, whose logics and arrangements they believed would destroy the prospect for substantive colonial emancipation. In this way, their timely "untimeliness" is just what allows us to think *with* them now about their world and ours.

## Actually Existing Internationalism

Since the end of the Cold War and the intensification of neoliberal globalization, the limits of state sovereignty (to create conditions for substantive freedom and human flourishing) and the failures of internationalism (to create conditions for global justice and human solidarity) have become everywhere evident. Even if populations manage to empower democratic popular assemblies to promote their social and economic well-being, crucial decisions that would determine their life chances are made elsewhere—by private economic actors, unaccountable international agencies, and technocratic experts.

The fictions of national self-determination and universal human rights are underscored by recent developments within Europe. Consider the EU's punitive treatment of Greece for trying to resist the authoritarian dictates of global finance through a popular left government. For many critics, this confirmed the priority that national sovereignty should have over international association.

But we might also read it in terms of the European Union's disastrous decision to constitute itself as an economic and administrative confederation of states led by technocrats and bankers rather than as a truly democratic federation led by a continental association of self-governing peoples for whom resources were shared, risks were socialized, and autonomy was meaningful.

At a different level is Fortress Europe's failure to respond adequately to the recent flow of refugees from the eastern Mediterranean. This crisis does not simply reveal the moral failure or hypocrisy of the West and the "international community," it makes clear that the existing global order, organized around and managed by the interlocking actions of nominally sovereign states, international agencies, and the U.S. imperium, cannot meet the most basic requirements of global coordination, democratic participation, self-management, human rights, and social justice. The existing *nomos* seems to be entering a moment of unsustainable crisis. Under such conditions, we cannot but think seriously about novel forms of political consociation that might be adequate to the plural, translocal, interdependent demands of our historical present.

The bankruptcy of international law is revealed by Israel's ongoing occupation of Palestine and Russia's annexation of eastern Ukraine. Such violations pale in comparison to the mass violence perpetrated by the U.S. state in the name of liberal internationalism, which is legitimized through UN-sanctioned doctrines and policies regarding human rights, humanitarianism, and the "responsibility to protect."

The dangers of cultural and territorial autarky have recently been demonstrated by massacres of foreign workers in South Africa, the mass deportation of Haitians in the Dominican Republic, the flight of Rohinga Muslims from Myanmar, and the internment of Central American children in the United States. Such dangers will surely be amplified by a Donald Trump administration, which may abandon liberal internationalism to act in the name of "America First." Immediately after assuming office, Trump pursued immigrant round-ups and Islamophobic travel bans, manufactured a military threat from Iran and antagonized China, expressed sympathy for Russian Crimea, and offered tacit approval for Israel's likely annexation of parts of Palestine. Trump's rule will likely underscore the limitations of international law and the lack of frameworks for long-distance solidarity today. The latter was certainly evident as the world watched the Islamic State's siege of Kobani in northern Syria in 2014–15.

In recent years, scholars have developed valuable critiques of existing forms of internationalism (and corresponding cosmopolitan ideologies).[8] Such criticism is warranted and welcome, especially when directed at pious acolytes of international legal procedure, righteous proponents of humanitarian intervention, patriotic defenders of Western civilization, and the unaccountable technocrats who administer the global order. Much of this work comports with the important critique of European internationalism developed by Carl Schmitt in *Nomos of the Earth*.[9]

Schmitt identifies the system of public international law and its humanist ideology as the legitimizing expression of a European imperium, which is based on the sanctity of property and the reality of great power politics. These, he argues, function perversely and paradoxically to legalizes extreme violence against non-European populations. But we should also recall that Schmitt regarded Europe's invidious humanist internationalism as inseparable from the nomos of sovereign states. Far from establishing a binary between internationalism and state sovereignty, he demonstrated how each required and enabled the other. Moreover, Schmitt developed this critique to advance a reactionary vision of imperial spheres of influence corresponding to civilization mandates. It was a brief for politics as permanent war undiluted by legal veils or liberal shibboleths.

This is not to suggest that critics of U.S.-UN internationalism are covert nativists or realpolitik opportunists. But it does underscore the inadequacy of one-sided critique that simply challenges internationalism from the standpoint of state sovereignty (or vice versa). It also reveals the limitations of a critique of existing arrangements that does not allow for the possibility of alternative forms of democratic and cosmopolitan internationalism. Such arguments tend to employ an either-or logic, tacitly conceding that existing forms of liberal internationalism stand for internationalism as such and implying that the only realistic alternative is an open-eyed acceptance of state sovereignty as a quasi-natural fact and territory-ethnicity-force as the inevitable truth of world politics.

Such false binaries are often employed by recent critics of liberal internationalism. Writing from a social democratic perspective, for example, Samuel Moyn makes the important point that national social rights were more substantive and therefore more appealing for most people after World War II than the minimal, abstract, and distant character of so-called human rights. He also acknowledges that various forms of cosmopolitanism emerged after the war. But he asserts, without support, that "the 1940s did not offer any version of a supranational welfarism that was practically effective then or ideologically plausible now."[10] He neither examines nonliberal forms of cosmopolitanism and internationalism nor explores how they may have created possibilities for the "transnational politics" whose current absence he bemoans. Rather, he simply declares that "the nation-state won as a political form and nationalism won as a political ideology."[11] This realist analytic leads him to ignore unrealized historical alternatives and present an either-or choice between actually existing liberal internationalism, human rights, and empty cosmopolitanism, on one side, and the national welfarism of sovereign states, on the other. (He thus implies that the historical "victory" of the UN human rights order has exhausted the space of, and ruled out the possibility for, any other form of cosmopolitan internationalism.)

Writing from the standpoint of radical anti-imperialism, Partha Chattejee, sets up a similar dichotomy and reaches a similar conclusion.[12] He argues that twentieth-century currents of liberal internationalism, Soviet-led communist internationalism, and the post-Bandung "internationalism of the non-aligned" created networks and alliances that promoted the aim of national self-determination, through state sovereignty, for all peoples. He then counterposes these forms of nationalist internationalism to current forms of liberal cosmopolitanism, which he traces back to Kant and uses a "discourse of human rights" to "justify intervention in the sovereign domain of non-Western governments by a global civic community acting on behalf of humanity itself."[13] Chatterjee rightly criticizes the "new forms of imperial power" that are enabled by these invidious types of "international politics" and "cosmopolitan imagining."[14] But he then dismisses cosmopolitanism as such, declaring it the "utopian dream" of "a global intellectual elite located principally in Europe and America"[15] He bases this position on three claims. First, that "the principal achievement of anti-imperialism in the twentieth century" was "the establishment of a universal civic constitution based on the formal equality of sovereign nation-states," which is institutionally "enshrined principally in the General Assembly of the United Nations." [16] Second, that "popular mobilizations" in Africa and Asia only "demand from postcolonial nation-states a rapid material improvement in their living standards and livelihood opportunities" and will likely resist any attempts at global regulation.[17] Third, that the social forces capable of instituting a cosmopolitan program will probably tilt in favor of the West. Finally, like Moyn, he professes a "realist perspective based on the actual record of history" to conclude that "cosmopolitanism as a concept . . . is extremely limited in its historical potential."[18] We are again presented with the false choice between actually existing liberal cosmopolitanism or sovereign national states.[19]

My point is neither to defend cosmopolitanism nor to criticize nationalism. It is to call into question the one-dimensional and binary thinking that underlies these arguments. It is to challenge the dubious idea that the real is rational (which abjures immanent critique and denigrates future-oriented political imagination). It is to push back against the dubious assertion that the arrangements and benefits associated with a future cosmopolitan internationalism would only be of value to liberal Westerners or comprador elites in the Global South, that all ordinary people ever really want is social benefits from a national state. How can we take ideas such as cosmopolitan internationalism, postnational democracy, and transnational polities off the table in a world characterized by imperial wars and occupations, mass displacement and labor diasporas, the criminalization of refugees and migrants, and imminent environmental catastrophe?

Both Moyn and Chatterjee adduce difficulty as proof of impossibility and riskiness as proof of reaction. Each ignores the variety of historical cosmopolitanisms and internationalisms that might point beyond or help us to think across the false dichotomy between liberal cosmopolitanism and national self-determination. And each summarily dismisses historical attempts to anticipate and enact such political forms as fantastic, unrealistic, utopian, lacking mass support, or having "lost out" historically. Both dismiss Senghor's program for a postimperial democratic socialist federation on the grounds that it lost out or was out of sync with the new global order.[20]

There is no disputing the fact that liberal internationalism has authorized new forms of Western imperialism and state violence, nor the fact that for colonized peoples national independence and state sovereignty were often hard-won victories that should be protected against American and European disregard. The UN General Assembly may indeed be a principal achievement of twentieth-century anti-imperialism, just as national welfarism may be understood as a victory of the nineteenth-century workers' struggle in Europe. But each has also served the oppressive status quo by preempting and containing more radical alternatives. Neither should be regarded as a fixed and unsurpassable horizon for anti-imperial and social justice thinking.

I suggest that categorical defenses of national sovereignty reproduce rather than engage the kinds of dilemmas raised by Crimea, Gaza, Greece, Syria, and the Mediterranean refugee crisis. These cases illuminate real problems that have haunted modern democratic politics from their inception; namely, how to fashion effective democratic frameworks through which accountability, legality, and justice might be pursued either on scales that exceed the boundaries of any particular political community or within plural or decentralized polities that seek to displace the model of a unitary sovereign state. Said in a different way: How can the good of popular sovereignty be reconciled with the demands of global solidarity or plural democracy, especially if one cannot be fully realized without the other? How can we conjugate a people's right to self-government with recognition that entwined histories, common futures, and a shared planet implicate seemingly separate peoples in each others' calamities and potentialities? How can we preserve the indisputable benefits of being a full citizen within a democratic political community *and* make claims (in one's own name or in solidarity with others) on distant actors and agencies whose practices circumscribe the life chances of that community? What political forms might guarantee a people's self-determination *and* accommodate the bonds of interdependence, reciprocity, and responsibility that bind it to seemingly disparate peoples and places?

Criticism of existing arrangements should be relentless, and the dangers of certain alternatives should be specified. But the fact that imagining alternative forms is difficult and risky should not be used to foreclose inquiry and reflection along such lines. Pointing out such difficulties and risks should be the starting point, not the concluding insight, of any serious analysis of internationalism and cosmopolitanism. Critiques of existing arrangements and warnings about possible alternatives neither resolve the political dilemmas cosmopolitan internationalism signals (and to which it seeks to respond) nor absolve us from the responsibility of engaging such questions directly in our scholarship. The fact that every experiment in cosmopolitan internationalism will be difficult, risky, contradictory, and unlikely to succeed are reasons *for* taking it seriously as an object of study and aim of praxis. It is precisely because the worldly dilemmas that a cosmopolitan internationalism needs to address are real that mechanical critiques of liberal internationalism from the standpoint of national self-determination are analytically and politically inadequate. We need to learn from historical attempts to identify these dilemmas and to elaborate alternative political forms through which real democratic internationalism oriented toward something like global justice were pursued.

## The Democratic Dilemma

In his writings on universal history, cosmopolitan rights, perpetual peace, and world federation, Kant certainly makes many dubious and, from our vantage point, outmoded claims that warrant criticism.[21] But summary rejections of Kant's political writings (whether as naively liberal, unforgivably conservative, or irredeemably Eurocentric) often have more to do with how he has been claimed by liberal internationalists than with what he actually wrote.

Kant's eighteenth-century reflections deserve our attention for at least two reasons. First, he wrote at a moment of global revolutionary transformation and democratic possibility. His epoch was marked both by the convergence of popular demands for self-government (or popular sovereignty) and unprecedented (commercial and imperial) intercourse among peoples. But which specific political forms would best institutionalize human freedom for the coming century remained to be worked out. We now inhabit an analogous world historical moment.

Second, he defined a democratic dilemma that continues to vex modern political life. On one hand, Kant argued that all humans have a right to be free within a self-governing polity. By this he meant full participation in the process through which that community defined the generally valid laws to which they would voluntarily subject themselves, on a basis of equality with all other citizens who would be governed by the same laws. According to this conception of political freedom (or self-determination), humanity would be composed of separate self-governing polities. Each would be sovereign insofar as it was only accountable to itself; no outside authority could rightfully legislate or rule in its place. For Kant, legally governed social relations and democratic self-government worked together to create a state of political freedom and public peace. On the other hand, he argued that insofar as there existed no overarching legal or constitutional order regulating relations *among* these separate polities, they lived under a permanent threat of unregulated outside aggression. He reasoned that neither political democracy nor human freedom could be fully realized, even for members of self-governing polities, under such lawless conditions within an agonistic international order.

In short, Kant explained that real freedom required the existence of separate sovereign states *and* that such sovereignty would make real human freedom impossible. Conversely, in his view, only the creation of a global political agency could guarantee freedom for self-governing peoples even as it would, by definition, undermine such freedom. His ambiguous response to this dilemma was to envision a federal world republic or world republican federation. By this he meant neither a world state nor a simple confederation of sovereign states agreeing to follow the rules of interstate behavior (as in commercial or nonaggression pacts). Rather Kant envisioned a self-governing federation of self-governing peoples on a worldwide scale. Through this ideal, he hoped that humanity would be able to reconcile popular sovereignty with planetary entanglement and cosmopolitan responsibility. (Insisting that all peoples had an original right to share the whole planet, Kant also argued there exists a realm of cosmopolitan right above national and international law, whereby all the world's citizens may interact with any foreign people without being treated as an enemy.) He thus attempted to envision a cosmopolitan arrangement in which self-determination would not require state sovereignty and in which popular sovereignty would not be violated by an unaccountable world government.

However we might now evaluate Kant's underspecified suggestions, we should appreciate that he defined a profound and persistent problem for democratic politics. This dilemma did not disappear following the French revolution, when the Jacobin model of a unitary national state enjoying total territorial sovereignty within its borders became the normal and desirable form through which peoples sought to protect or pursue self-determination. Nor did it disappear in the nineteenth century when the industrial revolution unfolded and capitalism increasingly transformed social relations throughout Western Europe and its overseas empires, and sovereign national states facilitated the growth of distinct national economies (and vice versa).

After the end of World War II, Kant's democratic dilemma reemerged as a concrete problem for global politics. Following Europe's self-implosion, the genocidal mass murder of its Jewish "minority" populations, and the dawn of mass movements for decolonization, intellectuals, activists, and policy makers engaged in public debates about the problem of freedom, asking how best to reconcile the imperatives of democratic self-government, national independence, state sovereignty, international law, and global justice. Hannah Arendt, for example, maintained that peoples' humanity depended on their place and participation in a concrete political community through which (public) action becomes (publicly) meaningful. Thus her celebration of the ancient Greek polis as an ideal form of political association.[22] But she reasoned that since citizenship in the modern West had become dependent on national identity, one's human rights could only be recognized and protected through the framework of a national state.[23] In her view, European history between 1917 and 1945 demonstrated that under existing conditions the concept of human rights was an empty and dangerous abstraction. But we should recall that this was simultaneously a critique of parochial nationalism as the agency that had degraded democratic politics in the modern period. She demonstrated that in a world order grounded in national xenophobia, race thinking, and imperialism, as growing numbers of people were compelled to reside within the boundaries of nation-states to which they did not legally or ethnically *belong*, nation-states became incapable of guaranteeing them concrete human rights in the form of real citizenship and political belonging.

Like Kant, Arendt recognized that sovereign states were indispensable for a human self-realization that they also made impossible. She demonstrated how this deep and persistent contradiction was revealed in the catastrophic twentieth century when European nation-states and the international order they comprised were unable to address the political problems that they themselves had created, as embodied by diasporic Jews, national minorities, stateless peoples, and refugees. Likewise, neither national nor international legal orders were capable of adequately conceptualizing, let alone addressing, the Nazi genocide as a crime against humanity.[24] She insisted that "the right of every individual to belong to humanity, should be guaranteed by humanity itself" even as she conceded that "for the time being a sphere that is above the nations does not exist."[25] She responded to this dilemma by proposing various forms of multinational federal democracy for European Jews and small states.[26]

At the inception of the postwar period, a range of political thinkers in and beyond Europe shared Arendt's concern with imagining frameworks for transnational solidarity and postnational democracy that would *not* invest already powerful states or a new superstate with quasi-imperial authority over other parts of the world. New arrangements would have to respect the autonomy of vulnerable peoples or nations while also allowing them to make claims on the international community, whether against local states or great powers. Thus Albert Camus demanded that the planned United Nations be constituted as a genuine "international democracy" with a true "world parliament" able to enact binding legislation; W. E. B. Dubois demanded that the United Nations remove colonies from imperial powers, declare itself unconditionally opposed to colonialism, and include delegates from colonized territories; Mahatma Gandhi envisioned a world federation of free, equal, and interdependent states through which the powerful nations would serve the weak, partly through resource redistribution, with the aim of creating "one world"; and Harold Laski insisted that a truly democratic world system could not be based on the principle of state sovereignty and required that capitalism itself be overcome.[27]

These debates about self-determination and internationalism for a new historical era circulated at a moment when colonized peoples, especially across the black Atlantic, were especially sensitive to how political freedom posed a set of genuine risks and problems for which there was no natural or necessary institutional solution. The shared aim was certainly to end imperialism and secure self-determination. But given the deep relations of entanglement and dependence that would continue to subordinate postcolonial societies to larger processes and stronger states, many wondered whether the sovereign national state was the only or best form in which to do so. This is the context in which Senghor and Césaire attempted to reconcile the imperatives of self-government, translocal interdependence, and human solidarity by envisioning new types of federal polities organized on non-national lines and on transcontinental scales.

Imperial states typically subjugated non-Europeans in the name of claims to protect populations, generalize liberty, ensure world peace, and improve humanity. They violated subject peoples' autonomy and territorial integrity on the erroneous grounds that they were not capable of self-government. This at a time when the logic of global politics held that a people could neither appear on the stage of world history nor even be recognized as a political actor without being organized as an independent national state. Under such conditions, state sovereignty, national independence, and territorial integrity certainly promised a robust alternative to, and protection against, colonial domination by foreign powers. Any international arrangement that would open the door to new forms of intercontinental paternalism and supranational authority would be rightly suspect.

Yet many non-European thinkers also recognized that formal political liberty could not protect formerly colonized peoples from the depredations of global capitalism, uneven development, great power geopolitics, and an ascendant American state. Political independence would certainly not automatically undo the knots of socioeconomic entanglement and relations of dependence that would continue to bind former colonized peoples to former imperial powers. Moreover, this history of entanglement meant that much of the West's wealth and prosperity, as well as the infrastructure for generating future wealth, was made possible by the exploitation of slave and colonial labor, the expropriation of overseas natural resources, and the relations of intercontinental inequality that imperial capitalism had instituted worldwide.

From this perspective, many colonial critics believed that there should be non- or supranational mechanisms through which this interdependence could be recognized, reciprocity guaranteed, and colonized peoples provided with an enduring claim on the wealth in which they already had a rightful share. They saw clearly that their countries' lack of resources would make impossible the forms of social democracy or state socialism then being attempted in Western and Eastern Europe. They reasoned that some mechanisms for international economic solidarity, political accountability, and justice were necessary to repair the harms of imperialism and prevent its reemergence in a different form. Such critics wondered whether it would be possible to insist on self-determination *and* to create a real parliament of peoples, new forms of transnational citizenship, or genuine plural democracies on the scales of former empires. Could such frameworks facilitate massive reconstruction or reparations projects through which the West might be compelled to assume responsibility for the social misery and mass poverty it had created and pay its historical debt rather than resubordinate new national states through financial debt for development projects? And shouldn't there be some mechanism for criminalizing public and private acts of neocolonialism and imperial domination?

We know that the U.S.-UN system that emerged to govern the postwar global order turned out to resemble the very type of "international dictatorship" of powerful states against which Camus and Du Bois warned contemporaries. Its primary aim was to ensure order among sovereign national states rather than provide a framework for social justice or democratic accountability on a planetary scale. The UN Charter did make provisions for checking state sovereignty, whereby it could punish national states for violating individuals' human rights. But these were usually defined according to a set of Western norms to which the West rarely held itself. And the subjects of this law were individuals rather than communities. In other words, the UN defined conditions under which the international community could interfere in the domestic affairs of a sovereign state, but it never attempted to create a democratic world order that would rethink territorial nationality or state sovereignty.

We also know that by the mid-1950s most colonized peoples—led variously by peasant mobilizations, radical trade unions, nationalist political parties, and urban intellectuals—pursued decolonization through struggles for national independence and state sovereignty. But we should also recall that once the movement for decolonization gained historical momentum, colonial powers, the United States, and the United Nations themselves insisted that separate national states should be the form through which colonized peoples would be emancipated and around which the postwar international order should be organized. Shouldn't this fact alone invite us to pause before any claim about anticolonial nationalism as necessarily emancipatory and internationalism as inevitably imperial?

Between 1945 and 1960, Césaire and Senghor pursued their programs for self-determination without state sovereignty as public intellectuals, party leaders in their respective territories, and deputies in the French National Assembly.[28] Their interventions proceeded from a belief that imperialism itself, by establishing deep relations of interdependence between seemingly disparate peoples and places, had created conditions for new types of transcontinental political association. Just as Marx believed that industrial production had itself opened the door to a postcapitalist form of socialism, they believed that empire itself had created pathways to a postnational form of democracy. Their proposals were fundamentally driven by a concern with substantive freedom, or what Marx called human emancipation, beyond formal national liberation.

If we are to grasp these initiatives historically, we need to recognize that their starting point was the entangled histories that bound overseas and metropolitan peoples and prospects to one another. Believing that European power and prosperity was partly created through the exploitation of African and Antillean labor and resources, they rejected any arrangement that would compel them, the day after independence, to approach the French state as foreigners asking for aid. Given this legacy of imperial entanglement *and* the new realities of postwar geopolitics and global capitalism, they believed that delinking for Africans and Antilleans was neither practically possible nor morally acceptable. In that historical conjuncture, Césaire and Senghor concluded, mere political separation would not end multiplex relations of economic, social, and cultural (inter)dependence between overseas and metropolitan societies. The crucial question was what the terms and form of that inevitable relationship would be. If decolonization did not also seek to revolutionize metropolitan social relations and reconfigure the very nomos of the global order, it followed that it could never lead to substantive emancipation. In their view, decolonization would have to overcome republican colonialism *and* unitary republicanism, empires *and* national states. Only a new type of postnational polity, they believed, would allow Africans and Antilleans to enjoy self-government, protect cultural specificity, and pursue humane and just forms of economic growth through democratic socialism.

Césaire and Senghor thus believed that imperialism had created a perversely cosmopolitan situation to which European national states and monoculturalists would now have to accommodate themselves by becoming something else entirely. The challenge was how to invent an emancipatory political form that would build upon, rather than retreat from or seek to untangle, imperial interdependencies and heterogeneities. Rather than allow metropolitan France to detach itself from, and renounce responsibility for, its former colonies, they sought to democratize the long-standing entanglements that they recognized would persist even if these countries were legally separate.

Accordingly, they pursued a constitutional struggle to transform the imperial republic into a decentralized federation that would abolish imperialism *and* revolutionize existing forms of republicanism *and* provide a model for an alternative world order. Socialist and democratic, transcontinental and multinational, this new type of state would include former colonies as freely associated and self-governing members. Each would possess a local territorial assembly and an autonomous administration through which to manage its own affairs. They would also send representatives to a federal parliament. Metropolitan France, Senghor explained, would become "one state among others, no longer the federator, but the federated." Overseas peoples would be self-managing and subject to their own civil law even as they also enjoyed full federal citizenship, juridical equality within the federation, and socioeconomic solidarity with the rest of France. They would also be charter members of the emergent European Economic Community.

Note that Senghor and Césaire were not simply demanding that overseas peoples be fully assimilated within the existing national state. They were proposing a type of revolutionary integration that would reconstitute France itself by quietly exploding the unitary state and monocultural republic. They also believed that the historical conditions and sociopolitical infrastructure for such transcontinental federal polities already existed. In Marxian terms, they regarded empire as federation in alienated form. Theirs was an immanent critique: rather than simply demand decolonization for Martinique or Senegal, they called on Caribbeans and Africans to *decolonize France*. The aim was to end colonialism, not in order to retreat into autarchic national states but to elevate the French imperial republic into a postnational federal democracy within which multiple peoples, civilizations, and legal orders would coexist. Legal pluralism, disaggregated sovereignty, and territorial disjuncture would be constitutionally grounded; culture, nationality, and citizenship would no longer have to align with one another. They believed that only such a cosmopolitan formation could ensure autonomy, socialism, and justice.

Rather than beg for charity as foreigners, Africans and Antilleans would be able to claim development and social welfare resources as citizens of an autonomous region. Rather than depend on the goodwill of international agencies to redress harms, they could prosecute claims in a federal justice system. Thus, through this postnational federation, they might have a framework for holding European imperial powers directly accountable for past injuries and ongoing forms of exploitation. It might also serve to protect them against future (that is, American-led) forms of imperial domination. This federal polity could also serve as a building block for an alternative global order that might allow humanity to pursue the dreams of solidarity and reciprocity proclaimed by different currents of postwar internationalism.

Of course their program for postnational democracy was never institutionalized. A wide consensus (which included not only the majority of anticolonial political movements but former imperial powers, the United States government, and the United Nations organization) held that self-determination required territorial sovereignty and that decolonization should lead to independent national states. And even if Césaire and Senghor *had* convinced the French state to effectively negate itself by joining their postnational democratic-socialist federation, it is likely that such an ambitious and idealistic arrangement would have created all manner of problems and reached any number of impasses. Moreover, historical conditions have shifted dramatically since the late 1940s. Their solutions then could not possibly be ours now. So why should we today pay serious attention to such seemingly fanciful propositions?

## Recognizing Futures Past

Post–Cold War developments have revealed that there is no necessary relation between state sovereignty and self-determination, let alone between being human and possessing rights. Under such conditions, human freedom has again become a public problem for which there is no self-evident institutional solution. This is precisely the insight that motivated Césaire's and Senghor's seemingly untimely and unrealistic (and supposedly insufficiently radical) programs for a different type of decolonization that could form the basis of an alternative global order.

However problematic their proposals were, they warned against the very nationalist internationalism, organized around unitary sovereign states, that was established in the postwar period. Given the entangled and interdependent character of a twentieth-century world shaped by global capitalism and colonial imperialism, social mobility and cultural mixture, they believed that such an anemic internationalism would merely allow powerful territorial states to continue to dominate nominally independent nations for whom genuine economic development, democratic socialism, and international standing would become impossible. Moreover, in a situation of global entanglements, they recognized that the expectation that territory, nationality, and state should align would make real democracy in plural societies impossible, whether in newly independent or continental European countries.

Césaire and Senghor hoped to transform the conditions created by imperialism into a world order organized around plural postnational democracies on the scale of intercontinental federations. Within them, legal pluralism and cultural coexistence could be accommodated. Self-government might be reconciled with economic solidarity, rights of work and mobility, political citizenship, and mechanisms for justice on supranational scales. Through them the false choice between, on one hand, sovereign national states, and on the other, either an unaccountable world state or a powerless set of international agencies and ethics might be avoided. Their initiatives were based on the conviction that in the mid-twentieth century, a decolonization that did not also seek to invent political frameworks that could democratize persisting linkages between former colonies and former metropoles on a planetary scale could never guarantee substantive freedom in what we now call the Global South.

As political actors, critical intellectuals, and *engagé* poets, Senghor and Césaire developed a pragmatic and experimental relationship to politics. Rather than make universal or transhistorical claims about the correct political arrangement, they were open to various possible means to best pursue the desired end of substantive freedom in a given world. At the same time, they practiced a proleptic and anticipatory relationship to politics, acting as if seemingly impossible futures were already at hand, precisely by recognizing transformative potentiality within existing arrangements. Their multifaceted interventions illuminate the affinity between immanent critique, political imagination, and poetic knowledge.

A steady stream of critics have dismissed their projects as "impossible" because they were never institutionalized. We should resist this as an empiricist, conservative, and ideological move, one that presupposes that only the real is rational, and attend rather to how Césaire's and Senghor's efforts invite us to rethink conventional assumptions about possibility and impossibility, realism and utopianism, failure and success, and pragmatism and principles.

Such orientations may help us grapple with the challenges of plural and federal democracy for our times. More substantively, their efforts also remind us that self-determination became sutured to state sovereignty through a *historical* process, but there is no *intrinsic* relation between them. This process also conflated territorial sovereignty (which is about jurisdiction, borders, and state logic) and popular sovereignty (which is about self-management, active and universal citizenship, and democratic logic). We should resist using the categories that were *produced* by this historical process to analyze the process itself.

Specifically, they identified transcontinental federalism as the best possible way to abolish colonialism and secure self-determination within a nonnational political formation that might be the elemental unit of a different kind of federated world order. If this historical example can serve as some kind of inspiration now, their efforts should also remind us that they were proposing a situated experiment that could only be worked out practically, and possibly itself be abandoned or transcended. We should also recall that their propositions about federalism were typically tied to corresponding propositions about socialism, which they regarded as the flip side of the same coin. Their legacy reminds us that these types of postnational arrangements should be in the service of, and could only be fully realized under, a set of postcapitalist social arrangements that bound wealthy and powerful peoples to poor and weak ones through relations of economic responsibility and accountability.

We should also learn from their shortcomings and blind spots; namely, their failure to recognize that this radical hope to reconstitute France, Europe, and world order could only have been realized if their constitutional efforts were linked to a corresponding social movement propelling these changes. Without direct pressure and mass popular support, existing states would not, and will not, constitutionalize themselves out of existence (pace Israel today). Similarly, we should beware of the illusion that even the most radical constitutional arrangements can themselves effect societal transformation.

If plural and federal democracies are to create conditions for substantive freedom, they must emerge from, and in turn nourish, a corresponding set of political practices. Constitutional initiatives must index a concrete political ethos or form of life (bound up with autonomy, interdependence, reciprocity, and solidarity). The work of crafting new political forms should proceed on the basis of an understanding of the dialectic between polity and politics, politics and ethics, ethics and subjectivity. In other words, federalist forms require federalist politics, federalist practices, and federalist subjects.

Finally, we should recall that there is nothing intrinsically emancipatory about federalism as such. Variants of federalist thinking have emerged out of liberal, republican, racialist, pan-ethnic, Marxist, and anarchist political traditions. So I suggest that we both pay attention to political form and avoid political formalism and make the claim that if federal and plural democracies are to overcome the unitary national state and create conditions in which self-managing communities can pursue substantive freedom in an interdependent world, if they are to model and help create new types of differential unities, translocal solidarities, and planetary politics, then constitutional arrangements need to emerge in conjunction with everyday practices and cultures of horizontal sociality, self-management, and popular democracy.

Césaire and Senghor were situated humanists, concrete cosmopolitans, and embodied universalists who regarded decolonization not only as a way to secure political liberty or improve material well-being but as an opportunity to transform the global order, to promote and model a new planetary politics based on mutuality, reciprocity, solidarity, and *métissage*. Just as they claimed to have heard the call of their predecessors in the 1790s and 1840s, we may now enter into dialogue with these flawed visionaries from the 1940s. Doing so not least because of the inability of either existing internationalism or its critics to adequately address the deep dilemmas that they, like Kant and Arendt, identified, which continue to plague contemporary global politics.

# Notes

1. Robert C. Hilderbrand, *Dumbarton Oaks: The Origins of the United Nations and the Search for Postwar Security* (Chapel Hill: University of North Carolina Press, 2001).
2. Documents from the First General Assembly may be found at http://research.un.org /en/docs/ga/quick/regular/1.
3. UN Charter, art. 2.7, para. 3 (October 24, 1945), http://www.un.org/en/sections/un -charter/chapter-i/index.html.
4. William Roger Louis and Ronald Robinson, "The Imperialism of Decolonization," *Journal of Imperial and Commonwealth History* 22, no. 3 (1994): 462–511; William Roger Louis and Ronald Robinson, "Empire Preserved: How the Americans Put Anti-Communism before Anti-Imperialism," in *Decolonization: Perspectives from Then and Now*, ed. Prasenjit Duara (New York: Routledge, 2004).
5. Neil Smith, *American Empire: Roosevelt's Geographer and the Prelude to Globalization* (Berkeley: University of California Press, 2004).
6. For an overview, see Evan Luard, *A History of the United Nations: Vol. 1, The Years of Western Domination, 1945–1955* (New York: St. Martin's Press, 1982). On the imperial genealogy of the UN, see Mark Mazower, *No Enchanted Palace: The End of Empire and the Ideological Origins of the United Nations* (Princeton, N.J.: Princeton University Press, 2009).
7. See Gary Wilder, *Freedom Time: Negritude, Decolonization, and the Future of the World* (Durham, N.C.: Duke University Press, 2015).
8. For example, Talal Asad, "Thinking About Terrorism and Just War," *Cambridge Review of International Affairs* 23, no. 1 (2010): 3–24; Talal Asad, "Reflections on Violence, Law, and Humanitarianism," *Critical Inquiry* 41, no. 2 (Winter 2015): 390–427; Ayça Cubukçu, "Thinking Against Humanity," *London Review of International Law* (in press); Richard Falk, *Humanitarian Intervention and Legitimacy Wars: Seeking Peace and Justice in the 21st Century* (New York: Routledge, 2015); Richard Falk et al., "Humanitarian Intervention: A Forum," *The Nation*, June 26, 2003, https://www .thenation.com/article/humanitarian-intervention-forum-0/; David Kennedy, *Of War and Law* (Princeton, N.J.: Princeton University Press, 2006); Samuel Moyn, *The Last Utopia: Human Rights in History* (Cambridge, Mass.: Harvard University Press, 2010); Samuel Moyn, "Soft Sells: On Liberal Internationalism," in *Human Rights and the Uses of History*, ed. Samuel Moyn (New York: Verso Press, 2014).
9. Carl Schmitt, *The Nomos of the Earth in the International Law of a Jus Publicum Europaeum* (Candor, N.Y.: Telos Press, 2006).
10. Samuel Moyn, "The Universal Declaration of Human Rights of 1948 in the History of Cosmopolitanism," *Critical Inquiry* 40, no. 4 (Summer 2014): 383.
11. Moyn, "The Universal Declaration of Human Rights," 369.
12. Partha Chatterjee, "Nationalism, Internationalism, and Cosmopolitanism: Some Observations from Modern Indian History," *Comparative Studies of South Asia, Africa and the Middle East* 36, no. 2 (2016): 320–34.
13. Chatterjee, "Nationalism, Internationalism, and Cosmopolitanism," 330.
14. Chatterjee, "Nationalism, Internationalism, and Cosmopolitanism," 332.
15. Chatterjee, "Nationalism, Internationalism, and Cosmopolitanism," 333.
16. Chatterjee, "Nationalism, Internationalism, and Cosmopolitanism," 332.
17. Chatterjee, "Nationalism, Internationalism, and Cosmopolitanism."

18.  Chatterjee, "Nationalism, Internationalism, and Cosmopolitanism," 332–33.
19.  For an account of nonliberal forms of Indian internationalism that belies the claims that twentieth century internationalisms either served the aim of national self-determination or were Eurocentric and elitist, see Manu Goswami, "Imaginary Futures and Colonial Internationalisms," *American Historical Review* 117, no. 5 (December 2012): 1461–85.
20.  Samuel Moyn, "Fantasies of Federalism," *Dissent* 62, no. 1 (Winter 2015): 145–51; Chatterjee, "Nationalism, Internationalism, and Cosmopolitanism," 326.
21.  Immanuel Kant, "Idea for a Universal History with a Cosmopolitan Purpose" and "Perpetual Peace: A Philosophical Sketch," in *Political Writings*, ed. H. S. Reiss (Cambridge: Cambridge University Press, 1991).
22.  Hannah Arendt, *The Human Condition*, 2nd ed. (Chicago: University of Chicago Press, 1998).
23.  Hannah Arendt, *The Origins of Totalitarianism* (New York: Harcourt, 1979).
24.  Hannah Arendt, *Eichmann in Jerusalem: A Report on the Banality of Evil* (New York: Penguin, 1977), 294.
25.  Arendt, *Origins of Totalitarianism*, 298.
26.  Hannah Arendt, *The Jewish Writings* (New York: Schocken Books, 2007).
27.  See Albert Camus, *Camus at "Combat": Writing 1944–1947* (Princeton, N.J.: Princeton University Press, 2006); W. E. B. Du Bois, *Color and Democracy: Colonies and Peace* (New York: Harcourt, Brace, 1945); Manu Bhagavan, *The Peacemakers: India and the Quest for One World* (New York: Harper Collins, 2012); Harold Laski, *Reflections on the Revolution in Our Time* (London: George Allen and Unwin, 1943); Harold Laski, "Towards a Universal Declaration of Human Rights," in *Human Rights: Comments and Interpretation: A Symposium*, ed. UNESCO (New York: Columbia University Press, 1949).
28.  The following account is elaborated fully in Wilder, *Freedom Time*.

# Bibliography

Arendt, Hannah. *Eichmann in Jerusalem: A Report on the Banality of Evil*. New York: Penguin, 1977.
——. *The Human Condition*, 2nd ed. Chicago: University of Chicago Press, 1998.
——. *The Jewish Writings*. New York: Schocken Books, 2007.
——. *The Origins of Totalitarianism*. New York: Harcourt, 1979.
Asad, Talal. "Reflections on Violence, Law, and Humanitarianism." *Critical Inquiry* 41, no. 2 (2015): 390–427.
——. "Thinking About Terrorism and Just War." *Cambridge Review of International Affairs* 23, no. 1 (2010): 3–24.
Bhagavan, Manu. *The Peacemakers: India and the Quest for One World*. New York: Harper Collins, 2012.
Camus, Albert. *Camus at "Combat": Writing 1944–1947*. Princeton, N.J.: Princeton University Press, 2006.
Chatterjee, Partha. "Nationalism, Internationalism, and Cosmopolitanism: Some Observations from Modern Indian History." *Comparative Studies of South Asia, Africa and the Middle East* 36, no. 2 (2016): 320–34.
Cubuckçu, Ayça. "Thinking Against Humanity." *London Review of International Law* (in press). Distributed ahead of print, http://eprints.lse.ac.uk/69640/.

Du Bois, W. E. B. *Color and Democracy: Colonies and Peace.* New York: Harcourt, Brace, 1945.

Falk, Richard. *Humanitarian Intervention and Legitimacy Wars: Seeking Peace and Justice in the 21st Century.* New York: Routledge, 2015.

Falk, Richard, Mary Kaldor, Carl Tham, Samantha Power, Mahmood Mamdani, David Rieff, Eric Rouleau, Zia Mian, Ronald Steel, Stephen Holmes, Ramesh Thakur, and Stephen Zunes. "Humanitarian Intervention: A Forum." *The Nation,* June 26, 2003, https://www.thenation.com/article/humanitarian-intervention-forum-0/.

Goswami, Manu. "Imaginary Futures and Colonial Internationalisms." *American Historical Review* 117, no. 5 (December 2012): 1461–85.

Hilderbrand, Robert C. *Dumbarton Oaks: The Origins of the United Nations and the Search for Postwar Security.* Chapel Hill: University of North Carolina Press, 2001.

Kant, Immanuel. "Idea for a Universal History with a Cosmopolitan Purpose. In *Political Writings,* ed. H. S. Reiss, 41–53. Cambridge: Cambridge University Press, 1991.

——. "Perpetual Peace: A Philosophical Sketch." In *Political Writings,* ed. H. S. Reiss, 93–130. Cambridge: Cambridge University Press, 1991.

Kennedy, David. *Of War and Law.* Princeton, N.J.: Princeton University Press, 2006.

Laski, Harold. *Reflections on the Revolution in Our Time.* London: George Allen and Unwin, 1943.

——. "Towards a Universal Declaration of Human Rights." In *Human Rights: Comments and Interpretation: A Symposium,* ed. UNESCO. New York: Columbia University Press, 1949.

Louis, William Roger, and Ronald Robinson. "Empire Preserved: How the Americans Put Anti-Communism before Anti-Imperialism." In *Decolonization: Perspectives from Then and Now,* ed. Prasenjit Duara, 152–61. New York: Routledge, 2004.

——. "The Imperialism of Decolonization." *Journal of Imperial and Commonwealth History* 22, no. 3 (1994): 462–511.

Luard, Evan. *A History of the United Nations. Vol. 1, The Years of Western Domination, 1945–1955.* New York: St. Martin's Press, 1982.

Mazower, Mark. *No Enchanted Palace: The End of Empire and the Ideological Origins of the United Nations.* Princeton, N.J.: Princeton University Press, 2009.

Moyn, Samuel. "Fantasies of Federalism." *Dissent* 62, no. 1 (Winter 2015): 145–51, https://www.dissentmagazine.org/article/fantasies-of-federalism.

——. "Soft Sells: On Liberal Internationalism." In *Human Rights and the Uses of History,* ed. Samuel Moyn. New York: Verso Press, 2014.

——. "The Universal Declaration of Human Rights of 1948 in the History of Cosmopolitanism." *Critical Inquiry* 40, no. 4 (Summer 2014): 365–84.

——. *The Last Utopia: Human Rights in History.* Cambridge, Mass.: Harvard University Press, 2010.

Schmitt, Carl. *The Nomos of the Earth in the International Law of a Jus Publicum Europaeum.* Candor, N.Y.: Telos Press, 2006.

Smith, Neil. *American Empire: Roosevelt's Geographer and the Prelude to Globalization.* Berkeley: University of California Press, 2004.

United Nations. Charter of the United Nations. October 24, 1945, http://www.un.org/en/sections/un-charter/chapter-i/index.html.

Wilder, Gary. *Freedom Time: Negritude, Decolonization, and the Future of the World.* Durham, N.C.: Duke University Press, 2015.

3

# FROM THE AMERICAN SYSTEM TO ANGLO-SAXON UNION

*Scientific Racism and Supranationalism in Nineteenth-Century North America*

JOSHUA SIMON

In the early years of the imperial crisis that culminated in the independence of the United States, the colonists of British North America insisted upon nothing more than the rights they bore as Englishmen and as the descendants of the conquerors of the New World. Inequities in the empire's systems of political representation and judicial review, imbalances of trans-Atlantic trade, and what colonists regarded as excessive taxes were all taken as evidence of a metropolitan conspiracy to deprive them of these cherished rights. Eventually, metropolitan persistence in this "design to reduce them under absolute Despotism" convinced enough colonists that only independence from Britain could secure their colonies' equal standing, as Thomas Jefferson famously put it, "among the powers of the earth," which is to say, within the Atlantic-spanning European state system as it stood at the end of the eighteenth century.[1]

In the course of their struggle to achieve independence, however, North American patriots came to embrace a more exciting idea: the New World and its inhabitants were not merely equal to the Old, but superior. North America's unsettled spaces were larger than Europe's. Its peoples' rustic customs were less corrupt than Europe's. The western hemisphere, long derided by European naturalists as an excessively humid home to degenerate plants, animals, and societies, was in fact a promised land, capable of sustaining political institutions that would permit greater liberty and achieve greater prosperity than the outdated monarchies of Europe.[2] When viewed from this perspective, the intensifying conflict with the British metropole was no mere colonial independence movement; it was a *revolution*. A patriotic victory would not just end British rule in North America, it would "begin the world over again," ushering in a new era of human civilization.[3]

Scholarship on the political thought of the American independence movement has usually emphasized how innovations in the design of domestic political institutions—written constitutions, federalism, bicameralism and the separation of powers, charters of basic rights, and so on—distinguished the early American republic from the monarchies of Europe, but a growing literature has shown that the leaders of the American Revolution were as concerned to advance beyond European accomplishments in the organization of international relations. Without entirely renouncing their earlier aspiration to a place within the existing European state system, in the first decades of their independence, American political thinkers began to imagine and then to construct a distinctively American state system—an improved mode of organizing interstate politics designed specifically to sustain republican governments. The most important American innovation in this domain aimed not only to set the New World apart from the Old but also to bring it together under the auspices of a federal union of former colonies.[4]

This essay traces the emergence and evolution of unionism as a mode of organizing interstate politics in North America, devoting particular attention to what Benedict Anderson helpfully described as the "scarcely-seen periphery of its vision"—the ways that North Americans understood the boundaries of the imagined community they were creating and the nature of the identity that they ascribed to its members.[5] I show that unionism was from the first a *supra-nationalist* imaginary, determinedly transcending political borders as well as cultural and linguistic differences, aspiring to a greater unity. However, I argue that North American supranationalism underwent an important transition in the course of the nineteenth century.

In the first fifty years after independence, influential statesmen aimed to forge a hemisphere-spanning "American System," a set of treaties and institutionalized alliances that would encompass all of the independent republics of the New World. The paradigm began to break down, however, as the domestic debate on slavery led some southerners to doubt that an American System would help preserve their peculiar institution. By the end of the nineteenth century, the ideology of Anglo-Saxon supremacism, already underpinning domestic politics, became part of the defense offered for policies ranging from unilateral intervention to outright conquest of Spanish America by the United States. But, in an ironic twist, at the turn of the twentieth century, this same ideology became the basis for a new supranational imaginary: an alliance or even union of the world's "English-speaking peoples"—primarily the United States and the United Kingdom, but also the former British colonies in South Africa and the antipodes.

The history of this shift in North Americans' supranational imaginary offers important insights for the political theory of supranational institutions. In particular, it highlights the role that regional identities, which aggregate populations larger than nation-states but smaller than the cosmopolis, play in legitimating supranational political institutions and raises a number of questions about how these identities form and change over time: What must polities and their citizens have in common if they are to be durably united under the auspices of an overarching federal state, confederation, or league? Are there particular circumstances that permit or encourage the construction of supranational institutions despite substantive heterogeneity amongst member states? Are there particular arguments or ideologies that can inspire populations to set aside their cultural differences? Conversely, what processes are likely to raise latent divisions to political salience and forestall or undo federative projects? Although the present essay offers only a modest exploration of these dynamics in a single context, I hope it provides an impetus for more systematic study.

## The International Argument for Federal Union

In the *Federalist Papers*, numbers six through eight, Alexander Hamilton makes his case for the federal union contemplated in the Constitution of 1787 as a superior mode of organizing the interactions of neighboring states. There, he describes the "dangers . . . which will in all probability flow from dissentions between the States" if their inhabitants declined to form a more perfect union and instead continued their alarming postwar progress toward becoming either "wholly disunited, or only united in partial confederacies." Against then—and still—fashionable theories promising that commercial interdependence and republican government would assure peace even in the absence of the proposed union, Hamilton argued that "to look for a continuation of harmony between a number of independent unconnected sovereignties, situated in the same neighbourhood, would be to disregard the uniform course of human events, and to set at defiance the accumulated experience of ages." The accumulated experience of ages demonstrated that trade could as easily form a pretense for conflict as for peace and that republics were "in practice" no "less addicted to war than monarchies."[6] The root cause of interstate conflict was "neighbourhood"—the very *proximity* of "unconnected sovereignties" to one another upon the Earth's surface—and history indicated that the ravages of interstate conflict could not be abated until this root cause was addressed.[7]

The history upon which Hamilton based his arguments was European history—a history, in Hamilton's telling, of near-constant warfare and destruction infrequently interrupted by short periods of peace, formalized in treaties that ultimately rested upon nothing more than a tenuous "balance of powers."

Anticipating and answering a defense of the European state system that Carl Schmitt would offer almost two centuries later,[8] Hamilton allowed that the European balance and its associated norms of interstate politics had *limited* warfare between Europeans, primarily by checking what military aggression could actually accomplish. Having "incircled" themselves "with chains of fortified places," European states could "impede" and "frustrate" enemy invaders. Consequently, the "history of war, in that quarter of the globe, is no longer a history of nations subdued and empires overturned, but of towns taken and retaken, of battles that decide nothing, of retreats more beneficial than victories."[9] However, Hamilton insisted—now anticipating an argument that Immanuel Kant would make famous less than a decade later[10]—that the balance of powers and its associated diplomacy could never conclude a true, lasting peace among the sovereign states situated in close proximity to one another on the European continent. What was more, the brakes that Europeans had managed to place upon warfare came at a heavy cost, creating a vicious cycle that was incompatible with republican government.

Even while at peace, Hamilton pointed out, the sovereign states comprising a balanced system faced a constant threat of invasion from their neighbors. The "continual effort and alarm attendant on a state of continual danger" forced each state to undertake preparatory measures, erecting immense military fortifications and raising large standing armies. To fund these expenditures, they imposed heavy taxes on their populations, creating bureaucracies with hearty police powers to enforce these extractions. Gradually, but inevitably, and despite periods of peaceful balance, within each polity comprising a balanced system the "military state becomes elevated above the civil . . . and by degrees, the people are brought to consider the soldiery not only as their protectors, but as their superiors." The fortifications and armies built to repel invasion and sustain independence become the motive and means for repressing the populations they were meant to protect. Within a neighborhood of sovereign states whose interrelations were governed by nothing more than a balance of powers, self-rule was impossible to sustain.[11]

Although trans-Atlantic isolation afforded a temporary respite, Hamilton argued that without a federal union the former colonies of North America would eventually become entangled in conflicting European alliances and replicate Europe's destructive history of interstate conflict. "America, if not connected at all, or only by the feeble tie of a simple league offensive and defensive, would by the operation of such opposite and jarring alliances be gradually entangled in all the pernicious labyrinths of European politics and wars."[12] Despite their "ardent love of liberty," Americans would, in time, be forced to "resort for repose and security, to institutions, which have a tendency to destroy their civil and political rights."[13] The federal union that the proposed Constitution would create offered an escape from this vicious cycle. By bringing the newly independent states of North America under a common government authorized to make and enforce laws concerning their interactions, the union would eliminate the tendency toward conflict inherent in the European balance of powers and allow Americans to enjoy freedoms that Europeans could not.

At this point, it is worth pausing to note the striking absence from Hamilton's defense of the proposed federal union of any appeal to the shared language, religion, or culture of the populations it proposed to unite.[14] The *Federalist* does not fabricate historical origins for a nation rising and reuniting under the proposed Constitution's common institutions. The argument is entirely focused on the former colonies' future. A federal union would solve the problems of interstate politics that had long impeded Europe's progress toward peace, freedom, and prosperity by bridging North America's heterogeneous populations, providing a framework that stabilized republican institutions, facilitated trade, and gradually won the allegiance of its subjects by demonstrating its beneficial effects upon their lives.

All this is not to say that Hamilton declined entirely to describe a political identity to which the federal union would correspond. He describes both the institutions that would comprise the federal union and the idea of an improved interstate politics that they reflected as "American." But what did this term describe? As Hamilton develops his argument for federal union as a means of organizing international politics, "America" is consistently set in opposition to "Europe," defined more by what it was not than what it was. Here Europe figures not only as a philosophical and historical foil, an Old World mired in conflict and stalled in its progress by an outdated form of international organization, but also as the greatest menace to Americans' newfound independence and thus a primary impetus for the federal union. That is to say, Hamilton appeals to a sense of solidarity among the inhabitants of the several states that were to comprise the union that rested on an account of both the essential differences between Europe and America and the common interests that Americans derived from their mutual exposure to the threat of European reconquest.

Also important, this account of what it meant to be American implied that America potentially extended well beyond the borders of the thirteen former British colonies that made up the United States. In *Federalist No. 11*, Hamilton led his readers "into the regions of futurity" to offer an even more ambitious vision of the incipient union's purposes and prospects:

> The world may politically, as well as geographically, be divided into four parts, each having a distinct set of interests. Unhappily for the other three, Europe by her arms and by her negociations, by force and by fraud, has, in different degrees, extended her dominion over them all. Africa, Asia, and America have successively felt her domination. The superiority, she has long maintained, has tempted her to plume herself as the Mistress of the World, and to consider

the rest of mankind as created for her benefit. . . . Facts have too long supported these arrogant pretensions of the European. It belongs to us to vindicate the honor of the human race, and to teach that assuming brother moderation. Union will enable us to do it. Disunion will add another victim to his triumphs.[15]

Here, rising into a rhetorical register that is rare in the *Federalist*, Hamilton situates the American struggle for independence in a global frame, describing a series of regional solidarities—Africa, Asia, and America—each of which is the *product* of European domination. That is to say, the common experience of imperial rule itself, and especially the common exposure to the "arrogant pretensions of the European," had invested the peoples of those regions with their "distinct set[s] of interests," creating continental political identities where none existed before.

At the end of the eighteenth century, this process offered Hamilton and his fellow Americans an extraordinary opportunity. He urged his readers to "vindicate the honor of the human race" by toppling European imperial rule and constructing a form of political community on its ruins unlike any the world had known before:

Let Americans disdain to be the instruments of European greatness! Let the thirteen States, bound together in a strict and indissoluble union, concur in erecting *one great American system*, superior to the control of all trans-atlantic force or influence, and able to dictate the terms of the connection between the old and the new World.[16]

Of course, Hamilton did not live to see a "great American system" extending throughout the western hemisphere and capable of insulating the entire New World from the vagaries of the Old. But in his own, foreshortened lifetime, Hamilton made notable efforts to build inter-American solidarity, using his formidable contacts and official powers to covertly support the Venezuelan dissident Francisco de Miranda, who hoped to lead Spanish America to independence. Hamilton's aim, in these machinations, was not, or at least not primarily, to serve the abstract "honor of the human race" but rather to ensure that Spanish American patriots did not achieve independence with the aid of Britain or France and forge alliances in the process that would invite Old World interference in New World affairs.[17] Even at this early date Hamilton had grasped that the problems inherent in the European system of balanced powers—the constant threats of invasion and warfare, with all the attendant difficulties they posed for republican institutions—that made the federal union necessary in North America would recur on a hemispheric scale if all the Americas were not bound by close, and perhaps even institutionalized, ties of allegiance. In the admittedly distant dream of "one great American System," he offered, once again, an opportunity to escape the impediments that the European system imposed upon its member states: a new, supranational mode of organizing interstate politics for the New World.


## American Systems

In the first decades of the nineteenth century, the French Revolution's imperial turn under Napoleon I, a second war with Britain, and the rise of a Concert of restored monarchs on the continent served to strengthen North Americans' sense of their essential differences with Europe. When the Spanish American colonies began, from 1811, to struggle in earnest for independence under republican forms of government, this sense blossomed into what the historian Arthur Whitaker has called the "Western Hemisphere idea": the "proposition that the peoples of this Hemisphere stand in a special relationship to one another which sets them apart from the rest of the world." As Whitaker observed, the contrast between Europe and the Americas was fundamental to the western hemisphere idea. "The proposition that the American peoples were 'set apart from the rest of the world' meant primarily 'set apart from Europe.' "[18] This *longitudinal* line of division along the Atlantic enabled a sense of hemispheric solidarity by encouraging Americans to deemphasize *latitudinal* variations in religion, language, and culture that would have divided the New World.

To take an important example, Thomas Jefferson, like many of his colleagues, was deeply suspicious of Catholicism and consequently skeptical of Spanish Americans' commitment to republicanism. In a letter to the Prussian naturalist Alexander von Humboldt, written shortly after news of the independence movements reached the United States, he despaired that "history . . . furnishes no example of a priest-ridden people maintaining a free civil government." Nonetheless, Jefferson had high hopes for the future of the hemisphere, which rested on an analysis of the novel interrelations that American states could establish amongst themselves after independence:

> In whatever governments they end they will be *American* governments, no longer to be involved in the never-ceasing broils of Europe. The European nations constitute a separate division of the globe; their localities make them part of a distinct system; they have a set of interests of their own in which it is our business never to engage ourselves. America has a hemisphere to itself. It must have its separate system of interests, which must not be subordinated to those of Europe.[19]

Here Jefferson echoes Hamilton's account of the longitudinal "divisions" between the Old and New Worlds. Like his rival, Jefferson contrasts Europe's "never-ceasing broils" with the possibility of peaceful interrelations among the American polities, ordered by a separate "system of interests." Spanish American envoys in North America helped to cultivate this connection, using diplomatic correspondence and newspaper reports to strategically emphasize the inspiration that the leaders of their independence movements had found in the example of the United States. Enthusiasm for the patriotic cause in Spanish America swept the country, exciting northerners and southerners, elites and masses, to toast their "sister republics" during their own Independence Day celebrations.[20] Some, including the abolitionist William Lloyd Garrison, were moved to imagine a future in which "the nations of North and South America may cordially unite, and be, as it were, but one government."[21]

This prospect remained remote, however, as Spanish and loyalist forces suppressed insurgents in New Spain and reversed patriotic gains in the Andes. Through more than a decade of fighting, North Americans debated whether to recognize the besieged republicans of the south. The Spanish American cause was popular, but strategic considerations weighed against recognition. Official neutrality conferred legal protection on U.S. ships, whose cargoes enriched traders along the Atlantic seaboard and the Gulf Coast. Recognition would also threaten ongoing negotiations between the United States and Spain concerning the Floridas, Texas, and the Pacific Northwest—territories that inhabitants of the western states looked forward to settling. Some statesmen were worried that the collapse of Spanish rule in the Americas would create an imperial vacuum that Britain was well positioned to fill. Others worried that the large numbers of slaves serving in both loyalist and patriotic armies might decide to pursue the course to their own liberation charted in Haiti.[22]

Against these reservations, the Kentucky congressman Henry Clay became Spanish America's foremost champion in the north by appealing to, and extending the same account of interstate politics and its perils that Alexander Hamilton developed in the *Federalist*. The fall of the Spanish Empire would introduce new sovereignties into the United States' neighborhood, making it inevitable that eventually the same problems that the federal union forged by the Constitution had been created to address would recur on a hemispheric scale. By recognizing patriots that aspired to create stable and prosperous republics, Clay argued, the United States could ensure that after achieving independence, the Spanish American governments "would be animated by an American feeling, and guided by an American policy, . . . obey[ing] the laws of the system of the New World, of which they will compose a part, in contradistinction to that of Europe." Following the line of thought that Hamilton had begun almost fifty years earlier, Clay argued that a hemisphere-spanning American System, in which international relations were governed by shared institutions, would finally free the New World from "the influence of that vortex in Europe, the balance of power between its several parts, the preservation of which has so often drenched Europe in blood."[23] Just as the federal union had helped insulate the states from the pernicious effects of interstate conflict and foreign interference, diplomatic recognition and support from the United States would help stabilize the Spanish American republics, preventing their regression to monarchical institutions and European alliances.

Spanish American independence and integration into the "system of the New World" would also diminish the United States' economic dependence on European markets and habitual deference to Europe in matters of foreign policy. Clay urged Congress to "break these commercial and political fetters" by building close commercial connections across two continents and forging an alliance "against all the despotism of the old world." The identity upon which this alliance would rest, and the form it would take, was by this time well understood: "Let us become *real and true* Americans," Clay exhorted his fellow members of Congress, "and place ourselves at the head of the American system."[24] For Clay, as for Hamilton before him, "American" was a hemisphere-spanning identity, premised not on language, religion, or national origin but on attachment to republican institutions and investment in the unionist framework of international relations that made self-rule possible. In March 1822, Clay finally got his way, and the United States became the first nation to recognize the independent republics of Chile and Peru, the sprawling federal union of Gran Colombia (comprising present-day Venezuela, Colombia, Panama, and Ecuador), the United Provinces of the Río de la Plata (comprising present-day Argentina, Uruguay, Paraguay, and Bolivia), and the Empire of Mexico (comprising present-day Mexico, Guatemala, El Salvador, Honduras, Nicaragua, and Costa Rica).

The despots of the Old World did not sit idly by as American upstarts dreamed of hemispheric union, freedom, peace, and prosperity. Meeting in Troppau, in October 1820, the Catholic monarchies of Europe asserted a joint prerogative to employ "peaceful means, or if need be arms" to bring any legitimate ruler afflicted by republican revolution back "into the bosom of the Great Alliance."[25] In April 1823, acting under the terms of the Troppau Protocol, the restored monarchy of France intervened in Spain to suppress a constitutionalist rebellion. Statesmen and diplomats from both the United States and Spanish America became concerned that the New World's republics would be next on the Holy Allies' agenda. Once again, heightened fears of European interference thickened inter-American solidarity. In his 1823 message to Congress, President James Monroe responded to these events, outlining what later became known as the "Monroe Doctrine" and giving new life to the idea of an American System adumbrated by Hamilton, Jefferson, and Clay.

The foundation of the Monroe Doctrine was a by now familiar longitudinal division of the world into rival "systems": Old and New, monarchical and republican, mercantilist and liberal. As Monroe put it, "the political system of the allied powers is essentially different . . . from that of America. This difference proceeds from that which exists in their respective Governments." Monroe laid particular emphasis on the "manifest" advantages that the United States had derived from the expansion of its union, noting that "by enlarging the basis of our system and increasing the number of States the system itself has been greatly strengthened. . . . Consolidation and disunion have thereby been rendered equally impracticable." For Monroe, following Hamilton, the peace and prosperity the United States enjoyed depended on its insulation from the Old World's invasions and intrigues, and on the assurance that the union provided against interstate conflict.

The success of the Spanish American independence movements offered the United States an opportunity to further "enlarge the basis of [its] system" by acts of diplomatic recognition if not by expansion of the union itself, but the crisis also provided a pretense for intervention by Europe's allied powers. So, in his famous address, Monroe took a major step beyond recognition. The United States would take no formal stance on the Holy Allies' efforts to maintain or restore monarchies in Europe,

> [but] in regard to [the Americas] circumstances are eminently and conspicuously different. It is impossible that the allied powers should extend their political system to any portion of either continent without endangering our peace and happiness; nor can anyone believe that our southern brethren, if left to themselves, would adopt it of their own accord. It is equally impossible, therefore, that we should behold such interposition in any form with indifference.[26]

Monroe's doctrine was *not* a mirror image of the Holy Allies' Troppau Protocol. It did not claim for the United States the authority to intervene in the affairs of other American states, even to liberate them from European rule. To the contrary, Monroe expressed great faith in his "southern brethren's" political commitments and capacities for self-rule. His "Doctrine," at least in its original articulation, was premised on the idea that, within a hemispheric system that enshrined nonintervention as a principle of international politics and eliminated, thereby, the vicious cycle of interstate conflict, Spanish Americans could be counted on to choose republican constitutions and align themselves with the New World against the Old.

## An American Amphictyony?

Monroe's address met with howls of protest across the Atlantic. Prince Metternich pronounced it "indecent." The British foreign minister George Canning declared that "the great danger of the time" was "a division of the world into

European and American, Republican and Monarchical; a league of worn-out
Gov[ernmen]ts on the one hand, and of youthful and stirring Nations, with the
Un[ited] States at their head, on the other."[27] Spanish Americans, by contrast,
greeted the message with enthusiasm, directing their representatives in Wash-
ington to propose formal treaties of defensive alliance with the United States.
The foreign minister of Colombia went a step further, inviting newly elected
President John Quincy Adams to send representatives to an "Amphictyonic"
Congress of the Spanish American republics in Panama.

The Panama Congress was the brainchild of the Venezuelan patriot Simón
Bolívar, who by 1824 had liberated five former colonies, formed the new state
of Colombia out of three of them, and begun planning even broader unionist
projects.[28] Very much in keeping with his counterparts in the United States,
Bolívar envisioned the Panama Congress as a model of a new and superior system of organizing international politics:

> The day on which our plenipotentiaries exchange credentials will mark the
> beginning of an immortal period in the diplomatic history of America. When,
> after a hundred centuries, posterity seeks the origin of our public law, and
> remember the pacts that consolidated their destiny, they will look with respect
> upon the protocols of the Isthmus: in them they will find the plan of the first
> alliances, which will trace the progress of our relations with the rest of the world.
> What then will the Isthmus of Corinth be, in comparison with that of Panama?[29]

Although wary of Bolívar's expansive ambitions, Adams and his secretary
of state, Henry Clay, were eager to see the United States represented. In his
first annual message to Congress, Adams praised the bilateral trade agreement
that the United States had already formed with Colombia as "indispensable to
the effectual emancipation of the American hemisphere from the thralldom
of colonizing monopolies and exclusions."[30] Both Adams and Clay viewed the
Panama Congress as an opportunity to continue building an American system
by forming similar pacts with the other newly independent states of Spanish
America.

But Adams and Clay encountered unexpected resistance in Congress when
they moved to nominate delegates and appropriate funds to finance their trip
to Panama. Concentrated largely in the south and west, and deeply dismayed
by the "corrupt bargain" that had denied Andrew Jackson the presidency in
1824, an opposition party was taking shape that would fundamentally shift the
terms in which the United States interacted with the rest of the western hemisphere.[31] Legislators from the slave states, in particular, decried any effort to
bind the United States more closely to the Spanish American republics, some
of which had adopted measures that would gradually emancipate their slaves
after independence. Even this half-hearted commitment to abolition offered an

implicit rebuke to the defenders of slavery in the United States and threatened southerners' long cherished plans to thicken ties among the slaveholding societies that rimmed the Caribbean.[32] Perversely echoing Monroe's vision of a New World united by shared ideals and interests against the Old, some southern statesmen denounced Spanish American abolitionism as evidence of growing British influence in the hemisphere. They staunchly opposed sending representatives to Panama and went so far as to call upon their colleagues to forge an alternative, slaveholding alliance with Spain and Imperial Brazil to defend their peculiar institution against outside interference.[33]

Importantly, the opponents of U.S. participation in the Panama Congress often made their case in terms that superficially resembled Thomas Jefferson's misgivings about Spanish Americans' political capacities, but they departed signally from these earlier arguments by locating the source of Spanish Americans' deficiencies in their *race* rather than their religion. Both the southern European origins of the region's colonists and the relative preponderance of African-descended and Native Americans within its population were treated as obstacles to the emergence of republican government in Spanish America and as reasons for the United States to avoid entangling alliances with their neighbors. Here, domestic and foreign agendas merged. At home, the ascendant pseudo-science of Anglo-Saxon supremacism helped to legitimize slavery in a supposedly free society and underpinned a shift from early efforts to assimilate the indigenous inhabitants of the North American interior to a new policy of "removal" and genocide. At the same time, Anglo-Saxon supremacism fatally undermined the prospect of a hemispheric American System of international politics, carving a latitudinal line of division across the New World and eventually aligning North Americans with Europe against their sister republics in the south.[34]

John Randolph, of Virginia, gave particularly piquant expression to these sentiments from the Senate floor, sarcastically expressing his hopes that the United States' representatives "may take their seat in Congress at Panama, beside the native African, their American descendants, the mixed breeds, the Indians, and the half breeds, without any offence or scandal at so motley a mixture." He emphasized that there was "a great deal of African blood in old Spain" and suggested that "a further deterioration" of racial purity was evident amongst "the Creole [that is, American-born] Spaniards, in all the Spanish and Portuguese possessions."[35] Randolph was joined in opposition to U.S. participation in the Panama Congress by other prominent southerners, including John C. Calhoun, who only two years before, as vice president, had helped draft Monroe's famous address. In his insistence that the United States must not accept any external limitation on its sovereignty, we can see Calhoun already developing the strong commitment to "states' rights" that would eventually make him famous.[36]

Ultimately, Congress did approve participation in the Panama Congress, but the U.S. representatives left late and carried a strictly limited mandate. It fell to none other than Henry Clay to write the delegates' official instructions. Some of Clay's old fervor for the American System is still visible in this document, as when he notes, by way of introduction, that the "assembling of a Congress at Panama composed of diplomatic representatives from independent American nations will form a new epoch in human affairs." But this prospect was swiftly undermined by Clay's pointed insistence that the Panama Congress was "to be regarded in all respects as diplomatic in contradistinction to a body clothed with powers of ordinary legislation."

> All notion is rejected of an amphictyonic council, invested with power finally to decide controversies between the American States, or to regulate in any respect their conduct. Such a council might have been well enough adapted to a number of small contracted States, whose united territory would fall short of the extent of the smallest of the American powers. The complicated and various interests which appertain to the nations of this vast continent can not be safely confided to the superintendence of one legislative authority. We should almost as soon expect to see an amphictyonic council to regulate the affairs of the whole globe.[37]

Here Clay derides the outermost but earnest aspirations of his predecessors to see the federal union formed by the U.S. Constitution extended first throughout the western hemisphere and then around the world. Even more remarkable, he rejects the logic of interstate politics that had inspired these aspirations, which he himself had done so much to develop, adopting an argument that the opponents of the federal union had developed in the ratification debates of the Constitution of 1787–88. The New World, far from being united in a common struggle against the Old, was riven by contrary interests reflecting their distinctive racial compositions and consequent levels of social, economic, and political development. The ideology of Anglo-Saxon supremacism had fatally undermined the basis for solidarity upon which the defense of the federal union as a means of organizing international politics had been built.

## English-Speaking Peoples of the World Unite

As U.S. military might increased over the course of the nineteenth century, Anglo-Saxon supremacism exercised a profound and sometimes contradictory influence on U.S. foreign policy. Monroe's successors invoked his doctrine to defend unilateral interventions and territorial expansions disconnected from any credibly unionist or anti-imperial agenda for the Americas. In 1845, President James K. Polk used his own Annual Message to describe the proposed annexation of Texas as "a peaceful and effective rebuke" to French and British efforts to assure that the breakaway Mexican province retained its independence.[38] Senator James Buchanan expressed no sympathy for the Republic of Mexico's claims on the territory, insisting that "the Anglo-Saxon blood" of the settlers that had declared Texas independent "could never be subdued by anything that claimed Mexican origin."[39] Eventually, of course, this outlook led to war between the United States and Mexico. Far from sharing their forefathers' concerns about the effects of interstate conflict upon the republic, supporters of the war in the United States insisted that victory would demonstrate the racial superiority of North America's Anglo-Saxon population.

However, in 1847, as U.S. troops closed in on Mexico City, now Secretary of State Buchanan found himself in the seemingly paradoxical position of arguing against taking full advantage of victory by annexing all of Mexico. Once again, race formed the crux of his concerns: "How should we govern the mongrel race which inhabits [Mexico]?" he asked. "Could we admit them to seats in our Senate and House of Representatives? Are they capable of Self Government as States of this Confederacy?"[40] Most of Buchanan's compatriots, including his political opponents, concurred in his own negative answers to these questions. Ultimately, the United States added only the sparsely populated northern half of Mexico to its union, and that only after a deliberate policy of settlement and discrimination had shifted the region's racial demographics.[41] Anglo-Saxonism, then, inspired a sort of double betrayal of the unionist ideal: the United States would now not only wage aggressive wars of conquest upon its neighbors but also refuse to incorporate the territories and peoples it conquered on equal terms.

In no context, perhaps, were the effects of Anglo-Saxon supremacism more apparent than in the arc of U.S. relations with Cuba. The island's location, just off the North American mainland and ideally situated within sea routes to the Caribbean and the Gulf of Mexico, made it a consistent object of close attention in the early republic. Thomas Jefferson discussed the possibility of "receiving Cuba into our union" with James Madison as early as 1809.[42] As settlers filled territories served by the Mississippi River, John Quincy Adams came to regard "the annexation of Cuba to our federal republic" as "indispensable to the continuance and integrity of the Union itself." So long as Cuba remained an outpost of European imperialism, it offered an effective means of disrupting critical trade routes, and consequently, of prying mid-westerners' loyalties away from the United States.[43] Independence and incorporation of the strategic island would provide security and consolidate the republic's spread across the continent.

The tide began to turn at the Panama Congress. Among the many projects Simón Bolívar hoped to organize in that forum was a joint Colombian-Mexican mission to liberate Cuba and Puerto Rico and add them to one or the other's union of former colonies. This proposal was emphatically rejected in the United States, primarily by southerners concerned to prevent yet another bastion of slavery's fall to the abolitionist onslaught. But northerners joined the outcry against the liberation of Cuba, worried that Britain might use the resulting upheaval as an opportunity to establish a naval base just off the U.S. coast. Thus, paying lip service to the letter, while entirely abandoning the original spirit of the Monroe Doctrine, Adams and Clay instructed their representatives in Panama to inform the Congress that if an attempt to liberate Cuba resulted in a war with any European power, "the United States . . . might find themselves, contrary to their inclination, reluctantly drawn by a current of events to [the European] side."[44] Later, the U.S. Civil War and the emancipation of first the United States' and then Cuba's slaves sapped what remaining attraction the island held for annexationists for the same reasons that had prevented the annexation of southern Mexico: if Cuba became a state, the island's African-descended majority would become citizens.

A solution to this problem would not arrive until 1885, when the Conference of Berlin Concerning the Congo, a meeting of Europe's great powers called to organize the conquest of sub-Saharan Africa, "introduced into international relations" the category of the "protectorate." The term *protectorate* had a long and varied historical usage prior to the nineteenth century, but the Berlin Conference defined the rights and responsibilities of the states to which it conceded "sovereignty or influence" over parts of Africa so they might increase the "moral and material well being of the indigenous populations."[45] As Europeans scrambled for Africa, the United States intervened in an ongoing conflict between insurgent Cuban patriots and Spanish forces, declaring war on Spain, occupying the island, and establishing a temporary protectorate before forcing Cubans to accept a Constitution that gave the United States control of the island's commerce and foreign policy.

In subsequent years, the United States established protectorates in Panama, Nicaragua, Honduras, and the Dominican Republic, and forged a more enduring connection short of statehood in Puerto Rico. Reflecting on these actions in his 1904 Annual Message to Congress, President Theodore Roosevelt, who won fame as a soldier in Cuba, conceded that "there are points of resemblance in our work to the work which is being done by the British in India and Egypt, by the French in Algiers, by the Dutch in Java, by the Russians in Turkestan, [and] by the Japanese in Formosa."[46] As this comment makes clear, Roosevelt's American System inverted its predecessors, openly imitating the forms of international politics modeled by the imperial powers of Europe rather than pursuing a distinctively American ideal.

It is a great irony of history, then, that in the decades surrounding the turn of the twentieth century the same ideology of Anglo-Saxon supremacism that fatally undermined the idea of a hemisphere-spanning American System became the basis for a new supranationalist project. As increasing numbers of North Americans made their way overseas as the military, diplomatic, and commercial corps of an incipient empire, they frequently found themselves in the company of their opposite numbers from Great Britain. Aboard naval vessels from the South Pacific to the Pei-ho River, in private clubs from Rangoon to Manila, and in the pages of literary and political magazines, these fellow travelers began to fashion an imagined diaspora: the "English-speaking peoples" of the world.[47] Roosevelt opened his triumphalist 1889 *The Winning of the West* by celebrating not a specifically *American* history of expansion and federation but rather "the spread of the English-speaking peoples over the world's waste spaces," a process he considered "not only the most striking feature in the world's history, but also the event of all others most far-reaching in its effects and its importance."[48] Convinced that racial and cultural superiority explained the unique success of Anglo-Saxon settler colonies from the United States to South Africa and the Antipodes, some observers of global affairs began to argue that the further advance of civilization could be best effected by the concerted effort of the world's predominant Anglo-Saxon powers: Britain and the United States.

The architects of this novel project drew upon a rich vein of writing by English liberals who, from the middle of the nineteenth century, had been developing plans to transform the British Empire's far flung colonies into a vast "imperial federation" modeled on the federal union of the United States.[49] Extending this logic, the influential naval historian and strategist Admiral Alfred T. Mahan, a close adviser to Theodore Roosevelt, broached the possibility of an "Anglo-American Reunion" in 1894, though he set it aside, regretting that the time was not yet ripe. The implicit, but still critical, support that Britain offered in the run-up to the Spanish American War seemed to many commentators to signal a ripening. In 1903, John R. Dos Passos, a lawyer, author, and father to the famous novelist, dedicated an entire monograph to outlining the institutions under which the "English-speaking people" of Britain and the United States should unite. The warrant for this project lay in the "peculiar and striking characteristic, or virtue, of the Anglo-Saxon people . . . that they understand the objects for which governments are instituted more directly, and apply them more successfully and broadly than other peoples." The "future of mankind" as a whole depended, Dos Passos argued, upon the "firm union of that race, on its steady co-operation, and on its undeviating adherence to its common ideals."[50]

Enthusiasm for the idea of a federation of English-speaking peoples built steadily through the end of the First World War and gained strength when it became apparent that the League of Nations would not accomplish its founders' aims.[51] In 1939, the *New York Times* correspondent Clarence Streit published *Union Now*, calling upon Britain and its former colonies to form the nucleus of a federal union comprising the world's democracies. Streit was widely hailed as a path-breaking progressive, but not all observers were equally impressed. Writing at the time, George Orwell recognized that Streit's commitments to peace and democracy were limited to the white populations of Europe and North America. He noted that the primary effect of the union would be to provide "fresh police forces" for Europe's struggling empires, "tightening-up the existing structure" of global politics rather than reorganizing it along new lines.[52]

We are left with two questions: *Why* did the United States adopt the impoverished account of federal expansion that it did in the middle of the nineteenth century? and, conversely, *Why* did the United States abandon the much more promising view that had been articulated in the course of its independence movement and elaborated in its aftermath? Two potential answers emerge from the literature: first, the United States came to recognize that its original idea was utopian, impossible; second, the rise of racism, particularly in its pseudo-scientific form, *caused* North American policy makers to change their perspective.

Here I want to suggest, without systematic argument, a third view: the shift in North American supranationalism in the nineteenth century was not *caused* by scientific racism. Rather, scientific racism provided a convenient justification for the adoption of a new policy that broke explicitly and profoundly with earlier outlooks—a language in which North Americans could explain to themselves and others what they were doing. The shift itself was caused, however, by the United States' rise to economic and military superiority within its hemisphere, and its approach to parity within the Atlantic world. So long, that is to say, as the United States was a weak and economically dependent collection of former colonies, it embraced a supranationalist idea of one kind, which we still find attractive today. However, soon after it became a powerful and economically independent state, it abandoned that idea in favor of another, much less attractive position. This speaks to the power of institutional situations to influence ideas. It offers a rather sorry commentary on the sources of global thinking in North America, but it also offers promise: the New World still contains militarily weak and economically dependent societies. If we are interested in seeing attractive notions of international order articulated, it is to those societies that we should direct our attention.

# Notes

1. For the international legal dimensions of the Declaration of Independence, see David Armitage, *The Declaration of Independence: A Global History* (Cambridge, Mass.: Harvard University Press, 2007).
2. For eighteenth-century debates on the effects of climate on the flora and fauna of the New World, see Antonello Gerbi, *The Dispute of the New World: The History of a Polemic, 1750–1900*, trans. Jeremy Moyle (Pittsburgh, Penn.: University of Pittsburgh Press, 1973).
3. Thomas Paine, "Common Sense," in *Paine: Political Writings*, ed. Bruce Kuklick (Cambridge, UK: Cambridge University Press, 2000), 44.
4. See especially Peter Onuf and Nicholas Onuf, *Federal Union, Modern World: The Law of Nations in an Age of Revolutions, 1776–1814* (Madison, Wis.: Madison House, 1993); Daniel H. Deudney, "The Philadelphian System: Sovereignty, Arms Control, and Balance of Power in the American States-Union, circa 1787–1861," *International Organization* 49, no. 2 (March 1995): 191–228; James E. Lewis Jr., *The American Union and the Problem of Neighborhood: The United States and the Collapse of the Spanish Empire* (Chapel Hill, N.C.: University of North Carolina Press, 1998); David C. Hendrickson, *Peace Pact: The Lost World of the American Founding* (Lawrence, Kans.: University Press of Kansas, 2003).
5. Benedict Anderson, *Imagined Communities: Reflections on the Origin and Spread of Nationalism*, rev. ed. (London: Verso, 2006), 65.
6. Alexander Hamilton, "Federalist No. 6," in *The Federalist with Letters of "Brutus,"* ed. Terence Ball (Cambridge: Cambridge University Press, 2003), 19–20, 22. See also Gerald Stourzh, *Alexander Hamilton and the Idea of Republican Government* (Stanford, Calif.: Stanford University Press, 1970), 138–53; and Joshua Simon, *The Ideology of Creole Revolution: Imperialism and Independence in American and Latin American Political Thought* (Cambridge: Cambridge University Press, 2017), 74–77. For the "*doux commerce*" thesis, which claims that international trade should have a pacifying effect on both interpersonal and international relations, see Albert O. Hirschman, *The Passions and the Interests: Political Arguments for Capitalism Before Its Triumph* (Princeton, N.J.: Princeton University Press, 1977), 56–63; and Turkuler Isiksel, "The Dream of a Commercial Peace," in *After the Storm: How to Save Democracy in Europe*, ed. Luuk van Middelaar and Philippe Van Parijs (Tielt, Belgium: Lannoo, 2005), 27–40. For the "democratic peace" thesis, which argues that liberal democracies should be more peaceful in their foreign affairs, see Michael W. Doyle, "Kant, Liberal Legacies, and Foreign Affairs," *Philosophy & Public Affairs* 12, no. 3 (Summer 1983): 205–35; Michael W. Doyle, "Kant, Liberal Legacies, and Foreign Affairs, Part 2," *Philosophy & Public Affairs* 12, no. 4 (Autumn 1983): 323–53. For the adherents of both theses in the early American republic, see David M. Fitzsimons, "Tom Paine's New World Order: Idealistic Internationalism in the Ideology of Early American Foreign Relations," *Diplomatic History* 19, no. 4 (Fall 1995): 569–82; and Robert W. Tucker and David C. Hendrickson, *Empire of Liberty: The Statecraft of Thomas Jefferson* (New York: Oxford University Press, 1990), 25–47. For historical precedents of Hamilton's skepticism toward the "*doux commerce*" thesis, see Istvan Hont, *Jealousy of Trade: International Competition and the Nation-State in Historical Perspective* (Cambridge, Mass.: Harvard University Press, 2005), 51–57, 185–87.
7. Hamilton cited the Abbé de Mably's 1757 treatise on the "Droit Public de l'Europe" as the source of the "axiom in politics, that vicinity, or nearness of situation, constitutes

nations natural enemies," and credited the Abbé not only for identifying "the EVIL" but also "suggest[ing] the REMEDY": confederation. Hamilton, *Federalist No. 6*, 24–25.

8. See Carl Schmitt, *The Nomos of the Earth in the International Law of the Jus Publicum Europaeum*, trans. G. L. Ulmen (Candor, N.Y.: Telos Press, 2003), 141–71.

9. Alexander Hamilton, *Federalist No. 8*, in *The Federalist with Letters of "Brutus,"* ed. Terence Ball (Cambridge: Cambridge University Press, 2003), 30–31.

10. See Immanuel Kant, "Perpetual Peace: A Philosophical Sketch," in *Kant: Political Writings*, ed. H .S. Reiss (Cambridge: Cambridge University Press, 1970), 93–130. For an analysis of the *Federalist*'s influence on Kant, see William Ossipow, "Kant's *Perpetual Peace* and Its Hidden Sources: A Textual Approach," *Swiss Political Science Review* 14, no. 2 (Summer 2008): 357–89.

11. Hamilton, *Federalist No. 8*, 31, 34.

12. Alexander Hamilton, *Federalist No. 7*, in *The Federalist with Letters of "Brutus,"* ed. Terence Ball (Cambridge: Cambridge University Press, 2003), 30.

13. Hamilton, *Federalist No. 8*, 31–32.

14. Note, however, that in an earlier number, John Jay observes, with "pleasure" and some poetic license, that "Providence has been pleased to give this one connected country, to one united people, a people descended from the same ancestors, speaking the same language, professing the same religion, attached to the same principles of government, very similar in their manners and customs." John Jay, *Federalist No. 2*, in *The Federalist with Letters of "Brutus,"* ed. Terence Ball (Cambridge: Cambridge University Press, 2003), 6.

15. Alexander Hamilton, *Federalist No. 11*, in *The Federalist with Letters of "Brutus,"* ed. Terence Ball (Cambridge: Cambridge University Press, 2003)51–52.

16. Hamilton, *Federalist No. 11*, 52. Emphasis added.

17. For Hamilton's correspondence with Miranda, see Simon, *Ideology of Creole Revolution*, 84–87.

18. Arthur P. Whitaker, *The Western Hemisphere Idea: Its Rise and Decline* (Ithaca, N.Y.: Cornell University Press, 1954), 1–2.

19. Thomas Jefferson to Alexander von Humboldt, December 6, 1813, in *The Works of Thomas Jefferson*, ed. Paul Leicester Ford, 12 vols. (New York: Knickerbocker Press, 1904–5), vol. 11, 351.

20. For Fourth of July toasts to Spanish America in the United States, see Caitlin Fitz's remarkable *Our Sister Republics: The United States in an Age of American Revolutions* (New York: Liveright, 2016), 119–25 and *passim*.

21. Cited in Fitz, *Our Sister Republics*, 133.

22. For U.S.-Spanish relations in the years of the Spanish American independence movements, see Lewis, *American Union*, 69–154. For the looming British threat, see Jay Sexton, *The Monroe Doctrine: Empire and Nation in Nineteenth-Century America* (New York: Hill and Want, 2011), 15–45.

23. Henry Clay, "Speech on the Emancipation of South America," March 24, 1818, in *The Life and Speeches of the Honorable Henry Clay*, ed. Daniel Mallory, 2 vols. (New York: Robert Bixby, 1843), vol. 1, 321. See also Randolph B. Campbell, "The Spanish American Aspect of Henry Clay's American System," *The Americas* 24, no. 1 (July 1967): 3–17.

24. Henry Clay, "Speech on the Mission to South America," May 10, 1820, in *Life and Speeches*, vol. 1, 430. Emphasis added.

25. "Preliminary Protocol of Troppau," November 15, 1820, in *Metternich's Europe*, ed. Mack Walker (London: Palgrave Macmillan, 1968), 127.

26. James Monroe, "Seventh Annual Message to Congress," December 2, 1823, in *The American Presidency Project*, ed. Gerhard Peters and John T. Woolley, http://www .presidency.ucsb.edu.

27. Cited in Sexton, *The Monroe Doctrine*, 62, 63–64.

28. For Simón Bolívar's political thought, see Joshua Simon, "The Republican Imperialism of Simón Bolivar: Another Ideology of American Revolution," *History of Political Thought* 33, no. 2 (Summer 2012): 280–304; and Simon, *Ideology of Creole Revolution*, 89–127.

29. Simón Bolívar, "Invitación del Libertador . . . al Congreso de Panamá," December 7, 1824, in *Documentos Sobre el Congreso Anfictiónico de Panamá*, ed. Germán A. de la Reza (Caracas: Biblioteca Ayacucho, 2010), 42.

30. John Quincy Adams, "First Annual Message," December 6, 1825, in Peters and Woolley, *The American Presidency Project*.

31. For the nineteenth-century origins and ideology of the Democratic Party, see Daniel Walker Howe, *What Hath God Wrought: The Transformation of America, 1815–1848* (Oxford: Oxford University Press, 2007), 203–84; and John Gerring, "A Chapter in the History of American Party Ideology: The Nineteenth-Century Democratic Party (1828–1892)," *Polity* 26, no. 4 (Summer 1994): 729–68.

32. Robert E. May, *The Southern Dream of a Caribbean Empire, 1854–1861* (Baton Rouge: Louisiana State University Press, 1973).

33. Matthew Karp, *This Vast Southern Empire: Slaveholders at the Helm of American Foreign Policy* (Cambridge, Mass.: Harvard University Press, 2016).

34. Jay Sexton has observed that the use of the phrase "South America" rose sharply during the debates on the Congress of Panama, displacing the conventional use of the single term "America" in reference to both continents. Sexton, *Monroe Doctrine*, 79. Walter L. Williams noted the connection between Indian Removal and the emergence of American imperialism in "United States Indian Policy and the Debate over Philippine Annexation: Implications for the Origins of American Imperialism," *The Journal of American History* 66, no. 4 (March 1980): 810–31. For the intellectual history of Anglo-Saxonism and its influence on American politics, see Reginald Horsman's monumental *Race and Manifest Destiny: The Origins of American Racial Anglo-Saxonism* (Cambridge, Mass.: Harvard University Press, 1981); and the essays assembled in Allen J. Frantzen and John D. Niles, eds., *Anglo-Saxonism and the Construction of Social Identity* (Gainesville: University of Florida Press, 1997).

35. John Randolph, Register of Debates, vol. 2, 19th Congress, 1st Session, 112 (1826).

36. For Calhoun's arguments in relation to the Panama Congress, see Sexton, *Monroe Doctrine*, 76–84. For Calhoun's famous contributions to the political theory of confederation, see Murray Forsyth, *Unions of States: The Theory and Practice of Confederation* (Leicester, UK: Leicester University Press, 1981), 120–32.

37. Henry Clay, "General Instructions to Richard C. Anderson and John Sergeant, esqs., appointed Envoys Extraordinary and Ministers Plenipotentiary of the United States to the Congress at Panama," May 8, 1826, Washington, D.C., *The American Annual Register for the years 1827–29*, 2nd ed. (New York: William Hackson and E. & G. W. Blunt, 1835), 29–55.

38. James K. Polk, "First Annual Message," December 2, 1845, in Peters and Woolley, *The American Presidency Project*.

39. Cited in Horsman, *Race and Manifest Destiny*, 217.

40. Cited in Horsman, *Race and Manifest Destiny*, 241.

41. Paul Frymer, " 'A Rush and a Push and the Land Is Ours': Territorial Expansion, Land Policy, and U.S. State Formation," *Perspectives on Politics* 12, no. 1 (March 2014): 119–44.

42. Thomas Jefferson to James Madison, April 27, 1809, in *Founders Online*, https://founders.archives.gov/documents/Jefferson/03-01-02-0140.

43. John Quincy Adams to Hugh Nelson, April 28, 1823, in Louis A. Pérez Jr., *Cuba in the American Imagination: Metaphor and the Imperial Ethos* (Chapel Hill: University of North Carolina Press, 2008), 25.

44. Henry Clay, "Instructions," May 8, 1826, in *Register of Debates in Congress, Twentieth Congress, Second Session* (Washington, D.C.: Gales and Seaton, 1830), appendix, 39.

45. "General Act of the Conference of Berlin Concerning the Congo," February 26, 1885, *The American Journal of International Law* 3, no. 1 (January 1909): 7–25.

46. Theodore Roosevelt, "Fourth Annual Message," December 6, 1904, in Peters and Woolley, *The American Presidency Project.*

47. Paul Kramer, "Empires, Exceptions, and Anglo-Saxons: Race and Rule between the British and United States Empires, 1880–1910," *The Journal of American History* 88, no. 4 (March 2002): 1315–53. See also Srdjan Vucetic, *The Anglosphere: A Genealogy of a Racialized Identity in International Relations* (Palo Alto, Calif.: Stanford University Press, 2011).

48. Theodore Roosevelt, *The Winning of the West: An Account of the Exploration and Settlement of Our Country from the Alleghenies to the Pacific,* 4 vols. (New York: Putnam, 1897), vol. 1, 1.

49. Duncan Bell, *The Idea of Greater Britain: Empire and the Future of World Order, 1860–1900* (Princeton, N.J.: Princeton University Press, 2007), 231–59.

50. John R. Dos Passos, *The Anglo-Saxon Century and the Unification of the English-Speaking People* (New York: Putnam, 1903), 63, 47.

51. See, for example, George Louis Beer, *The English-Speaking Peoples: Their Future Relations and Joint International Obligations* (New York: Macmillan, 1917).

52. George Orwell, "Not Counting Niggers," *The Adelphia* (July 1939).

## Bibliography

*The American Annual Register for the years 1827–9,* 2nd ed. New York: William Hackson and E. & G. W. Blunt, 1835.

Anderson, Benedict. *Imagined Communities: Reflections on the Origin and Spread of Nationalism,* rev. ed. London: Verso, 2006.

Armitage, David. *The Declaration of Independence: A Global History.* Cambridge, Mass.: Harvard University Press, 2007.

Beer, George Louis. *The English-Speaking Peoples: Their Future Relations and Joint International Obligations.* New York: Macmillan, 1917.

Bell, Duncan. *The Idea of Greater Britain: Empire and the Future of World Order, 1860–1900.* Princeton, N.J.: Princeton University Press, 2007.

Bolívar, Simón. "Invitación del Libertador . . . al Congreso de Panamá," December 7, 1824. In *Documentos Sobre el Congreso Anfictiónico de Panamá,* ed. Germán A. de la Reza, 40–42. Caracas: Biblioteca Ayacucho, 2010.

Campbell, Randolph B. "The Spanish American Aspect of Henry Clay's American System." *The Americas* 24, no. 1 (July 1967): 3–17.

Deudney, Daniel H. "The Philadelphian System: Sovereignty, Arms Control, and Balance of Power in the American States-Union, Circa 1787–1861." *International Organization* 49, no. 2 (March 1995): 191–228.

Dillon, Elizabeth Maddock, and Michael Drexler, eds. *The Haitian Revolution and the Early United States: Histories, Textualities, Geographies.* Philadelphia: University of Pennsylvania Press, 2016.

Dos Passos, John R. *The Anglo-Saxon Century and the Unification of the English-Speaking People*. New York: Putnam, 1903.

Doyle, Michael W. "Kant, Liberal Legacies, and Foreign Affairs." *Philosophy & Public Affairs* 12, no. 3 (Summer 1983): 205–35.

——. "Kant, Liberal Legacies, and Foreign Affairs, Part 2." *Philosophy & Public Affairs* 12, no. 4 (Autumn 1983): 323–53.

Fitz, Caitlin. *Our Sister Republics: The United States in an Age of American Revolutions*. New York: Liveright, 2016.

Fitzsimons, David M. "Tom Paine's New World Order: Idealistic Internationalism in the Ideology of Early American Foreign Relations." *Diplomatic History* 19, no. 4 (Fall 1995): 569–82.

Ford, Paul Leicester, ed. *The Works of Thomas Jefferson*, 12 vols, vol. XI. New York: The Knickerbocker Press, 1904–05.

Forsyth, Murray. *Unions of States: The Theory and Practice of Confederation*. Leicester, UK: Leicester University Press, 1981.

Frantzen, Allen J., and John D. Niles, eds. *Anglo-Saxonism and the Construction of Social Identity*. Gainesville: University of Florida Press, 1997.

Frymer, Paul. " 'A Rush and a Push and the Land Is Ours': Territorial Expansion, Land Policy, and U.S. State Formation." *Perspectives on Politics* 12, no. 1 (March 2014): 119–44.

"General Act of the Conference of Berlin Concerning the Congo," February 26, 1885. *The American Journal of International Law* 3, no. 1 (January 1909): 7–25.

Gerbi, Antonello. *The Dispute of the New World: The History of a Polemic, 1750–1900*, trans. Jeremy Moyle. Pittsburgh, Penn.: University of Pittsburgh Press, 1973.

Gerring, John. "A Chapter in the History of American Party Ideology: The Nineteenth-Century Democratic Party (1828–1892)." *Polity* 26, no. 4 (Summer 1994): 729–68.

Hamilton, Alexander. In *The Federalist with Letters of "Brutus*," ed. Terence Ball. Cambridge: Cambridge University Press, 2003.

Hendrickson, David C. *Peace Pact: The Lost World of the American Founding*. Lawrence: University Press of Kansas, 2003.

Hirschman, Albert O. *The Passions and the Interests: Political Arguments for Capitalism Before Its Triumph*. Princeton, N.J.: Princeton University Press, 1977.

Hont, Istvan. *Jealousy of Trade: International Competition and the Nation-State in Historical Perspective*. Cambridge, Mass.: Harvard University Press, 2005.

Horsman, Reginald. *Race and Manifest Destiny: The Origins of American Racial Anglo-Saxonism*. Cambridge, Mass.: Harvard University Press, 1981.

Howe, Daniel Walker. *What Hath God Wrought: The Transformation of America, 1815–1848*. Oxford: Oxford University Press, 2007.

Isiksel, Turkuler. "The Dream of a Commercial Peace." In *After the Storm: How to Save Democracy in Europe*, ed. Luuk van Middelaar and Philippe Van Parijs, 27–40. Tielt, Belgium: Lannoo, 2005.

Jay, John. In *The Federalist with Letters of "Brutus*," ed. Terence Ball. Cambridge: Cambridge University Press, 2003.

Kant, Immanuel. "Perpetual Peace: A Philosophical Sketch." In *Kant: Political Writings*, ed. H. S. Reiss, 93–130. Cambridge: Cambridge University Press, 1970.

Karp, Matthew. *This Vast Southern Empire: Slaveholders at the Helm of American Foreign Policy*. Cambridge, Mass.: Harvard University Press, 2016.

Kramer, Paul. "Empires, Exceptions, and Anglo-Saxons: Race and Rule between the British and United States Empires, 1880–1910." *The Journal of American History* 88, no. 4 (March 2002): 1315–53.

Lawson, Gary, and Guy Seidman. *The Constitution of Empire: Territorial Expansion and American Legal History*. New Haven, Conn.: Yale University Press, 2004.

Lewis, James E., Jr. *The American Union and the Problem of Neighborhood: The United States and the Collapse of the Spanish Empire*. Chapel Hill: University of North Carolina Press, 1998.

Lorca, Arnulf Becker. "International Law in Latin America or Latin American International Law?: Rise, Fall, and Retrieval of a Tradition of Legal Thinking and Political Imagination." *Harvard International Law Journal* 47, no. 1 (Winter 2006): 283–305.

May, Robert E. *The Southern Dream of a Caribbean Empire, 1854–1861*. Baton Rouge: Louisiana State University Press, 1973.

Obregón, Liliana. "Completing Civilization: Creole Consciousness and International Law in Nineteenth-Century Latin America." In *International Law and Its Others*, ed. Anne Orford, 247–264. Cambridge: Cambridge University Press, 2006.

Onuf, Peter, and Nicholas Onuf. *Federal Union, Modern World: The Law of Nations in an Age of Revolutions, 1776–1814*. Madison, Wis.: Madison House, 1993.

Ossipow, William. "Kant's *Perpetual Peace* and Its Hidden Sources: A Textual Approach." *Swiss Political Science Review* 14, no. 2 (Summer 2008): 357–89.

Paine, Thomas. "Common Sense." In *Paine: Political Writings*, ed. Bruce Kuklick, 1–46. Cambridge: Cambridge University Press, 2000.

Pérez, Louis A., Jr. *Cuba in the American Imagination: Metaphor and the Imperial Ethos*. Chapel Hill: University of North Carolina Press, 2008.

——. *The War of 1898: The United States and Cuba in History and Historiography*. Chapel Hill: University of North Carolina Press, 1998.

Peters, Gerhard, and John T. Woolley, eds. *The American Presidency Project*, http://www.presidency.ucsb.edu.

Register of Debates, Vol. 2, 19th Congress, 1st Session (1826).

Scarfi, Juan Pablo. "In the Name of the Americas: The Pan-American Redefinition of the Monroe Doctrine and the Emerging Language of American International Law in the Western Hemisphere, 1898–1933." *Diplomatic History* 40, no. 2 (April 2016): 189–218.

Schmitt, Carl. *The Nomos of the Earth in the International Law of the Jus Publicum Europaeum*, trans. G. L. Ulmen. Candor, N.Y.: Telos Press, 2003.

Sexton, Jay. *The Monroe Doctrine: Empire and Nation in Nineteenth-Century America*. New York: Hill and Want, 2011.

Simon, Joshua. "The Americas' More Perfect Unions: New Institutional Insights from Comparative Political Theory." *Perspectives on Politics* 12, no. 4 (December 2014): 808–828.

——. *The Ideology of Creole Revolution: Imperialism and Independence in American and Latin American Political Thought*. Cambridge: Cambridge University Press, 2017.

——. "The Republican Imperialism of Simón Bolivar: Another Ideology of American Revolution." *History of Political Thought* 33, no. 2 (Summer 2012): 280–304.

Stourzh, Gerald. *Alexander Hamilton and the Idea of Republican Government*. Stanford, Calif.: Stanford University Press, 1970.

Tucker, Robert W., and David C. Hendrickson. *Empire of Liberty: The Statecraft of Thomas Jefferson*. New York: Oxford University Press, 1990.

Vucetic, Srdjan. *The Anglosphere: A Genealogy of a Racialized Identity in International Relations*. Palo Alto, Calif.: Stanford University Press, 2011.

Walker, Mack, ed. *Metternich's Europe*. London: Palgrave Macmillan, 1968.

Whitaker, Arthur P. *The Western Hemisphere Idea: Its Rise and Decline*. Ithaca, N.Y.: Cornell University Press, 1954.

Williams, William Appleman. *The Tragedy of American Diplomacy*. New York: Norton, 1972.

Williams, Walter L. "United States Indian Policy and the Debate over Philippine Annexation: Implications for the Origins of American Imperialism." *The Journal of American History* 66, no. 4 (March 1980): 810–31.

**4**

# CONSTITUTIONS AND FORMS OF PLURALISM IN THE TIME OF CONQUEST

*The French Debates Over the Colonization of Algeria in the 1830s and 1840s*

EMMANUELLE SAADA

Theoretical discussions of pluralism and its connections to constitutionalism often evoke the history of European imperialism as a counterexample: the modern empires of the nineteenth and twentieth centuries have implemented a hierarchical and exclusionary form of pluralism that should be distinguished from a richer and more desirable kind, historically associated with federations.

This perspective applies to the period of "high imperialism" in the first half of the twentieth century, marked by a very strong "rule of difference."[1] In her analysis of the defining features of "nation-state imperialism," Jean Cohen powerfully synthesizes this commonly held view:

> Insofar as it extended neither its republican political forms nor the rule of law to the colonies, [these features] are its differential and unequal categories of citizenship, status based legal pluralism and police state, executive/administrative modes of rule in the colonies justified by racialized, civilizational categories. War and conquest are the mechanism, annexation, boundaries, hierarchical rule, assimilation, together with the construction and maintenance of difference and inferiority between full citizens in or from the metropolis and subject indigenous populations overseas, the outcome.[2]

This analysis of modern European nation-state imperialism, which owes much to the pioneer work of Mahmood Mamdani, insists on the dichotomy between "civil society," reserved to European citizens in the colonies, and "customary power," exercised over natives.[3] It neglects important counterexamples: in the several territories colonized during the French Ancien Régime, such distinctions were not implemented in the nineteenth and twentieth century. In the "old colonies" of Martinique, Guadeloupe, French Guiana, and Réunion, all inhabitants were made full citizens when the Second Republic abolished slavery in 1848. Although these colonies were not spared multiple forms of institutional racism, a unitary conception of citizenship prevailed, and no customary power was recognized: a more complex "politics of difference" was at play there. Conversely, in other territories conquered by the French crown in the eighteenth century, citizenship rights were granted irrespective of participation in French civil law: in 1848, inhabitants of the French establishments on the coast of India and Senegal were given voting rights without having to abandon their personal status, the system of local norms regulating family and domestic life, as well as a wide range of social interactions. In other words, Hindus and Muslims in India and Senegal who were subjected not to the *Code civil* but to local bodies of legislation were authorized to send representatives to the French parliament. In 1916, in an attempt to facilitate local military recruitment, French legislators went further and granted full citizenship rights to the inhabitants of the *Quatre Communes du Sénégal* without requiring that they renounce their personal status: civil society and customary power were intertwined.[4]

Using the example of the first years of the French conquest of Algeria, in the 1830s and 1840s, in this paper I propose another way of nuancing the stark dichotomy between civil society and customary power in the imperial context and, in doing so, aim to enrich our understanding of legal pluralism in the context of modern European imperialism. I emphasize the hesitations that paved the way before a strict "rule of difference" was applied in Algeria and show that the emerging French colonial state envisaged a form of pluralism that was not purely hierarchical and status based. This historical account can enrich our political lexicon, and it notably blurs the lines between "empire" and "federation."

Algeria ended up being an example of the most repressive form of settler colonialism, in which the legal discrimination between "citizen" and "subject" tainted all aspects of the relations between colonizer and colonized, especially after the 1880s. However, other modes of interacting with and governing natives had been put on the table in the early years of the French presence in Algeria in which a form of "ethos of plurality" could be detected.[5] At the time when the French state was waging a very violent war of conquest, its political elite discussed these options in the context of debates about the constitutional form colonialism should take, the legality of French rule of Algeria, and the judicial organization of the territory.

This exploration of the establishment of modern European rule is not a purely antiquarian effort: it sheds light on continued internal tensions and points to fissures in the "politics of difference." It also indicates the existence of heated debates among the French political elite of the time regarding the different ways in which to organize relations between groups and legal systems within an emerging French Empire. That they were not all exclusively based on hierarchy and exploitation and that the conception of a larger polity inclusive of "different civilizations" was debated, if not enacted in the long term, strongly resonates with contemporary debates on pluralism in France.

## Pluralism and the Politics of Difference in the French Empire

This focus on the first years of rule in Algeria offers a temporal counterpoint to the recent historical reappraisal of the federative moment in the post–World War II period, associated with the important works of Frederick Cooper and Gary Wilder on decolonization in the French Empire.[6] With very different epistemological assumptions and archives, both have insisted that a new field of political possibilities opened in the immediate postwar period in France, and especially during the constitutional debate of 1944–46. Wilder has powerfully pointed to the emergence of new forms of political imagination, which owed much to interwar negritude but whose coordinates were also firmly linked to the postwar context.

Cooper and Wilder both show how French national imperialism was radically challenged by proponents of the federation as a way to establish new forms of solidarity within the territory of the former empire by articulating, for the first time, political equality and cultural difference. The federation they had in mind (if not the one implemented in the Constitution of the Fourth Republic in 1946 and later reformed with the Loi-cadre of 1956) was a challenge to the traditional concepts of state and empire in the French context. And it largely rested on a strong version of pluralism: all inhabitants of the federation should receive full citizenship rights irrespective of their "personal status."

But what exactly opened in the years following World War II? What concrete historical formations did this new imagination push against? Was the French colonial empire that was abolished at the time only the territorial extension of a unitary nation-state, in which forms of legal pluralism were purely hierarchical?[7] Or had more robust forms of pluralism already been discussed at different points in its history?

It is clear that a long philosophical and constitutional republican tradition has privileged the unitary state over federative forms in France: the "indivisibility" of the Republic has long been affirmed in French Constitutions since 1791 and valued in the republican doctrine to the point that the objective existence of the empire has been denied by legal theorists, including specialists of colonial law, and is not mentioned in the text of French constitutions.[8] For most of the nineteenth and twentieth centuries, the Republic was thought of as a phenomenon circumscribed to the European borders of France; the oversea territories were considered as an ensemble of colonies, strictly separated from the Republic, under "special" legislation and exceptional rule, not as part of a unified empire. From this perspective, legal pluralism was regarded as a residual phenomenon, an expedient necessary to the government of very diverse native populations, not a political or constitutional principle.

The recent works of Cooper and Wilder reconsidering the process of decolonization represent an important challenge to this account. That the French political conversation was able to shift so quickly to a political and constitutional discussion of a federation in the aftermath of World War II was, of course, in large part the result of the transformation of the field of imperial and global forces during the war, with a recognition of both France's reliance on its empire and the growing constraints imposed by other world powers. But it also reveals that the unitary ideology was not so strong after all and that the French republican doctrine and institutions could at least logically accommodate a large degree of pluralism.

Describing the debates over pluralism at the other end of the historical arc of republican imperialism can contribute to this reconsideration of pluralism in the French context. This call for historical nuance necessitates distinguishing different kinds of pluralism, at least between what could be called a minimal and hierarchical form of pluralism and a more substantive form that implies some degree of parity between different systems. The "minimal" pluralism is often the result of a discourse on the "necessity" to maintain local legal norms: it is either viewed as a temporary necessity, before the process of "civilization" has made it possible to extend metropolitan laws overseas, or a more permanent one because the differences between civilizations are considered too ingrained to ever be erased. In this case, pluralism is marked by a strong asymmetry because local norms are considered to be of lesser value, and their sphere of application is progressively limited. A typical example of this is the kind of pluralism described by Mahmood Mamdani: local populations were subjected to their "customs" only in the domestic and private spheres because colonial administrators considered them unable to follow the more sophisticated European legal norms.[9] A more substantive pluralism would involve a valorization of local legislation and more symmetrical relations between different systems, and even include the possibility for individuals to opt for one system or the other, irrespective of their status. It could also involve a constitutional recognition of the different legal systems and of their autonomy.

## Questioning the Historical Shift from Assimilation to Association

Although there is currently a historiographical consensus on the existence of a strong politics of difference within the modern French empire, the literature presents considerable hesitations regarding its scope and its chronology. Traditionally, historians of the French Empire have distinguished between a first period during which "assimilation" prevailed, generally until the end of the nineteenth century, and a period of "association," starting after World War I. According to this chronology, in the first period, a strong revolutionary belief in the universality of French republican values translated into the colonial doctrine of the "mission to civilize." French constitutional, legal, and administrative systems were to be gradually exported to the colonies.[10] That the horizon of assimilation was in practice constantly receding was not considered as a contradiction to the principle.[11]

Starting at the end of the century, "association," often compared to British indirect rule, displaced the ideal of "assimilation" as a way of letting local civilization "evolve" following its own path. This shift has been described as the consequence of the rise of scientific discourses on race and evolutionism, as well as the sobering of "civilizing" ambitions after colonial administrators were confronted with the very concrete difficulties of ruling over vastly different populations.[12] A similar trend can be identified in British colonial doctrine: the civilizing project of English liberals gave way to a more separatist vision in the second half of the nineteenth century.[13] This periodization is important when discussing the history of pluralism: assimilation implies either a rejection of pluralism or the implementation of its poorest, most hierarchical form, whereas association makes space for a richer and more open form of pluralism.

Yet this historical sequencing raises several difficulties. The first problem concerns the timing of the shift from assimilation to association, which varies considerably within this literature. Such fuzziness is obvious in the case of the British Empire. The "turn" has been identified in India in the late nineteenth century but also in the middle of the eighteenth century when English administrators, after studying ancient Indian laws, decided that they were best suited for Indians.[14] This discrepancy might be indicative of a historical process that is more complex than a mere turn.

In the French case, the policy of "the Arab Kingdom" proclaimed by Napoléon III in the 1860s is sometimes considered as a first turn to association: after visiting Algeria in 1860 and 1865, inspired by a few orientalist officers, he claimed to be "as much the Emperor of the Arabs as the emperor of the French people." Yet this shift was mostly rhetorical. In spite of Napoleon's claims of "tolerance, justice and respect for the differences of mores, religions and races," the imperial state imposed the privatization of land in 1863 and consecrated legally the difference of status between "citizens" and "subjects" in 1865.[15] Other historians consider that the policy of "protectorate" in Tunisia and in the Indo-chinese peninsula in the 1880s marks such a turn and locate the official displacement of assimilation by association in the 1920s.

A large body of scholarship is implicitly skeptical of the very existence of a turn. Borrowing more or less explicitly from Said's critique of orientalism, some historians have insisted on a continued rule of difference, fully formed before the conquest and identified as a cause of the very colonial project in the first place. In the case of France, eighteenth-century representations of the Orient would have been at the foundation of Napoleon's campaign in Egypt, which, in turn, cast a long shadow on the conquest and colonization of Algeria.[16] Exclusionary practices were a constant staple of French colonial governance, and the project of assimilation never existed outside of the political rhetoric served to the French public.

Finally, the very idea of a shift from assimilation to association does not resist the multiple "tensions of empire" and the resulting dialectics of "inclusion" and "exclusion." In his study of Saint-Simonian administrators in Algeria, for example, Osama Abi-Mershed has shown that in the first forty years of rule in Algeria (1830–1870) attempts at "civilizing" natives were not contradictory with administrative practices that essentialized native culture.[17]

To make things more complex, a completely different sequential model also exists on the market of historical ideas. Here, pluralism does not follow but, on the contrary, *precedes* more unitary forms. Historians have identified such an arc in the field of international law. From the sixteenth to the eighteenth century, "international law both in theory and in practice had been far more inclusive than it was to become in the nineteenth century."[18] As Charles Alexandrowicz suggested a long time ago—before positivism and the civilizational norm solidified in the nineteenth century—many non-European political entities were considered as legitimate powers and worthy partners.[19] It is only in the nineteenth century that new European imperial dynamics led to an exclusion from international law of state formations deemed "below" the standard of civilization.[20] Historians, legal scholars, and political scientists have suggested a similar arc to describe the relations between European powers and native populations in North America: an "ethos of pluralism" prevailed in the eighteenth century, but a more clearly colonial ideology led to much hierarchical and oppressive relations in the following one.[21] In this literature, it is not entirely clear whether this ethos corresponds to a necessity made virtue or to a genuine respect for different legal norms; Europeans had not yet solidified their self-perception as the beacon of civilization and legitimate rulers of the world.[22]

Recent historical work on colonial legal pluralism has adopted a very similar view: in a context of layered, incomplete, and patchy sovereignty, pluralism prevailed in a first phase of imperialism not as a conscious program of government but as the result of "jurisdictional politics"; it mostly reflected the inability of colonial states to impose a unified legal system.[23] In this perspective, the rise of territorial sovereignty coincided with the demise of legal pluralism, even though neither of these two processes was ever complete.

This paper is intended to contribute to the historical understanding of pluralism, both as a program and as a set of practices in the early years of the conquest of Algeria. The general backdrop for this history is a deeply ambivalent presence of law in the French Empire. On one hand, the principle of "legislative exception" (spécialité législative), which persisted throughout the history of the modern French Empire, means that French law did not apply universally or automatically to colonial territories: these were under "special laws." This principle was first affirmed in the Constitution of 1791 and was reaffirmed in all subsequent constitutional texts except that of 1793. Instead of being voted by the parliament, colonial legislation primarily constituted in decrees redacted by the executive branch. The principle was reaffirmed in the very important law of 1833 on the legislative regime of the colonies, then known as "the colonial charter," which distinguished between the "old colonies" of Martinique, Guadeloupe, Réunion, and French Guiana, subjected to legislative power, and the territories in India and Africa, which continued to be ruled by royal ordinances. This was reaffirmed in the July 1834 ordinance officially annexing Algeria to France: "French possessions in Africa are ruled by ordinances." Legislative exception was reaffirmed in constitutional texts during the Second Republic in 1848, the Second Empire, and the Third Republic. It implied that specific legislation applied to colonial territories and, in particular, to native populations: it was the main constitutional foundation of colonial pluralism.

But "exception" did not mean that the empire was outside of the law, ruled by administrative fiat and by the power of the sword, as is sometimes implied by our common representations of high imperialism. On the contrary, at least in the early years of the French presence in Algeria, "legality" was a constant preoccupation of colonial actors: they often reflected on the legality of conquest, occupation, and colonization and on the status of colonial territories in the constitution; they debated at length the most appropriate legal system to put in place in the colonies. All these debates involved discussions of pluralism in that they included discussions of the value and use of local systems of legal norms and their relationship with the laws imposed by the French. Very much like the period of rapid transformation that became known as "decolonization," the first years of the French colonization in Algeria show a very different picture than that of high imperialism—a moment of deep instability and hesitation in which a wide array of different options was discussed.

## Capitulation, Constitutionalism, and Pluralism

July 5, 1830, in the last days of the Restoration, which ended later in the month with the July Revolution, French troops seized the Regency of Algiers (the city of Algiers and the territory surrounding it), which had been under loose Ottoman rule. Often interpreted as the desperate gesture of a weakened regime to divert public opinion from domestic issues, the conquest of Algiers did not correspond to a precise plan of colonization of North Africa. For the next fifteen years, the army considerably expanded this first conquest, beginning with the cities on the coast and the plain bordering it in the south. During that time, one of the most debated questions in Paris political circles was whether France should colonize the Regency, and under which terms, or whether "decolonization" was on order. This debate continued after the official annexation of the Regency to France in July 1834 and was the occasion of the introduction of the word *decolonization* in French in 1836.[24] As late as 1841, the French parliament was discussing the issue and sent Alexis de Tocqueville to Algeria to settle the question. His response was that the French state should practice "complete domination" toward the native populations while "partially colonizing" the country with the settling of a French population made mostly of farmers. He called for the replacement of military rule by a civilian government and the import of French law and political and administrative organization, to the benefit of settlers only. Native Algerians were to live separately under a mix of military rule and customary arrangements.[25] This vision, which closely resembles the dichotomous colonial rule of high imperialism, was not fully implemented in Algeria until the 1870s. The first forty years of French rule were an experiment in a less clear division between colonizer and colonized and a more complex form of pluralism.

The seizure of Algiers in 1830 was preceded by a series of proclamations to the population of the territory and ended with a treaty of capitulation signed by the general in chief De Bourmont and the last *Dey* of Algiers, Hussein Dey. The rhetoric of the proclamations was very much inspired by Napoleon's promises to the Egyptians to free them from the tyranny of Ottoman rule and to protect them. The convention of capitulation used a similar rhetoric and evoked both "protection" and "respect":

The General in Chief of the French Army pledges to his Highness the Dey to allow him the freedom and possession of all his personal property. . . .
The General in Chief guarantees to all the soldiers of the militia the same advantage and the same protection. . . . The exercise of the Muslim Religion shall be free. The liberty of the inhabitants of all classes, their religion, their

property, their business and their industry shall remain inviolable. Their women shall be respected. The General in Chief makes this engagement in his honor.

This convention did not prevent the soldiers from sacking a large part of Algiers in the first weeks of the occupation. The occupation forces also desecrated several mosques, which were used for military purposes, and at least one cemetery outside of Algiers, which was demolished to build a road to be used by the army to access the rural outskirts of the city.

This breach of the convention was justified by advocates of the use of violent methods of colonization as a prerogative of the military victor. They considered that the convention had only been a tactical means to speed the conquest of the city of Algiers, by reassuring its inhabitants and convincing them that the French conquest did not have the "barbarian character" they feared. As a consequence, it did not bind French forces beyond the seizure of Algiers. Moreover, inhabitants of the Regency outside of the city had proven that they themselves did not feel bound to the convention, maintaining armed resistance to the progression of the army in the outskirts of Algiers and—in the following years—in the cities of Bone, Oran, and Bougie.[26]

In the early 1830s, proponents of the right of conquest were a minority. More voices opposed the interpretation of the 1830 convention as an empty promise, and others gave it a foundational status and criticized the forces of occupation for not respecting its prescriptions. One of the most articulate and powerful of these voices was Hamdan Khodja, a legal scholar and businessman of Algiers who had strong links to the Ottoman administration prior to 1830. In 1833 he published a long accusation against the French occupation, written originally in Arabic but immediately translated into French under the title "*Le Miroir*" (The Mirror).[27] Affirming what has been called in other contexts a form of "global liberal constitutionalism," Khodja insisted on a universal form of *jus gentium* that bound the French state to respect its own convention. Quoting Benjamin Constant, Khodja faulted the French for betraying one central principle of "civilization"—the rule of law. Although the exact circumstances of the redaction of the text are not known, it is likely that Khodja was in close contact with French liberals while sojourning in Paris. And it appears that his opinions were shared by many members of the French political elite, who also denounced the breach of the 1830 convention. In their critique of the violence of the conquest, they evoked the respect for the Charter of 1830, the constitutional text that served as a foundation to the Monarchy of July and had strongly reinforced the legislative power of the parliament. Even if the Charter did not apply to Algeria, which remained under the regime of royal ordinances, it was to serve as a guide for the colonial administration. This is what

Frédéric-Gaëtan, marquis de la Rochefoucault-Liancourt, and deputy of the Cher department, affirmed in front of the parliament in 1835:

> It would be shameful for the victorious French to pillage the vanquished. This is what capitulation meant from the first day of the conquest. It is hard to imagine how administrators, in the 19th century with the Charter in hand, even though it was not extended to Algiers, under a representative government, were able to adopt and support other principles.[28]

In 1833, the critiques of the conquest were strong enough that a commission was sent to Algiers to inquire about the situation, and a parliamentary commission was later formed in Paris to "guide the government on whether to keep the Regency and how to organize its colonization."

The two main questions had to do with the nature of occupation: Should Algiers remain a military outpost, or become a trading post or even a colony? And what should be done with the population? Was it appropriate to "displace native populations" from conquered territory and "substitute a European population for the Muslim population," or should they "include natives into the forces which could foster the success of the French implantation in Algeria?"[29] To answer these questions, the commission in Algiers interviewed many witnesses and participants to the conquest and occupation: officers, civil administrators, several members of the local elites, including an interpreter, the "mufti of the Moors," and a rabbi presented as the leader of the "Jewish nation." In Paris, the list of interviewees included Khodja, who reiterated his strong critiques of the French occupation.

The question of legality was central to the debates of both commissions. Most remarkably, nobody evoked seriously the right of conquest, described as a thing of the past, belonging to another era of colonialism, symbolized by the darkest hours of Spanish conquest of the New World. On the contrary, the text of the capitulation was the common reference to understand what the French were bound to do in Algeria. On several occasions, the debaters also evoked the French constitution of the time, the "Charter," as the reason they should abide by the convention: "To seize the property (of the Turks) today would be a true confiscation. A people governed by the French Charter must not provide such an example."[30]

The 1830 convention remained an essential text throughout the nineteenth century for the French colonial state in Algeria. Members of the Algerian elite constantly evoked it to claim rights. The French administration did the same and used the convention as a quasi-constitution, a standard to judge subsequent legislation. Later it was used primarily as an instrument of spoliation of the natives, as the colonial administrators insisted that all rebellions were breaches of the convention that justified the sequestration of the land of entire tribes and redistribution of the land to settlers.

But what exactly was covered by the convention? What did the expression of "respect" imply? What did it obligate the French administration to do? Introducing a connection that will become central to French rule in Algeria, the majority of the Algiers commission affirmed that "by leaving natives the free exercise of their religion, it must be understood that we also guarantee them their laws, institutions, and customs identified with them. For Muslims, the law of the prophet is also political law."[31]

As is well known, the connection between religion and law later served to exclude Algerians and other colonial populations from political rights. Progressively between the 1830s and the 1860s, colonial law produced a differentiation between subject and citizen that was predicated on the presumed inability and unwillingness of natives to follow French civil law because of their obedience to the Qu'ran, which was viewed as inextricably a religious and legal text.

Even though members of the commission realized and lamented that the convention would be "an obstacle to the exercise of our sovereignty," in the early 1830s the articulation of political and religious law was not yet used to justify limiting the rights of natives.[32] On the contrary, it deeply shaped attempts to include local elites in government and to institutionalize forms of legal pluralism.

Far from being viewed as pure subjects, native Algerians were considered to have a distinct legal personality. The word *nationality* was in use in the 1830s debates in reference to the specific statuses of Algerian natives populations. For example, in 1836, Prime Minister Adolphe Thiers mentions the "Arab nationality" in the parliament when discussing the budget of occupation in Algeria.[33] Introduced in French in 1807 by Germaine de Staël and popularized by the Romantic historians of the 1830s, such as Guizot, Michelet, and Thierry, the word *nationality* (*nationalité*) at the time conjured cultural and political dignity, without necessarily implying sovereignty. As late as 1896, the French highest civil court, the Cour de Cassation, mentions the "national legislation" of Muslims and Jews in Algeria as synonymous with their "mores and customs" (*moeurs et coutumes*).[34]

This recognition of local nationalities might explain why the majority of members of the 1833 commission discarded the options of exterminating or displacing natives, expressed at the time in other forums. On the contrary, they promoted a paternalist "equal protection to the properties and work of all inhabitants, be they Arabs, Turks, Moors or Europeans."[35] The institutional translation of this ideal was a protectorate, granting a large fraction of autonomy to local elites. There were projects for other forms of shared government as well: in 1833, in the first town council of Algiers, there were as many native members as there were Europeans, and they had a deliberative voice in the use of city taxes.[36] This system of shared government, which took British rule in India as a model, prevailed for several years, in large part because the violent and costly war of conquest necessitated an alliance with local groups against others: again, it was a political and military necessity. But the debates of the 1833 and 1834 commissions also indicate that a more robust version of pluralism was at work. According to them, the "text of the capitulation has left the natives with their natural judges."[37] They pleaded for an "absolute tolerance" toward local normative systems, similar to the tolerance practiced by the Ottoman Empire toward the Jews, in spite of "its despotism."[38] This tolerance was possibly facilitated by the perception of similarities between French and Algerian legal principles: Laurence, the commissions' rapporteur on legislation and justice, insisted on the influence of Roman law on the "content and form of Quran's prescriptions"—a point that seems exotic today. According to him, as a consequence, French and native laws were necessarily going to be intertwined in Algeria.[39] This type of position translated into institutions as early as 1830 when a mixed court with French, Moor, and Jewish judges was put in place, albeit for a short year. Starting in 1831, each population had its specific court, with French judges intervening in appeal procedures. For a few years, though, far from being organized hierarchically, there was a form of symmetry between the two systems: French laws or local laws applied depending on the matter and on the intentions of the individuals involved in a specific interaction.[40] This fluidity did not last long, but that it existed at all at the beginning of the colonization in Algeria indicates at least of a form of tolerance toward pluralism that is often overlooked by those who focus on a later period of French rule. Later, for reasons that merit ampler scrutiny, pluralism evolved toward a more hierarchical and pragmatic form. In this first phase, it was important for colonial judges to reaffirm "respect" for the legitimacy of local norms. It is striking that this rhetoric is still present in an 1854 judgment of the Imperial Court of Algiers:

> All the while substituting its sovereignty for that of the Deys, France maintained the internal regime of Algeria and guaranteed the faith, laws, and properties of the natives. In acting thus, France without doubt gave in to the generous tendencies of its nature and rendered new homage to the law that prevailed in Europe—as fixed by the treaties of Westphalia, Reswick, and Utrecht. But one can no more doubt that the need to diminish the sacrifices of the conquest as well as the costs of occupation also contributed to its conduct.[41]

Here principles of international law (and, strangely enough, the implicit recognition of Algerian sovereignty) as well as the economic imperative to rule an empire on the cheap converged to justify pluralism.

Of course, in reality, "the generous tendencies" of France meant a long and violent war of conquest, which wiped out a quarter to a third of the Algerian population. But in this first period the imperatives of a continued war and the necessity to maintain order and security are not yet evoked in debates on the constitutional organization of Algeria. These ideas were developed over the next thirty years.

## Toward a Republican "Rule of Difference"

In the history of pluralism in Algeria, the constitutional debates of 1848 constitute an important shift. In mid-June 1848, barely a week before the June days uprising, the Constituent Assembly discussed at length the status of Algeria. The debate hinged on the application of the Constitution being drafted to Algeria. For some representatives, including deputies from Algeria, the goal was to make Algeria an "integral part of France" (*partie intégrante*). They argued that the "strength of a nation results from the reunion, under a *homogenous* government of a largest possible territory, inhabited by a compact population of citizens."[42] Here Algeria was not to be a colony but an extension of France. Consequently, as indicated by the qualifier "homogenous," the application of the Constitution to Algeria was not turning France into an empire but into a larger and more powerful nation-state. Advocates of what was dubbed "assimilation" also conjured the memory of the French Revolution, which had declared in September 1789 that Corsica was to be an "integral part of France" to which the future Constitution would apply, and it was turned into a French department in January 1790. The push for applying the Constitution to Algeria was also related to the newly minted male universal suffrage: even if special legislation persisted, the argument went, French citizens in Algeria would fight it and be able to demand the full application of constitutional protections. A last and ubiquitous argument was more practical: the introduction of the French Constitution as well as the metropolitan administrative apparatus in Algeria would offer guarantees to prospective settlers, whereas the continuation of arbitrary power would discourage emigration to and colonization of the country. The example of the inclusion of Oregon into the United States was mentioned several times during the debates: paraphrasing with some inaccuracy the doctrine of Manifest Destiny, French constituents commented on the apocryphal story of a 1844 Congress decision to grant state status to Oregon after the settling of five thousand pioneers. For them the conclusion was clear: " institutions given in advance" attract settlers and produce statehood.[43]

Several members of the Constituent Assembly fiercely opposed the project of the assimilation of Algeria. Général Cavaillac, intervening at the Constituent Assembly as the minister of war of the provisional government, was the most prominent voice against it. One of the main actors of the Algerian conquest, he was also one of the most violent ones, suffocating to death entire villages in caves, women and children included. A week after the debate on Algeria, he led the bloody crushing of the June uprising. His main arguments against the assimilation of Algeria were twofold: first, Algeria was in a state of war, which required special legislation; second, and more important, the presence of highly "diverse populations" made it very difficult to know the long-term effects of the application of the French Constitution to Algeria. He refused to grant Algeria the right to "make demands on France."[44] Other high-ranking officers who participated in the conquest of Algeria, and among them General Lamoricière, another advocate of violent conquest who introduced the generalized used of "razzias" as well as civilian proponent of a military administration in Algeria, made similar points: they all insisted on the presence of "Arabs" (no longer distinguished from "Moors" or "Turks" as they were in the 1830s) as the main reason for the need to maintain Algeria under exceptional legislation. Algeria could not be French as long as it was "still covered with Barbarians."[45] These opponents to assimilation also evoked the Oregon model. They insisted that the peaceful settlement of pioneers had been possible only because of the absence of a threatening armed population led by a personality of the caliber of Abd-el-Khader.

Interestingly, a very few deputies opposed the assimilation with a more generous attitude toward native Algerians. They also mentioned the Oregon case, but only to remind the assembly that "Indians" had all been exterminated by the "Anglo-Americans."[46] Because France refused to commit such crimes, it was forced to keep natives under a distinct legal regime.

Finally, all deputies agreed that the republican constitution should apply to the French citizens of Algeria only, "not to the foreigners," thereby continuing to implicitly recognize a form of sovereignty to the Algerian people.[47] But the disagreement over the mention that Algeria was an "integral part of France" persisted. The 1848 Constitution reflected this lack of consensus: it affirmed both the assimilation and the exception. Article 109 declared Algeria and other colonies "French territories" but "ruled by specific laws until a special law applies the present constitution to them"—a special law that was never passed.

Constitutional silence persisted over time: the imperial Constitution of 1852 called again for a special law (*senatus-consulte*) to elaborate the "Constitution of the colonies and of Algeria." Such texts were voted for the "old colonies" in 1854 and 1866, but none was drafted for Algeria. The Third Republic's constitutional texts were no more precise, even though in practice the parliament began to intervene more often in Algerian affairs.

Exception remained the rule in Algeria, but its rationale changed radically in the 1850s and 1860s. In the first years of the conquest, the exception was used as a consequence of a deep uncertainty over the term and nature of French rule in Algeria. It was also related to the recognition of the complexity of local legal norms and to an "ethos of pluralism." By the 1850s, after completion of the first phase of conquest, and even more after the massive uprisings of 1871, the question of security became central to discussions and the legal exception became more clearly related to the necessity of maintaining order and was associated to a poorer version of pluralism. "Difference" became a rule.

Obviously, one could say with reason that the most robust form of pluralism, which implied reciprocity and the recognition of the dignity of native legislations, was only a short-lived exception due to the relative weakness and lack of organization of the burgeoning colonial state at a moment of intense hesitation regarding the form of rule in Algeria. And one could argue that the transition to a more minimal and hierarchical version of pluralism was the unavoidable consequence of the strengthening of colonial power. But, at a minimum, the debates of the early 1830s and 1840s illustrate that, in a formative moment for liberalism in France and elsewhere, pluralism was compatible with empire. Far from being the product of a ready-made orientalist ideology, the divide between citizen and subject was not a given of modern imperialism. It was the product of thirty years of rule in Algeria, and it was preceded by the possibility of a much stronger form of pluralism.

## Notes

1. Partha Chatterjee, *The Nation and Its Fragments* (Princeton, N.J.: Princeton University Press, 1993).
2. Jean Cohen, *Globalization and Sovereignty: Rethinking Legality, Legitimacy, and Constitutionalism* (Cambridge: Cambridge University Press, 2012), chap. 2.
3. Mahmood Mamdani, *Citizen and Subject: Contemporary Africa and the Legacy of Late Colonialism* (Princeton, N.J.: Princeton University Press, 1996).
4. Mamadou Diouf, "Assimilation coloniale et identités religieuses de la civilité des originaires des quatre communes (Sénégal)," *Canadian Journal of African Studies* 34, no. 3 (2000): 565–87.
5. I am borrowing this notion from Patrick Macklem, "Indigenous Peoples and the Ethos of Legal Pluralism in Canada," in *From Recognition to Reconciliation: Essays on the Constitutional Entrenchment of Aboriginal and Treaty Rights*, ed. Patrick Macklen and Douglas Sanderson (Toronto, Canada: University of Toronto Press, 2016), http://ssrn.com/abstract=2403909 or http://dx.doi.org/10.2139/ssrn.2403909. He is himself indebted to Bruce Duthu's *Shadow Nations: Tribal Sovereignty and the Limits of Legal Pluralism* (Oxford: Oxford University Press, 2013).
6. Frederick Cooper, *Citizenship Between Empire and Nation: Remaking France and French Africa, 1945–1960* (Princeton, N.J.: Princeton University Press, 2014); Gary Wilder, *Freedom Time: Negritude, Decolonization, and the Future of the World* (Durham, N.C.: Duke University Press, 2015).

7.  For a classical discussion of the different forms of legal pluralism, see John Griffiths, "What Is Legal Pluralism?," *Journal of Legal Pluralism and Unofficial Law* 18, no. 24 (1984): 1–55.

8.  Olivier Beaud, "L'Empire et l'empire colonial dans la doctrine publiciste française de la IIIe République," *Jus Politicum* 14 (June 2015): 1–77, http://juspoliticum.com /article/L-Empire-et-l-empire-colonial-dans-la-doctrine-publiciste-francaise -de-la-IIIe-8239-Republique-991.html; and Emmanuelle Saada, "The Absent Empire: The Colonies in the French Constitutions," in *Endless Empires: Spain's Retreat, Europe's Eclipse, and America's Decline,* ed. Alfred W. McCoy, Josep M. Fradera, and Stephen Jacobson (Madison: University of Wisconsin Press, 2012), 205–15.

9.  Mamdani, *Citizen and Subject.*

10.  Raymond Betts, *Assimilation and Association in French Colonial Theory, 1890–1914* (New York: Columbia University Press, 1961).

11.  Damien Deschamps, *La République aux colonies: le citoyen, l'indigène et le fonction- naire (vers 1848, vers 1900)* (PhD diss., University of Grenoble, 1998), http://www.theses .fr/1998GRE21009.

12.  Alice L. Conklin, *A Mission to Civilize: The Republican Idea of Empire in France and West Africa, 1895–1930* (Stanford, Calif.: Stanford University Press, 1997).

13.  Karuna Mantena, *Alibis of Empire: Henry Maine and the Ends of Liberal Imperialism* (Princeton, N.J.: Princeton University Press, 2010).

14.  Mantena, *Alibis of Empire*; and Bernard S. Cohn, "Law and the Colonial State in India," in *Colonialism and Its Forms of Knowledge* (Princeton, N.J.: Princeton University Press, 1996), 57–75.

15.  Georges Spillman, "Napoléon III et le royaume arabe d'Algérie," *Revue des Travaux de l'Académie des Sciences Morales et Politiques et Comptes Rendus de Ses Séances* 129, no. 1 (1976): 242.

16.  Henry Laurens, *Orientales I: autour de l'expédition d'Égypte* (Paris, France: CNRS, 2004).

17.  Osama W. Abi-Mershed, *Apostles of Modernity: Saint-Simonians and the Civilizing Mission in Algeria* (Stanford, Calif.: Stanford University Press, 2010).

18.  Jennifer Pitts, "Empire and Legal Universalisms in the Eighteenth Century," *The American Historical Review* 117, no. 1 (2012): 99.

19.  Charles Alexandrowicz, *The European-African Confrontation: A Study in Treaty Making* (Leiden, Netherlands: Sijthoff, 1973).

20.  Martti Koskenniemi, *The Gentle Civilizer of Nations: The Rise and Fall of International Law, 1870–1960* (Cambridge: Cambridge University Press, 2004); and Antony Anghie, *Imperialism, Sovereignty, and the Making of International Law* (Cambridge: Cambridge University Press, 2004).

21.  Macklem, "Indigenous Peoples"; Duthu, *Shadow Nations*; Saliha Belmessous, *Assimila- tion and Empire: Uniformity in French and British Colonies, 1541–1954* (Oxford: Oxford University Press, 2013); Richard White, *The Middle Ground* (Cambridge: Cambridge University Press, 1991).

22.  For White, the French Empire's reach in North America was too weak to warrant anything else than accommodation with local powers. White, *Middle Ground.* Belmessous grants more ideological weight to the idea of assimilation, which she identifies as a recurring tendency in the *longue durée* history of French imperialism. Belmessous, *Assimilation and Empire.*

23.  Lauren Benton, *Law and Colonial Cultures: Legal Regimes in World History, 1400–1900* (Cambridge: Cambridge University Press, 2002).

24. Charles-Robert Ageron, "Décolonisation," *Encyclopedia Universalis*, http://www.universalis.fr/encyclopedie/decolonisation/.
25. Alexis de Tocqueville, "Second Letter on Algeria" (1837) and "Essay on Algeria" (1841), in *Writings on Empire and Slaver*, ed. and trans. Jennifer Pitts (Baltimore, Md.: Johns Hopkins University Press, 2001).
26. *Procès-verbaux et rapports de la commission, nommée par le Roi, le 7 juillet 1833 pour aller recueillir en Afrique tous les faits propres à éclairer le gouvernement sur l'état du pays et sur les mesures que réclame son avenir* (Paris, France: Imprimerie Royale, 1834), 69 (hereafter "Algiers report").
27. Hamdan ibn Utman Huqad, "Le miroir," in *Aperçu historique et statistique sur la régence d'Alger*, ed. Abdelkader Djeghloul (Arles, France: Actes Sud, 2003). On Hamdan Khodja, see Jennifer Pitts, "Liberalism and Empire in a Nineteenth Century Mirror," *Modern Intellectual History* 6, no. 2 (August 2009): 287–313.
28. Marquis de la Rochefoucault-Liancourt, *Note sur l'administration d'Alger* (Paris, France: Imprimerie A. Henri, 1835), 11.
29. *Procès-verbaux et rapports de la commission d'Afrique instituée par ordonnance du roi du 12 décembre 1833* (Paris, France: Imprimerie Royale, 1834), 8 (hereafter "Paris report").
30. Paris report, 168.
31. Algiers report, 70.
32. Algiers report, 21.
33. Quoted by Pitts, "Liberalism and Empire," 288.
34. Cour de cassation, report from attorney-general Sarrut, 18 to 22 April 1896, 173–190, *Revue Générale d'Administration*, 1896, Bibliothèque nationale de France, Département Philosophie, histoire, sciences de l'homme, 8-LC5-92 (13). http://gallica.bnf.fr/ark:/12148/cb32859773c/date18960101#resultat-id-1.
35. Paris report, 277.
36. Paris report, 337.
37. Paris report, 305.
38. Paris report, 306.
39. Algiers report, 183–84.
40. Paris report, 323.
41. Quoted in A. Sabatery, *Eléments de droit musulman concernant l'exposé de l'organisation de la justice dans le Pachalik d'Alger avant 1830* (Alger: Paysant, 1866), 31.
42. Debate at the National Constituent Assembly, June 15th, 1848, reproduced in *Histoire parlementaire de l'Assemblée nationale*, vol. 2 (Brussels: Bureaux de l'Association des Ouvriers typographes, 1848), 231.
43. National Constituent Assembly, 1848, 233.
44. National Constituent Assembly, 1848, 236.
45. National Constituent Assembly, 1848, 291.
46. National Constituent Assembly, 1848, 295.
47. National Constituent Assembly, 1848, 241.

# Bibliography

Abi-Mershed, Osama W. *Apostles of Modernity: Saint-Simonians and the Civilizing Mission in Algeria.* Stanford, Calif.: Stanford University Press, 2010.
Ageron, Charles-Robert. "Décolonisation." *Encyclopedia Universalis.* http://www.universalis.fr/encyclopedie/decolonisation/.

Alexandrowicz, Charles. *The European-African Confrontation: A Study in Treaty Making*. Leiden, Netherlands: Sijthoff, 1973.

Anghie, Antony. *Imperialism, Sovereignty, and the Making of International Law*. Cambridge: Cambridge University Press, 2004.

Beaud, Olivier. "L'Empire et l'empire colonial dans la doctrine publiciste française de la IIIe République." *Jus Politicum* 14 (June 2015): 1–77. http://juspoliticum.com/article /L-Empire-et-l-empire-colonial-dans-la-doctrine-publiciste-francaise-de-la-IIIe-8239 -Republique-991.html.

Belmessous, Saliha. *Assimilation and Empire: Uniformity in French and British Colonies, 1541–1954*. Oxford: Oxford University Press, 2013.

Benton, Lauren. *Law and Colonial Cultures: Legal Regimes in World History, 1400–1900*. Cambridge: Cambridge University Press, 2002.

Betts, Raymond. *Assimilation and Association in French Colonial Theory, 1890–1914*. New York: Columbia University Press, 1961.

Chatterjee, Partha. *The Nation and Its Fragments*. Princeton, N.J.: Princeton University Press, 1993.

Cohen, Jean. *Globalization and Sovereignty, Rethinking Legality, Legitimacy, and Constitutionalism*. Cambridge: Cambridge University Press, 2012.

Cohn, Bernard S. "Law and the Colonial State in India." In *Colonialism and Its Forms of Knowledge*, 57–75. Princeton, N.J.: Princeton University Press, 1996.

Conklin, Alice L. *A Mission to Civilize: The Republican Idea of Empire in France and West Africa, 1895–1930*. Stanford, Calif.: Stanford University Press, 1997.

Cooper, Frederick. *Citizenship Between Empire and Nation: Remaking France and French Africa, 1945–1960*. Princeton, N.J.: Princeton University Press, 2014.

Deschamps, Damien. *La République aux colonies: le citoyen, l'indigène et le fonctionnaire (vers 1848, vers 1900)*. PhD diss., University of Grenoble, 1998. http://www.theses.fr /1998GRE21009

Diouf, Mamadou. "Assimilation coloniale et identités religieuses de la civilité des originaires des quatre communes (Sénégal)." *Canadian Journal of African Studies* 34, no. 3 (2000): 565–87.

Duthu, Bruce. *Shadow Nations: Tribal Sovereignty and the Limits of Legal Pluralism*. Oxford: Oxford University Press, 2013.

Griffiths, John. "What Is Legal Pluralism?" *Journal of Legal Pluralism and Unofficial Law* 18, no. 24 (1984): 1–55.

*Histoire parlementaire de l'Assemblée nationale*, Vol. 2. Bruxelles: Bureaux de l'Association des Ouvriers typographes, 1848.

Koskenniemi, Martti. *The Gentle Civilizer of Nations. The Rise and Fall of International Law, 1870–1960*. Cambridge: Cambridge University Press, 2004.

Laurens, Henry. *Orientales I : autour de l'expédition d'Égypte*. Paris, France: CNRS, 2004.

Macklem, Patrick. "Indigenous Peoples and the Ethos of Legal Pluralism in Canada." In *From Recognition to Reconciliation: Essays on the Constitutional Entrenchment of Aboriginal & Treaty Rights*, ed. Patrick Macklen and Douglas Sanderson, chap. 1. Toronto, Canada: University of Toronto Press, 2016.

Mamdani, Mahmood. *Citizen and Subject: Contemporary Africa and the Legacy of Late Colonialism*. Princeton, N.J.: Princeton University Press, 1996.

Mantena, Karuna. *Alibis of Empire: Henry Maine and the Ends of Liberal Imperialism*. Princeton, N.J.: Princeton University Press, 2010.

Muthu, Bruce. *Shadow Nations: Tribal Sovereignty and the Limits of Legal Pluralism*. Oxford: Oxford University Press, 2013.

Pitts, Jennifer. "Empire and Legal Universalisms in the Eighteenth Century." *The American Historical Review* 117, no. 1 (2012): 92–121.

——. "Liberalism and Empire in a Nineteenth Century Mirror." *Modern Intellectual History* 6, no. 2 (August 2009): 287–313.

*Procès-verbaux et rapports de la commission d'Afrique instituée par ordonnance du roi du 12 décembre 1833.* Paris, France: Imprimerie Royale, 1834.

*Procès-verbaux et rapports de la commission, nommée par le Roi, le 7 juillet 1833 pour aller recueillir en Afrique tous les faits propres à éclairer le gouvernement sur l'état du pays et sur les mesures que réclame son avenir.* Paris, France: Imprimerie Royale, 1834.

*Revue Générale d'Administration.* 1896. Département Philosophie, histoire, sciences de l'homme, 8-LC5-92 (13). Bibliothèque nationale de France, http://gallica.bnf.fr/ark:/12148/cb32859773c/date18960101#resultat-id-1.

Marquis de la Rochefoucault-Liancourt. *Note sur l'administration d'Alger.* Paris, France: Imprimerie A. Henri, 1835.

Saada, Emmanuelle. "The Absent Empire: The Colonies in the French Constitutions." In *Endless Empires: Spain's Retreat, Europe's Eclipse, and America's Decline,* ed. Alfred W. McCoy, Josep M. Fradera, and Stephen Jacobson. Madison: University of Wisconsin Press, 2012.

Sabatery, A. *Eléments de droit musulman concernant l'exposé de l'organisation de la justice dans le Pachalik d'Alger avant 1830.* Alger: Paysant, 1866.

Spillman, Georges. "Napoléon III et le royaume arabe d'Algérie." *Revue des Travaux de l'Académie des Sciences Morales et Politiques et Comptes Rendus de Ses Séances* 129, no. 1 (1976): 139–242.

de Tocqueville, Alexis. *Writings on Empire and Slaver.* ed. and trans. Jennifer Pitts. Baltimore, Md.: Johns Hopkins University Press, 2001.

ibn Utman Huqad, Hamdan. "Le miroir." In *Aperçu historique et statistique sur la régence d'Alger,* ed. Abdelkader Djeghloul. Arles, France: Actes Sud, 2003.

Wilder, Gary. *Freedom Time: Negritude, Decolonization, and the Future of the World.* Durham, N.C.: Duke University Press, 2015.

White, Richard. *The Middle Ground.* Cambridge: Cambridge University Press, 1991.

# PART II

---

# NEW FEDERAL FORMATIONS AND SUBSIDIARITY

# 5

# THE CONSTITUTIONAL IDENTITY OF INDIGENOUS PEOPLES IN CANADA

*Status Groups or Federal Actors?*

PATRICK MACKLEM

Indigenous legal norms are beginning to influence the constitutional relationship between indigenous peoples and the Canadian state, inviting questions about potential forms of legal pluralism that might structure this relationship in the future. Indigenous legal norms possess increased salience in constitutional litigation where what is at stake are claims to indigenous territory, treaty rights, and rights of self-government. Indigenous legal norms act as evidence that an indigenous community has occupied its ancestral lands in a manner sufficient for a claim of aboriginal title to such lands. Indigenous legal perspectives assist in providing meaning to the terms and conditions of treaties between indigenous peoples and Canada. In addition, the Canadian judiciary increasingly refers to the fact that there were and continue to be indigenous legal orders operating alongside the Canadian legal order.

This last development is the focus of this chapter because its institutional implications relate directly to the themes structuring this volume. One way to coordinate the plurality of indigenous legal orders with the Canadian legal order is to conceive of them in status group terms, or as multicultural jurisdictions, whose power and authority emanates from indigenous cultural identities that predate the establishment of the Canadian state. Another vehicle of coordination is to conceive of indigenous legal orders as federal actors in the Canadian federation. This chapter begins with a history of the demise and rise of legal pluralism as an animating feature of the relationship between indigenous peoples and the Canadian state.[1] Then distinctive institutional and normative challenges are indentified that status group pluralism and federalism pose in the context of constitutional recognition of indigenous governing authority.

## Legal Pluralism

Scholars refer to "legal pluralism" as a concept that denotes the existence of a plurality of legal orders existing within or across the territorial boundaries of a sovereign state.[2] Many institutional mechanisms give formal expression to the presence of a plurality of legal orders. A federal system constitutionally vests lawmaking authority in two levels of government, each relatively autonomous in the production of legal norms. A state can also devolve power to regional and local levels of government, enabling the exercise of delegated lawmaking authority to a subsection of its population. Forms of minority protection also may promote legal pluralism to the extent that they contemplate a minority community having a measure of lawmaking authority relatively shielded from the legislative power of the broader political community in which it is located.

Canada manifests strong commitments, in theory[3] and in practice, to legal pluralism. The most obvious example lies in the federal nature of its constitutional order, which divides legislative, executive, and judicial power between two levels of government, each sovereign within its spheres of authority, protecting the distinctive cultural and linguistic identity of Quebeçois people by making them a majority in the province in which they reside. Many point to the federal nature of the Canadian state as a contributing factor to the rise of a secessionist movement in Québec by hardening cultural and linguistic differences into legal entitlements and by empowering political actors to capitalize on national, ethnic, religious, and linguistic differences to gain political power. But Canadian federalism as an instrument that fosters "exit" is supplemented by a set of countervailing constitutional arrangements designed to foster "voice" in national institutions, including a commitment to bilingualism, guaranteed seats on the Supreme Court of Canada for judges from Québec, and extensive representation of Québec in the House of Commons and Senate.[4]

A less familiar commitment to legal pluralism lies in the constitutional relationship between indigenous peoples and the Canadian state. The pluralism relevant in this context is one in which the sources of legal validity themselves are plural in nature. In the previous examples, norms produced by legal actors other than the central government appear to possess legal validity by a plurality of sources. A provincial law is legally valid because it was enacted by a legislature possessing jurisdiction to enact it. A municipal bylaw is legally valid because it was enacted in accordance with relevant enabling legislation. A law promulgated by a minority community possesses legal validity because the community has a legal right to promulgate it. But ultimately the legal validity of each of these norms is derived from a singular source, the constitution of the state itself. In contrast, the legal pluralism that captures salient properties of indigenous-settler relations is one of "constitutional pluralism," to use Jean Cohen's phrase, in which a plurality of constitutional orders exists within and, conceivably, across state boundaries.[5] In such an environment, there are multiple legal norms of different content, multiple sites of legal norm production, multiple legal sources for these sites, and multiple forms of norm enforcement. As a result, "legal reality," according to John Griffiths, is "an unsystematic collage of inconsistent and overlapping parts, lending itself to no easy legal interpretation." [6]

At the time of initial contact between indigenous peoples and imperial powers and their colonial representatives, "legal reality" appeared receptive to an ethos of constitutional pluralism. Manifold indigenous legal orders exercised lawmaking authority over territories and peoples in the Americas. The legal norms that constituted these legal orders specified and regulated the economic, social, and political practices of individuals and groups belonging to distinct indigenous nations as well as relations between and among indigenous nations. The legal validity of these norms lay in the nature of the legal orders from which they emanated. European settlement imported colonial legal norms whose validity ultimately depended on the legal systems of France and the United Kingdom. Colonial settlement also marked the genesis of a series of intersocietal encounters, some friendly, others hostile, with mistrust, trust, suspicion, and expectation alike participating in the formation of a pluralist ethos characteristic of their relations. In the words of Jeremy Webber, "the distinctive norms of each society furnished the point of departure, determining the spirit of interaction, colouring the first interpretations of the other's customs, and shaping the beginning of a common normative language."[7]

Contact thus set the stage for constitutionally plural relationships between indigenous peoples and colonial powers. Treaties negotiated early in the history of European expansion formalized efforts to achieve peaceful coexistence between indigenous nations and newcomers to the continent. A 1665 peace treaty between the French Crown and four indigenous nations belonging to the Iroquois Confederacy, for example, confirmed a cessation of conflict and a state of peace between the parties. The text of the treaty indirectly acknowledged the First Nations' continuing title to their territories and certain territorial rights of the French Crown in the settlements of Montréal, Trois-Rivières, and Québec City.[8] Such early treaties reveal a nascent constitutional pluralism at play among the parties. Premised on mutual recognition, they stand as formal markers of early encounters and interactions that had the potential— if deepened and multiplied—to evolve into a durable form of constitutional pluralism structuring indigenous-settler relations on the continent.

The promise of a "common normative language" informing this relationship, however, remains unfulfilled. There are many complex reasons for its absence—reasons that span many domains, including epistemology, economics, politics, and law. One account merits our attention, even though it glosses over the complexity of what it seeks to explain. The ethos of constitutional pluralism immanent in early encounters between indigenous and colonial peoples failed to take root and was replaced by its antithesis: a monistic account of constitutional order with decidedly non-indigenous sources of legal authority, initially grounded in British law and subsequently grounded in the Constitution of Canada.

Why did constitutional pluralism fail to take root? Although the Crown initially entered into treaties with indigenous people to secure their precarious legal and factual footing on indigenous territories by acts of mutual recognition, the Crown soon began to negotiate treaties for different reasons. International law had come to stabilize claims of sovereignty by imperial powers over indigenous territory. Constitutional law assumed a singular, hierarchical conception of sovereignty incapable of comprehending multiple sovereign actors on a given territory. As a result, the Crown no longer regarded a treaty as necessarily being linked to its sovereignty over indigenous territory.[9]

During the nineteenth century, perhaps as a result of the dramatic shift in demography and in the balance of military and economic power between indigenous peoples and the Crown, the treaty process from the Crown's perspective became a means of facilitating the relocation and assimilation of indigenous people. The Crown increasingly saw the treaty process as a means of formally dispossessing indigenous peoples of ancestral territory in return for reserve land and certain benefits to be provided by state authorities, rendering remote the possibility of constitutional pluralism becoming a "legal reality."

Moreover, although early treaties signaled a nation-to-nation relationship of mutual respect, the parties did not initially regard them as creating legal rights enforceable in a court of law. Instead, the treaty served as evidence of an ongoing relationship; rights and obligations flowed not from the document itself but from the relationship formalized by the treaty.[10] This early process of generating norms of conduct and recognition operated against the backdrop of a colonial legal imagination that had yet to experience a radical separation of law and politics, in which certain issues are regarded as legal and others as political.

When law gradually emerged as a relatively autonomous sphere of social life, the judiciary began to address the legal consequences of the treaty process. Judicial interpretation of treaties only started to occur in Canada in the late 1800s, when courts held treaties to be political agreements unenforceable in a court of law. International law provides that an agreement between two "independent powers" constitutes a treaty binding on the parties to the agreement.[11] But because courts regarded indigenous nations as uncivilized and thus not independent, they refused to view Crown promises as legally enforceable obligations under international or domestic law. This view was gradually replaced by a more accommodating approach that regarded a treaty as a form of contract.[12] Indigenous people were imagined as possessing legal personality similar to that possessed by non-indigenous people in Canada and were therefore capable of entering into domestically binding agreements with the Crown.

But because treaties assumed the legal form of contract, their terms were subject to the exercise of unilateral legislative authority. Prior to 1982, this had the effect of permitting legislatures to unilaterally regulate or extinguish existing treaty rights. Moreover, when courts viewed treaties as contractual agreements, they initially interpreted their substance in a manner that was blind to indigenous expectations of the treaty process. Treaty rights were interpreted solely by reference to non-indigenous legal norms and values. In the words of Dale Turner, treaties were "textualized in the language of the dominant European culture."[13]

Despite its nascent presence in early treaties, constitutional pluralism did not take root in Canada because the Crown, protected by a robust, monist conception of sovereign authority, began to negotiate treaties for reasons antithetical to pluralism's promise. When treaties assumed legal form in Canadian law, Canadian legal institutions did not comprehend them as instruments of mutual recognition in which each party acknowledged a measure of legitimacy of the legal order of the other and accordingly made arrangements for the coexistence and interaction of legal norms emanating from the two or more legal communities they represented. Their legal form as contracts rendered them unintelligible as instruments of mutual recognition. As contracts, they assumed a hierarchical legal relation between the Crown and indigenous parties, given that the Crown in its legislative capacity had the authority to unilaterally override their terms. Their substance, too, rendered them unintelligible to constitutional pluralism because indigenous legal norms played no role in clarifying their terms.

Another set of factors contributing to the failure of constitutional pluralism relates to how Canadian law comprehended the legality of indigenous interests in their territories. With British sovereignty came underlying Crown title, with a particularly brutal twist. The fiction of underlying Crown title was developed in feudal times to legitimate the then-existing kaleidoscopic pattern of landholdings in England by treating the Crown as the original occupant and actual landholders as holding title by way of (mostly fictional) grants from the Crown. Its transplantation to the colonial context was not accompanied by the complementary fiction that the actual indigenous landholders held title by way of a grant from the Crown. As a result, the Crown enjoyed full title to all of the territory of its British colonies in North America. The fiction of underlying Crown title became a legal technology of indigenous dispossession, radically disrupting the actual pattern of indigenous landholding in British North America.

In the late 1800s, Canadian law belatedly accepted a tepid conception of aboriginal title at common law, which acknowledged that indigenous peoples lived on and occupied the continent prior to European contact and that, by the Royal Proclamation of 1763, they possessed certain interests worthy of legal protection.[14] This body of law prescribed ways of handling disputes between indigenous and non-indigenous peoples, especially disputes over land. It recognized, in common law terms, indigenous occupation and use of ancestral lands,[15] described rights associated with aboriginal title in collective terms vesting in indigenous communities,[16] and purported to restrict settlement on indigenous territories until these territories had been surrendered to the Crown.[17] It prohibited sales of indigenous land to non-indigenous people without the approval of and participation by Crown authorities.[18] And it prescribed safeguards for the manner in which such surrenders can occur and imposed fiduciary obligations on government in its dealings with indigenous lands and resources.[19]

The common law of aboriginal title, however, historically failed to protect indigenous territories from settlement and exploitation. The law's inability to protect indigenous territories was in part a function of broader social and historical realities associated with colonial expansion. Governments, courts, and settlers either misunderstood or ignored the law of aboriginal title. Crown respect for the law of aboriginal title was eroded by the decline of the fur trade and the waning of indigenous and non-indigenous economic interdependence. Increased demands on indigenous territories occasioned by population growth and westward expansion, followed by a period of paternalistic administration marked by involuntary relocations, only exacerbated the erosion of respect.

In addition to these external factors, the law's failure to protect indigenous territories also can be internally traced to legal choices of the judiciary. On more than one occasion, the judiciary suggested that indigenous territorial claims might not possess any independent legal significance at all.[20] The possibility that indigenous territories might not generate legal recognition by the Canadian legal order served as a legal backdrop for more than a century of relations between the Crown and indigenous peoples, shaping legal expectations of governments, corporations, citizens, and other legal actors. It contributed to a perception that governments and third parties were relatively free to engage in a range of activity on ancestral lands—a perception that, in turn, legitimated unparalleled levels of government and third-party development and exploitation of indigenous territories, which continues relatively unabated today.

Moreover, until recently, the legal significance that the judiciary attached to indigenous territorial interests was minimal. Courts resisted characterizing aboriginal title in proprietary terms, preferring instead to characterize it as a right of occupancy or a personal or usufructuary right,[21] or, more recently, as a *sui generis* interest.[22] Constructing aboriginal title as a nonproprietary interest enabled its regulation and indeed its extinguishment by appropriate executive action,[23] disabled indigenous titleholders from obtaining interim relief,[24] and frustrated access to the common law presumption of compensation in the event of expropriation.[25] Courts also indicated a willingness to view aboriginal title as a set of rights to engage only in traditional practices on indigenous territory, that is, those practices that indigenous people engaged in at the time the Crown acquired territorial sovereignty.[26] Each of these legal choices had a profound effect on the ability of indigenous peoples to rely on Canadian law to protect ancestral territories from non-indigenous incursion. Each represented another nail in constitutional pluralism's coffin.

## Constitutional Pluralism

Notwithstanding this history, the Canadian constitutional environment is demonstrating renewed receptivity to conceiving of indigenous-Canadian relations in accordance with the ethos of constitutional pluralism that animated their origins. There are currently more than five hundred treaties between indigenous peoples and the Crown in Canada from the shores of the Atlantic Ocean to the Yukon in the western Canadian Arctic. In most of British Columbia, where territories have not yet been subject to treaty, indigenous peoples are negotiating new treaties to structure their relationships with federal and provincial authorities. With enactment of section 35(1) of the Constitution Act, 1982, which recognizes and affirms "the existing aboriginal and treaty rights of the aboriginal peoples of Canada,"[27] treaty rights now assume the form of constitutional rights. No longer enforceable merely in the face of Crown inaction, treaties now constrain the exercise of legislative authority.

To illustrate, in *R. v. Badger*,[28] at issue was whether the right to hunt contained in Treaty 8 provided a defense to a charge under Alberta's Wildlife Act, which prohibited hunting out of season and hunting without a license. The Supreme Court of Canada held that Treaty 8 protected hunting for food on private property that was not put to a "visible, incompatible use," and that the right to hunt was a treaty right within the meaning of section 35(1) of the Constitution Act. The Court stated that "a treaty represents an exchange of solemn promises. . . [and] an agreement whose nature is sacred."[29] It reiterated that treaties should be interpreted in "a manner which maintains the integrity of the Crown" and that ambiguities or doubtful expressions in the wording of the treaty should be resolved in favor of indigenous people.[30] *Badger* marks a significant transformation in the judicial understanding of a treaty's form and substance. No longer mere political agreements or contractual agreements, treaties now possess formal constitutional status. Their substance is to be determined in a manner consistent with indigenous legal understandings and expectations, flexible to evolving practices, inclusive of reasonably incidental practices, and in ways that best reconcile the competing interests of the parties.

*Badger's* requirement that treaties be interpreted in a manner consistent with indigenous understandings implicitly rests on an ethos of constitutional pluralism. Though each treaty is unique in its terms and scope of application, indigenous understandings of treaties are relatively uniform. Indigenous people entered into treaties with the Crown to formalize a relationship of continental coexistence. They initially sought military alliances before and during the war between Britain and France and also sought to maximize benefits associated with economic interdependence. As the nineteenth century progressed, indigenous peoples sought to maintain their autonomous legal orders and traditional ways of life in the face of railway construction, surveying activity, non-indigenous settlement of indigenous territories, and an unprecedented rise in hunting, fishing, and trapping by non-indigenous people. They sought to retain traditional authority over their territories and to govern their communities in the face of colonial expansion. In James [Sákéj] Henderson's words, "Aboriginal nations entered into the treaties as the keepers of a certain place."[31] Indigenous people regarded the treaty process as enabling the sharing of land and authority with non-indigenous people while at the same time protecting their territories, economies, and forms of government from non-indigenous incursion.

The new constitutional status of treaties also recovers the promise of constitutional pluralism. Understanding treaties as constitutional instruments opens the pluralist legal door to comprehending treaties as constitutional accords. As constitutional accords, they articulate basic terms and conditions of social coexistence and make possible the exercise of constitutional authority. Unlike legal contracts between the Crown and private citizens, which distribute power delegated by the state to private parties in the form of legally enforceable rights and obligations, treaties establish the constitutional parameters of state power itself.[32] Accordingly, treaties do not distribute delegated state power, they distribute constitutional authority. Treaties are therefore as much a part of the constitutional history of Canada as the Constitution Act, 1867, which distributes legislative power between the federal and provincial governments. Treaty rights are constitutional rights that flow to indigenous people in exchange for allowing European nations to exercise a measure of sovereign authority in North America.

The judiciary has begun to conceive of treaties in similar terms. In *Haida Nation v. British Columbia*, the Supreme Court of Canada concluded that British Columbia has a legal duty to consult with the Haida people about the harvest of timber from lands subject to a claim by them of aboriginal title.[33] More generally, the Court held that where treaties remain to be concluded the Crown is required to participate in negotiations "leading to a just settlement of Aboriginal claims."[34] According to the Court, "treaties serve to reconcile pre-existing Aboriginal sovereignty with assumed Crown sovereignty."[35]

As constitutional accords, treaties operate as instruments of mutual recognition. Negotiations occur against a backdrop of competing claims of constitutional authority. The Crown enters negotiations under the assumption that it possesses jurisdiction and rights with respect to the territory in question; a First Nation enters negotiations on the assumption that it possesses jurisdiction and rights with respect to the same territory. The treaty process is a means by which competing claims of authority and right can be reconciled with each other by each party agreeing to recognize a measure of the authority of the other.[36] Recognition can occur geographically, as with a number of contemporary land claims agreements that distribute jurisdiction between the parties based on different geographical categories of land within the territory in question. Recognition also can occur by subject, whereby the parties distribute jurisdiction between themselves based on various subject matters suitable for legislation. As an instrument of mutual recognition, a treaty is an ongoing process, structured but not determined by the text of the original agreement, by which parties commit to resolving disputes that might arise in the future through a process of dialogue and mutual respect.

Viewing treaties as constitutional accords is consonant with recent scholarly attempts to construct alternative legal histories of indigenous-Crown relations.[37] Legal histories typically trace the legal position of indigenous people under Canadian law over time to demonstrate the redemptive potential, or lack thereof, of Canadian law for protecting indigenous peoples from assimilation. What such histories lack, and what recent scholarship attempts to provide, is an appreciation of how indigenous people actively participated in the production and reproduction of legal norms that structured their relations with non-indigenous people on the continent. This scholarship is consistent with "critical legal pluralism," an approach introduced by Kleinhaus and MacDonald that "focuses the spotlight on the citizen-subject and views them as sources of normativity in the sense that they are *law inventing*, not merely *law abiding*, forces within a society."[38]

James Tully, for example, has interpreted the treaty process as a form of "treaty constitutionalism" whereby indigenous people participate in the creation of constitutional norms governing aboriginal-Crown relations.[39] Robert Williams has written of the "long-neglected fact that . . . Indians tried to create a new type of society with Europeans on the multicultural frontiers of colonial North America."[40] Henderson has interpreted the treaty process as producing "treaty federalism"—a constitutional order grounded in the consent of indigenous and non-indigenous people on the continent and established well before confederation.[41] In Henderson's words, treaty federalism "represents a belief in autonomous zones of power, freedom, and liberties in consensual and dynamic order, rather than the unexamined essence of divine sovereignty and its imposed hierarchies or parliamentary sovereignty."[42] What such scholarship shares is an appreciation of the active participation by indigenous people in the production of basic legal norms governing the distribution of constitutional authority in North America.[43] Viewed through the prism of constitutional pluralism, the treaty process is a formal manifestation of such participation through its active production of constitutional accords that distribute constitutional authority on the continent.

The second development relates to the form and substance of aboriginal title and rights. With the enactment of section 35(1) of the Constitution Act, 1982, and confirmed by the Supreme Court of Canada in *Delgamuukw v. British Columbia*,[44] aboriginal title shed its common law status and assumed the form of a constitutional right. An indigenous community that possesses aboriginal title to its ancestral lands holds title to the land itself, including surface and subsurface resources, and federal or provincial laws or actions that interfere with aboriginal title must meet fairly searching constitutional standards before they are held to possess constitutional validity. Although the Court in *Delgamuukw* extensively described the nature and scope of aboriginal title and the circumstances under which it can be justifiably interfered with by the Crown, it offered little insight into why aboriginal title merits constitutional protection, holding simply that a "plain meaning" of the Constitution and precedent were conclusive of the issue.[45]

But a deeper account of the constitutional status of aboriginal title rests on an ethos of constitutional pluralism. On this account, aboriginal title is a constitutional—as opposed to a common law or statutory—norm because it is an entitlement that is not conditional on the exercise of judicial and legislative authority. Instead, it is logically and historically antecedent to the exercise of judicial and legislative authority and owes its origins to facts and norms that predate the establishment of the Canadian state. Indigenous peoples possessed title to their territories according to their own laws prior to the establishment of a sovereign entity that assumed the legislative power to redistribute title to its citizens. In the words of Swepson and Plant, "rights of ownership already accrue to Indigenous populations, and are not ceded to them through the actions of nation-states."[46] Canada became a sovereign state against the backdrop of a preexisting distribution of territory among indigenous nations. By recognizing and affirming aboriginal title, section 35(1) extends constitutional validity to indigenous legal norms that inform and make sense of this preexisting distribution of indigenous territory. It ensures that state power will be exercised in a manner that respects these indigenous legal norms and the indigenous legal orders to which they owe their existence.

Also relevant to a recovery of constitutional pluralism's promise is a shift in how the judiciary assesses the validity of a claim of aboriginal title. Indigenous legal norms can participate in establishing the requisite exclusive occupation on which aboriginal title rests. In the words of Chief Justice Lamer in *Delgamuukw*:

> If, at the time of sovereignty, an aboriginal society had laws in relation to land, those laws would be relevant to establishing the occupation of laws which are the subject of a claim of Aboriginal title. Relevant laws might include, but are not limited to, a land tenure system or laws governing land use.[47]

Elsewhere in his reasons, Chief Justice Lamer stated that indigenous laws governing trespass and conditional land use by members of other indigenous nations, as well as treaties between and among indigenous nations, also might assist in establishing the occupation necessary to prove aboriginal title.[48]

These passages were instrumental to the Court's recent decision in *Tsilhqot'in Nation v. British Columbia* to grant a declaration of aboriginal title to the Tsilhqot'in people, a collectivity of six communities sharing a common culture and history and living in a remote valley bounded by rivers and mountains in central British Columbia.[49] The Court held that the Tsilhqot'in manifested sufficient and exclusive occupation and exclusive control of the land in question required for a declaration of aboriginal title. Sufficiency of occupation was established by evidence at trial of a strong presence on or over the land claimed, manifesting itself in acts of occupation that demonstrated that the land in question belonged to, was controlled by, or was under the exclusive stewardship of the Tsilhqot'in. Exclusivity of occupation was established by evidence that Tsilhqot'in laws excluded others from the land, except when they were allowed access to the land with the permission of the Tsilhqot'in. The presence of indigenous laws emanating from an indigenous legal order, in other words, stands as evidence that indigenous peoples possess aboriginal rights in the Canadian constitutional order.

Constitutional recognition of indigenous legal norms is not restricted to the proof of aboriginal title. Elsewhere the Court has suggested that indigenous laws compatible with the assertion of Crown sovereignty survived its assertion, were "absorbed into the common law as rights," and, if not surrendered or extinguished, received constitutional recognition as aboriginal rights by section 35(1).[50] This suggests that at least part of the reason something is an aboriginal right in Canadian law is because it was an indigenous legal norm at the time of the assertion of Crown sovereignty. Understanding aboriginal rights as indigenous legal norms renders section 35(1) a provision performative of constitutional pluralism by formally acknowledging the constitutional significance of indigenous legal orders.

In addition, Chief Justice McLachlin, in *Haida Nation* and *Taku River*, wrote of treaties as instruments that "reconcile pre-existing Aboriginal sovereignty with assumed Crown sovereignty" or "*de facto* Crown sovereignty."[51] The Court regularly refers to "the pre-existing societies of aboriginal peoples,"[52] indigenous "legal systems,"[53] "pre-existing systems of aboriginal law,"[54] and "aboriginal peoples occupying and using most of this vast expanse of land in organized, distinctive societies with their own social and political structures."[55] And, in the following passage, Chief Justice McLachlin, in her dissent in *Van der Peet*, clearly summoned the spirit of legal pluralism:

> The history of the interface of Europeans and the common law with aboriginal peoples is a long one. As might be expected of such a long history, the principles by which the interface has been governed have not always been consistently applied. Yet running through this history, from its earliest beginnings to the present time is a golden thread—the recognition by the common law of the ancestral laws and customs of the aboriginal peoples who occupied the land prior to European settlement.[56]

This passage seems to suggest that constitutional pluralism has always characterized "the interface of Europeans and the common law with aboriginal peoples." But history tells us otherwise. Canadian courts describing relations between indigenous peoples and Canada as constitutionally plural, as important as this development is, does not make them so. Constitutional recognition of indigenous governments would be a precondition of the reanimation of the ethos of constitutional pluralism in relations between indigenous peoples and Canada.

Under Canadian law, indigenous government authority is currently exercised by Indian band councils that exercise delegated statutory authority pursuant to the federal Indian Act.[57] But the enactment of section 35 of the Constitution Act, 1982, together with the emergent discourse of pluralism animating jurisprudential characterizations of the relationship between indigenous peoples and the Canadian state, raise the spectrum of constitutional recognition of indigenous government authority. As elaborated below, two potential forms of constitutional recognition lie on this spectrum that merit scrutiny.[58] The first is to conceive of indigenous legal orders as status groups, grounded in distinctive indigenous cultural identities that predate the establishment of the Canadian state. The second is to conceive of them as constituting a third order of government in the Canadian federation. There is no hard and fast distinction between these models. One could imagine a federal model that recognizes lawmaking authority in indigenous governments along status group lines, where indigenous jurisdiction relates solely to the preservation of indigenous culture,[59] and one could imagine alternative—or supplementary—forms of constitutional recognition of indigenous governing authority.[60] These models are also formal in nature, but their form will affect the scope and content of indigenous governing authority and the relationship between indigenous governments and the Canadian state.

## Multicultural Jurisdictions

In 1985, the Eagle Lake First Nation, whose members live on a reserve in western Ontario, passed a resolution enacting a lottery law that authorized and regulated gaming activities on the reserve. The First Nation then began to conduct regular bingo games that attracted a significant number of non-indigenous participants and generated an annual profit of over a million dollars. The operation enabled the First Nation to build a community arena, a resort, a lodge, a conference center, and a local school and gymnasium. But federal law prohibits certain forms of gaming without provincial authorization. The Eagle Lake First Nation, acting on the assumption that it possessed the authority to make laws in relation to the regulation of economic activity on the reserve, did not seek Ontario's authorization for its activities.

Members of the First Nation were charged with and convicted of keeping a common gaming house contrary to the Criminal Code. Before the Supreme Court of Canada, in R. v. Pamajewon,[61] the First Nation unsuccessfully argued that it possessed an aboriginal right to make laws governing economic affairs on its reserve land free of federal and provincial interference. According to Chief Justice Lamer, "assuming that section 35(1) encompasses claims to self-government, such claims must be considered in light of the purposes underlying the provision and must, therefore, be considered against the test derived from consideration of those purposes."[62] At the time the Court rendered its decision, the test for determining the content of an aboriginal right was that found in R. v. Van der Peet, which defined an aboriginal right as an element of a custom, practice, or tradition integral to the distinctive culture of an aboriginal nation. The Court rejected the Eagle Lake First Nation's characterization of its claim as an assertion of a broad right to regulate the use of its reserve lands; instead, it characterized the claim as involving the assertion of a narrow right to participate in and regulate high-stakes gambling on the reserve. It concluded that the claim did not relate to a custom, practice, or tradition integral to the distinctive culture of the First Nation at the time of contact.

The judiciary has not yet explicitly confirmed that indigenous communities possess a constitutional right of self-government. Were it to do so, or were a treaty to be negotiated to this effect,[63] such an outcome could assume at least two different forms. The first, alluded to in the approach adopted by Chief Justice Lamer in Pamajewon, would be a form of status group legal pluralism in which the assignees of an aboriginal right of self-government are a plurality of multicultural jurisdictions identified by their indigenous status. Chief Justice Lamer held that, assuming that the First Nation could assert a right of self-government, such a right would be narrowly construed—as a right to regulate a practice, custom, or tradition integral to the distinctive culture of the community at the time of contact. Such a right would comprehend lawmaking authority over matters that lie at the core of indigenous cultural identity.

An alternative form of constitutional recognition of indigenous governing authority is to conceive of indigenous legal orders in federal terms, as federal actors in the Canadian federation.[64] To see how this might be the case, it is useful to theorize the potential implications of *Mitchell v. M.N.R.*, where at issue was whether section 35 protects a Mohawk practice of cross-border trade. The Court held that the Mohawk nation failed to establish that it was integral to their distinctive culture at contact to carry goods from New York to Ontario across the St. Lawrence River for trade purposes. For present purposes, what is relevant is another dimension of the judgment alluded to in McLachlin C.J.'s majority decision and expressly addressed by Binnie J.'s concurring reasons. The government had contended that section 35(1) extends constitutional protection only to those indigenous practices, customs, and traditions that are compatible with the historical and modern exercise of Crown sovereignty. Pursuant to what was referred to as the doctrine of "sovereign incompatibility," the government argued further that any Mohawk practice of cross-border trade, even if established on the evidence, would be barred from recognition under section 35(1) as incompatible with the Crown's sovereign interest in regulating its borders.[65]

McLachin C.J. refused to address the merits of the doctrine of sovereign incompatibility as the respondent had not proven its claim to an aboriginal right. Nonetheless, Binnie J. concurring, characterized British colonial law as presuming that the Crown intended to respect aboriginal rights that were not incompatible with the sovereignty of the Crown. In his view, this notion of incompatibility with Crown sovereignty is a defining characteristic of sovereign succession and therefore operates as a limit on the scope of aboriginal rights. A fundamental attribute and incident of sovereignty is a state's control over the mobility of persons and goods across its border. According to Binnie J., the international dimension of the asserted aboriginal right was incompatible with the historical attributes of Canadian sovereignty and cannot be said to be an "existing" right within the meaning of section 35.

Binnie J. regarded the doctrine of sovereign incompatibility to be consistent with section 35's purpose of reconciliation. In his words, the government's "claim relates to national interests that all of us have in common rather than to distinctive interests that for some purposes differentiate an aboriginal community." Binnie J. saw the task of defining the nature and scope of the aboriginal right as one that required reconciling competing sets of interests. On one hand, the case implicates interests associated with Canadian sovereignty "that all of us have in common;" on the other hand, it also implicates interests associated with cross-border trading that, for historical reasons, "differentiate an aboriginal community" from other Canadians. For Binnie J., the nature and scope of aboriginal rights are to be determined by reconciling these competing interests, and "reconciliation of these interests in this particular case favours an affirmation of our collective sovereignty."[66]

Binnie J. is quick to argue that the doctrine of sovereign incompatibility does not foreclose constitutional protection of interests associated with indigenous sovereignty in the form of an aboriginal or treaty right of self-government. Although careful not to express any opinion on the subject, Binnie J. discusses at length the concept of "shared sovereignty," and quotes the report of the Royal Commission on Aboriginal Peoples as follows:

> Shared sovereignty, in our view, is a hallmark of the Canadian federation and a central feature of the three-cornered relations that link Aboriginal governments, provincial governments and the federal government. These governments are sovereign within their respective spheres and hold their powers by virtue of their constitutional status rather than by delegation. Nevertheless, many of their powers are shared in practice and may be exercised by more than one order of government.[67]

Given that "the constitutional objective is reconciliation not mutual isolation,"[68] section 35 does not warrant a claim to unlimited governmental powers or to complete sovereignty, such as independent states are commonly thought to possess. As with the federal and provincial governments, aboriginal governments operate within a sphere of sovereignty defined by the Constitution. In short, the aboriginal right of self-government in section 35(1) involves circumscribed rather than unlimited powers.[69]

The Royal Commission on Aboriginal Peoples proposed that aboriginal government authority could be clarified by distinguishing between a core and a periphery. The commission identified the core of aboriginal jurisdiction as the authority to make laws in relation to matters of vital concern to the life and welfare of the community, that do not have a major impact on adjacent jurisdictions, and that are not otherwise the object of overarching federal or provincial concern. Such a core would prevent Parliament and provincial legislatures from enforcing against aboriginal people laws that regulated matters central to aboriginal identity. Subject to the above principles, aboriginal governments would have the authority to establish a national constitution, governmental and judicial institutions, and citizenship criteria, and enact laws in relation to education, health, family matters, and certain economic activity as well as aspects of criminal law and procedure. On the other hand, matters that do not fall within the core of aboriginal jurisdiction could support overlapping and duplicative laws enacted by all three levels of government. Aboriginal authority over matters on the periphery of aboriginal jurisdiction, such as those that would have a major impact on adjacent jurisdictions, would require intergovernmental agreement.[70]

Organized as federal actors, indigenous governments' authority would, in some respects, resemble that of Indian tribal governments in the United States, whose inherent sovereignty obtains legal expression through the concept of "domestic dependent nations" status. The Constitution of the United States is understood as recognizing Indian nations as legally free to exercise inherent jurisdiction over their internal affairs, subject to limitations inherently flowing from the overriding sovereignty of the United States[71] and an overriding or plenary power of Congress.[72] For present purposes, the relevant point of convergence is the fact that indigenous jurisdictional authority would not be tailored to the distinctive cultures of the communities over which it is exercised. Instead, the nature and scope of jurisdictional authority would be uniform across indigenous legal orders, just as it is with respect to Indian nations in the United States, and just as provincial authority in Canada is uniform across provinces. All indigenous governments, in other words, would possess the same legislative authority to make laws in relation to territory and persons.

There are several reasons to prefer the federal model over status group pluralism. The temporal gaze of status group pluralism—in the form discussed here—is backward in time, rooting indigenous legal authority in its significance to the distinctive cultural identity of an indigenous community at the time of contact. Such significance cannot be in doubt, but it has little relevance to the nature and scope of governing authority an indigenous community needs in the present to effectively govern itself into the future. Such authority includes powers to maintain and reproduce the distinctive cultures of indigenous communities, but, to be effective, it also should include territorial authority, the capacity to foster economic and resource development, and the ability to raise revenue.

The backward gaze of status group pluralism also risks freezing—and essentializing—indigenous cultural norms concerning government authority. Cultures can undergo deep transformations over time. According to Eric Wolf, "in the rough-and-tumble of social interaction, groups are known to exploit the ambiguities of inherited forms, to impart new evaluations or valences to them, to borrow forms more expressive of their interests, or to create wholly new forms to answer to changed circumstances."[73] Indigenous cultures include cultural forms, practices, and ways of life that have been affected, transformed, and even generated in response to contact with non-indigenous society. To the extent that colonization can be understood in part as a process that involved the construction of indigenous people as culturally different than, and inferior to, settlers, many scholars view contact and colonization as actually producing certain aspects of indigenous cultural identities.[74] Attempts to define indigenous cultural identities solely by reference to precontact ways of life not only risk stereotyping indigenous peoples in terms of historical differences with non-indigenous peoples that may or may not have existed in the distant past but also profoundly underdescribe important aspects of contemporary indigenous identities.

Given the cultural heterogeneity of indigenous communities, if constitutional recognition of indigenous government authority takes the form of status group pluralism, indigenous governments would not enjoy uniform lawmaking authority by virtue of their status as indigenous peoples. The jurisdiction of each government would be tailored to the distinctive cultural identity and history of each community. In contrast, the federal model does not condition the nature and scope of indigenous government authority on what it might have looked like at the time of contact—or on establishing a link to past cultural identity. The distribution of legislative authority would also be general, not specific, and yet would leave indigenous governments with room to exercise it in ways that attend to the specificities of their communities. Its scope and content can be delineated in contemporary terms, with a functional eye to present and future needs. As "federal and provincial divisions that the Crown has imposed on itself are internal to itself,"[75] recognition of indigenous governments as federal actors would leave intact the distribution of legislative and executive authority between federal and provincial governments and superimpose an additional indigenous order of government onto the Canadian federation. And the level of autonomy constitutionally assigned to indigenous federated actors would likely be much greater than that currently possessed by indigenous governments and what they might possess as status groups.[76]

Perhaps most important, while conceiving of indigenous governing authority would perform an act of recognition—of the fact of a plurality of indigenous legal orders that have and continue to operate thus far in the shadow of the Canadian state—the federal form that it would assume would enable indigenous peoples to make credible political claims for redistribution: claims that are currently marginalized by the structure of fiscal politics in Canada. The greatest threat to the vitality of indigenous communities are their social and economic conditions. Indigenous peoples experience greater poverty, receive less education, suffer from much poorer health, enjoy shorter life spans, receive fewer social services of lower quality, have higher suicide rates, and have higher incarceration rates than non-indigenous people.[77]

Section 36(1) of the Constitution Act, 1982 commits the federal and provincial governments to "providing essential public services of reasonable quality to all Canadians," and section 36(2) commits the federal government to the principle of making equalization payments to ensure that provincial governments have sufficient revenues to provide reasonably comparable lev-els of public services at reasonably comparable levels of taxation.[78] To this end, the federal government currently makes financial transfers to the prov-inces in support of their spending initiatives to correct both horizontal fiscal imbalances among provinces and vertical fiscal imbalances between the fed-eral government and provinces. Although they too are tasked with providing essential public services to their citizens, indigenous governments receive no mention in these provisions. Accordingly, there is no political space in the dis-course of equalization for indigenous political actors to make credible claims for redistribution.

Conceiving of indigenous governments as a third order of government would enable indigenous political actors to leverage demands for redistribu-tion into claims that indigenous governments, like provinces, should receive equalization payments to correct both horizontal and vertical imbalances in the delivery of social services.[79] Framing the gross inequalities that exist between indigenous and non-indigenous communities in the discourse of equalization would provide political credibility to indigenous redistributional demands. In contrast, although the interest group pluralism model contemplates indigenous autonomy in the delivery of social services, it risks becoming an instrument of privatization of state responsibilities.[80]

Recognizing indigenous governments as federal actors thus would reconstitute the federation by institutionalizing indigenous government authority and regen-erating a measure of their original and continuing sovereignty over their territo-ries and peoples.[81] But "the essence of federalism is not found in a particular set of institutions;" it lies instead "in the institutionalization of a particular kind of rela-tionship among the participants in political life."[82] In this sense, too, federalism is a far better model than status group pluralism. Both models recognize differences that exist between indigenous and non-indigenous people, but federalism struc-tures their relations in ways that facilitate coexistence.[83] Such structuring, in Jean Leclair's words, acknowledges that "our individual identities are complex and that they comprise more than a single allegiance."[84] As Leclair also notes, this is why instruments that establish both self-rule and shared rule are critical to federalism's success. Recognition of indigenous governments as possessing a constitutional sphere of autonomy over people and territory, on its own, would not institutional-ize a relationship of coexistence. Institutional arrangements would also be needed to instantiate the plural allegiances of all federal actors.[85] Conceiving of indige-nous governments as federal actors in the Canadian federation would foster a politics of exit unless it is supplemented by a set of countervailing constitutional arrangements designed to foster indigenous voice in Canadian institutions, such as guaranteed representation in Parliament and perhaps provincial legislatures, and in key government agencies and offices.[86]

Recognizing indigenous governments as federal actors might also lead to a deepening of institutional relationships that currently exist among federal actors in the federation.[87] Although the judiciary occasionally characterizes federal-provincial relations in terms of cooperative federalism, the cooperative federalism that animates the Canadian federation is not similar to that of a number of other federations. In Germany, for example, "the federal principle by its nature creates not only rights but also obligations." One such obligation "consists in financially strong states having to give assistance within certain limits to poor financially weaker states."[88] Moreover, all parties to the federation "are bound to cooperate according to the nature of this union and to contribute to its consolidation and to the preservation of its interests and well-known interests of its members."[89] In contrast, in Canada the dominant view is that, with a few exceptions, federal and provincial governments can exercise their legislative and executive authority in ways that need not take the interests of the other level of government into account.[90]

Extensive consultation duties currently structure the relationship between indigenous peoples and the Crown, requiring the Crown to exhibit "loyalty, good faith in the discharge of its mandate," and "full disclosure appropriate to the subject matter" when exercising legislative or executive authority in ways that might adversely affect indigenous interests associated with aboriginal or treaty rights.[91] Indigenous peoples are not under a corresponding and reciprocal set of duties, but they "must not try to frustrate the Crown's reasonable good faith attempts, nor should they take unreasonable positions to thwart governments from making decisions or acting in cases where, despite meaningful consultation, agreement is not reached."[92]

Conceiving of indigenous governments as federal actors would mean that their status and authority would be roughly formally equal to that of other federal actors, in which case the duties that the Crown owes to them might be seen as no longer necessary now that they are full and formally equal members of the Canadian federation. Alternatively, whether due to a commitment to precedent or principle, the judiciary might be reluctant to discard such obligations—in which case, such duties might be reconceived as reciprocal due to the formal equality that would exist between and among indigenous governments and other federal actors. This, in turn, might have a cascading effect on the relations between and among other federal actors, rendering the federation more amenable to the principle of cooperative federalism in a more robust way.

The history of the constitutional relationship between indigenous peoples and Canada is one of a rise, demise, and resurgence of constitutional pluralism. At contact, manifold indigenous legal orders exercised lawmaking authority over territories and peoples in the Americas. The legal norms that constituted these legal orders specified and regulated the economic, social, and political practices of individuals and groups belonging to distinct indigenous nations as well as relations between and among indigenous nations. The legal validity of these norms lay in the nature of the legal orders from which they emanated. European settlement imported colonial legal norms whose validity ultimately depended on the legal systems of France and the United Kingdom. The relationships between and among these legal orders reveal a nascent constitutional pluralism that was gradually replaced by its opposite: a singular, hierarchical conception of sovereignty incapable of comprehending multiple sovereign actors on a given territory. Protected by this monist conception, the Crown began to negotiate treaties for reasons antithetical to pluralism's promise. The judiciary began to interpret treaties in ways that rendered them unintelligible as instruments of mutual recognition. The fiction of underlying Crown title became a legal technology of indigenous dispossession, radically disrupting the actual pattern of indigenous landholding in British North America. Superimposed on Crown title was a weak form of aboriginal title at common law, which left governments and third parties relatively free to engage in a range of activity on ancestral lands, resulting in unparalleled levels of government and third-party development and exploitation of indigenous territories.

However, indigenous legal norms are beginning to influence the constitutional relationship between indigenous peoples and the Canadian state. Indigenous legal norms possess increased salience in constitutional litigation where claims to indigenous territory, treaty rights, and rights of self-government are at stake. Indigenous legal norms act as evidence that an indigenous community has occupied its ancestral lands in a manner sufficient for a claim of aboriginal title to such lands. They assist in providing meaning to the terms and conditions of treaties between indigenous peoples and Canada. And the Canadian judiciary increasingly makes reference to the fact that there were and continue to be indigenous legal orders operating in Canada alongside the Canadian legal order.

This essay has sought to identify and evaluate modes of constitutionally coordinating the fact of a plurality of indigenous legal orders and with the existence of the Canadian legal order. One mode of coordination is to conceive of indigenous legal orders in status group terms, or as multicultural jurisdictions, whose power and authority emanates from indigenous cultural identities that predate the establishment of the Canadian state. This mode is consistent with the jurisprudential tendency to define aboriginal and treaty rights recognized and affirmed by section 35 of the Constitution Act, 1867 in terms of the distinctive cultural identities of indigenous peoples at the time of contact or treaty. It shares many of the flaws of this judicial tendency. Its backward temporal gaze is of little relevance to the nature and scope of the governing authority an indigenous community needs in the present to effectively govern itself into the future. And it risks freezing and essentializing indigenous cultural norms concerning government authority.

Another vehicle of coordination is to conceive of indigenous legal orders as federal actors in the Canadian federation. This mode of coordination has a more durable precedent: the Canadian federation itself. It would not condition the nature and scope of indigenous government authority on what it might have looked like at the time of contact—or on establishing a link to past cultural identity. The distribution of legislative authority would also be general, not specific, and yet would leave indigenous governments with room to exercise it in ways that attend to the specificities of their communities. Its scope and content can be delineated in contemporary terms, with a functional eye to present and future needs. And it would enable indigenous people to leverage and make credible political claims for redistribution by casting them in the discourse of equalization. It might also have the effect of deepening constitutional commitments to the principle that constitutional actors owe a duty of loyalty to each other in the exercise of legislative and executive power. To be successful, this mode of coordination would need to be supplemented with instruments of shared rule to instantiate indigenous allegiances in federal—and perhaps provincial—governing institutions.

## Notes

1   This part of the chapter draws from Patrick Macklem, "Indigenous Peoples and the Ethos of Legal Pluralism in Canada," in *From Recognition to Reconciliation: Essays on the Constitutional Entrenchment of Aboriginal & Treaty Rights*, ed. Patrick Macklem and Douglas Sanderson (Toronto, Canada: University of Toronto Press, 2016), 17–34.

2.  "The legal pluralist is intensely interested in identifying the forms of normative ordering, including legal systems, that have meaning to the socially plural societies occupying the same social field and examining the operation of those normative ordering systems in relation to the power of the state." Bruce Duthu, *Shadow Nations: Tribal Sovereignty and the Limits of Legal Pluralism* (New York: Oxford University Press, 2013), 11–12. For further discussion of legal pluralism, see Paul Schiff Berman, *Global Legal Pluralism: A Jurisprudence of Law Beyond Borders* (Cambridge: Cambridge University Press, 2012); Boaventura de Sousa Santos, *Toward a New Legal Common Sense: Law, Globalization and Emancipation* (Cambridge: Cambridge University Press, 2002); Carol Weisbrod, *Emblems of Pluralism: Cultural Differences and the Law* (Princeton, N.J.: Princeton University Press, 2002); William Connolly, *The Ethos of Pluralization* (Minneapolis: University of Minnesota Press, 1995).

3.  See, for example, James Tully, *Strange Multiplicity: Constitutionalism in an Age of Diversity* (Cambridge: Cambridge University Press, 1995); Will Kymlicka, *Multicultural Citizenship: A Liberal Theory of Minority Rights* (Oxford: Oxford University Press, 1996); Harry Arthurs, *"Without the Law": Administrative Justice and Legal Pluralism in Nineteenth Century England* (Toronto, Canada: University of Toronto Press, 1985); Roderick A. MacDonald, "Metaphors of Multiplicity: Civil Society, Regimes and Legal

Pluralism," *Arizona Journal of International and Comparative Law* 15, no. 1 (1998): 69–92; Tim Schouls, *Shifting Boundaries: Aboriginal Identity, Pluralist Theory, and the Politics of Self-Government* (Vancouver, Canada: University of Vancouver Press, 2003); David Schneiderman, "Canadian Constitutional Culture: A Genealogical Account," in *The Oxford Handbook on the Canadian Constitution*, ed. Peter Oliver, Patrick Macklem, and Nathalie Des Rosiers (Oxford: Oxford University Press, 2017).

4. On exit and voice mechanisms, see Albert O. Hirschman, *Exit, Voice, and Loyalty: Responses to Decline in Firms, Organizations, and States* (Cambridge, Mass.: Harvard University Press, 1970).

5. Jean L. Cohen, *Globalization and Sovereignty: Rethinking Legality, Legitimacy, and Constitutionalism* (Cambridge: Cambridge University Press, 2012), 45.

6. John Griffiths, "What Is Legal Pluralism?" *Journal of Legal Pluralism and Unofficial Law* 18, no. 24 (1986): 4. Legal scholars, myself included, have often cited this article as a classic articulation of legal pluralism. David Schneiderman's work on the British legal and political pluralists, including F. W. Maitland, Harold Laski, and John Neville Figgis, of the early twentieth century reveals Griffiths to have been a relative latecomer to the field. See David Schneiderman, "Harold Laski, Viscount Haldane, and the Law of the Canadian Constitution in the Early Twentieth Century," *University of Toronto Law Journal* 48, no. 4 (Autumn 1998): 521–60. See also David Schneiderman, "Haldane Unrevealed," *McGill Law Journal* 57, no. 3 (2012): 597–626.

7. Jeremy Webber, "Relations of Force and Relations of Justice: The Emergence of Normative Community Between Colonists and Aboriginal Peoples," *Osgoode Hall Law Journal* 33, no. 4 (1995): 627.

8. *Treaty of Peace Between the Iroquois and Governor de Tracy*, New York Papers 111 A28. The text of the treaty can be found in Clive Parry, ed., *The Consolidated Treaty Series*, vol. 9 (Dobbs Ferry, N.Y.: Oceana, 1969–86), 363; and E. B. O'Callaghan, ed., *Documents Relative to the Colonial History of the State of New York*, vol. 3 (Albany, N.Y.: Weed, Parsons, 1856–61), 21. For more discussion of the treaty, see Royal Commission on Aboriginal Peoples, *Treaty Making in the Spirit of Co-Existence: An Alternative to Extinguishment* (Ottawa, Canada: Minister of Supply and Services Canada, 1995), 18–20.

9. Compare this statement with McHugh's statement that "constitutional lawyers and courts intellectually drawn to the unitary common law model of sovereignty— itself . . . largely a nineteenth-century model—were unable to recognize a shared or multiple version." P. G. McHugh, *Aboriginal Societies and the Common Law: A History of Sovereignty, Status, and Self-Determination* (New York: Oxford University Press, 2004), 65.

10. Compare with Blackstone's vision of a contract as being dependent on the existence of a social relation and preexisting rights and obligations. William Blackstone, *Commentaries on the Laws of England*, vol. 1 (Oxford: Clarendon Press, 1765–69), 428. See also Atiyah's statement that eighteenth-century legal consciousness invoked the notion of promise "to support an independently existing duty." Patrick Atiyah, *The Rise and Fall of Freedom of Contract* (Oxford: Clarendon Press, 1979), n. 40, 143; and Kahn-Freund's statement that "the contract is only an *accidentale*, not an *essentiale* of the relation." Owen Kahn-Freund, "Blackstone's Neglected Child: The Contract of Employment," *Law Quarterly Review* 93 (1977): 512 (offprint).

11. See, for example, Ian Brownlie, *Principles of Public International Law*, 8th ed. (Oxford: Clarendon Press, 2012), 58–70. Even if treaties between the Crown and First Nations constituted treaties in international law, this fact alone would not render them enforceable in domestic courts; implementing legislation would be required; see *A.G. Canada v. A.G. Ontario (Labour Conventions)*, [1937] A.C. 326 (P.C.).

12. "The right acquired by the Indians in those treaties was . . . necessarily subject to restriction through acts of the legislature, just as the person who acquires from the Crown a grant of land is subject in its enjoyment to . . . legislative restrictions." *Pawis v. The Queen* (1979), 102 D.L.R. (3d) 602 (F.C.T.D.), 610.

13. Dale Turner, "From Valladolid to Ottawa: The Illusion of Listening to Aboriginal People," in *Sacred Lands: Aboriginal World Views, Claims, and Conflicts*, ed. Jill Oakes et al. (Edmonton, Canada: Canadian Circumpolar Institute, 1998), 64. A good example of this phenomenon is in *Pawis v. The Queen*, which *interpreted* a treaty provision establishing a "full and free privilege to hunt and fish" to mean that "no consideration is to be extracted from those entitled to hunt and fish." *Pawis v. The Queen*, 609–10.

14. King George III issued the Royal Proclamation of 1763 to governmental administrations in the North American territories formally ceded by France to Britain in the Treaty of Paris of the same year, following the Seven Years' War. It also stipulated that "whereas it is just and reasonable, and essential to our Interest, and the Security of our Colonies, that the several Nations or Tribes of Indians with whom We are connected, and who live under our Protection, should not be molested or disturbed in the Possession of such Parts of Our Dominions and Territories as, not having been ceded to or purchased by Us, are reserved to them, or any of them, as their Hunting Grounds." *Royal Proclamation, 1763,* R.S.C., 1985, App. II, No. 1.

15. *Hamlet of Baker Lake v. Minister of Indian Affairs and Northern Development*, [1980] 1 F.C. 518 (F.C.T.D.).

16. *Amodu Tijani v. Secretary, Southern Nigeria*, [1921] 2 A.C. 399 (P.C.).

17. "The purpose of this surrender requirement is clearly to interpose the Crown between the Indians and prospective purchasers or lessees of their land, so as to prevent the Indians from being exploited." *Guerin v. The Queen*, [1984] 2 S.C.R. 335, at 383.

18. Aboriginal title cannot be transferred, sold, or surrendered to anyone other than the Crown. *Canadian Pacific Ltd. v. Paul*, [1988] 2 S.C.R. 654, at 677.

19. Aboriginal title "gives rise upon surrender to a distinctive fiduciary obligation on the part of the Crown to deal with the land for the benefit of the surrendering Indians." *R. v. Guerin*, [1984] 2 S.C.R. 335, at 382; also, "the Government has the responsibility to act in a fiduciary capacity with respect to Aboriginal peoples," *R. v. Sparrow*, [1990] 1 S.C.R. 1075, at 1108.

20. Aboriginal rights with respect to land and resources did not predate but were created by the Royal Proclamation and, as such, are "dependent on the good will of the Sovereign." *St. Catherines Milling v. The Queen* (1888), 14 A.C. 46 (P.C.).

21. *St. Catherines's Milling v. The Queen*, 54; see also *Smith v. The Queen*, [1983] 1 S.C.R. 554.

22. Aboriginal title refers to an "Indian interest in land [that] is truly *sui generis*." *Canadian Pacific Ltd. v. Paul*, 658; see also, "[c]ourts must be careful . . . to avoid the application of traditional common law concepts of property as they develop their understanding of . . . the *sui generis* nature of Aboriginal rights." *R. v. Sparrow*, 1112.

23. "Whatever may have been the situation upon signing of the Robinson-Huron Treaty, that right was in any event surrendered by arrangements subsequent to that treaty by which the Indians adhered to the treaty in exchange for treaty annuities and a reserve." *Ontario (A.G.) v. Bear Island Foundation*, [1991] 2 S.C.R. 570, at 575.(

24. A number of cases held that aboriginal title does not constitute an interest in land sufficient to support the registration of a caveat or certificate of *lis pendens*, which would temporarily prevent activity on ancestral territory pending final resolution of a dispute. See, for example, *Uukw v. A.G.B.C.* (1987), 16 B.C.L.R. (2d) 145 (B.C.C.A.); *Lac La Ronge Indian Band v. Beckman*, [1990] 4 W.W.R. 211 (Sask. C.A.); *James Smith Indian Band v. Saskatchewan (Master of Titles)*, [1994] 2 C.N.L.R. 72 (Sask. Q.B.); but see *Ontario (A.G.) v. Bear Island Foundation*.

25. Per Lord Atkinson, "a statute is not to be construed so as to take away the property of a subject without compensation." *British Columbia v. Tener*, [1985] 1 S.C.R. 533, at 559, quoting *Attorney-General v. De Keyser's Royal Hotel Ltd.*, [1920] A.C. 508, at 542.

26. For example, "the common law . . . can give effect only to those incidents of that enjoyment that were . . . given effect by the [aboriginal] regime that prevailed before." *Baker Lake v. Minister of Indian Affairs*, [1980] 1 F.C. 518, at 559; also, "the essence of Aboriginal rights is the right of Indians to live on the lands as their forefathers lived." *A.G. Ont. v. Bear Island Foundation*, [1985] 1 C.N.L.R. 1, 3 (Ont. S.C.).

27. Constitution Act, 1982, being Schedule B to the Canada Act 1982 (UK), 1982, c 11, section 35(1).

28. *R. v. Badger*, [1996] 1 S.C.R. 771.

29. *R. v. Badger*, para. 41.

30. *R. v. Badger*.

31. James Youngblood Henderson, "Interpreting Sui Generis Treaties," *Alberta Law Review* 36, no. 1 (December 1997): 64.

32. Williams stated, "In American Indian visions of law and peace, a treaty connected different peoples through constitutional bonds of multicultural unity." Robert A. Williams Jr., *Linking Arms Together: American Indian Treaty Visions of Law & Peace, 1600–1800* (New York: Oxford University Press, 1997), 105.

33. *Haida Nation v. British Columbia (Minister of Forests)*, [2004] 3 SCR 511.

34. *Haida Nation v. British Columbia*, para. 20.

35. *Haida Nation v. British Columbia.* See also *Taku River Tlingit First Nation v. British Columbia (Project Assessment Director)*, [2004] 3 SCR 550, para. 42.

36. See, generally, Royal Commission on Aboriginal Peoples, *Treaty Making in the Spirit of Co-Existence*.

37. The classic text remains James Henderson and Russel Barsh, *The Road: Indian Tribes and Political Liberty* (Berkeley: University of California Press, 1980).

38. Duthu, *Shadow Nations*, 77 (emphasis in original), drawing from Martha-Marie Kleinhans and Roderick A. MacDonald, "What Is a *Critical* Legal Pluralism?," *Canadian Journal of Law & Society* 12, no. 2 (Fall 1997): 25–46.

39. James Tully, *Strange Multiplicity*, 117.

40. Williams, *Linking Arms Together*, 9.

41. James Sákéj Youngblood Henderson, "Empowering Treaty Federalism," *Saskatchewan Law Review* 58, no. 2 (1997): 241–330.

42. James Sákéj Youngblood Henderson, "*Sui Generis* and Treaty Citizenship," *Citizenship Studies* 6, no. 4 (2002): 422.

43. See, generally, Webber, "Relations of Force and Relations of Justice." See also Sidney L. Harring, *White Man's Law: Native People in Nineteenth Century Canadian Jurisprudence* (Toronto, Canada: Osgoode Society for Canadian Legal History, 1998).

44. *Delgamuukw v. British Columbia*, [1997] 3 S.C.R. 1010.

45. The Court held that the text of section 35(1) and *R. v. Van der Peet*, [1996] 2 S.C.R. 507 both suggest that section 35(1) provides constitutional status to those rights that were "existing" prior to 1982 and, given that aboriginal title was a common law right existing in 1982, section 35(1) accords it constitutional status.

46. Lee Swepston and Roger Plant, "International Standards and the Protection of the Land Rights of Indigenous and Tribal Populations," *International Labour Review* 124, no. 1 (1985): 97.

47. *Delgamuukw v. British Columbia*, para. 148.

48. *Delgamuukw v. British Columbia*, para. 157.

49. *Tsilhqot'in Nation v. British Columbia*, [2014] 2 SCR 257. For a critique, see John Borrows, "The Durability of Terra Nullius: Tsilqot'in Nation v. British Columbia," *University of British Columbia Law Review* 48, no. 3 (2015): 701–43.

50. *Mitchell v. MNR*, [2001] 1 S.C.R. 911, para. 10 per McLachlin C.J.

51. *Haida Nation v. British Columbia*, para. 20; *Taku River Tlingit First Nation v. British Columbia*. For an extended reflection of this approach, see Felix Hoehn, *Reconciling Sovereignties: Aboriginal Nations and Canada* (Saskatoon, Canada: Native Law Centre, University of Saskatchewan, 2012). See also Mark Walters, "Looking for a Knot in the Bulrush: Reflections on Law, Sovereignty, and Aboriginal Rights," in *From Recognition to Reconciliation: Essays on the Constitutional Entrenchment of Aboriginal & Treaty Rights*, ed. Patrick Macklem and Douglas Sanderson (Toronto, Canada: University of Toronto Press, 2016), 35–62.

52. *R. v. Van der Peet*, para. 39, per Lamer C.J.

53. *R. v. Sappier; R. v. Gray*, [2006] 2 S.C.R. 686, para. 45, per Bastarache J.

54. *Delgamuukw*, para. 145, per Lamer C.J.

55. *Mitchell v. MNR*, para. 9, per McLachlin C.J.

56. *R. v Van der Peet*, para. 263.

57. Indian Act, R.S.C. 1985, c. I-5. For the view that indigenous governments are better characterized as participants in regimes of multilevel governance layered over the existing federal structure without altering its foundations, See Martin Papillon, "Adapting Federalism: Indigenous Multilevel Governance in Canada and the United States," *Publius* 42, no. 2 (2012): 289–312.

58. For extended treatments of these models, see Cohen, *Globalization and Sovereignty*, chaps. 1 and 2, respectively.

59. For a discussion and critique of such model, see Schouls, *Shifting Boundaries*, 128–131.

60. For example, treaty federalism, where there exists a free-standing and uniform "core" of indigenous jurisdiction supplemented by jurisdiction negotiated by treaty, as proposed by the Royal Commission on Aboriginal Peoples. Royal Commission on Aboriginal Peoples, *Final Report*, vol. 2, *Restructuring the Relationship* (Ottawa, Canada: Ministry of Supply and Services, 1996), 215. For a discussion of this approach, see Hoehn, *Reconciling Sovereignties*, 140–46.

61. *R. v. Pamajewon* [1996] 2 S.C.R. 821. *R. v. Pamajewon* also involved the trial and conviction of, and subsequent appeals by, members of the Shawanaga First Nation for similar violations of the Criminal Code.

62. *R. v. Pamajewon*, 832.

63. The 1998 Nisga'a Final Agreement, for example, recognizes that the "Nisga'a Nation has the right of self-government." It recognizes two levels of Nisga'a government, Nisga'a Lisims Government and Nisga'a Village Government. Nisga'a Lisims Government constitutes the government of the Nisga'a Nation as a whole; it can make laws in relation to a wide range of subject matters, including citizenship, culture, Nisga'a lands, employment, social services, health services, child and family services, and education. Nisga'a Village Governments are local governments of four existing Nisga'a villages and any additional village on Nisga'a lands established in accordance with the terms of the agreement; they possess the authority to make laws in relation to a number of local matters. Generally speaking, the agreement also provides that in the event of an inconsistency or conflict between a Nisga'a law and a federal or provincial law, the Nisga'a law prevails to the extent of the inconsistency.

64. "It is indeed plausible to surmise that the institutionalization of Aboriginal self-governments in Canada, either actual or potential, could lead to the creation of a

quasi-federal relationship with the federal and provincial governments, or, at the very least, could induce the development of such a dynamic." Jean-François Gauldrealt-DesBiens, "The Ethos of Canadian Aboriginal Law and the Potential Relevance of Federal Loyalty in a Reconfigured Relationship Between Aboriginal and Non-Aboriginal Governments: A Thought Experiment," in *Fédéralisme et gouvernance autochtone /Federalism and Aboriginal Governance*, ed. G. Otis and M. Papillon (Québec, Canada: Presses de l'Université Laval, 2013), 57. For an illuminating analysis of the federal model in the context of the indigenous peoples of Australia, see Dylan Lino, *Constitutional Recognition of Australia's Indigenous Peoples: Law, History and Politics* (PhD diss., Melbourne Law School, January 2017).

65. *Mitchell v. M.N.R.*

66. *Mitchell v. M.N.R.* para. 164.

67. *Mitchell v. M.N.R.*, para. 130, quoting Royal Commission on Aboriginal Peoples, *Final Report*, 240–41.

68. *Mitchell v. M.N.R.*, para. 133.

69. *Mitchell v. M.N.R.*, para. 143, quoting Royal Commission on Aboriginal Peoples, *Final Report*, 214.

70. Royal Commission on Aboriginal Peoples, *Final Report*, 219. For an analysis of this proposal, see Hoehn, *Reconciling Sovereignties*, 143–44. The *Charlottetown Accord* also proposed to define a core of aboriginal jurisdiction. Matters essential or "integral" to an aboriginal community's ability "to safeguard and develop" its language, culture, economy, identity, institutions, and traditions and "to develop, maintain and strengthen" its relationship to its land, water, and environment, were to fall within the exclusive jurisdiction of aboriginal governments. The *Accord* was a proposed set of constitutional amendments agreed to by the federal and provincial governments in 1992 but defeated in a public referendum in the same year. See *Consensus Report on the Constitution: Final Text*, Charlottetown, August 28, 1992.

71. Indian nations do not exercise criminal jurisdictional authority over non-Indians. *Oliphant v. Suquamish Indian Tribe*, 435 U.S. 191 (1978).

72. United States recognizes congressional plenary power over Indian nations in relation to major crimes. *United States v. Kagama*, 118 U.S. 375 (1886).

73. Eric R. Wolf, *Europe and the People Without History* (Berkeley: University of California Press, 1982), 387. See also Kukathas, who stated, "because they are the product of interaction, and are subject to numerous influences, cultures are . . . mutable." Chandran Kukathas, "Explaining Moral Variety," *Social Philosophy and Policy* 11, no. 1 (Winter 1994): 6; and Williams, who stated, "cultures, subcultures, fragments of cultures, constantly meet one another and exchange and modify practices and attitudes." Bernard Williams, *Ethics and the Limits of Philosophy* (London: Fontana Collins, 1985), 158.

74. On the production of indigenous identities, Jung states that indigenous identity is a political achievement. Courtney Jung, *The Moral Force of Indigenous Politics* (Cambridge: Cambridge University Press, 2008). It also has been argued that colonization was a process that forged non-aboriginal identity. For example, Riles states that "this essentialized European identity depended . . . upon an opposition of Europe to non-Europe that articulated in symbolic terms inequalities of power between Europeans and their colonial subjects." Annelise Riles, "Aspiration and Control: International Legal Rhetoric and the Essentialization of Culture," *Harvard Law Review* 106, no. 3 (1993): 737.

On the production of cultural identities generally, Scott states that "subjects are produced through multiple identifications, . . . [and] the project of history is not to

reify identity but to understand its production as an ongoing process of differentiation, . . . subject to redefinition, resistance and change." Joan Scott, "Multiculturalism
and the Politics of Identity," in *The Identity in Question*, ed. John Rajchman (New York:
Routledge, 1995), 3, 11; Brown states that persons cannot be "reduced to observable
social attributes and practices defined empirically, positivistically, as if their existence
were intrinsic and factual, rather than effects of discursive and institutional power."
Wendy Brown, *States of Injury: Power and Freedom in Late Modernity* (Princeton, N.J.:
Princeton University Press, 1995), 66; and Gupta and Ferguson call for scholarship that
explores "the processes of *production* of difference in a world of culturally, socially,
and economically interconnected and interdependent spaces" (emphasis in original).
Akhil Gupta and James Ferguson, "Beyond Culture: Space, Identity and the Politics of
Difference," *Cultural Anthropology* 7, no. 1 (February 1992): 14.

75. *Mitchel v. Peguis Indian Band*, [1990] 2 S.C.R. 85, 108–109. For more discussion of the
implications of this conclusion, Hoehn infers that "there is no constitutional barrier
to judicial recognition of the sovereignty of an Aboriginal nation." Hoehn, *Reconciling
Sovereignties*, 54.

76. Gauldrealt-DesBiens states that "pragmatic reasons make it worthwhile to examine
the potential links between Aboriginal self-government claims and federalism, as even
within the Canadian framework the level of autonomy constitutionally assigned to
federated units is much greater than that afforded to self-governing Aboriginal peoples."
Gauldrealt-DesBiens, "The Ethos of Canadian Aboriginal Law and the Potential Relevance
of Federal Loyalty," 58.

77. See Canadian Human Rights Commission, *Report on the Equality Rights of Aboriginal
People* (Ottawa, Canada: Minister of Public Works and Government Services, 2010).

78. Constitution Act, 1982, section 36.

79. The *Charlottetown Accord*, section 50, proposed a constitutional amendment committing the federal and provincial governments to the principle of providing indigenous
governments peoples with fiscal or other resources, such as land, to assist those
governments to govern their own affairs and to meet the commitments listed above,
taking into account the levels of services provided to other Canadians in the vicinity
and the fiscal capacity of governments of aboriginal peoples to raise revenues from
their own sources.

80. "By locating culture at the center of political voice, indigenous peoples . . . risk being
backed into demands for cultural protection and the preservation of tradition, which
do not issue a fundamental challenge to many of the structural relations that are the
condition of their disadvantaged position. The claims of culture issue scant challenge
to the neo-liberal economic order, for instance, or to the structural location of
indigenous populations at the bottom of that order. Some states may even be eager to
confer self-government on their indigenous populations, using territorial autonomy
to abjure state responsibility for providing development and social services." Jung,
*The Moral Force of Indigenous Politics*, 249. On the politics of distribution versus
politics of recognition more generally, see Nancy Fraser, "Social Justice in the Age of
Identity Politics: Redistribution, Recognition, and Participation," in *Redistribution or
Recognition? A Political-Philosophical Exchange*, ed. Nancy Fraser and Axel Honneth
(New York: Verso, 2003), 7.

81. Slattery states, that "the duty to consult embodies . . . a 'generative' constitutional
order which sees section 35 as serving a dynamic and not simply static function." *Rio
Tinto Alcan Inc. v. Carrier Sekani Tribal Council*, [2010] 2 S.C.R. 650, para. 38, quoting
Brian Slattery, "Aboriginal Rights and the Honour of the Crown," *Supreme Court Law*

*Review: Osgoode's Annual Constitutional Cases Conference* 29, no. 2 (2005): 440; see also Brian Slattery, "The Generative Structure of Aboriginal Rights," *Supreme Court Law Review* 38, no. 2 (2007): 595–628. Compare also Macdonald's statement that Canada is a "reconstitutive federation." Roderick A. Macdonald, "Kaleidoscopic Federalism," in *States and Moods of Federalism: Governance, Identity and Methodology*, ed. Jean-Francois Gaudreault-DesBiens and Fabien Gélinas (Montréal, Canada: Éditions Yvon Blais: 2005), 264.

82.  Daniel Elazar, *Federalism and Political Integration* (New York: Turtledove, 1979), 2.

83.  Jean Leclair, "Envisaging Canada in a Disenchanted World: Reflections on Federalism, Nationalism, and Distinctive Indigenous Identity," *Constitutional Forum* 25, no. 1 (2016): 20.

84.  Jean Leclair, "Federal Constitutionalism and Aboriginal Difference," *Queen's Law Journal* 31, no. 2 (2006): 534.

85.  The final Report of the Truth and Reconciliation Commission of Canada, released in 2015, obliquely alludes to this requirement in its call to "reconcile Aboriginal and Crown constitutional and legal orders to ensure that Aboriginal peoples are full partners in Confederation." Truth and Reconciliation Commission, *Calls to Action* (Winnipeg, Canada: Truth and Reconciliation Commission of Canada, 2015), call to action 45(iv). The mandate of the Truth and Reconciliation Commission was to inform Canadians about what happened in the residential schools system—a system created to remove indigenous children from the influence of their own culture and place them in boarding schools for the purpose of assimilation. It issued a sweeping series of calls to action, ranging from matters relating to child welfare, to education, language and culture, health, and justice.

86.  The Charlottetown Accord proposed guaranteed indigenous representation in the Senate, and a possible double majority power in relation to certain matters materially affecting indigenous people. See *Charlottetown Accord*, section 9. The Royal Commission on Aboriginal Peoples proposed the creation of an Aboriginal Parliament, leading eventually to a House of First Peoples, to "stimulate greater direct participation in the decision-making processes of Canadian Institutions of government." Royal Commission on Aboriginal Peoples, *Final Report*, 374.

87.  This idea is a corollary of the work of Jean-Francois Geaudrault-DesBiens in "The Ethos of Canadian Aboriginal Law," which engages with the doctrine of federal loyalty to reflect on some of the possible normative consequences of the establishment of a more egalitarian relationship between indigenous and federal and provincial governments.

88.  *Finance Equalization Case 1*, 1 BVerFGE 117 (1952).

89.  *Housing Funding Case*, 1 BVerFGE 299 (1952), trans. in Donald R. Reich, "Court, Comity, and Federation in West Germany," *Midwest Journal of Political Science* 7 (1963): 209, and quoted in Gaudreault-DesBiens, "The Ethos of Canadian Aboriginal Law," 66.

90.  As exceptions, Gaudreault-DesBiens points to the extraterritorial application of otherwise valid provincial legislation (*Morguard Investments Ltd. V. De Savoye*, [1990] 3 S.C.R. 1077); a presumption of federal-provincial cooperation (*City of Montreal v. Montreal Street Railway* (1912) A.C. 333 (B.C.C.A.); the duty to negotiate the terms of secession (*Reference Re Secession of Quebec* [1998] 2 S.C.R. 217); and the constitutional convention requiring substantial provincial consent to a federal initiative involving constitutional amendment introduced in Westiminster (*Reference Re Patriation to Amend the Constitution*, [1981] 1 S.C.R. 753). To these one might add section 36(2) of the Constitution Act, 1982, which commits the federal government to the principle of making equalization payments to ensure that provincial governments have sufficient

revenues to provide reasonable comparable levels of public service at reasonably comparable levels of taxation.
91. *Wewaykum Indian Band v. Canada*, [2002] 4 S.C.R. 344, para. 86.
92. *Haida Nation v. British Columbia*, para. 42. For a comprehensive treatment of this subject, see Dwight Newman, *The Duty to Consult: New Relationships with Aboriginal Peoples* (Saskatoon, Canada: Purich, 2009).

## Bibliography

A.G. Canada v. A.G. Ontario (Labour Conventions), [1937] A.C. 326 (P.C.).
A.G. Ont. v. Bear Island Foundation, [1985] 1 C.N.L.R. 1, 3 (Ont. S.C.).
Amodu Tijani v. Secretary, Southern Nigeria, [1921] 2 A.C. 399 (P.C.).
Arthurs, Harry. *"Without the Law": Administrative Justice and Legal Pluralism in Nineteenth Century England*. Toronto, Canada: University of Toronto Press, 1985.
Atiyah, Patrick. *The Rise and Fall of Freedom of Contract*. Oxford: Clarendon Press, 1979.
Attorney-General v. De Keyser's Royal Hotel Ltd., [1920] A.C. 508.
Baker Lake v. Minister of Indian Affairs, [1980] 1 F.C. 518.
Berman, Paul Schiff. *Global Legal Pluralism: A Jurisprudence of Law Beyond Borders*. Cambridge: Cambridge University Press, 2012.
Blackstone, William. 1 *Commentaries on the Laws of England*. Vol. 1. Oxford: Clarendon Press, 1765–69.
Borrows, John. "The Durability of Terra Nullius: Tsilqot'in Nation v. British Columbia." *University of British Columbia Law Review* 48, no. 3 (2015): 701–42.
British Columbia v. Tener, [1985] 1 S.C.R. 533.
Brown, Wendy. *States of Injury: Power and Freedom in Late Modernity*. Princeton, N.J.: Princeton University Press, 1995.
Brownlie, Ian. *Principles of Public International Law*. 8th ed. Oxford: Clarendon Press, 2012.
Canadian Human Rights Commission. *Report on the Equality Rights of Aboriginal People*. Ottawa, Canada: Minister of Public Works and Government Services, 2010.
Canadian Pacific Ltd. v. Paul, [1988] 2 S.C.R. 654.
City of Montreal v. Montreal Street Railway (1912) A.C. 333 (B.C.C.A.).
Cohen, Jean L. *Globalization and Sovereignty: Rethinking Legality, Legitimacy, and Constitutionalism*. Cambridge: Cambridge University Press, 2012.
Connolly, William. *The Ethos of Pluralization*. Minneapolis: University of Minnesota Press, 1995.
Delgamuukw v. British Columbia, [1997] 3 S.C.R. 1010.
Duthu, Bruce. *Shadow Nations: Tribal Sovereignty and the Limits of Legal Pluralism*. New York: Oxford University Press, 2013.
Elazar, Daniel. *Federalism and Political Integration*. New York: Turtledove, 1979.
Finance Equalization Case 1, 1 BVerFGE 117 (1952).
Fraser, Nancy. "Social Justice in the Age of Identity Politics: Redistribution, Recognition, and Participation." In *Redistribution or Recognition? A Political-Philosophical Exchange*, ed. Nancy Fraser and Axel Honneth, 10–31. New York: Verso, 2003.
Gauldrealt-DesBiens, Jean-François. "The Ethos of Canadian Aboriginal Law and the Potential Relevance of Federal Loyalty in a Reconfigured Relationship Between Aboriginal and Non-Aboriginal Governments: A Thought Experiment." In *Fédéralisme et gouvernance autochtone/Federalism and Aboriginal Governance*, ed. G. Otis and M. Papillon, 51–81. Québec, Canada: Presses de l'Université Laval, 2013.

Griffiths, John. "What Is Legal Pluralism?" *Journal of Legal Pluralism and Unofficial Law* 18, no. 24 (1986): 1–55.

Guerin v. The Queen, [1984] 2 S.C.R. 335.

Gupta, Akhil, and James Ferguson. "Beyond Culture: Space, Identity and the Politics of Difference." *Cultural Anthropology* 7, no. 1 (February 1992): 6–23.

Haida Nation v. British Columbia (Minister of Forests), [2004] 3 SCR 511.

Hamlet of Baker Lake v. Minister of Indian Affairs and Northern Development, [1980] 1 F.C. 518 (F.C.T.D.).

Harring, Sidney L. *White Man's Law: Native People in Nineteenth Century Canadian Jurisprudence.* Toronto, Canada: Osgoode Society for Canadian Legal History, 1998.

Henderson, James [Sákéj] Youngblood. "Empowering Treaty Federalism." *Saskatchewan Law Review* 58, no. 2 (1997): 241–330.

———. "Interpreting Sui Generis Treaties." *Alberta Law Review* 36, no. 1 (December 1997): 46–96.

———. "*Sui Generis* and Treaty Citizenship." *Citizenship Studies* 6, no. 4 (2002): 415–40.

Henderson, James [Sákéj] Youngblood, and Russell Barsh. *The Road: Indian Tribes and Political Liberty.* Berkeley: University of California Press, 1980.

Hirschman, Albert O. *Exit, Voice, and Loyalty: Responses to Decline in Firms, Organizations, and States.* Cambridge, Mass.: Harvard University Press, 1970.

Hoehn, Felix. *Reconciling Sovereignties: Aboriginal Nations and Canada.* Saskatoon, Canada: Native Law Centre, University of Saskatchewan, 2012.

Housing Funding Case, 1 BVerFGE 299 (1952).

James Smith Indian Band v. Saskatchewan (Master of Titles), [1994] 2 C.N.L.R. 72 (Sask. Q.B.).

Jung, Courtney. *The Moral Force of Indigenous Politics.* Cambridge: Cambridge University Press, 2008.

Kahn-Freund, Owen. "Blackstone's Neglected Child: The Contract of Employment." *Law Quarterly Review* 93 (1977): 508–28.

Kleinhans, Martha-Marie, and Roderick A. MacDonald. "What Is a *Critical* Legal Pluralism?" *Canadian Journal of Law & Society* 12, no. 2 (Fall 1997): 25–46.

Kukathas, Chandran. "Explaining Moral Variety." *Social Philosophy and Policy* 11, no. 1 (Winter 1994): 1–21.

Kymlicka, Will. *Multicultural Citizenship: A Liberal Theory of Minority Rights.* Oxford: Oxford University Press, 1996.

Lac La Ronge Indian Band v. Beckman, [1990] 4 W.W.R. 211 (Sask. C.A.).

Leclair, Jean. "Envisaging Canada in a Disenchanted World: Reflections on Federalism, Nationalism, and Distinctive Indigenous Identity." *Constitutional Forum* 25, no. 1 (2016): 15–28.

———. "Federal Constitutionalism and Aboriginal Difference." *Queen's Law Journal* 31, no. 2 (2006): 521–35.

Lino, Dylan. *Constitutional Recognition of Australia's Indigenous Peoples: Law, History and Politics.* PhD diss., Melbourne Law School, January 2017.

Macdonald, Roderick A. "Kaleidoscopic Federalism." In *States and Moods of Federalism: Governance, Identity and Methodology,* ed. Jean-François Gaudreault-DesBiens and Fabien Gélinas, 261–87. Montréal, Canada: Éditions Yvon Blais, 2005.

———. "Metaphors of Multiplicity: Civil Society, Regimes and Legal Pluralism." *Arizona Journal of International and Comparative Law* 15, no. 1 (Winter 1998): 69–92.

Macklem, Patrick. "Indigenous Peoples and the Ethos of Legal Pluralism in Canada." In *From Recognition to Reconciliation: Essays on the Constitutional Entrenchment of Aboriginal & Treaty Rights,* ed. Patrick Macklem and Douglas Sanderson, 17–34. Toronto, Canada: University of Toronto Press, 2016.

McHugh, P. G. *Aboriginal Societies and the Common Law: A History of Sovereignty, Status, and Self-Determination.* New York: Oxford University Press, 2004.

Mitchel v. Peguis Indian Band, [1990] 2 S.C.R. 85.

Mitchell v. MNR, [2001] 1 S.C.R. 911.

Morguard Investments Ltd. V. De Savoye, [1990] 3 S.C.R. 1077.

Newman, Dwight. *The Duty to Consult: New Relationships with Aboriginal Peoples.* Saskatoon,, Canada: Purich, 2009.

O'Callaghan, E. B., ed. *Documents Relative to the Colonial History of the State of New York.* Vol III. Albany, N.Y.: Weed, Parsons, 1856–61.

Oliphant v. Suquamish Indian Tribe, 435 U.S. 191 (1978).

Ontario (A.G.) v. Bear Island Foundation, [1991] 2 S.C.R. 570.

Papillon, Martin. "Adapting Federalism: Indigenous Multilevel Governance in Canada and the United States." *Publius* 42, no. 2 (2012): 289–312.

Parry, Clive, ed. *The Consolidated Treaty Series.* Vol. 9. Dobbs Ferry, N.Y.: Oceana, 1969–86.

Pawis v. The Queen (1979), 102 D.L.R. (3d) 602 (F.C.T.D.).

Reference Re Patriation to Amend the Constitution, [1981] 1 S.C.R. 753.

Reference Re Secession of Quebec [1998] 2 S.C.R. 217.

Reich, Donald R. "Court, Comity, and Federation in West Germany." *Midwest Journal of Political Science* 7 (1963): 42–61.

Riles, Annelise. "Aspiration and Control: International Legal Rhetoric and the Essentialization of Culture." *Harvard Law Review* 106, no. 3 (1993): 723–40.

Rio Tinto Alcan Inc. v. Carrier Sekani Tribal Council, [2010] 2 S.C.R. 650

Royal Commission on Aboriginal Peoples. *Final Report: Vol. 2, Restructuring the Relationship.* Ottawa, Canada: Ministry of Supply and Services, 1996.

Royal Commission on Aboriginal Peoples. *Treaty Making in the Spirit of Co-Existence: An Alternative to Extinguishment.* Ottawa, Canada: Minister of Supply and Services Canada, 1995.

Royal Proclamation, 1763, R.S.C., 1985, App. II, No. 1.

R. v. Badger, [1996] 1 S.C.R. 771.

R. v. Guerin, [1984] 2 S.C.R. 335.

R. v. Pamajewon [1996] 2 S.C.R. 821.

R. v. Sappier; R. v. Gray, [2006] 2 S.C.R. 686.

R. v. Sparrow, [1990] 1 S.C.R. 1075.

R. v. Van der Peet, [1996] 2 S.C.R. 507.

Schneiderman, David. "Canadian Constitutional Culture: A Genealogical Account." In *Oxford Handbook on the Canadian Constitution*, edited by Peter Oliver, Patrick Macklem, and Nathalie Des Rosiers. Oxford: Oxford University Press, 2017.

———. "Haldane Unrevealed." *McGill Law Journal* 57, no. 3 (2012): 597–626.

———. "Harold Laski, Viscount Haldane, and the Law of the Canadian Constitution in the Early Twentieth Century." *University of Toronto Law Journal* 48, no. 4 (Autumn 1998): 521–60.

Schouls, Tim. *Shifting Boundaries: Aboriginal Identity, Pluralist Theory, and the Politics of Self-Government.* Vancouver, Canada: University of Vancouver Press, 2003.

Scott, Joan. "Multiculturalism and the Politics of Identity." In *The Identity in Question*, ed. J. Rajchman, 3–12. New York; Routledge, 1995.

Slattery, Brian. "Aboriginal Rights and the Honour of the Crown." *Supreme Court Law Review: Osgoode's Annual Constitutional Cases Conference* 29, no. 2 (2005): 433–45.

———. "The Generative Structure of Aboriginal Rights." *Supreme Court Law Review* 38, no. 2 (2007): 595–628.

Smith v. The Queen, [1983] 1 S.C.R. 554.

de Sousa Santos, Boaventura. *Toward a New Legal Common Sense: Law, Globalization and Emancipation*. Cambridge: Cambridge University Press, 2002.

St. Catherines Milling v. The Queen (1888), 14 A.C. 46 (P.C.).

Swepston, Lee, and Roger Plant. "International Standards and the Protection of the Land Rights of Indigenous and Tribal Populations." *International Labour Review* 124, no. 1 (1985): 91–106.

Taku River Tlingit First Nation v. British Columbia (Project Assessment Director), [2004] 3 SCR 550.

Truth and Reconciliation Commission. *Calls to Action*. Winnipeg, Canada: Truth and Reconciliation Commission of Canada, 2015.

Tsilhqot'in Nation v. British Columbia, [2014] 2 SCR 257.

Turner, Dale. "From Valladolid to Ottawa: The Illusion of Listening to Aboriginal People." In *Sacred Lands: Aboriginal World Views, Claims, and Conflicts*, ed. Jill Oakes et al., 53–68. Edmonton, Canada: Canadian Circumpolar Institute, 1998.

Tully, James. *Strange Multiplicity: Constitutionalism in an Age of Diversity*. Cambridge: Cambridge University Press, 1995.

United States v. Kagama, 118 U.S. 375 (1886).

Uukw v. A.G.B.C. (1987), 16 B.C.L.R. (2d) 145 (B.C.C.A.).

Walters, Mark. "Looking for a Knot in the Bulrush: Reflections on Law, Sovereignty, and Aboriginal Rights." In *From Recognition to Reconciliation: Essays on the Constitutional Entrenchment of Aboriginal and Treaty Rights*, ed. Patrick Macklem and Douglas Sanderson, 35–62. Toronto, Canada: University of Toronto Press, 2016.

Webber, Jeremy. "Relations of Force and Relations of Justice: The Emergence of Normative Community Between Colonists and Aboriginal Peoples." *Osgoode Hall Law Journal* 33, no. 4 (1995): 623–60.

Weisbrod, Carol. *Emblems of Pluralism: Cultural Differences and the Law*. Princeton, N.J.: Princeton University Press, 2002.

Wewaykum Indian Band v. Canada, [2002] 4 S.C.R. 344.

Williams, Bernard. *Ethics and the Limits of Philosophy*. London: Fontana Collins, 1985.

Williams, Robert A., Jr. *Linking Arms Together: American Indian Treaty Visions of Law & Peace, 1600–1800*. New York: Oxford University Press, 1997.

Wolf, Eric R. *Europe and the People Without History*. Berkeley: University of California Press, 1982.

# 6

# FEDERACY AND THE KURDS

*Might This New Political Form Help Mitigate Hobbesian Conflicts in Turkey, Iraq, and Syria?*

ALFRED STEPAN AND JEFF MILEY

Unregulated guns, violence, and ISIS increasingly flow across the stateless border between Syria and Iraq, and this conflict threatens to widen as Turkey violates international borders to attack Kurds in Iraq and Syria to stop them from creating an independent Kurdish state out of this chaos. Can we imagine any possible political solutions to these current Hobbesian conflicts in Syria? We hope this essay expands your imagination by considering a difficult but not impossible set of national and international scenarios involving a relatively new political form we call "federacy."[1]

We begin by describing how the first fully developed federacy emerged to manage conflicts over who had the right to rule a certain territory. We call this right to rule by the contested name of "sovereignty." Far from being "indivisible," sovereignty could only help resolve a range of potential conflicts in the first federacy if it was constitutionally embedded and was *divided* between a unitary nation-state and one distant part of its territory that was culturally, linguistically, and historically radically "other." Furthermore this first federacy is of special relevance because it emerged only through elaborate negotiations, much of it international, about how to create a new peaceful and democratic physical space in a changing world.

Between 1917 until 1923 (with important constitutional refinements in 1951 and 1991) there was contested sovereignty between Sweden, Russia, Finland, France, the UK, and the United States about a single strategically located space, the Aland Islands. The Aland Islands illustrates very well some of the conditions and processes leading to the creation of a federacy that is embedded in laws, treaties, international agreements, and, increasingly, in the constitutions of a unitary state and its federacy.[2] Ruth Lapidoth, in her valuable book on varieties of autonomy, sets out very nicely the geopolitical importance of the 6,500 islands and skerries that make up the Aland Islands: "The islands are located in a strategically important area in the Baltic Sea between Sweden and Finland, at the entrance to the Gulf of Bothnia. This location also dominates the access to St. Petersburg, and is thus of great importance for the defense of three states: Sweden, Finland, and Russia."[3]

The history of the islands reflects the contributing role of geography and geopolitics as well as the tensions between two powerful forces in international politics—nationalism and self-determination of peoples versus state building and state maintenance. The institutional arrangements, their processes of enactment, and the role of international actors exemplify how federacies can emerge.

Here are the seven major players (five states, one alliance of three powerful states, and one major new international organization) and their contesting goals about sovereignty concerning the Aland Islands.

1. Sweden: From the Middle Ages until 1809 the Aland Islands were under Swedish rule and were Swedish in language and culture. Finland was also under Swedish rule, and the Aland Islands were administered by a governor from Abo, a city on the Finnish coast.

2. Imperial Russia: In 1809 Sweden was forced to yield Finland and the Aland Islands to Russia. Within Imperial Russia, the Aland Islands were part of the Grand Duchy of Finland, an entity that had a degree of democratic self-government and its own parliament.

3. Finland, after the fall of Imperial Russia: In the turmoil following the March 1917 Revolution in Russia, Finland broke lose from Russia to become an independent nation-state, and it asserted sovereignty over the Aland Islands.

4. The Aland Islanders and Sweden: The Alanders feared Finnish dominance of their culture and polis and looked upon union with Sweden as the surest guarantee for the preservation of their distinctive culture. Sweden encouraged this prospect. Indeed, Sweden, a well-armed regional power, sent a naval expedition to the Aland Islands in 1918. For their part, the Aland Islanders sent political delegations to Sweden, which were well received. If the principle of self-determination had resulted in a plebiscite, few authorities or contemporary observers doubt that the Alanders would have voted to be put under Swedish sovereignty.[4]

5. France, the UK, and the USA: These three countries were the major winning powers of WWI, and they shared a goal, devised by the French Prime Minister Georges Clemenceau, of containing the diffusion of the newly revolutionary forces of the USSR by constructing a demilitarized "cordon sanitaire" on the

northern borders of the USSR and in the Baltic Sea. Finland felt that such an internationally protected demilitarized space was in their interest, but Sweden, a much stronger military force, wanted to defend itself and did not indicate that it would join the demilitarized cordon sanitaire.

6. The USSR: The Soviets were opposed to granting sovereignty of the Aland Islands to Sweden. They believed Sweden, with its powerful Navy, would gain great leverage over the Soviet Union's access to the Baltic Sea as well as securing direct access to St. Petersburg.

7. The League of Nations: This newly created international organization was given a major role by the victorious powers of WWI to help resolve the contesting claims to the Aland Islands. But the league was itself conflicted by the clash between the principles of self-determination, which favored the Aland Islanders' right to join Sweden, and the League of Nation's goal of promoting a zone of peace, neutrality, and disarmament, which favored awarding the Aland Islands to Finland.

The solution ultimately devised by the League of Nations, and supported by the three winning powers of WWI, was to create the first constitutionally embedded and internationally guaranteed federacy in world history. The League of Nations awarded the Aland Islands to Finland in their 1921 "Act of Autonomy of Aland." The league negotiated with the Aland Islanders and Finland, getting both bodies to accept and sign an extremely detailed list of the exclusive sovereignty rights for the federacy on their own territory, and the league became the guarantor of these rights. A leading scholar has described the Autonomy Act as the "most radical form of international guarantee for a national minority ever to have been drawn up. In no other treaty have such far-reaching guarantees been given for the preservation of a national minority's language and culture and for the protection of the national character of the area inhabited by the minority."[5]

To date nine other constitutionally embedded federacies have been created,[6] and the following six protections of minority rights described in the 1991 Autonomy Act, which is currently in force, are found in all of them. Most of these federacies had some international guarantors, and all of them incorporated variants of the features found in the Aland Autonomy Act of 1921, and in the increasingly codified and consensually expanded Autonomy Acts of 1951 and 1991. These six constitutionally embedded, culture making, and identity sustaining prerogatives are explicitly given to the Government of Aland and its self-governing legislature in chapter 5 of the act.

1. The official language of Aland shall be Swedish. The language used in state administration shall be Swedish. (section 36)

2. The language of education in schools maintained by public funds or sub-sidized by funds shall be Swedish, unless otherwise provided by an Act of Aland. (section 40)

3. The power to grant the right of domicile is vested in the Government of Aland. (section 7)

4. Only a person with the right of domicile may participate in elections of the Aland Parliament, the municipal councils, and the other positions of trust in the Aland and municipal administration. (section 9)

5. The right of a person without the right of domicile to exercise a trade or profession in Aland for personal gain may be limited by an Act of Aland. (section 11)

6. The limitations of a person without the right to domicile to acquire real prop-erty or property of a similar nature in Aland with full legal title or with the right to enjoy are as provided in the [quite restrictive] Act on the Acquisition of Real Property in Aland. (section 10)

## Federacy as an Ideal Type

Our ideal definition of *federacy* is the following:

> A federacy is a political administrative unit in an independent unitary state with exclusive power in certain areas, including some legislative power, constitutionally or quasi-constitutionally embedded, that cannot be changed unilaterally and whose inhabitants have full citizenship rights in the otherwise unitary state.

The minimal agreed set of arrangements for such a federacy, as an ideal type, would have to satisfy four defining institutional requirements:

*Defining Characteristic 1: Federal-like division of state and federacy functions.* In order that the federacy, unlike other parts of the unitary state, can pass special self-governing laws and administer their polity in such a way that it can address many of the areas of greatest tension with the unitary state, there must be a classic federal-like agreement concerning the division of powers in the polity. These federal-type arrangements are: (1) explicit powers that fall in the exclusive domain of the federacy; (2) powers that remain in the center; and (3) powers that might be shared or even remain with the center but that can be progressively transferred permanently to the federacy.

*Defining Characteristic 2: Constitutionally, or quasi-constitutionally embed-ded political autonomy of the federacy.* The territorially concentrated minority population in the federacy has an embedded degree of political autonomy well beyond that found in any other part of the unitary state. Ideally, the legislatures of the unitary state and the newly created federacy would *both* agree to the new autonomy arrangements, but at an absolute minimum, it would be stipulated that the act of autonomy, or federacy agreement, would not be able to be unilaterally altered without substantial supermajorities on both sides.

*Defining Characteristic 3: Existence of dispute resolution procedures.* The federacy and the state, as part of the eventual autonomy agreement, would have binding dispute resolution procedures about their respective powers and prerogatives.

*Defining Characteristic 4: Reciprocal representation between the unitary state and the federacy.* The goal of the federacy arrangement is to create a high level of trust, voice, and loyalty between the federacy and the center. Citizens of the autonomous units are full citizens of the state, vote in statewide elections, and have representatives in the parliament of the state as well as in their own parliament. Only citizens of the federacy can vote in the federacy, but the center would have an official representative in the federacy who would coordinate those activities in the federacy that fall under central state powers.

*Defining Characteristic 5: The federacy is part of an internationally recognized independent state.* The autonomy agreement is an internal law of the unitary state and not part of international law. The autonomy agreement might be derived from international agreements, but it is not part of international law (unless the state makes a specific exception) and would not create a "subject" of international law.

If these five requirements are functioning, federacy arrangements *may* additionally contain and legitimate two peace and development facilitating features not normally found in unitary or federal states.

*Facilitating Characteristic 1: Role of international guarantors in the founding of the federacy.* A federacy arrangement, especially if it emerges in the context of a geopolitical conflict, may well combine elements of two of the greatest principles in conflict since the late nineteenth century: the right of state sovereignty and the right of self-determination of populations. In such cases, federacy arrangements, more than in unitary or federal states, may involve some participation of concerned neighboring states and international organizations in their emergence and even in the establishment of some arrangements, particularly the distinctive cultural rights of the federacy's population.

*Facilitating Characteristic 2: Role of the federacy in international treaties signed by the center.* More than in a federation, and totally unlike a unitary state, it is possible that the very existence of a federacy may facilitate the federacy's advocacy and creation of some 'opt-out' arrangements of treaties into which the unitary state enters. This will be most likely if the leaders of the federacy, with the support of the unitary state, believe that certain provisions of the treaty would be hurtful to the preservation of the distinctive economy and way of life of the population that the federacy had been created to protect. No other part of the unitary state would have the status to construct such opt-out arrangements with the participation and help of the center that normally negotiates them.

## Federacy's Conceptual Distinctiveness as a Political Form from Unitary States, Asymmetrical Federations, Confederations, or Associated States

Federacy as a political form is quite different from the ideal type of a unitary state. The high degree of a federacy's constitutionally embedded autonomy and prerogatives are not enjoyed by other jurisdictions of the unitary state. However, as we have seen, a unitary state can enter a federacy agreement; indeed, such an agreement may be a particularly useful formula for managing a small or medium-sized unitary nation-state's problems with a territorially concentrated minority population or nation.

"Unitary states," not federal states, may need federacies. In any type of federal system, *every major political unit* in the polity is part of a federation. An "asymmetrical" federal system does not need a federacy because the specific prerogatives obtainable for minority populations can be established within it. Witness the vast number of special prerogatives India has negotiated and delivered for Mizoram, where a once war-torn secessionist society now has a high degree of voice and loyalty inside India. However, a "symmetrical" federal system with a federacy is either a contradiction in terms or is an "asymmetrical" federal system.

Contrary to what some readers may assume, federacies are fundamentally different from confederations. A "confederation" is an agreement *between* states. A federacy is an agreement *within* a state. In a confederation, a member state may make a *unilateral* decision not to participate in a collective foreign policy endeavor, unless such a decision violates the specific treaty creating the confederation. However, in a federacy, opting out of a decision unilaterally is not constitutional. Opt outs by a federacy can only be undertaken with the *prior agreement and help* of the center.

Finally, some observers might feel that federacies and "associated states," which do not qualify for membership in the United Nations (or even some colonies), are analytically the same. However, our ideal type federacy has the requirement that citizens resident in the autonomous unit participate fully in elections for the central government of the polity, have their own representatives in the parliament, and thus in a parliamentary system can play a role in government formation. In a presidential system, citizens who reside in the autonomous unit have the right to participate in the election of the president. In any case, if the autonomous unit were still a colony, this would violate our ideal type stipulation that the federacy is an integral part of an independent state.

We do not claim to have invented the word *federacy*. Discussions regarding it have been with us since the Greeks, but to date the term has been insufficiently developed, theoretically or empirically. Even now federacy is used in so many ways that nothing like a cumulative literature in comparative politics can emerge unless an endeavor at closure is made of the sort we have just attempted. [7]We believe the concept and, even more, the *practice* of federacy can expand the repertoire of democratic and constitutional ways to handle deeply different, territorially concentrated minorities in unitary states. But can it, and has it, traveled beyond the small democratic countries of Scandinavia? Yes, it played a crucial role in reconstructing deeply divided postauthoritarian Italy at the end of World War II.

## The Role of Federacies in the Italian Postwar Democratic Transition

Italy's economy, politics, and unitary state at the end of World War II were all facing crises.[8] Due to Mussolini's alliance with Hitler, Italy's international and domestic legitimacy was dangerously low. Partly in response to Mussolini's authoritarian centralizing policies, in the country's peripheries, territorially concentrated minority populations in five different areas had leaders and movements seeking exit or self-government from the Italian state. These areas were German-speaking South Tyrol, where the vast majority of the population wanted to rejoin the irredentist neighbor, Austria; the French-speaking province of Valle D'Aosta on the alpine border with France, which had recently sent troops and agents to the province, making annexation a live issue; Friuli-Venezia Giulia on the border with Yugoslavia, with many Slovene speakers, much of the territory of which the Allies' war partner Tito was occupying and claiming as part of Yugoslavia; and the islands of Sicily and Sardinia, with their very distinctive social structures and problems. In 1944–45, Italy was a "politically robust multinational polity" governed by a unitary state. Let us examine how federacy played a key role in helping solve what many considered the politically most dangerous case, South Tyrol.

South Tyrol, in what is now the province of Bolzano, is adjacent to the strategically valuable Brenner Pass connecting the Alps with northeastern Italy. Before World War I this territory was part of Austria, with a population approximately 86 percent German-speaking, 8 percent Italian-speaking, and 4 percent Ladino-speaking. In the 1919 Treaty of St. Germain, the territory was given to Italy as part of a secret agreement (later published) for joining the Allies in World War I. Mussolini's fascist regime imposed a particularly harsh and authoritarian set of unitary state and Italian nation-building policies on South Tyrol. The German schools were closed, Italian was made the only official language, there was extensive state-sponsored Italian immigration into the area, and the name of the territory was changed to Alto Adige. In 1926 Mussolini proudly announced, "The Germans of the Alto Adige are not a national minority but an ethnic remnant."

Not so. German speakers were still the largest and most politically organized part of the population in South Tyrol (Alto Adige) in 1945. Almost immediately after the war, the German-speaking South Tyrolean People's Party (Sudtiroler Volkspartei, SVP) was formed and rapidly became the dominant social movement and political party in South Tyrol. In the name of self-determination, the SVP demanded a plebiscite over their status. With the strong domestic political and international diplomatic irredentist support of Austria, the SVP's goal was to exit Italy and accede to Austria. The Italian-speaking minority in South Tyrol and the Italian-speaking majority in Italy were deeply suspicious of the German speakers of South Tyrol. Hitler and Mussolini had arranged for a plebiscite of sorts in South Tyrol in which German speakers could opt to retain Italian nationality or migrate to Hitler's Reich and receive German citizenship. Out of a total number of the 229,500 inhabitants of Bolzano entitled to opt out of Italy and to migrate to the Reich, 166,488 did so.

How was Italy to respond to this challenge to its unitary state authority? The political history of unified Italy did not offer much in the way of a useable past. In theory, federalism, especially asymmetrical federalism, would have seemed to have offered the most possibilities. However, none of Italy's major unification leaders—Cavour, Garibaldi, or Mazzini—were sympathetic to federalist ideas.

South Tyrol reveals a lot about some of the special international and national arrangements that can be negotiated once the possibility of a federacy is on the table. The origin of the special statute for South Tyrol (which is close to our ideal type of a federacy) was not in a constituent assembly but in the De Gasperi-Gruber Accord, signed by the foreign ministers of Italy and Austria on September 5, 1946, and linked to the Paris Peace Treaty (which involved the United Nations). Some of the specific commitments were expanded and constitutionalized in 1948 and 1972 in further special statutes. The De Gasperi-Gruber Accord was helpful in defusing the crisis, especially in the area of equal cultural, political, and employment rights for German-speaking citizens. Some of the key agreements that allowed Karl Gruber, the Austrian foreign minister, to stress that the accord would significantly improve the rights of the German-speaking former Austrian citizens in South Tyrol were the following:

1. German-speaking inhabitants of the Bolzano Province . . . will be assured a complete equality of rights with the Italian-speaking inhabitants within the framework of special provisions to safeguard the ethnical character and the cultural and economic development of the German-speaking element.

     In accordance with legislation already enacted or awaiting enactment the said German-speaking citizens will be granted in particular:

     (a) elementary and secondary teaching in the mother-tongue;
     (b) parification of the German and Italian languages in public offices and official documents;
     (c) The right to re-establish German family names which were Italian-ized in recent years;
     (d) Equality of rights as regards the entering upon public offices with a view to reaching a more appropriate proportion of employment between the two ethnical groups.
2. The populations of the above mentioned zones will be granted the exercise of autonomous legislative and executive regional power. The frame within which the said provisions will apply will be drafted in consultation also with the local representative German-speaking elements.

The accord enabled Austrian political leaders to not be too adamant in their irredentist drive. It also enabled Alcide de Gasperi, the Italian foreign minister, to stress that the major concessions to German speakers would strengthen Italy's frontiers and protect its electrical resources while ensuring the language rights of the Italian minority in South Tyrol. These and many other issues were included in the Special Statute for the Trentino-Alto Adige as Constitutional Law on February 2, 1948.

This Constitutional Law meets our embeddedness requirement for a federacy. Article 88 of this statute stresses its constitutional embeddedness by stating: "For the amendment of the present law the procedure established by the Constitution shall be applied." Articles 4 through 17 spell out the federal-like constitutionally embedded powers of the region. Citizens of Bolzano are full citizens of Italy, and since 1948 they have received six seats in the Italian parliament: four in the lower house and two in the upper house. As in the Scandinavian federacies, the unitary state is represented in the federacy by a commissioner.

Notwithstanding these gains, a major point of contention remained in the new federacy. It was solved in a novel form of dispute settlement involving substantial international participation. The population of Bolzano were in a German majority province. However, not really in the spirit of the De Gasperi-Gruber Accord, Bolzano was joined with the more populous Italian-speaking province Trentino, making the Trentino-Alto Adige Region. In 1960 Austria appealed to the United Nations, stating that some of the Paris Peace Treaty provisions implied in the De Gasperi-Gruber Accord, which was attached to the Paris Peace Treaty, had not been fully honored. In response to Austria's complaints, the UN General Assembly adopted a resolution urging Italy and Austria to reopen negotiations. Italy then created a mixed commission, with substantial South Tyrolean, German-speaking representation, which produced a 137-point agreement approved by both the Austrian and Italian parliaments. This agreement was incorporated in the new 1972 autonomy statute. The last of its 137 measures went into force in 1988, and in a 1992 exchange of notes to the United Nations, Austria and Italy confirmed that all outstanding issues had been settled.

Some of the key outcomes were a treaty recognizing the jurisdiction of the International Court of Justice for some disputes; public posts to be filled on a proportional basis according to self-identified language groups (as of the 1981 census, this meant that 65 percent of the posts went to German speakers); and the explicit right granted to Bolzano to challenge state legislation in case of infringement of the region's constitutionally embedded autonomy.

Political party institutions played a key role in the conflict resolution by negotiation. The central party in South Tyrol since 1945 has been the SVP. It was initially strongly secessionist and wanted to rejoin irredentist Austria. However, in the context of the de Gasperi-Gruber Accord and sensing that the victorious Allied powers, for their own geopolitical interests, were gradually aligning themselves with Italian state-building and state-maintenance principles instead of with German-speaking self-determination and nation-building principles, the SVP shifted its stance from a politics of secession to a politics of autonomy.

The SVP can justly claim many of the achievements gained by the autonomy statutes of 1948 and 1972 and the robust economic growth of Bolzano. Important for our understanding of the possibilities of federacies being able to contribute to multicultural accommodation, a review of late 1990s public opinion surveys indicates that 78 percent of the German-speaking voters responded that they were happy with the work of the regional federacy government, and an impressive 62 percent of Italian speakers and 60 percent of Ladino speakers also expressed satisfaction with the regional government. But can the practice of federacy travel to a Muslim majority country?

## Did the Idea of Federacy Play a Crucial Role in the Peace and Democratization Process in Indonesia and Aceh?

In 1998, when the thirty-two-year-long military regime of General Suharto fell in Indonesia, the world's most populous Muslim majority country, democratization was one possible outcome. But by 2003, a fourth Indonesian president since Suharto was already on the horizon; the new political managers of the state's two-thousand-mile archipelago were trying to manage secessionism in its eastern periphery of Papua and in its northwestern periphery of Aceh; East Timor had already won its struggle for independence; Muslim-Christian riots (with some military and police complicity) had occurred on islands such as Ambon and Sulawesi; and massive al-Qaeda-linked explosions had killed 202 in Bali and wounded approximately 170 in the Marriott Hotel in Jakarta. Although democratization was still a possibility, crises of "stateness," intensified religious conflicts, and growing military autonomy were other possibilities.

To many in the country's capital, Jakarta, the crisis in Aceh presented particularly dangerous problems for the unitary state of Indonesia. Except for the absence of irredentism, Aceh scores relatively high on most of the variables that make it difficult to manage politics democratically and peacefully in a unitary state. Many of Aceh's people pride themselves on practicing a stricter form of Islam than in the Indonesian heartland of Java; many think of themselves as members of the Acehnese, not Indonesian, nation; many want more control over their oil resources; and Aceh as a territory has had a long history of resistance to, and armed repression by, the unitary state. Many Acehnese gave active or at least passive support to the armed resistance to colonial rule in the late nineteenth century and to armed rebellions and separatist or independence movements in the 1950s and for much of the last thirty years. The most recent insurgent group, the Gerakan Aceh Merdeka (GAM), started an insurrection in 1976 and intensified their struggle for independence in 1999 in the political and coercive spaces created by the fall of Suharto.[9] A tentative "Cessation of Hostilities Agreement" began in December 2002, but the government of Indonesia, convinced that GAM was only using the ceasefire to strengthen its guerrilla forces, declared martial law in May 2003. The chief of the armed forces, General Endriartono Sutarto, told troops their mission was "destroying GAM forces down to their roots" and "finishing off, killing those who still engage in armed resistance."[10]

Yet, in 2005 a relatively enduring comprehensive peace treaty was signed. By 2009 the World Bank office in Aceh judged that the "political commitment to the peace process remains strong on both sides"; Indonesia was ranked as one of the two most politically democratic of the world's forty-seven Muslim majority polities; and scholarly debates were less about the challenges of "stateness," or political Islam, than about what still needs to be done before Indonesia is democratically consolidated.

Did the *idea* of federacy contribute to this startling change, especially peace in Aceh? We believe we can make a strong case that it did.

One of the major reasons the cessation of hostilities broke down in 2003 was the continuing clash of fundamental goals. The central government and the military were worried about the territorial fragmentation of Indonesia and were deeply suspicious of any formula other than a unitary state. GAM, for their part, could not see how they could advance their social and developmental goals outside of independence. But on February 23, 2005, just as another peace negotiation was about to collapse, GAM suddenly announced that their "demand for independence is no longer on the table."

What contributed to this major compromise on the part of GAM? It would seem that the *idea* of federacy-type arrangements broke the bargaining deadlock. Why, how, and with what consequence?

More has to be written by key participants, but it seems that on the eve of the second round, the head of the Helsinki mediation team, the former president of Finland, Martti Ahtisaari, in a television address on February 20, 2005, alluded to "self-government" for Aceh as a possible goal of the negotiations. The next day GAM renounced independence and accepted a goal of self-government.[11]

It may be that Ahtisaari's informal conversations with the GAM were even more important than his television address. One of the key GAM negotiators in Helsinki, Nur Djuli, told Stepan why he personally came to believe that an Aland Island type of arrangement could lead to self-government. One evening Nur Djuli and some other GAM negotiators were sitting with Ahtisaari looking out at the sea. They respected Ahtisaari, who among many other accomplishments had been nominated for the Nobel Peace Prize for his peacekeeping achievements in the Balkans as a high official of the United Nations.[12] Ahtisaari noticed a ship going by and asked Nur Djuli if he recognized the flag the ship was flying. Djuli said he did not. Ahtisaari said the flag was that of the Aland Islands. Ahtisaari went on to say that the Aland Islands were a part of the unitary state of Finland with special self-governing arrangements. He said that he, as president, could not send a Finnish ship to the Aland Islands without the permission of the legislature of the Aland Islands. He said further that no major domestic law or treaty affecting the Aland Islands could go into effect without the *consultation and consent* of the government and legislature of the Aland Islands. Djuli later insisted that he and some of the other GAM negotiators virtually did not sleep that night. They spent the night looking up the Aland Islands, and then Greenland, on the Internet. They may or may not have heard of the word *federacy*, but they increasingly began to feel that the Finnish-Aland Islands federacy arrangement might produce a serious form of "self-government" for Aceh.

A non-zero-sum game was now on the table. If GAM were able to negotiate for a federacy of the Aland Islands type, they believed many of their goals concerning self-government could be met. If the central government's negotiators were able to get such a federacy, their central goal of peacefully keeping Aceh inside of the unitary state of Indonesia would be met. Such a mutually acceptable treaty, called the "Memorandum of Understanding between the Government of the Republic of Indonesia and the Free Aceh Movement" (MoU), was signed on August 15, 2005, and witnessed by Martti Ahtisaari.[13]

The major goal of the central government was achieved in the second paragraph of the MoU Preamble: "The parties commit themselves to creating conditions within which the government of the Acehnese people can be manifested through a fair and democratic process *within the unitary state and constitution of the Republic of Indonesia*" (emphasis added).

In addition to forgoing their independence claims, GAM agreed to demobilize "all of its 3000 military troops" and to undertake "the decommissioning of all arms, ammunition and explosives held by the participants in GAM activities" under the supervision of the newly created EU-ASEAN-led "Aceh Monitoring Mission," no later than December 31, 2005.

The quid pro quo for GAM were new federacy prerogatives, many quite similar to those agreed to in the Aland Islands–Finland federacy, that were to be the principles of a new Law on the Governing of Aceh. Four of our five defining characteristics of a federacy, and both of our facilitating features, are clearly involved in the MoU.

## In a Democratic China Might Two Federacies Be Useful?

If China ever becomes a democracy, it is likely that one of its most intractable problems will be Tibet. Many of the democratic countries in the world and many Human Rights organizations will probably demand that China quit violating the rights of the Tibetans and give greater self-governing rights to the territorially concentrated Tibetan minority. On a number of occasions, the Dalai Lama has indicated that he would accept federacy-type arrangements. Of course, if China continues "Cromwellian" policies of encouraging Han immigration into Tibet and Chinese nationalism grows more intense, there might not be sufficient political space for such initiatives even in a democratic China. But as the conversation facing the sea off the coast of Finland between the Aceh independence leaders and the former president of Finland shows, possibilistic political theories with successful examples might someday be emulated with surprising speed and success.

It is even possible that a majority of the citizens in Taiwan and a newly democratic government of China might feel it is in their mutual interest to begin exploratory conversations about a federacy relationship.

## Federacy for the Kurds in the Middle East?

On the one hundredth anniversary of the Sykes-Picot Agreement, sovereignty and borders are the subjects of increasing contention in the Middle East. Postinvasion Iraq has been plagued by sectarian bloodshed, even cleansing, and a crisis of "stateness" that continues to this day. Indeed, with the emergence of ISIS and its "Caliphate," much of the border separating Iraq from Syria effectively vanished.

Meanwhile, in Syria the ongoing civil war has been devastating. Over a quarter of a million people have died, close to five million are refugees, close to seven million are internally displaced, fully a quarter of the population has been forced to flee. To make matters worse, the dynamics of instability and violence in Syria have contributed to the recent resurgence of widespread hostilities in neighboring Turkey between the state and the Kurdish militants in the southeast.

Given the scope of destruction and the intensity of the polarization under way, the task of even imagining, much less constructing, a peaceful and stable alternative to tyranny and chaos for the region is certainly daunting. We are not naive optimists about the prospects for peace and democratic stability anytime in the near future. Even so, we think it important to try to imagine beyond the current catastrophe, to look ahead for potential ways out. We believe that the institutional arrangement of federacy merits close attention in this regard.

As we have seen, over the past century, the institutionalization of federacy arrangements has proven useful in Finland and in Italy, as well as most recently in the world's largest Muslim state, Indonesia. In these successful cases, federacy arrangements have been enshrined at the end of the nightmare of interstate or civil war and have facilitated postconflict transitions to democracy. Federacy could well prove useful to the Middle East as well.

Iraq, Syria, and Turkey all qualify as "politically robust multinational polities" containing territorially concentrated ethnic and religious minorities. Any stable scenaro, and certainly any stable *democratic* scenario, in these three states would require a transformation of belligerent nationalist and dogmatic sectarian mentalities, mentalities reflected and perpetuated by institutional arrangements unwilling to recognize or respect cultural and confessional diversities. Of particular salience, in all three states, the Kurdish question remains unresolved.

We think a federacy arrangement might provide a way forward in Iraq, where autonomy for the Kurds has already been effectively achieved and constitutionally embedded. In this we concur with Brendan O'Leary, who noted in 2005 that the Kurdish region of Iraq was likely to evolve into a "federacy."[14] Indeed, in Iraq, a federacy arrangement could help secure the territorial integrity of the state (a major concern not only in Baghdad but also in Ankara) while continuing to guarantee a high degree of autonomy for the Kurds. In addition, it could help resolve ongoing disputes over sharing resources, as well as the related unsettled and potentially explosive issue of the status of oil-rich Kirkuk.

In Syria, the case for federacy is at least as strong. Such an arrangement could help consolidate the only space in the country not dominated by obviously tyrannical forces. In addition, the recognition of Kurdish autonomy in a Syrian constitution would reassure Kurds of their continuing autonomy after the Russians and Americans pull out. Finally, the precedent of minority protections would bode well for other minorities in a potential post-Assad, post-ISIS scenario.

In our judgment, it is highly unlikely that Syria will ever again come remotely close to a unitary nation-state. For now, statelessness and violence remain the order of the day. One cannot think of creating a federal system in a semistateless, Hobbesian situation. Where there are major areas of statelessness, there cannot be a democracy. But perhaps democracy could be built up in a few areas, such as the space in the north controlled by the Kurdish Freedom Movement, the territory also known as Rojava.

Since the descent into civil war in Syria, Kurdish forces inspired by Abdullah Öcalan and his model of "democratic confederalism" have taken control of Rojava, the de facto Kurdish region in northern Syria, consisting originally of three noncontiguous cantons. After the Assad government decided to withdraw regime forces from the region, Kurdish forces seized control, city by city. The first city to declare its freedom was Kobane, which gives added weight to the symbolic significance of its heroic defense against the onslaught by ISIS that lasted from September 2014 through January 2015.

One encouraging sign about developments in Rojava is that the Syrian Kurdish forces in control there have consistently insisted that their "democratic confederal" model is not about dissolving state borders but, instead, about transcending them. This non-zero-sum posture stands in striking contrast to the secessionist agenda openly embraced by Barzani and his Kurdish Regional Government in Iraq. Indeed, the Syrian Kurdish forces claim that their model both respects existing boundaries and guarantees autonomy as well as multicultural and multiconfessional accommodation for ethnic and religious minorities within it. In this crucial respect, the Syrian Kurdish model of "democratic confederalism," which they sometimes refer to as "democratic autonomy," already converges quite closely with our model of federacy.

The biggest obstacle to the recognition of Kurdish autonomy in Syria comes not from Damascus but from Ankara. The Erdogan government and the Turkish military fear that recognition of autonomy for a territory on its border controlled by forces inspired by the imprisoned Kurdish leader Abdullah Öcalan constitutes a direct threat to the territorial integrity of the Turkish state.

Given the strength and belligerence of the Turkish nation-state mentality, a federacy arrangement for the Kurds in Turkey remains highly unlikely in the near future. Nevertheless, we do believe that, at the very least, a softening of the Turkish nation-state mentality can be achieved in a post-Erdogan scenario. Such a softening could be channeled and constructively reinforced via a negotiated retreat of the PKK into the Kandil mountains across the border into the Kurdish region of Iraq, such as advocated recently by Abdullah Öcalan, or into Rojava, in exchange for recognition of cultural and linguistic rights for the Kurds alongside freedom for the widely revered leader who has been a consistent voice for peace and has also renounced secessionism for more than a decade now. We believe recognition of cultural and linguistic rights for the Kurds and other minorities in Turkey is the only arrangement compatible with democracy, and the only way to end the dangerous polarizing conflagration currently under way.

## Notes

1. For a more elaborate discussion of federacy with a detailed discussion of how nine federacies came into being, see Alfred Stepan, Juan J. Linz, and Yogendra Yadav, "Federacy: A Formula for Democratically Managing Multinational Societies in Unitary States," in *Crafting State Nations: India and Other Multinational Democracies* (Baltimore, Md.: Johns Hopkins University Press, 2011), 203–256.
2. Four different combinations of spellings and accents for the Aland Islands are used in the English-language literature. We follow the spelling used in the League of Nations official documents and in most English-language scholarly articles.
3. Ruth Lapidoth, *Autonomy: Flexible Solutions to Ethnic Conflicts* (Washington, D.C.: U.S. Institute of Peace Press, 1997), 70.
4. Tore Modeen, "Aland Islands," in *Encyclopedia of Public International Law*, vol. 12, ed. Rudolph Berhardt (Amsterdam: North Holland, 1990), 1.
5. Tore Modeen, "The International Protection of the National Identity of the Aland Islands," *Scandinavian Studies in Law* (1973): 175–210, at 178–79. Also see the well-documented book by James Barros, *The Aland Islands Question: Its Settlement by the League of Nations* (New Haven, Conn.: Yale University Press, 1968).
6. We briefly discuss them later, and all are discussed in great detail in Stepan, Linz, and Yadav, "Federacy."
7. Elazar did the most to introduce the concept of federacy in the modern political science literature, but he created great conceptual and empirical confusion about federacies. He gave only three examples of a federacy relationship, India and Bhutan, India and Jammu-Kashmir, and Puerto Rico's relationship to the USA. Daniel J. Elazar, *Federal Systems of the World: A Handbook of Federal, Confederal and Autonomy Arrangements* (New York: Longman 1999), esp. xvi–xvii, and 209. However, *none of these three relationships* is remotely close to a federacy as we have just defined it. Bhutan and India have been independence states since 1949 and 1947, respectively. Bhutan's and India's elected bodies and judicial system are fully separate from each other. Bhutan, which borders China, has, if you will, "outsourced" many, but not all, of its defense tasks to India. Elsewhere, Elazar classifies Jammu and Kashmir as a "federacy" of India, but it is actually a disputed component of an "asymmetrical" federal system. The United States and Puerto Rico does not meet our definition of a federacy for two reasons. First, Puerto Rico (unlike any federacy we discuss) does not have any elected representatives at the center, and Puerto Ricans do not have full voting rights. They cannot vote for the president of the United States unless they live on the mainland. Second, a federacy is a special territory in an otherwise unitary state, and the USA is a federal state.

8. Our discussion of existing federacies does not include endnotes; interested readers are referred to the extensive notes in Stepan, Linz, and Yadav, "Federacy."
9. For documentation and analysis of Aceh's conflicts with Indonesia and the eventual creation of what we call a federacy, see Edward Aspinall, *Islam and Nation: Separatist Rebellion in Aceh Indonesia* (Stanford, Calif.: Stanford University Press, 2009).
10. Edward Aspinall and Harold Crouch, *The Aceh Peace Process: Why It Failed* (Washington, D.C.: East-West Center, 2003), 1.
11. Aspinall and Crouch, *Aceh Peace Process*, 27.
12. In 2008, Ahtisaari was awarded the Nobel Peace Prize, in part because his work was "central to the solution of the complicated Aceh question in Indonesia." See "The Nobel Peace Prize for 2008," www.novelprize.org/nobel_prizes/peace/laureates/2008/press.html.
13. A complete English copy of the MoU is available in Edward Aspinall, *The Helsinki Agreement: A More Promising Basis for Peace in Aceh?* (Washington, D.C.: East-West Center, 2005), 75–84.
14. Brendan O'Leary, "Power-Sharing, Pluralist Federation, and Federacy," in *The Future of Kurdistan in Iraq*, ed. Brendan O'Leary, John McGarry, and Khaled Salih (Philadelphia, Penn.: University of Pennsylvania Press, 2005), 47–91.

## Bibliography

Alsopp, Harriet. *The Kurds of Syria: Political Parties and Identity in the Middle East.* London: I. B. Taurus, 2014.
Andrews, Peter A., ed. *Ethnic Groups in the Republic of Turkey.* Wiesbaden, Germany: Dr. Ludwig Reichert Verlag, 1989.
Angrist, Michael P. "Turkey: Roots of the Turkish-Kurdish Conflict and Prospects for Constructive Reform." In *Federalism and Territorial Cleavages*, ed. Ugo M. Amoretti and Nancy Bermeo, 387–416. Baltimore, Md.: Johns Hopkins University Press, 2004.
Aspinall, Edward. *The Helsinki Agreement: A More Promising Basis for Peace in Aceh?* Washington, D.C.: East-West Center, 2005.
——. *Islam and Nation: Separatist Rebellion in Aceh Indonesia.* Stanford, Calif.: Stanford University Press, 2009.
Aspinall, Edward, and Harold Crouch. *The Aceh Peace Process: Why It Failed.* Washington, D.C.: East-West Center, 2003.
Barros, James. *The Aland Islands Question: Its Settlement by the League of Nations.* New Haven, Conn.: Yale University Press, 1968.
"Casualties of Syrian Civil War." Wikipedia. https://en.wikipedia.org/wiki/Casualties_of_the_Syrian_Civil_War.
Cockburn, Patrick. *The Age of Jihad.* London: Verso, 2016.
Elazar, Daniel J. *Federal Systems of the World: A Handbook of Federal, Confederal and Autonomy Arrangements.* New York: Longman 1999.
Gunter, Michael. *Kurds Ascending.* London: Palgrave MacMillan, 2008.
Kirmanj, Sherko. *Identity and Nation in Iraq.* Boulder, Colo.: Lynne Reinner, 2013.
Knapp, Michael, Anja Flach, and Ercan Ayboga. *Revolution in Rojava. Democratic Autonomy and Woman's Liberation in Syrian Kurdistan.* London: Pluto Press, 2016.
Lapidoth, Ruth. *Autonomy: Flexible Solutions to Ethnic Conflicts.* Washington, D.C.: U.S. Institute of Peace Press, 1997.
Le Billon, Philippe. "Oil, Secession, and the Future of Iraqi Federalism." *Middle East Policy Council* 22, no. 1 (Spring 2015): 68–76.

McDowall, David. *A Modern History of the Kurds.* London: I. B. Taurus, 1996.

Miley, Thomas Jeffrey. "State Terror, Human Rights Violations, and Authoritarianism in Turkey: Report of the Third Imrali Peace Delegation." March 2017. http://www.mbl.is /media/99/10299.pdf.

Modeen, Tore. "Aland Islands." In *Encyclopedia of Public International Law.* Vol. 12, ed. Rudolph Berhardt, 1. Amsterdam: North Holland, 1990.

——. "The International Protection of the National Identity of the Aland Islands." *Scandinavians Studies in Law* (1973): 175–210.

"The Nobel Peace Prize for 2008." Official website for the Nobel Prize. www.nobelprize.org /nobel_prizes/peace/laureates/2008/press.html.

Öcalan, Abdullah. *Democratic Confederalism.* London: Transmedia, 2011. http://www .freeocalan.org/wp content/uploads/2012/09/Ocalan-Democratic-Confederalism.pdf.

O'Leary, Brendan. "Power-Sharing, Pluralist Federation, and Federacy." In *The Future of Kurdistan in Iraq,* ed. Brendan O'Leary, John McGarry, and Khaled Salih, 47–91. Philadelphia: University of Pennsylvania Press, 2005.

Safi, Louay. "Nationalism and the Multinational State." *American Journal of Islamic Social Sciences* 9, no. 3 (Fall 1992): 338–50.

Stepan, Alfred, Juan J. Linz, and Yogendra Yadav. "Federacy: A Formula for Democratically Managing Multinational Societies in Unitary States." In *Crafting State Nations: India and Other Multinational Democracies.* Baltimore, Md.: Johns Hopkins University Press, 2011.

"Syria's Refugee Crisis in Numbers." Amnesty International, December 2016. https://www .amnesty.org/en/latest/news/2016/02/syrias-refugee-crisis-in-numbers/.

Wimmer, Andreas. "Democracy and Ethno-religious Conflict in Iraq." *Survival: Global Politics and Strategy* 45, no. 4 (Winter 2003–04): 111–34.

"World Directory of Minorities and Indigenous Peoples: Syria." Minority Rights Group International, 2011. http://www.refworld.org/docid/4954ce5ac.html.

Yahiaoui, Dorra, and Akram Al Ariss. "Diversity in the Arab World: Challenges and Opportunities." In *Management and Diversity: International Perspectives on Equality, Diversity, and Inclusion.* Vol. 3, ed. Mustafa Özbilgin et al., 249–60. Bingley, UK: Emerald Publishing, 2017.

Yildiz, Güney. "Why Did Turkey's Peace Process with the PKK Rebels Fail? How Can It Be Resurrected?" MPhil. diss., University of Cambridge, June 2017.

7

# EUROPE—WHAT'S LEFT?

*Toward a Progressive Pluralist Program for EU Reform*

ROBERT HOWSE

A transnational federation that precludes war and orders the relations between peoples through law and rights has been a liberal progressive dream since Kant's *Perpetual Peace*. Kant's evocative essay gave little institutional detail about how the federation would work, but implied that such a union was the logical outcome, on one hand, of the idea of cosmopolitan right, and, on the other, of the historical experience of violence. Some have purported to see such a project imprinted on governance constellations such as the United Nations or its predecessor, the League of Nations. In these cases, it soon became clear that the legal constructs did not depart from Westphalian sovereignty in their real operation (except perhaps the UN Security Council, but in an ineffective manner because implementation of its decisions still depended entirely on state sovereignty).

For many, the European Union, which began with the European Steel and Coal Community, then morphed into the European Economic Community (EEC), then the European Community (EC), and finally the EU, is the first and original example of a transnational federation. From its founding, the project of European integration was intended as a response to the most brutal and destructive outbreak of violence among the European nations: World War II and the Holocaust. There is little question that the most compelling telos of union was to connect the peoples and states of Europe in such a way as to turn such violent hatreds into a thing of the past. The project began through legal guarantees of economic mobility-free movement of goods, services, capital, and persons. But even from the early years of interpretation by the European

Court of Justice, it was clear that the European treaty of union created rights for citizens that were directly enforceable in the European Court, the judgments of which would be directly applicable in the Member States; the treaty thus had a kind of constitutional dimension embedding a form of transnational legality that departed from Westphalian interstate international law in creating a direct and meaningful relationship between the citizen and the transnational order. This seemed to go further than anything yet devised in the direction of what Kant had called *cosmopolitan right*.

In addition, as became ever clearer as the union evolved, and the ambit of the treaty expanded, the EU project not only constitutionalized, in effect, certain rights but also entailed the division of sovereignty that for many federal theorists is the true essence of federalism. Thus, certain competences were assigned exclusively to the European institutions (such as external commercial trade policy and competition policy), and others were to be exercised jointly. On the other hand, even though the union had a Parliament, the exercise of the union-level competences was achieved through a pooling or joint exercise of national sovereignty, intergovernmental decision making in the European Council above all. Thus began an endless debate among scholars of federalism as to whether, in truth, the EU was a federation or a confederation.

Such discussion has crosscut controversies about whether the EU is or should become a constitutional polity in the full sense—is this possible without Europe having or being a single "demos," the will of which can find direct expression in European governance through the European Parliament? As the EU level competences have expanded into many fields of policy, including labor and social standards, environment, and food safety, the relative weakness of democratic legitimacy (that is, in comparison to national institutions involved in these kinds of policy making) has become apparent, creating a concern with the democratic deficit. National governments generally have an ideological orientation of some sort. But is it really possible to conceive of the EU as a governance space that is ideologically neutral, or blind? In the post–WWII generation that was involved in getting the European project going, and also rebuilding the European polities as liberal democracies, there was a rather solid consensus on the goal of preventing another outbreak of murderous hatred among European peoples, as well as facilitating the building of stable mixed economies and democratic political institutions within European states. The original blueprint of the four freedoms plus intergovernmental cooperation and coordination on a range of commercial and industrial policies was an authentic expression of this consensus. It was able to accommodate most of the ideological spectrum—leftists like Alexandre Kojève were able to imagine the European project as a form of socialist internationalism; liberals as a stage toward the Kantian ideal of transnational federalism; and moderate nationalist conservatives a la De Gaulle as "L'Europe des patries"—in which the European nations would, despite being caught between the two superpowers, nevertheless realize great things not in competition and rivalry with one another but through concerted action.

But as the European project has evolved, the anchoring original consensus has given way to ideological struggle over Europe and what it means. In the 1980s and 1990s, Europe came to be seen by some as a WTO on steroids, removing inefficient regulations through harmonization and aggressively tackling the problem of regulatory barriers to economic mobility. Such a neoliberal view of the project of "deeper integration" understandably met with skepticism on the left, or alternately as with Jürgen Habermas a demand that depth of social integration equal that of economic integration. And indeed in many areas, EU-level regulatory initiatives began to appear more as harmonization toward the top rather than the bottom, as it were. This in turn began to alarm nationalist conservatives, especially when the EU became entangled in matters of social regulation, family benefits, migration, and so on, which were of considerable sensitivity for nationalist conservatives. And today, manifested in Brexit, and anti-European right politics in a number of Member States, this ideological challenge to Europe has a certain vitality. On the other hand, the project of monetary union, unaccompanied by social solidarity, with the imposition of "austerity" in the wake of financial crisis through the hegemony of Germany/North Europe in the Eurozone institutions, has created a severe crisis of legitimacy for Europe on the left.

My thesis in this essay is that the response to this predicament, particularly on the left, should not be the one that is usually preferred by law professors and legal and political theorists; namely, to urge a new constitutional moment for Europe, a rebuilding of the architecture, a more truly federal or constitutional design, which would somehow cabin or address arguments about lack of democracy or respect for sovereignty, whether on the right or the left. The ideological struggle needs to play itself out; it is not so much a function of faulty architecture or incomplete constitutionalization of Europe but of genuine sociological difference across a vast territory comprising many peoples, and it is also connected to more general struggles about globalization, neoliberalism, and neonationalism that are happening beyond the confines of Europe's borders. From the perspective of the left, which is my own, there remains a constructive progressive agenda in and for the European Union, and what advancing this agenda requires is political imagination and shrewdness more than legal or institutional ingenuity (although some institutional innovation may be appropriate within the overall existing architecture).

Thus, my thesis is that the multifaceted crisis of Europe today provides the occasion for thinking about Europe in *concrete* political terms rather than in abstractions; relating values, material realities, institutions, and policies in a rigorous manner, without escape into airy terms such as constitutionalism or messianism. This concrete thinking has, in fact, begun to emerge on the left, although its influence on, and presence in, mainstream EU legal scholarship is at best marginal. Philosophers such as Étienne Balibar and Giorgio Agamben and economists such as Thomas Piketty and Yannis Varoufakis have taken the lead. But this work of intellectuals has not been unrelated to the practice and strategy of the political left in Europe in response to crisis, above all, to austerity. I further argue that, like much of the best thinking, the grappling by the left with the future of Europe has come out of internal struggle and wrestling with profound dilemmas; unlike much of the legal theorizing, its root is in the appreciation of value conflicts and material contradictions rather than the desire to impose order or harmony through juridical forms, howsoever labeled. Finally, I claim that the pro-EU forces who seek not only survival but renewal of the European project (perhaps most clearly exemplified by French President Emmanuel Macron) cannot do without the ideas and political support of the new or newer left in Europe. The very crisis in which the values of the left were most betrayed by Europe (Greece/austerity) has led, in combination with other developments, to a situation in which the left may have an extraordinary opportunity to shape the future of Europe.

## The Left and the European Project: Past and Future

The roots of commitment of the left to the European project run deep. First of all, as was developed by the Marxist Hegelian philosopher Alexandre Kojève, the rational ideal of social equality implies, at least in principle, some kind of world society in which social and economic opportunity are not arbitrarily determined or apportioned on the basis of national boundaries or socioeconomic class, in Kojève's phrase, the universal and homogenous state.[1] Second, and a very strong consideration for the first decades of European integration, the project of Europe comes to sight as a response to the destruction and self-destruction of the national political and economic ideal in fascism. The national state is regressive, it asserts ethno-national unity to suppress class struggle and tends to scapegoat national minorities for social and economic problems caused by capitalism. Third, for the social democratic left, and really for all but the communists, a united Europe seems the only hope, postwar, of maintaining some independent space in a world dominated by American power on one side and Soviet power on the other. It is this space that is required for social democracy or democratic socialism, and all the variants. Finally, as globalization took off in the 1980s and 1990s, there is hope that a united Europe will have the power to resist or tame the more extreme forms of neoliberal globalization.

None of these considerations is entirely meaningless or wrongheaded, even today. But as it became increasingly evident that Europe's direction was coming from technocrats with an essentially neoliberal mentality, and that the technocrats along with centrist and center-right politicians were quite content to use the European project to implement the neoliberal agenda and align Europe with economic globalization, the left faced some hard choices. For some on the left, such as Jürgen Habermas, the problem was in large measure the structures that enabled the technocracy, facilitating fundamental decisions and choices cut off from true democratic self-determination. The cure: a democratic constitutional overhaul of the EU architecture.[2] If the architecture was fundamentally flawed, then organized popular resistance to an EU neoliberal agenda, and new movements in favor of a progressive agenda for Europe, would get nowhere because they would be defeated by technocrats beyond the direct control of the people. Habermas veered in the direction of more European integration, but others on the left, for instance, Wolfgang Streeck, developed into left Euroskeptics, viewing the EU project as fatally tainted by neoliberalism as its driving spirit.[3] At one point in the 1980s, Britain's Labour Party had exit from the European Union in its policy platform. But, in fact, neither the Habermastype constitutional proposal nor the Euroskeptic reaction could be translated into political effectiveness for the left. In the first case, the project was too philosophical and too removed from concrete demands that could be linked to a policy platform or manifesto. In the second case, most of the Euroskeptics, apart from some fringe far left parties, stopped short of declaring a full program for exit from, or dismantling of, the EU. Partly this goes to the deep discomfort of the European left in the postwar period with the idea of adopting a strong discourse on nationalism. Second, a program for exiting the EU would need to be accompanied, if it were to be plausible, with a strategy for rebuilding a damaged social welfare state in a world in which globalization was not going to go away, certainly not in the foreseeable future. The situation increasingly became one in which the left could not live with the EU as it was nor construct a politically viable alternative. The left thus became politically impotent, by and large, on European issues. And it could always blame the "democratic deficit," the fundamental architecture of the Union, for its lack of influence.

The Eurozone crisis, austerity, and its culmination in the punitive treatment of Greece changed this. The stakes were no longer about a better future, or how much of the social welfare state one could recover or protect under conditions of globalization. The southern countries in Europe were faced with an all-out assault from Brussels, Frankfurt, and Berlin on social justice in their societies, indeed, even basic human security was menaced. Homes were lost on a massive scale, pensioners lacked for food, middle-class people were plunged into poverty and radical social insecurity. In these circumstances, a progressive response was urgent. If the left could not lead in opposition or resistance to the most punitive and cruel capitalist agenda since the depression, according to Wolfgang Schäuble and Jeroen Dijsselbloem, then it had lost its soul and perhaps also its mind. Moreover, the people in the southern countries were being made to pay for the defects and excesses of a Eurozone finance system that was designed to serve the interests of Germany above all, as well as of big banks, both within Europe and globally.[4]

It was the immediate question of Grexit—Should Greece say enough is enough, default on its loans, throw off the punitive discipline of the Eurogroup, and exit the EU?—that summoned forth clearer thinking on the left about the EU, in the first instance by making more manifest or transparent the differences of view that had emerged over a long period of time, but that were never well thrashed out. Yannis Varoufakis, Greece's celebrity finance minister, broke from the government after a referendum in which a majority of Greek voters said NO to austerity. Tsipras, supported by the bulk of his cabinet, decided to pull back from Grexit and attempt to work once again with the European institutions. By exiting the EU, or at least the Eurozone, Greece would be able, it was argued by Varoufakis and his supporters, to regain its social and economic sovereignty, and the left party Syriza would be able to govern in a manner true to its values. Tsipras and his followers countered that leaving would mean rejecting not only austerity and the neoliberal version of European integration but the ideals of the European project that were part of vision of the left (and became visible in Greece's reception of refugees, even in the worst years of the crisis). More pragmatically, exiting the EU when Greece was in full crisis mode would have made the crisis of confidence in basic social and economic institutions even more acute, and might well have led to the fall of the government, chaos, and a new regime of the right or center-right. But there was another factor too: Wolfgang Schäuble actually embraced Grexit as an opportunity to get rid of at least one big thorn in the side of what he takes to be a fiscally conservative, neoliberal concept of monetary union and economic integration.

I weighed in on this disagreement in a piece that was published in Greek translation and discussed in Syriza circles. In support of Tsipras, I wrote:

> Given Schäuble was maneuvering in the Eurogroup to bring about Grexit, Tsipras needed a commitment of political leaders to Europe as a community of fate, where cleansing of any of its nations is an unthinkable betrayal of European values and of the lessons of history. To get such a commitment required raising the Greek crisis to the level of an ontological and moral crisis for Europe, which would concentrate minds at the top political levels as well as those of European and global opinion-makers. This morning Tsipras got the commitment. Grexit as an option, even in the confused "temporary" version that was part of the deceptive rhetoric of Schäuble, is unmentioned in today's agreement; it has become unmentionable. The EU has made a significant moral and political

re-investment in Greece, and through its resolution of the ontological crisis, made the salvation of Greece into a test of the viability and justification of the European project. This being the case, the costs to Europe of a further failure or breakdown going forward with Greece have been upped considerably, especially at a time when European unity is being tried on *many* fronts.[5]

In the end, Greece managed to put some limits on the demands to dissemble its labor laws and pension system, and it got promises of debt relief, unfulfillable so far because of Schäuble and internal German politics. But Germany is now isolated as the only intractable opponent of meaningful debt relief for Greece. Now, finally, Greece is growing again economically, albeit slowly and with the least advantaged still suffering real hardship. But a sense of social stability and basic confidence in domestic institutions has returned, if, admittedly, mitigated by a feeling of exhaustion and defeat that is shared by many.[6] The Greeks may not have suffered in vain. There is now a widespread belief in Europe, among all but the Germans and the most die-hard neoliberals, that Greece was treated indecently in the crisis, and for many it represented a moment as shameful as the failure to stop genocide in the Balkans, at Europe's own front door. By apparently going on the cross, Greece may have prepared the moral premise of the resurrection of Europe. Something of Europe's humanity seemed to have been lost in its punitive conduct toward Greece, which, as Etienne Balibar articulates it, was not merely a neoliberal economic formula for solving a debt crisis but was "accompanied by a delirious stigmatization of the Greek people."[7] In fact, austerity was "collective punishment" of the Greek people for the mistake and corruption of their past political elites, which, in fact, in electing a nonestablishment left party, Syriza, the Greek people had themselves thrown out of power. If Europe's institutions are to be reformed in a progressive direction, and especially the Eurozone, it will be much more due to the cry of "never again" as regards what happened to Greece and not by virtue of the dreamy constitutionalism of EU jurists (and some philosophers). This is why the present moment is of such importance, and why, I believe, the thinking of much of the left about the future of Europe has taken on a concreteness and lucidity that it had arguably been lacking for some time. At the present moment, the EU establishment needs the pro-Europe left to counter right-wing populist nationalism, by giving the European project itself a genuine populist thrust, one obviously opposite to the ethno-nationalist and exclusionary populism of the right.

## Agamben, Streeck, the Latin Empire, and "Social Europe"

As noted previously, the Marxist-Hegelian philosopher Alexandre Kojève, who was an early architect of the EU (and the GATT) as an influential French policy adviser, held as the ultimate goal the universal and homogenous state: a world social and juridical order. But Kojève, writing at the end of World War II to Charles de Gaulle, argued that "the era where all of humanity together will be a political reality still remains in the distant future. The period of national political realities is over. This is the epoch of Empires, which is to say of transnational political unities, but formed by affiliated nations."[8] But rather than imagining Europe as one such transnational political unity, Kojève saw different parts of Europe as belonging to different potential transnational constellations, based on varying affinities. In particular, Kojève drew a contrast between the Slav nations, the Anglo-Saxon world, and the Latin world. Germany would be allied with the Anglo-Saxon world and its version of capitalism, rather puritanical. France, Kojève suggested to de Gaulle, should consider founding and leading the Latin Empire, based on a less materialistic sensibility, a kind of secularized Catholicism that yielded a welfare state that respected not only work but family, leisure and quality of life. Kojève envisaged this empire as a constellation of democracies, wherein democratic equality would be the principle of relations among the constituent parts of the "empire." Although the details are somewhat limited, Kojève would appear to have in mind a federal structure, with a common defense and foreign policy, as well as a redistributive function.

At the height of the Greek crisis, the Italian philosopher Giorgio Agamben sought to revive Kojève's Latin Empire concept, arguing that "if we do not want Europe to inevitably disintegrate as many signs seem to indicate it is, it would be appropriate to ask ourselves, without delay, how the European Constitution (which is not a constitution under public law, but rather an agreement between states, either not submitted to a popular vote or—as in France—flatly rejected [by 54.67 percent of French voters]) can be reconfigured anew."[9] It is crucial here that Agamben conceives the Latin Empire concept not as an *alternative* to the EU, or a way of dismantling it, but as the key to a new configuration. The premise of the configuration would be: "Not only is there no sense in asking a Greek or an Italian to live like a German, but even if this were possible, it would lead to the destruction of a cultural heritage that exists as a way of life." Agamben's "Latin Empire" op-ed got a great deal of attention and was published in many languages, but he later backed off from transforming his concept into a concrete proposal for EU reform. One of its implications might be the dismantling of the Eurozone as currently operated, wherein the Latin Empire countries, including France, would float an alternative currency underpinning a common, more or less social democratic understanding of the proper parameters of macroeconomic policy and perhaps some form of solidarity mechanism or fund to ensure that in time of crisis an individual member of this "Latin" currency zone would have the resources available to address the crisis without sacrificing basic commitments to social justice. Instead of multiple Eurozones, Wolfgang Streeck has suggested a return to national currencies altogether that would

allow the "Mediterranean" countries to have currencies suited to "their economic and social structures"(that is, a less individualist, fiscally conservative,
or economic growth-oriented approach to capitalism and the welfare state).[10]
Joseph Stiglitz has devised, with Greece's case in mind, a mechanism to allow
for a smooth transition from the euro to a new national currency. We know
as a historical fact that the single market and much of the EU *acquis* does not
depend on monetary union as the UK and other EU states are not part of the
euro. As Streeck argues (and Stiglitz agrees), it is questionable whether any EU
member state apart from Germany really benefits significantly from the euro;
the legal and institutional autonomy of the Eurozone from the other elements
of the EU make its dismantlement quite feasible, especially with a carefully
devised transitional arrangement to prevent financial speculation and even
chaos. Amputation of the monetary union, in sum, is a cure that will not kill
the patient (the European project as a whole). The removal of the transactions
costs entailed in the existence and use of multiple currencies within Europe is
a laudable goal taken in abstraction, but one that could be sacrificed to save or
enhance the legitimacy of a project that serves broader aims, as we have seen.

But the Latin Empire concept has implications other than European currency dis-union. One is that the Latin countries could as a bloc diverge from
EU policies that tilt in a neoliberal direction: deregulation of financial services, pro-privatization policies, and so forth. This would require true variable
architecture or, more precisely, new forms of it in the European treaties. With
variable architecture, arguably, the Latin countries, or perhaps any EU Member
State that shares their social-democratic spirit, could demand specific social
safeguards in free trade agreements negotiated by the EU, at least in areas of
mixed competence. Indeed, the effective activism of Paul Magnette in the face
of the Canada-EU trade agreement, CETA, produced something of this kind,
even at the *sub*national level, a declaration specifically addressing the concerns
of the Walloons. The idea of attempting to develop common positions of or
Mediterranean EU members on the future of Europe is being pursued by the
Tsipras government itself—the Latin Empire[11] as a route to voice rather than
exit from the core of Europe. On the occasion of holding a Euromed summit
in Athens, Tsipras remarked: "Economic stagnation, social cohesion problems,
the rise of Euroscepticism and isolationism, the strengthening of far-right populist phenomena, are issues that we cannot bypass in a serious debate on the
future development of European integration. In such a debate, Europe's Mediterranean countries can and must raise their voice. The way to have a bigger say
is to seek a common approach and common positions. Having that in mind, we
turned to the leaders of France, Italy, Spain, Portugal, Cyprus and Malta, for a
first meeting in Athens. I believe that regardless of the political origin of each
of us, there is ground for joint action."[12] On the same occasion, Tsipras further
recounted: "in the recent meeting of socialist heads of states and governments

in Paris, where I participated as an observer, I suggested the creation of a forum for dialogue, meaning that the Socialists, the European Left and the Greens can sit on the same table and explore things that unite them."

Tsipras's remarks again raise the question of how much of the neoliberal tilt is built into the EU architecture and attributable to the "democratic deficit." Here one must distinguish the Eurozone, the governance of the monetary union, which as Hennette et al. suggest, represents a "democratic black hole,"[13] from EU governance in general, where the Parliament now provides an important role of democratic supervision and accountability. For some, such as Joseph Weiler, the parliament is risible as a democratic institution because it does not appear to be an effective transmission belt for citizen preferences in the manner of representative democracy within sovereign states.[14] Yet the parliament and even EU intergovernmentalism as currently practiced, which is not inconsistent with public consultations by the commission or the Member States on EU issues, can provide real fora to subject to scrutiny the projects of neoliberal-oriented technocrats, and tame them. The dominance of German and other North European technocrats, with their fiscal conservative ideology, in the Eurogroup and the ECB was guaranteed by the nontransparent manner of governance of these bodies and the *lack* of parliamentary supervision. Thus, Hennette et al. argue that the fundamental democratic deficit to be addressed urgently is with the Eurozone specifically, which should be subject to control by a separate democratic body in the EU.

Setting aside for now the merits of this particular proposal, an existing normative framework outside of the monetary union can be used to counter the neoliberal agenda, but it needs to be mobilized by like-minded left governments and civil society movements in Europe, ideally through the kind of common position of the left advocated by Tsipras. This is the so-called Social Europe, which ironically was developed in the same period of EU development as the Eurozone, more or less. Ironically, because this framework declares as basic social rights for all Europeans precisely the kinds of social protections that were subject by the Eurogroup to sustained assault in its austerity campaign against Greece and to some extent Spain and Portugal as well. The framework includes the Charter of Fundamental Rights, the range of directives on minimum standards for worker's rights, collective bargaining, and social protection, and the Social Chapter annexed to the Treaty of Maastricht, as well as such ILO Conventions as could be regarded as incorporated into EU or Member State law. Indeed, opposition to this framework has been a hallmark of Euroskeptics on the right, including the Brexit movement.

Although the framework has been put in question by austerity, it remains in legal force and has been used as a shield in various ways by the Tsipras government, perhaps rather late in the day in the reform process. Thus, the government insisted that demands from the Eurozone institutions for reform of important aspects of Greek labor law be stalled until an independent expert group examined possible reforms against European standards of labor protection and made recommendations.[15] With the initiative coming very much from Paris and Athens, there is an active effort to transform the diffuse normative framework of Social Europe into a European Pillar of Social Rights.[16] Of course such initiatives can amount to mere verbiage, or be marginalized by stronger, more brutal forces in the European space. My point is that they can be *one* normative focal point for a common program of action of left governments and parties in Europe. Again, what I seek to question is the notion that, from a progressive point of view, the future of Europe is frozen or paralyzed absent a fundamental overhaul of the basic architecture, the implantation of a plan for democratic utopia in the EU, along the lines long argued for by Habermas.

## Varoufakis and DIEM25; Etienne Balibar

Yannis Varoufakis himself has gone from the champion of Grexit to an advocate for a reformed and renewed EU (and Eurozone) in the name of progressive democratic values. He has given stern lectures to those on the left in the EU who espouse Brexit in response to neoliberalism and austerity as the long-ascendant forces in the EU, warning that they are playing into the hands of reactionary nationalists and populists, and that no real progressive agenda emerges from the proposition of exiting the EU. Varoufakis has found DIEM25, the Democracy in Europe Movement 2025. Adopting some of the Habermas constitutional democratization agenda, and calling for a constitutional assembly of the European people(s) to be elected directly on "transnational tickets," which would refound Europe as a federal democratic polity by 2025, DIEM25's manifesto includes more realistic shorter term actions. These include transparency in existing decision-making institutions immediately (including better control of lobbyists) and concerted action in five areas within a year: public debt, banking, investment, migration, and poverty. This would "Europeanize all five while limiting Brussels' discretionary powers and returning power to national Parliaments, to regional councils, to city halls and to communities."

There is an extremely important point to be discerned in what at first glance is paradoxical in this language. A common progressive agenda for Europe need not mean "more" Europe or more integration, political and social. That would be viewing the agenda through the "ever closer union" lens. Instead, Europeanization can entail providing the common action and solidarity necessary to allow national and subnational communities to protect and rebuild their own institutions for social justice, countering the neoliberal ascendency in EU technocratic decision making. In other words, concerted action should be seen as enabling the effective exercise of sovereignty once again, in light of globalization and new economic, environmental, and technological realities—not as diminishing sovereignty or transferring it to supranational institutions, however democratic they may be made to appear. This idea of recovering sovereignty (of peoples not states) through revitalizing the European project was developed by Emmanuel Macron in his Athens speech in early September 2017. Common interests unite large numbers of citizens across Europe (for example, combating climate change), where the sovereignty of the peoples, the effective exercise of power to achieve one's ends, is enhanced by the ability to act together. Nation-state sovereignty alone is less effective, or may even present a barrier, if interests opposing change have too much of a handle on power in particular Member States. Thus, Macron's proposal of multinational tickets for European Parliament elections to give the opportunity for parties and movements to form representing the interests of large blocs of citizens across the Member States.

Here, I believe, Etienne Balibar is correct to state that "even if Habermas presents himself as fundamentally opposed to the power of finance of which the 'governance' today tends to neutralize the political, his discourse throws a sort of veil of ignorance over the conflict of interests which determines the material constitution of Europe today and which pervades the nations themselves. To retrieve legitimacy for a federal project can't allow dispensing with an alternative social and political economy, which requires organized concerted action."[17]

A little democracy goes a long way, albeit not far enough. Already we see examples of the European Parliament and civil society and progressive governments mobilizing in the EU to block the lock-step relationship between expansion of Brussels' powers, the intensification of neoliberalism, and the aggressive projection of the neoliberal globalization model in the EU's external economic relations. The example of investor-state dispute settlement (ISDS) is a recent one. This regime has, more or less plausibly, been painted as a network of secret or "shadow" courts dominated by a clique of elite arbitrators motivated not by justice but by personal wealth acquisition, a system where multinational corporations unleash blue chip law firms on some of the poorest countries in the world, forcing multimillion-dollar settlements or winning awards that are even larger, sometimes more than an impoverished nation's entire annual budget for health, education, and public security. The fear of such payouts has understandably had a chilling effect on legitimate government regulation in many countries; inconsistently interpreted by arbitrators in different cases, the general norms in investment treaties have been read to go far beyond compensation for takings that aim to extract rents from investors and are likely inefficient, extending to regulatory changes that respond to many valid policy concerns but a negative economic impact on some particular foreign investor.

Many individual EU Member States had signed on to treaties offering ISDS, whether to other member states or to non-EU states. With the Treaty of Lisbon, exclusive EU competence was created over investment policy. But as the EU began to formulate its approach, the civil society movement against ISDS gained strength. In July 2015, in its guidance to the Transatlantic Trade and Investor Partnership (TTIP) negotiators, the European Parliament recommended that TTIP investment disputes be settled by a standing judicial body rather than through conventional methods of investor-state arbitration.[18] More generally, the Parliament made clear that it would not accept any EU agreement on investment that did not safeguard domestic policy interests. Following this, the European Commission undertook an online consultation; the consultation produced an astonishing number of responses—something like 150,000—with a huge number of them indicating hostility to investor-state dispute settlement. In the result, the commission developed a policy of rejecting across the board investor-state arbitration in its trade and investment agreements and adopting, instead, a judicial model (in addition to a range of substantive safeguards of domestic regulatory autonomy). Now much of civil society is skeptical that this represents a genuine shift from neoliberalism as opposed to window dressing or a placebo for a the left. Without resolving that controversy, it is notable that the further activism of Walloon leader Paul Magnette resulted in a further commitment to ensure that the dispute settlement provisions on investment effectively shut down the possibility of global corporations menacing the regulatory autonomy of Member States. What will be the end result? It is unclear, but a major institution of neoliberal globalization was effectively delegitimized through democratic activism in response to Brussels' exercise of competences. Whatever the debates about the adequacy of proposed substitutes, ISDS will never come back to Europe.

I invoke this example not to scrape the bottom of the barrel for good news for the left, but only to indicate that (as Varoufakis and Balibar each in their own way suggest) whatever the prognosis of a democratic utopian agenda for the EU, struggle within the existing institutional framework for progressive values and progressive policies is not simply futile. The left is not, and should not, be reduced to either waiting for the constitutional messiah or jumping on the Euroskeptic bandwagon without an alternative that clearly distinguishes it from the nationalism of the right. (After all, the likes of Marie Le Pen also have their discourse of social protection).

## Enter Emmanuel Macron, Center Stage

Emmanuel Macron is reviled as a globalist and neoliberal by the hard left, the latter now best represented domestically by Jean-Luc Melanchon of *La France Insoumise*. Less noticed is that none other than Yannis Varoufakis berated the hard left for not rallying around Macron as the alternative to the populist xenophobic right. This, in effect, is basically an admission that a left Euroskeptic agenda of destroying the EU cannot in good conscience be pursued because the risk is too high that its ultimate result will be catastrophic for the left: the anti-Europe platform will be captured by the right and facilitate the ascendancy of a xenophobic reactionary or even fascist political agenda. Varoufakis, with the DIEM25, seemed to have assimilated this lesson before Brexit, but Brexit must surely reinforce it.

Also behind Varoufakis's endorsement of Macron was Macron's support for Greece against the German/Eurogroup austerity agenda. In fact, even before his election as French president, Macron had set out a proposal that included the control of the Eurozone by a new parliamentary institution, which would have a parliament, a finance minister, and a budget controlled by the parliament and to which the finance minister would be responsible. In effect, Macron seems to have adopted Piketty's idea for reform of the Eurozone in the wake of austerity. Vulnerable with the upcoming elections in Germany and also due to Brexit depriving Germany of a strong neoliberal ally in Europe (even if the UK is not in the Eurozone itself), Merkel had little choice but not to reject out of hand Macron's proposals.[19]

Macron's globalist, neoliberal reputation (clearly overstated in my view by his opponents on both left and right) should not blind the left to the progressive potential of his initiative. Properly exploited, the innovations in question would allow the Eurozone to be harnessed to progressive social values, with a Parliament making decisions about spending and transfers, not technocrats. But, even beyond this, Macron has made a bold dare. He has proposed that, before the end of 2017, democratic assemblies ("conventions democratiques") be instituted throughout the EU with a view to the reconstruction of Europe.[20] Moreover, Macron claims to have obtained the support of Chancellor Merkel for this initiative. Truly astute, Macron calculated that Merkel could not really afford to be the spoiler of this overture for a democratic refounding of Europe. Macron is fearless, it seems. But how terrified Merkel and Schäuble must be of the loss of control over the outcome that is risked by this kind of open-ended democratic process. I wonder if this is a gambit: Germany can quickly back France in pushing through the Eurozone reforms including a Eurozone parliament (swallowing its austerity ideology to retain power and control at the core of Europe), or it can face the prospect of Macron going to the people and indeed inviting the people(s) elsewhere in Europe to rise up and demand their own democratic conventions! Unlike Habermas's proposals for redesign of the legal and constitutional architecture, Macron envisages the conventions as largely spontaneous and immediate.

If this were not enough, Macron has added yet another item to the policy agenda for the EU that has a significant progressive potential—the harmonization of corporate income tax in Europe.[21] The operation of jurisdictions such as Luxembourg and Ireland as tax havens within the EU has allowed multi-national corporations with major activities and consumer markets in many European countries to avoid their share of social responsibility. This erosion of the tax base for the funding of progressive social programs is not as dramatic and intentionally cruel as austerity, but arguably it has even broader and longer-term negative consequence for left governance in EU Member States. Again, here, Macron has reached out to Merkel and obtained the support of Germany as the beginning point of this initiative. He has, probably correctly, calculated that Germany's desire for power in Europe is more fundamental than the attachment to neoliberal/austerity ideology. Working with Macron, Germany has a chance to retain its power in Europe post-Brexit. Working against Macron, and in the shadow of Europe's shame about the treatment of Greece, Germany is diminished. This risk to Germany is especially real if one takes into account that, in the face of German noncooperation, France always has the Latin Empire option of leading the Latin, or Mediterranean, European nations in opposition to the "German ideology" (to use a phrase of Marx in a different sense). Under previous French administrations, socialist ones, Germany was able to buy relative acquiescence of France to its Eurozone agenda by not making an issue about France exceeding the legal fiscal disciplines of the Eurozone (that is, not making the required budgetary targets for the monetary union). In effect, France was blackmailed out of truly standing up to Germany on austerity and the direction of European monetary union generally. One can look at the Macron government's proposed budget cuts as just another instance of imposing neoliberal discipline, but perhaps it is more astute to regard this initiative as a way of emerging from the German blackmail and gaining a decisive voice on the future of the Eurozone.

## Europe and the Left Need Each Other

A fundamental dilemma for the left in Europe arises from its own discourse that European integration and globalization have served the hollowing out of the progressive state and are in the grip of neoliberal ideology. If this is true, how much progressive change can *any* given left political party credibly promise, if terms of social and economic life are so much set at levels of "governance" largely beyond its control or influence? The attempt at a radical rupture with the EU order, heroic but ultimately likely to result either in chaos or a victory not for progressivism but for nationalism, including its xenophobic regressive variations, has understandably become the platform of only very marginal parties and movements on the left. Indeed, even Yannis Varoufakis, its most brilliant and charismatic advocate, has now set out in another direction. Rupture from the EU would still leave one exposed to globalization; opting out of which seems mythic or delusional, whether suggested by Marie Le Pen or her equivalents on the marginal left.

Although any given left political party or government cannot plausibly say that it can change the terms of social and economic life as they are shaped by the EU, common or concerted action of left parties, movements, and governments in the EU have this potential. As I have attempted to sketch here, both in thinking and in practice, elements in the European left have begun to move beyond the "false necessity" of the Habermas-type position that a deep structural democratic defect simply excludes voices other than neoliberal technocratic ones from any capacity to shape today's Europe, and thus one must advocate for and await a democratic constitutionalist transformation of the EU architecture to realize progressive hopes. Too much ink has been spilled on what the model would actually look like, how it would align with what theory of democracy or legitimacy, as if the frustration of citizens to which the left needs to address itself is at bottom not about un- or underemployment, the erosion of social protections, and so forth, but about the failure of the EU treaties and the governance they produce to align with some theoretical republican model of democratic self-determination. This does not take away from the need to introduce greater democratic accountability into the institutions and greater control of technocratic agents, whose interests and ideological outlook are not necessarily those of the principals—the citizens and their elected representatives. But this, as Varoufakis and others have suggested, can be done simultaneously with pressing a common or concerted progressive policy agenda within the existing legal and institutional structures. Indeed, as Macron's call for "conventions democratiques" in Member States suggests, spontaneous democratizing initiatives with opening up potential can be conducted without constitutional changes to the legal and institutional structures. Macron's proposal is consistent with Kalypso Nicolaidis's "demoicracy" theory of European democracy as *co*-determination by the various peoples, *demoi*, of Europe, of EU values, principles, and policies.[22] Unlike Habermas-type constitutionalist theories that imply the formation of a people that gives itself a constitution, and a representative government with different branches, elevating republicanism to the supranational level, the Nicolaidis conception has the advantage that it can breathe democratic life into the existing architecture by facilitating codetermination among the "demoi." The parliament already represents a kind of agora for such an activity, but so would the simultaneous operation of "conventions democratiques" in the various Member States à la Macron. And, finally, the demoicracy model seems to point to the logic of the formation of common positions among the democratic forces in the different Member States; here, the notion of a common front or concerted agenda of left parties and movements in the various Member States.

But I would make the further point that, at this particular juncture, the left has leverage. The European elites committed to the EU project (apart from the most blind and self-satisfied technocrats of the Juncker variety) see the project in terms of the moral energy it can harness is running on close to empty. Original the authority for the project, if it did not come from the bottom up (obvious), certainly derived from its representation as saying never again to sanguinary militant nationalism in Europe. This legitimacy from the task of overcoming the darkness of Europe's twentieth century of total wars and genocide was already wearing thin when the EU turned out to be incapable of preventing or halting genocide in the Balkans. Conveniently, though, the end of the Cold War also meant the end of history in the Francis Fukuyama sense, that is, in the supposed ideological triumph of some version (in Fukuyama's mind the American) of late twentieth-century capitalism and liberal democracy over the political and economic alternatives. During this period, aligning itself with neoliberal ideas of modernization or streamlining of governance, and turning to incentive-based regulation, privatization, and so forth, was arguably, on balance, legitimatizing rather than delegitimizing for the EU elites. Indeed, at conferences at that time, one often heard laments by globalist neoliberals that the multilateral economic institutions (the GATT and others) were behind at the kind of "deep integration" that was happening in Europe with the harmonization of national laws with a view to efficiency and low-transaction cost movement of the factors of production.

On balance, neoliberalism as a full policy and ideological program is now *de*legitimating. It is a target, and indeed one of the main targets, of populism on the left and the right. Of course, many people respond to it through anxious resignation. Anti-neoliberalism is the creed behind active and lively resistance to everything that is done in Brussels, even if it is not accurate or fair to describe any particular measure or initiative as neoliberal. On the right, the alternatives to the status quo that are proposed are almost entirely anti-EU or entail forms of nationalism, in rhetoric or reality, that are antithetical to any kind of reenergizing of the European project.

In these circumstances, I doubt that the EU elites really have anywhere to go other than to the left to find new energy and idealism for the European project; and they have the enormous task of shifting the left's identification today of that project with the disgrace of the Eurozone's treatment of Greece. It is not surprising, therefore, that the astute Emmanuel Macron has focused his proposals for revitalizing the EU on reforming the Eurozone as an urgent priority. (Hennette et al. [2017], relying on jurisprudence of the ECJ, point out that as long as reforms do not alter the exclusive competences of the EU itself, they are legal without treaty amendment, that is, without "constitutional" change[23]). Germany, as I have suggested, has little choice but to go along; its hegemonic power in Europe has depended on the premise of that power not being directly challenged by France and largely being supported by the UK (the support of which is, of course, now fundamentally compromised by Brexit).

As Chancellor Merkel surely knows, and is shown by the fragmentation of left and right parties in the German opinion polls, her political popularity is not due to any national consensus around her specific program or her party's ideological orientation. It is a reward for her maintaining Germany's hegemonic power in Europe and influence in the world, and wielding it in Germany's perceived immediate national interests. Her career and her political constellation would not, I reckon, withstand a revitalized France under a willful and effective leader aggressively promoting a countervision of Europe in alliance with the left across the continent, or at least Mediterranean or Latin (in spirit) Europe.

In Germany, historically, ideology only lasts as long as it supports German power.[24] If Macron wills it, "austerity" is finished. Hence, carpe diem.

## Notes

1. See Robert Howse, "Kojève's Latin Empire: From 'the End of History' to 'the Epoch of Empires,'" *Policy Review* 126 (August–September 2004): 41–48.
2. Jürgen Habermas, *The Crisis of the European Union: A Response* (Cambridge: Polity Press, 2012).
3. Wolfgang Streeck, *How Will Capitalism End?* (London: Verso Books, 2016).
4. To my mind the best description of what happened and how it unfolded from the economic and political logic of the euro is in Joseph Stiglitz's book *The Euro: How a Common Currency Threatens the Future of Europe* (New York: Norton, 2016), which combines economic rigor with clear-sighted analysis of power politics and interests in Europe and at the plane of globalization as well. As Stiglitz explains, the economic construct upon which "austerity" was based is "internal devaluation." Under this view, if a country's imports exceed exports, such that it is forced to borrow to finance the difference, the standard corrective mechanism of currency devaluation—which is unavailable in a currency union like the euro—can be replaced by austerity policies, whereby the government is discouraged or prevented by fiscal restraints from stimulating the economy and reducing unemployment. High unemployment will drive down wages eventually as workers are desperate to accept even poorly paying jobs. Lower wages will then mean lower prices, and lower prices will make the country's exports competitive to the point where imports and exports are balanced. In other words, adjustment through misery.

    Stiglitz gives a cogent explanation as to why this did not work in the case of Greece and elsewhere in the Eurozone (and why it should not have been expected to work). Growth in exports was disappointing, and decreases in GDP were much larger than predicted. Given the large differences among the economies within the Eurozone, it was likely that they would face different economic shocks at different times. Given that the normal tools of adjusting exchange rates and interest rates were not available within the currency and monetary union, and given that fiscal stimulus was also constrained by the required budgetary targets, to be successful at managing economic crises the Eurozone would have required *social solidarity* among its members: a willingness to share the burden of a crisis in one or several countries through commonly financed investments in afflicted countries and through backing their social safety nets through the adjustment process.

5. Robert Howse, "The Deal on Greek Debt: Political Gamechanger for Europe, Tactical Retreat (Not Surrender) for Tsipras," *Verfassungsblog: On Matters Constitutional* 15 (July 2015), https://verfassungsblog.de/the-deal-on-greek-debt-political-gamechanger -for-europetactical-retreat-not-surrender-by-tsipras/.

6. These observations derive from conversations in a recent visit to Athens, July 2017, after the successful resolution of Greece's negotiations with the creditor institutions.

7. Étienne Balibar, *Europe, crise et fin?* (Paris: Editions Le bord de l'eau, 2016), 36.

8. Alexandre Kojève, "Esquisse d'une doctrine de la politique française" (1945), *La règle du jeu* 1 (1990), trans. Erik De Vries, "Outline of a Doctrine of French Policy," *Policy Review* (2004): 3–40.

9. Giorgio Agamben, "The 'Latin Empire' Should Strike Back," *Liberation* (March 26, 2013), http://www.voxeurop.eu/en/content/article/3593961-latin-empire-should-strike-back.

10. "Wolfgang Streeck: Why Europe Can't Function as It Stands," *Verso Books* (Blog), November 7, 2016, https://www.versobooks.com/blogs/2926-wolfgang-streeck-why -europe-can-t-function-as-it-stands.

11. It should be emphasized that Kojève understood the Latin Empire as, in principle, encompassing the entire Mediterranean basin, including the Islamic countries there.

12. Sarantos Michalopoulos, "Tsipras: Euro-Med Summit Will Unite Europe, Not Divide It," *EURACTIV*, September 9, 2016.

13. Stephanie Hennette, Thomas Piketty, Guillaume Sacriste, and Antoine Vauchez, "*Pour un traite de democratization de l'Europe* (Paris: Seuil, 2017), 7 (author's translation).

14. Joseph H. H. Weiler, "On 'Political Messianism', 'Legitimacy' and the 'Rule of Law,'" *Singapore Journal of Legal Studies* (December 2012): 248–68.

15. See "Recommendations Expert Group for the Review of Greek Labour Market Institutions," September 27, 2016, http://www.ieri.es/wp-content/uploads/2016/10/Final -Report-Greece-September-2016.pdf.

16. Joint Declaration of Ministers, European Social Conference, Paris, March 2, 2016, http:// www.gouvernement.fr/en/european-social-conference-joint-declaration-of-ministers.

17. Balibar, *Europe, crise et fin?*, 218 (author's translation).

18. European Parliament Resolution containing the European Parliament's recommendations to the European Commission on the negotiations for the Transatlantic Trade and Investment Partnership, July 8, 2015 (2014/2228 (INI)).

19. Thomas Wieder, "Angela Merkel soutient Emmanuel Macron dans sa volonté de réformer la zone euro," *Le Monde*, June 21, 2017, http://www.lemonde.fr/europe /article/2017/06/21/angela-merkel-soutient-emmanuel-macron-dans-sa-volonte-de -reformer-la-zone-euro_5148324_3214.html#LDFs2OGpsut3eQVw.99.

20. "Le discours d'Emmanuel Macron au Congres de Versailles," July 3, 2017, http://www .bfmtv.com/politique/texte-le-discours-d-emmanuel-macron-au-congres-de -versailles-1200523.html.

21. See Ivan Illan, "The Irish Jig Is Up," *Equities*, August 11, 2017, https://www.equities.com /news/the-irish-jig-is-up. Macron's initiative seems like a moderate or gradualist version of Piketty's proposal for a European tax on capital. See Thomas Piketty et al., "Our Manifesto for Europe," *The Guardian*, May 2, 2014.

22. Kalypso Nicolaidis, "The Idea of European Demoicracy," in *Philosophical Foundations of European Union Law*, ed. Julie Dickson and Pavlos Eleftheriadis (Oxford: Oxford University Press, 2012), chap. 2.

23. Hennette, Piketty, Sacriste, and Vauchez, "*Pour un traite de democratization de l'Europe*, 13–20.

24. Leo Strauss, "Re-education of Axis Countries Concerning the Jews," *The Review of Politics* 69, no. 4 (Fall 1943): 530–38.

# Bibliography

Agamben, Giorgio. "The 'Latin Empire' Should Strike Back." *Liberation* (March 26, 2013). http://www.voxeurop.eu/en/content/article/3593961-latin-empire-should-strike-back.

Balibar, Étienne. *Europe, crise et fin?* Paris: Editions Le bord de l'eau, 2016.

"Le discours d'Emmanuel Macron au Congres de Versailles." July 3, 2017. http://www.bfmtv .com/politique/texte-le-discours-d-emmanuel-macron-au-congres-de-versailles -1200523.html.

Habermas, Jürgen. *The Crisis of the European Union: A Response.* Cambridge, Mass.: Polity Press, 2012.

Hennette, Stephanie, Thomas Piketty, Guillaume Sacriste, and Antoine Vauchez. *"Pour un traite de democratization de l'Europe.* Paris: Seuil, 2017.

Howse, Robert. "The Deal on Greek Debt: Political Gamechanger for Europe, Tactical Retreat (Not Surrender) for Tsipras." *Verfassungsblog: On Matters Constitutional* 15 (July 2015). https://verfassungsblog.de/the-deal-on-greek-debt-political-gamechanger-for -europetactical-retreat-not-surrender-by-tsipras/.

——. "Kojève's Latin Empire: From 'the End of History' to 'the Epoch of Empires.'" *Policy Review* 126 (August–September 2004): 41–48.

Illan, Ivan. "The Irish Jig Is Up." *Equities.* August 11, 2017. https://www.equities.com/news /the-irish-jig-is-up.

Joint Declaration of Ministers, European Social Conference, Paris. March 2, 2016. http:// www.gouvernement.fr/en/european-social-conference-joint-declaration-of-ministers.

Kojève, Alexandre. *Esquisse d'une doctrine de la politique française* (27.8.1945). Published in *La règle du jeu* 1 (1990). English translation by Erik De Vries, "Outline of a Doctrine of French Policy," *Policy Review* (2004): 3–40.

Michalopoulos, Sarantos. "Tsipras: Euro-Med Summit Will Unite Europe, Not Divide It." *EURACTIV.* September 9, 2016.

Nicolaidis, Kalypso. "The Idea of European Demoicracy." In *Philosophical Foundations of European Union Law*, ed. Julie Dickson and Pavlos Eleftheriadis, chap. 10. Oxford: Oxford University Press, 2012.

Piketty, Thomas, et al. "Our Manifesto for Europe." *The Guardian.* May 2, 2014.

"Recommendations Expert Group for the Review of Greek Labour Market Institutions." September 27, 2016. http://www.ieri.es/wp-content/uploads/2016/10/Final-Report-Greece -September-2016.pdf.

Stiglitz, Joseph. *The Euro: How a Common Currency Threatens the Future of Europe.* New York: Norton, 2016.

Strauss, Leo. "Re-education of Axis Countries Concerning the Jews." *The Review of Politics* 69, no. 4 (Fall 1943): 530–38.

Streeck, Wolfgang. *How Will Capitalism End?* London: Verso Books, 2016.

Weiler, Joseph H. H. "On 'Political Messianism,' 'Legitimacy' and the 'Rule of Law.'" *Singapore Journal of Legal Studies* (December 2012): 248–68.

Wieder, Thomas. "Angela Merkel soutient Emmanuel Macron dans sa volonté de réformer la zone euro." *Le Monde.* June 21, 2017. http://www.lemonde.fr/europe/article/2017/06/21 /angela-merkel-soutient-emmanuel-macron-dans-sa-volonte-de-reformer-la-zone -euro_5148324_3214.html#LDFs2OGpsut3eQVw.99.

"Wolfgang Streeck: Why Europe Can't Function as It Stands." *Verso Books* (Blog). November 7, 2016. https://www.versobooks.com/blogs/2926-wolfgang-streeck-why-europe -can-t-function-as-it-stands.

# 8

# SUBSIDIARITY AND THE CHALLENGE TO THE SOVEREIGN STATE

NADIA URBINATI

Until recently, subsidiarity has been more widely practiced than theorized. Conceived by some as a chapter in global governance and not merely a system for local-level decision making,[1] it has been adopted through the years in numerous countries, most of them democratic.[2] It is listed as a case of federalization (both functional and territorial) within two large categories: the "coming together" and the "holding together" of states.[3] The former is peculiar to a supranational integration of states (for example, the European Union), and the latter is peculiar to the internal decentralization of states (Canada being the most cited example).[4] In this chapter I analyze the paradigm of subsidiarity and its main principles and problems within the European context and present it as a process of social federalization whose success is in and by itself a challenge to the sovereign state form, and particularly to its social functions. The practice of subsidiarity rests on some theoretical assumptions whose ambition is transforming the sovereign state from within.

## Anti-Sovereignism

Subsidiarity has been defined as "the soul of federalism" although its relationship to federation as a project of political unity is ambivalent.[5] It is a paradigm of federalization of social agencies (private persons, communities, corporations, and local administrations of the state) that coordinate their functions in relation to their specific objectives (assisting those who are in need, performing services from schooling to health, and so forth) and generate practices and norms that bind them while consolidating their cooperation. The European Union is an interesting case of how federalization of social functions can strengthen cooperation through time with no need of a federal state. Article 4 of the European Charter of Local Self-Government (signed October 15, 1985) states: "Public responsibilities shall generally be exercised, in preference, by those authorities that are closer to the citizen. Allocation of responsibility to another authority should weigh up the extent and nature of the task and requirements of efficiency and economy."

The EU reveals the ambiguity and complexity of subsidiarity, which expands the role of administration, vindicates the idea that a corporate society can subsist without the need of an overacting state, and cultivates the ambition of making political pluralism the first step toward a much more radical process of legal pluralism.[6] At the same time, its claim for the primacy of lower-level decision-making agencies and "multiple criteria for allocating authority" is primed to unravel the democratic deficit of existing institutions rather than repair it. In addition, it may justify centralized forms of authority in order to contain the process of pluralism.[7] The EU helps us test these conundrums and proves that subsidiarity can be controlled in its radical consequences by being hierarchically subordinated to a system of rights, and that it can foster union with no need of creating a supranational political federation, not to mention a full-fledged democratic polity. Despite being a modern expression of anti-sovereignism, the EU shows that subsidiarity does not reject every kind of government. (What kind of political government the EU is exactly remains the issue of an enormous and still growing literature.)

I argue that to grasp the meaning and implications of today's arguments in favor of subsidiarity we have to think of it as part of a struggle that opposes the pluralist paradigm of social communities against the unitary and bipolar paradigm of individual/state that constitutes political democratic sovereignty.[8] The implications of this project promise to be enormous: "As in the European Union," subsidiarity's strongest supporter writes, "so in international law subsidiarity can be understood to be a conceptual alternative to the comparatively empty and unhelpful idea of state sovereignty.[9] As to its philosophical roots, certainly the myth of a self-governed society that can mediate the general principle of human dignity with the factual conditions in which dignity can be fulfilled is shared by diverse traditions, religious and secular, and intersects various national experiences.[10] Focusing on the European context allows us to disclose subsidiarity's main religious roots, in particular in Reformed Christianity and Catholic Christianity, the protagonists of the early clash of authorities that marked the postmedieval age and the formation of the territorial sovereign states.

Relaunched in 1931 within neo-Thomism as a polemical category against a totalizing state and within a future vision of constitutional democracy that would reshape the political order after WWII, subsidiarity has become a sophisticated chapter in the global phenomenon of governance. Indeed, it enabled the devolution of the welfare state (particularly its social democratic form), the gradual lessening of the power of lawmaking and the expansion of the prerogatives of administration (bureaucracies) and justice (the courts). The European project profited from subsidiarity's aim of deflating politics and led democratic societies throughout their institutional transformation from more deliberative forms to more executive forms.[11] On the Old Continent, Julien Barroche thus writes:

> Subsidiarity has contributed in reorienting our thinking beyond sovereignty as the site and form of the legitimate authorizing power to make decisions to the holding together of the several different functions that compose a collective and articulate themselves in ascending layers of decisions by social actors, within various contexts and on specific issues—this baroque architecture can be given the name of *fédéralisme d'éxecution*.[12]

Today, subsidiarity is praised for several concurrent reasons: for expanding the liberty of society from state interference in the distribution of economic, social, and symbolic resources; for making justice a project of valorization of social diversity and pluralism, not simply adjudication of the rights of individuals; for reducing the role of parliaments and their unavoidable partisan interests and expanding that of courts whose decisions seldom indicate that protecting local "mores" may be a viable strategy for strengthening social harmony in multiethnic and multicultural societies; and finally, for educating feelings of solidarity, responsibility, and charity by encouraging persons' direct participation in performing social tasks.[13] As Carozza wrote, subsidiarity is a "paradoxical principle" that "limits all social bodies (the state included) at the same very time it strengthens and legitimates them. It restrains [state] intervention and yet asks for [state] assistance. It expresses a vision of the role of the superior [state] structures that is both positive and negative and much broader than that which competes to the individual."[14]

Subsidiarity belongs in the genre of federation but is not a form of state federation; its core value is society in relation to which the state should play at most an auxiliary function. Its conflicting relationship with the state form is the factor that bridges subsidiarity's ideological traditions, which are ostensibly opposite, such as liberalism and Catholicism. Thus, claiming the priority of the social and contesting the principle of political sovereignty doesn't make subsidiarity retrieve the myth of a premodern kind of federalism. Subsidiarity did not develop in the age of the disintegration of the medieval order but when the nation-state was already an existing reality. Although its inspiring principles predate the construction of the territorial state and are ideally rooted in the corporate, pluralist, and unequal societies that inhabited the cosmopol-itan-imperial order of the Middle Ages, subsidiarity is truly modern. It was defined and perfected in the golden age of sovereignty, not before. It emerged along with the construction of the nation-state in the model of a constitutional government whose legitimacy sprung directly from the consent of its subjects through suffrage, and whose prerogatives were limited by the declaration of rights. Subsidiarity is as modern as its rival and is tied to it as its negative other.

## The Priority of the Social

Subsidiarity does not denote a political order. It is a relational practice that is parasitical on and presumes the existence of a jurisdictional authority that it wants to contain, not fully overcome. Let us illustrate its structural dynamic in its relationship to social subunits and the state.

The term *subsidiarity* comes from military vocabulary. It was used in the late Roman Empire to denote subsidiary troops (*subsidiarii*), or troops in reserve (of *prima acies*), who did not serve on regular bases and in ordinary times but only in exceptional circumstances or when there was a need for supplementary forces. When used during war, these troops worked as "reinforcements"; in peace time they were used as "reserves." In both cases, they were secondary and acces-sory (in relation to the official ones), and supplementary and complementary (thus useful and actually necessary). In today's practice of subsidiarity, the public seems to play the role of *subsidium* as a troop in reserve in relation to the regular forces, which are the social or local or private or nonstate actors. The norm and the exception follow a new hierarchy of values in which social and local commu-nities come first, and the harmonious integration of their diverse functions is the desired consequence that the state should help to achieve.

Subsidiarity presumes a *vertical* relationship between "superior" and "infe-rior" institutional levels that it regulates in view of achieving an optimal hierar-chical order in which the "inferior" becomes progressively more autonomous and the "superior" retains only the traditional sovereign's function of security and coercion. Verticality intersects with a *horizontal* scheme of integration among the various social actors; this makes subsidiarity a chapter in demo-cratic organization as it presumes self-responsibility and the inclusion of volun-tary actors in performing the decided social tasks (this was also the doctrinal pillar of the European democratic Christian parties post-WWII).[15] Vertical and horizontal relations are obtained by means of two strategies that the state must adopt, one *negative* and one *positive*. Subsidiarity orders the state never to inter-vene in the place of the social groups or communities when the latter can act by themselves and to intervene only when they are incapable of fulfilling their own task.

Self-help and the duty toward the community are the guidelines of *subsidium*, and charity and care are the ethical motivations, Christian in character, from which subsidiarity derives its moral justification. State nonintervention and noninterference are the *sine qua non* conditions for the "inferior" levels to prevent them from being destroyed by the "superior" ones. Hence, the state is to intervene only after verifying the actual capabilities of the subunits and must orient its decision in view of preserving and strengthening them. Subsidiarity's norm and primary goal is the care of the social agents; the state plays an essentially instrumental and auxiliary function.

The valuation of what is "inferior" and what is "superior"—in fact, the implications of the priority of the social—depends on the two subsidiary's normative qualifying criteria of *proximity* (of the agent(s) to given problems or needs and the people bearing them) and *self-responsib*ility (of the agents toward their primary and closer community first).[16] For example, the Catholic argument is that the value that justifies subsidiarity resides in "the good" it protects and promotes—namely, persons' responsibility toward the communities to which they belong, and in particular the life of the ethical communities of the family and the parish—without which persons cannot pursue the good life as the Church commands. When translated into subsidiarity policy, the protection of the family requires the state to provide for family allowances or to supplement inadequate family wages, but it does not endorse policies of job opportunities for women as the social democratic welfare state does. The state is not supposed to ensure "family justice but to increase its [family's] responsibility and independence" from the public. A good social policy should aim not to substitute for the family in its care and educational roles but to make it easy for spouses and parents to perform these duties.[17]

Subsidiarity is not inspired by equal rights and the distribution of equal opportunity, which are actually held responsible for corroding social communities and individual corporate responsibility.[18] Its motivational engine is dignity, which is not identical to equality of individual rights. In the Marshall model of social justice, citizenship rests on the "reconciliation of liberty and equality, . . . egalitarian possibilities of politics in correcting the inequalities produced by the market without decisively disrupting the freedom of the individual." But subsidiarity requires state intervention "only to the extent that the organic and natural order of society is restored by providing relief for poverty or by recreating solidarity—or rather harmony—between various social groups."[19]

The subsidiarity principle of protecting social subunits from state interference lacks normative legitimacy; it is a form of prudential politics for protecting the existing (*status quo*) arrangements of social power within given communities. In its genuine structure, the subsidiarity's paradigm of social federalization can display potentially dramatic (and worrisome) implications if we consider that its plan is that of inducing the state to devolve portions of its political and social functions to subunits. Its ambiguity emerges whenever we consider the standards for legitimate associations and the way disagreements and contestations with the state over the allocation of resources and the fulfillment of social functions are resolved. Subsidiarity's supporters are less worried and believe that by rejecting the bipolar sovereign paradigm of individual/state, subsidiarity is in a better position to reconcile universal values (such as liberty, equality, and rights) with cultural diversity.[20] It would thus seem that its attentiveness to the actual social conditions makes subsidiarity better equipped to govern social pluralism than the sovereign state with its abstract rights because of the former's inherent tendency to accommodate empirical cases and suggest policies that are functional to the preservation of the "inferior" entities. Yet compromising on equal rights in the name of the preservation of social subunits opens the door to legal and moral problems that gravely endanger the state's commitment to rights and the rule of law. Within this context, the EU's corrective has been a crucial step in redirecting subsidiarity toward liberal and democratic constitutionalism. As we shall see, the EU's several treaties make clear that subsidiarity must be subjected to the guarantee of rights that both the Member States and the European court have to ensure.[21] Precisely because of its internal lack of legitimacy, subsidiarity tends to produce an expansion of judicial or quasi-judicial (read bureaucratic) fora.

## Liberty, Equality, and Pluralism

Subsidiarity is essentially a claim of liberty and pluralism, not equality. This makes its relation to liberalism and democracy possible, but ambiguous and problematic. Concerning its relation to liberalism, we have to consider that subsidiarity embodies two readings of liberty that can find a natural home in liberalism and liberal republicanism: liberty as noninterference and liberty as nondomination. They spring from the principle of self-responsibility yet are predicated to social subunits or communities, not to individuals. As we shall see in the following section, subsidiarity is imbued with an anti-individualistic philosophy, and its faithfulness to individual rights is shaky. Nonetheless, it can play a function that economic liberalism would not dislike because the negative liberty of social subunits translates quite naturally into a containment of welfare state and the privatization of many publicly performed functions of assistance and social insurance. It is correct to say that subsidiarity sets the conditions for an alliance between economic liberalism and religious groups (Christian and Catholic in particular) on issues that are connected to the devolution of the state authority's social functions, the expansion of private and social charity, and the reward of corporate philanthropy and compassionate solidarity.[22] Distant as to their founding principles, Christianity and liberalism are close in their unfriendliness to the state and the ambition of politics to claim a superior authority over religion and economic interests (a similarity that Karl Marx had already detected in his *Jewish Question*).

When we move to democracy, we see that because of its preference for diversity rather than unity subsidiarity has been frequently and enthusiastically identified with a quest for more substantive democracy, and for this reason it has attracted supporters in participatory democracy.[23] Its early admirers in the 1980s welcomed subsidiarity as a "democratic constitutionalization of society" that would actualize the promises of extending democracy beyond the state, enhancing decentralization, and strengthening local communities and civil associations over delegation and state institutions.[24] The recognition of subsidiarity by the European Charter of Local Self-Government reinforced that democratic hope: "Local authorities, acting within the limits of the law, are to be able to regulate and manage public affairs under their own responsibility in the interests of the local population."

Yet things are surely more complex. Although subsidiarity may claim faithfulness to democratic principles as it treasures the actors' voluntary engagement and direct responsibility as paramount, subsidiarity does not entail the same kind of equality as political democracy does, which is rigorously individualistic (one head/one vote) and blind to differences (at least when it distributes the basic self-governing power). As mentioned previously, subsidiarity prioritizes the respect for socially diverse actors, the capabilities of the persons involved, and the contextual evaluation of their specific needs, which are never equal. Contrary to democratic citizens, subsidiary's persons are not presumed to be equal in their social powers and responsibility, and their functional differences are assumed as a good to be preserved when they entail individuals' unequal contribution to the functions that communities ask for and reward. In Aristotle's words, we would say that subsidiarity replaces arithmetical equality (which belongs to political democracy) with proportional equality (which belongs to a corporatist notion of society).

The final issue to be analyzed is pluralism, a pillar of subsidiarity that issues from the principles of proximity and self-responsibility. Similar to liberty and equality, subsidiarity's pluralism needs to be qualified. As I said earlier, vertical and horizontal relations define subsidiarity's contribution to social pluralism, in particular to horizontal and vertical pluralism. Horizontal pluralism delineates "the autonomy of the 'life circles' and encourages these 'circles not to neglect their own capacity,'" and vertical pluralism delineates the permission that "different spiritual families" have to follow their own ways of life within their respective groups.[25] The former affirms the priority that subsidiarity ascribes to social units over its members; the latter affirms the disquieting implications that this may have in relation to the principle of the individual's liberty and equal consideration. The relative autonomy of social organizations in the context of a pluralistic society can exist because these organizations are "glued together by a morality that is supposed to provide harmony or solidarity between the various groups" that the state assists and subsidizes.[26] Thus, certain homogeneity internal to groups and between them is assumed and necessary. I return to this issue when analyzing the Catholic contribution to subsidiarity and its ethical conception of the unifying of the good. It is important here to observe that the value of social units' inner harmony and the value of individual liberty are not on the same footing and, moreover, are not easily accommodated with this kind of pluralism. A classical example on liberal pluralism is James Madison's argument in *The Federalist 10* of liberty meeting pluralism insofar as it recognizes the healthy tension between local power and national power. It does not, however, think that the life of the small unit is in itself a desirable condition for individual liberty. If groups are a contribution to liberty, it is because a central political system of institutions and legal rights guarantees that individuals are free to exit from a subunit and choose otherwise. Thus the pluralist offer in the free market of subunits is the condition of liberty, not the individual's identification with one of them. Subsidiarity's primacy of social communities is not in and by itself a guarantee that rights and individual freedom will be protected because pluralism does not descend from the principle of individual freedom. It is predicated on a corporate society, in which the good is to be protected first.

To conclude, subsidiarity's conflicting relationship with the two main constructions of modernity—the state and the individual—explains its tension with, and sometimes even explicit opposition to, the principle of state sovereignty in a constitutional liberal democracy in relation to liberty, equality, and pluralism. The relationship between social subunits (in whose name subsidiarity is claimed) and the persons that belong to them (in whose name basic rights are proclaimed) is the locus to which we should turn our attention if we want to grasp the ambiguities of subsidiarity in relation to rights and their equal enjoyment by individuals. Indeed, because its paradigm overturns the hierarchy of the political order when it claims the primacy of the social, subsidiarity is primed to highlight and exacerbate the tension between subunits and the criterion of generality that the law proclaims in a constitutional democratic state. Social subunits cannot be taken for granted, and when they vindicate allocation of functions and powers, they have to be screened and judged on account of the equal respect they owe to all their members. Thus, unless the state is given a superior authority in determining the boundaries internal to social groups, the latter are not in and by themselves secure enough for the individual.

This is in line with the subsidiarity paradox: either the social subunits regulate their inner relations according to the principles of individual autonomy and equal rights, and in this case they are like all other civil associations or an expression of civil society, or they are corporate communities that in order to protect their autonomy are willing sometimes to compromise with individual rights for reasons of prudence. In the first case, subsidiarity would entail the acceptance of the principles of legal justice at the cost of sacrificing the primacy of the social; in the second case, subsidiarity would entail the *status quo* acceptance of social units as a good to be protected and allow that compromising rights can sometimes help to protect them. This conundrum can hardly be solved from within the paradigm of subsidiarity.

## The Philosophical-Political Context of Subsidiarity

It is by now clear that subsidiarity is a claim of pluralism, yet it is not necessarily a celebration of the individual right to choose to join associations and unite with others to attain common objectives. It does not share completely in the logic of civil society, but it conveys the following ambition: contesting the priority of the sovereign authority and redrawing the relationship between the social and the political. To paraphrase John Rawls, subsidiarity questions the separation between the right and the good and presumes a conception of the ethical life that prioritizes the communal life as the good for the person that can be protected only if issues that belong to it can be governed by it, with limited or no interference by the state. Respect for "traditions" and social "mores" is most of the time the reason that supporters of subsidiarity adduce for liberty as noninterference, a reason that embodies a polemical core against the philosophy that claims the priority of the individual and the principle of equal rights against all external authority, from the state down to social units. Liberal pluralism and subsidiarity's social pluralism are different (a difference that recalls that between liberalism and communitarianism).

The pluralist paradigm has put on several identities, depending on the direction that the contested paradigm of sovereignty took, whether (state) liberalism or (state) socialism or social welfare (state) democracy. As part of its persistent and broad process of sovereign state containment, the pluralist paradigm in which subsidiarity belongs has through the years overlapped with the moderate components of liberalism, socialism, and democratic welfarism. For instance, it overlapped with a stream of liberal thought (in the tradition of Hume and Montesquieu against Rousseau and Kant) that tried to relocate individual rights (and the right to private property in particular) within the architecture of social pluralism and division of powers that aimed at countering centralization and socialist ambitions (von Hayek, Milton Freedman). Moreover, it overlapped with social corporatism, a project of pluralism, harmony, and state containment that belonged also to secular projects outside the Catholic camp, such as non-Marxist socialism (inspired by Fourier and Proudhon), liberal constitutionalism and some federalist branches of republicanism (Sismondi), and socialism (Cole and Laski).[27] These several ideas sought, in their own way, to oppose individualism and the risks of despotism that state absolutism seemed to incubate.[28] In a word, the pluralist paradigm includes several trends of criticism of that rich constellation of social functions that, with the making of the nation-state after the French revolution, liberal governments started planning and managing, at the beginning in order to meet the exigencies of an industrial and market economy that was still in its infancy, and later on, with democratization, in order to create the social conditions for effective political citizenship.[29]

The "divine Montesquieu" was the authoritative bridging author of these various projects, certainly of the liberal and the republican ones, because his theory of moderate government with the containing function played by intermediary social bodies was meant to be a corrective to sovereign state absolutism and its principle of a legally perfect equality of all the subjects (Bodin and Hobbes). Later on, with democratization and the "mad passion" of the equality of social conditions driving an atomistic society of electors, Alexis de Tocqueville would follow in Montesquieu's steps and indicate pluralism of civil associations and state federalism as the two most viable strategies that could moderate popular sovereignty in a time in which (that is, after Rousseau and the French Revolution) the heavy burden of political majorities could build a new oppressive (because consented to) power over a society made weak by its individualistic fragmentation. The rich and multifaceted twentieth-century liberal-republican literature against the totalitarian project and its metamorphoses in mass democracy (Arendt, Maritain, Mounier, Furet and Hayek) completed within the secular camp the plan of neutralizing the political and ethical culture of the enlightenment. Subsidiarity is situated within this complex political-philosophical anti-sovereignism as "*statophobie post-totalitaire*."[30]

We may thus say that subsidiarity is a paradigm of social federalization whose proponents have endorsed it as an alternative to the bipolar paradigm of individual/state governing the modern doctrine of sovereignty in its post–French Revolution experience. To paraphrase Philip Pettit's scheme of the two modern political traditions—one inspired by republicanism as containment of the effects of centralization of state power (liberty as nonarbitrary interference or nondomination) and one inspired by republicanism as the construction of political freedom through the conquest of state power (liberty as self-government of equal citizens or popular sovereignty)—we may say that subsidiarity has evolved as an answer against the latter, yet without necessarily succeeding by itself in promoting the former.

This is in synthesis the philosophical-political context of subsidiarity, as a chapter in the struggle against the modern sovereign both in its claim of holding an absolute power of making laws and in its claim of receiving legitimacy by its very subjects as the outcome of a foundational consent that involved not social communities but the individuals, all of them equally and as equals. As Jean-Jacques Rousseau explained in the closing of his *Social Contract*, for such a sovereign to hold its collective identity through time without resorting to a transcendental binding authority, a new binding force was needed: the civil religion of the republic. Rousseau's injunction can be rendered in the following maxim: the sovereign cannot tolerate polytheism; it can tolerate at the most civil associations within an unquestioned acceptance of the same unitary source of the law (more or less the same was Madison's argument of pluralism within the frame of a federal state). Legal pluralism would thus be a blasphemy. Not by chance, in proposing subsidiarity in his *Quadragesimo Anno* (1931), Pope Pius XI put on trial first and foremost the religion of the state (*statolatria*) as the ultimate source of individualism because it denied all intermediary forms of life within which the abstract individual could achieve an existential and moral substance as a person.

## Auxilium, Subsidium, and the State: Two Models of Social Federalization

Julien Barroche proposes that we see subsidiarity as the merging of the religious and the secular reactions against the "phobie de l'État."[31] As such, subsidiarity has a long and a short history. The long history brings us back to the Renaissance and the emergence of territorial states, which eroded the two cosmopolitan and federal institutions that since the fall of the Western Roman Empire had unified the continent, the Church of Rome and the Empire; in this sense, subsidiarity is part of the various alternatives to state formation.[32] The short history brings us to the nineteenth-century construction of the nation-state.

In its religious genesis, subsidiarity developed along two major trajectories, one within Protestant Christianity and one within Catholic Christianity. They never ceased to inspire Europeans through the centuries and, in particular, in the decades between the nation-state formation in the nineteenth century and the reaction against its totalitarian aberration in the interwar period.

Johannes Althusius belonged to a Christian reformed version of federalism, which was inspired by John Calvin's movement of religious and civic communities' self-determination and a federative republicanism that radiated from Geneva.[33] The renaissance of Althusius's corporate thought in Germany after the French Revolution coincided with two crucial historical conjunctures: the process of German unification (and the then unfulfilled project of political federalism as envisaged among others by Otto von Gierke, who rediscovered Althusius's work) and the reaction against totalitarianism, which stirred legal and political scholars to recover Althusius's principle of liberty based on the primacy and autonomy of society over the central authority of the state (Martin Buber and Carl Friedrich).[34]

Althusius's *Politica* (1603) is one of the early statements of a model of territorial unification based on *plural foedera* of communities as the basic *subsidia* for the spiritual and material needs of the individuals. Rather than a covenant among single persons, political authority was, according to Althusius, a covenant among communities and associations, the result of which was a government whose primary function was that of *coordinating* and *securing the symbiosis* of the several kinds of corporate bodies composing society. The government had to provide for "execution and administration of (1) public duties and (2) private occupations necessary and useful to social life and symbiosis."[35] The goal of the political larger unit was harmony and peace, which was achieved by protecting subunits' *status quo* and thus by practicing liberty and toleration. The principle of utility justified liberty as noninterference and toleration by the magistrates with the choices of the communities and the individuals; the magistrates regulated their decisions by "common consent," and the free exchange of services was "performed by one citizen for another."[36] "This is done according to the manner, order, and procedure that was agreed upon and established among the members and citizens. And such communication of things is rightly called the sinews of the city."[37] The *Politica* did not provide for a general criterion of intervention in the case social units lacked normative legitimacy: "what should the central authorities do if one or more provinces are able but unwilling to act so as to secure the requisite objectives?"[38] To Althusius, the "harmonious exercise of social life" and cooperation among subgroups was the goal and was the primary good that the very subunits would fulfill by themselves in a climate absent of state constraints and toleration.

This radical pluralism could open two scenarios: on one hand, a robust autonomy of the social units, and on the other, the possibility of discretion in decision making by the magistrates in their attempt to preserve the federative unit. Through Althusius we can detect the major problem mentioned in the beginning: subsidiarity's lack of a central source of an authoritative legitimacy principle that can guide judgments and decisions in the case of disagreement between social units and between them and the federative magistrates.

Within the tradition of Thomism, Catholic theology would propose a solution to the problem of radical pluralism by providing for a standard of legitimacy that was meant to inspire and rule both the communities and the persons belonging to them. The Catholic solution was found in the unanimous adhesion to a substantive good, which was a single one, dictated by God's will through the natural law down to the other legal orders, civil and moral. The meaning of the good was detected and imposed by the magisterial authority of the Church on all subjects, individual and collective. Subsidiarity could thus have a centralized face and actually produce or justify a centralized authority with the power of determining and imposing objectives that the member units did not choose or want but had to endure and follow. If harmony was the good, the way it was achieved became secondary—on some occasions subsidiarity could be a strategy for imposing the goal of the whole over and above its parts. According to some contemporary critics of the EU, the centralizing vice contaminates fatally all kinds of subsidiarity (including its secular version), which can be thus a clever process of centralization, because "instead of providing a method to balance between Member State and Community interests, [it] assumes the Community goals, privileges their achievement absolutely, and simply asks who should be the one to do the implementing work."[39]

The EU's subsidiarity originally came from Catholicism rather than Protestantism. It is a historical fact that its template was the encyclical *Quadragesimo Anno*, which allowed the German syntagma *Subsidiarität* to deliver the Latin word to European languages in conjunction with the German redactions of the Pontifical document. The diffusion of this concept in the post-/anti-totalitarian context of Europe's democracy reconstruction was mediated by the Germano-Catholic tradition of corporatism and social solidarity.[40]

The Catholic project of social federalization took place within a political and juridical context that was already occupied by the modern state and the liberal culture of rights and the market, organized, that is to say, within the bipolar paradigm of citizen/state. It achieved its first doctrinal imprimatur in Pope Leo XIII's *Rerum Novarum* (1891), was rigorously explicated in Pope Pius XI's *Quadragesimo Anno* (1931), and after WWII reappeared in Vatican Council documents, in particular *Mater et Magistra* (1961).

Subsidiarity marked a turning point as it inaugurated a new Church strategy, which closed the book on frontal hostility to and the refusal of the nation-state (see, for instance, *The Syllabus of Errors*, 1864) in favor of a reconquering of the liberal society. Leo XIII coordinated the social doctrine of the Church, which, situated in a revived Thomism, held that the conditions for the compromise with modernity included a corporatist conception of society and a rejection of the contractarian and egalitarian justification of political authority. Social corporatism defined the conditions for reestablishing a dogmatic link between authority and hierarchy in modern times. The Catholic fascination with fascism after WWI was the child of their common condemnation of both the liberal state and socialism, individualism and a class-based conception of society. Therefore, the totalitarian experience in the intrawar period marked a crucial turning point in the Catholic social doctrine.

Pope Pius XI's *Quadragsimo Anno* (a celebration of the *Rerum Novarum*'s fortieth birthday) disqualified both fascism and communism as totalitarian aberrations springing from the myth of the state, which became the major target. *Statolatria* (the worshiping of the state) was incubated in the modern doctrine of sovereignty: Pius XI's alternative against it was subsidiarity, not simply the separation of state and society as with liberalism. Much more radically, subsidiarity projected a new conception of self-management of society that aimed at restoring dignity to the person through the reaffirmation of the principles of responsibility and charity. A corporate society could not provide for an answer to the vices of modernity (individualism and socialism) *if* the state did not renounce its primacy and accept a role merely as a coordinating commander in presiding and protecting persons' ethical and religious life.

Advancing an argument that Cold War liberals would resume in the 1970s against the democratic welfare state (the *Trilateral Committee*), the *Quadragesimo* held the totalitarian state responsible of weakening the authority of the state as it compelled the latter to become the agent of too many and too demanding tasks: the state "has been overwhelmed and crushed by almost infinite tasks and duties" (QA n. 78). Thus, to restore authority to state institutions would require debunking the state-totalizing vocation and making society responsible for its needs through the direct participation of the persons and their communities, private or corporate agents. Self-caring according to the principle of proximity resulted in a radical restructuring of the entire collective edifice, from the state to civil society.

Within the plan of restricting the role of the state, the 1931 encyclical defined the idea of subsidiarity as a logical consequence of a vision of justice that pivoted on individual responsibility, not state redistribution (QA n. 80). From this conception of justice, the definition of subsidiarity came:

> The supreme authority of the State ought, therefore, to let subordinate groups handle matters and concerns of lesser importance, which would otherwise dissipate its efforts greatly. Thereby the State will more freely, powerfully, and effectively do all those things that belong to it alone because it alone can do them: directing, watching, urging, restraining, as occasion requires and necessarily demands. Therefore, those in power should be sure than the more perfectly a graduated order is kept among the various associations, in observance of the principle of "subsidiary function." The stronger social authority and effectiveness will be the happier and more prosperous the condition of the State. (QA n. 80)

The Catholic strategy of reconquering the liberal society achieved two additional goals: it redescribed society not in liberal language or as the home of individual rights (as "civil" society) but in terms of an organic ethical life or as a federation of communities; and it made room for economic liberalism, which became a precious ally of subsidiarity against state intervention in social relations. *Quadragesimo* declared that social groups and interests had to be able "to cooperate amicably," and, in addition, that their cooperation would rearrange the whole society according to principles that were neither liberal nor social-ist: "guilds" and unified interests (common to workers and masters) "in the whole Industry or Profession" were depicted by Pius XI as the right associations that could make society central yet also a place of harmony, not conflict (QA n. 85). "Not "hostile classes" but "harmonious cooperation," not "enmity and strife" but integration of forces and aims. The Catholic corporate social theory reinterpreted the main categories of modernity and assessed quite an extra-ordinary score: emancipating corporatism from the state-centered doctrine (Fascist totalitarianism) and making it compliant with a market economy and economic liberalism, thus becoming a valid alternative to the social democratic models of aggregation and redistribution after WWII.

Concluding this quick overview of the Catholic contribution to subsidiarity, some clarification is needed to bring us back to the issue of the overlap of the concepts of pluralism and association with liberalism. Although liberalism and Catholicism have a common enemy (the sovereign state form), the way they conceptualize pluralism and association is different. Concerning the former, the kind of pluralism that Catholic subsidiarity has proclaimed since 1891 is not internal to a liberal perspective because it is not the outcome of the indi-vidual freedom of choice in view of satisfying preferences or achieving some specific aims. Pluralism in Catholic corporatism was not part of an individu-alistic philosophy (Locke's conception of individual rights was the main target of neo-Thomism); it was engrafted not in consent and the principle of indi-vidual freedom but in the person's duties toward the community: the family *in primis*, and then the communal life of neighbors, the voluntary cooperation and charitable mutuality among workers and industrialists, and agrarians and peasants. As for association, the community to which Catholic subsidiarity referred as the substance of pluralism was not reducible to an interest-based form of agreement among interest bearers as with unionism, for instance, or other instrumental associations in civil society. Community entailed a denial of voluntary agreement, the basic condition of the liberal paradigm of asso-ciation. The Catholic notion of the community figures as a form of ethical life in which the person chooses only partially: for instance, the family is a natural association yet not in the sense in which Locke would have it or as a voluntary union among two persons who autonomously choose to unite and eventually separate. In Thomism, the family is a natural community insofar as it is not based on individual agreement but on a sacrament of the Church, a binding command to actuate God's will that coincides with the good of the persons. Family is a domain of duties, not rights. More profoundly than all other social communities, family is a place of harmony and love (caritas) within which the person can pursue sainthood or salvations and form their social sentiments.

The renaissance of Thomism after WWII testified to Catholicism's hege-monic project of redirecting the discourse of human rights by situating it within an anti-contractarian perspective so as to, on one hand, cure the discourse of rights of the malaise of individualism, and on the other, cure the malaise of the political theology of immanentism (legitimacy by consent) and restore the monoarchic authority of the Church in setting limits on rights and liberty and redefining social justice.[41] The image of a struggle between "integral humanism" and "totalitarian humanism" (expressions that are rooted in Catholic philosophy thanks to Jacques Maritain and that have been recently refurbished by Charles Taylor[42]) permeates and is somehow complementary to the otherwise complex and multifaceted Catholic antiliberal project, which after WWII Democratic Christian Parties took onto themselves to actualize.[43] Subsidiarity's moderation of the prerogative of the sovereign state would play a crucial role in the process of European integration, two tasks that lived in symbiosis through the years (as it is claimed also by EU's founding fathers, the large majority of whom were Catholic, including Alcide De Gasperi, Konrad Adenauer, and Robert Schumann).[44]

## Refederalizing European Societies

The social federalization that an ancient cosmopolitan institution such as the Catholic Church fostered in the course of its confrontation with the sovereign state resonates with its renaissance in contemporary Europe, which is the home of a new form of cosmopolitan federalization that includes social and local communities and the several stages of bureaucratic governance for the management of many of the functions that the nation-state had performed for several decades. As Barroche writes, subsidiarity became the name of a political strategy of European unification that was meant to favor governance over government and management over politics yet without denying democracy, which acquired the meaning of a social system as Tocqueville had envisaged—a bottom-up project of integration relying on the voluntary cooperation of social actors and local administrations, from the communes up to the regions, the Member States to the Union.[45] It was in fact politics that subsidiarity contained, not the democratic ideal of voluntary participation, and it was the lawmaking institutions of the state it wanted to diminish, not the state's administrative, judicial, and coercive functions. Subsidiarity became through the years the name of an alternative to parliamentary democracy, with its politicization of public and social issues and its resistance against sacrificing national constituency's interests to the prerogatives of a regulatory community.[46]

The European strategy of subsidiarity succeeded in deflating the burden of political federalism (as a state-based project) while deepening administrative integration (as a governance project), which meant de facto bringing subsidiarity back to its original Catholic spirit: expanding the power of social and territorial communities, not in order to disintegrate society in its micro-components (radical pluralism) but in order to strengthen its union through a complex and hierarchical system of indirect responsibilities and mutual conveniences. From the point of view of doctrine, secular or European subsidiarity reconfigured Catholicism's original task of making society capable of governing itself. In this sense, it is not an exaggeration to interpret the EU as the major project coming from the antitotalitarian as anti-Enlightenment revision of politics that began in the interwar period. That a Catholic politician actively engaged in Catholic unionism, Jacques Delors, became a key figure in the EU politics of subsidiary confirms and actually completes this picture. To Delors we owe the switch in both the conception and the vocabulary of the EU's social project from social democratic to social Christian.[47]

In the history of the EU, subsidiarity marched together with the building of several layers of administrative authorities ("multilevel governance") that comprised local and regional autonomy according to the principles of proximity and self-responsibility.[48] The steps in the process of subsidiary integration have been consistently defined from the Charter of local and regional governance (1985) to the Regional Conference (1991). Finally, the Treaty of The Union (Maastricht) declares subsidiarity and proportionality to be the two principles that rule the EU competences and intervention and that put in action proximity and self-responsibility (article 5). Without being and becoming a political federation, the EU federalized itself in its functions—and only subsidiarity could make that possible. Thus we may legitimately say that subsidiary is the engine that moves and directs the EU.

The EU equipped itself to solve the problems existing in the two forms of Christian subsidiarity we have revisited, radical pluralism and a pluralism tamed by a unitary and central command: on one hand, the good of subunits came first, and on the other, the good of subunits was engrafted *within* a common notion of the good that unified the whole in a top-down process of command. The latter scheme offered a viable indication for a revisionist interpretation of the sovereignty of the Member States: the jurisdictional problem needed to be settled before the conception of subsidiarity—the standards and objectives of the social order were given in relation to which subsidiary was implemented. As we read in Article 4 of the European Treaty: "The Member States shall facilitate the achievement of the Union's tasks and refrain from any measure which could jeopardize the attainment of the Union's objectives."

The EU common notion of the good was redefined in terms of human rights. In the treaty, the fundamental rights and principles of subsidiarity are treated separately with a clear indication that the former are not and cannot be an object of bargaining. In effect, subsidiarity is justified insofar as local and associational units can better meet human rights' requirements than can a centralized state sovereignty. Somehow these two sets of principles—universal and local—have been conceived so as to neutralize the risks that federalization embodies: that of centralization (which subsidiarity may provoke if central authorities have to determine the objectives and impose them against subunits' preferences or interests if needed) and that of fragmentation (when the lack of a method for balancing between the Union and the local interests translates into an unbalanced power of the local goals over the communal ones). From the human rights point of view, fragmentation is an even greater risk than centralization because communities entail unequal powers within and in relations among each other: "This is a reason why many hold that a principle of subsidiarity must be supplemented with human rights protection against the subunit authorities."[49] The European Convention on Human Rights is supposed to do exactly that.

In a socially federalized Europe without a federal state, the condition for equal rights protection is delegated to the Court, which acquires a prominent role, higher than political institutions, and whose legitimacy springs from the declaration of rights in the several treaties that have being sealing the European Union since the Treaty of Rome (1957) and from each national constitution. Subsidiarity is thus acknowledged as the strategy that can only allow the sovereign states to amend their territorial limitation in applying human rights and to work for accommodation that is primed to "justify the necessity of international cooperation, assistance, and intervention": "The doctrine of the 'margin-of-appreciation', first developed by the European Court of Human Rights (ECHR), is the most notable example."[50]

Based on premises that are at once universalistic and particularistic (inspired by a notion of the person that transcends the citizen status and is attentive to her concrete life conditions), the European politics of subsidiarity generated a cascade phenomenon and penetrated all Member States in a top-down process of juridical and administrative adaptation. After Maastricht, national parliaments became the "official guardians of the acceptance of the principle of subsidiarity."[51] In Italy, for instance, the insertion of subsidiarity (both vertical and horizontal) in law administration in 1997 achieved constitutional recognition with the important reform of the Constitution (Title V) in 2000, which redesigned the powers and prerogatives of central State, Regions, Provinces, and Municipalities. That reform was welcomed as an example of a kind of social reformism that would amend the universalistic ambitions of the welfare state with a strategy of succour attentive to the specific needs (managed preferably by private secular and religious organizations) with the public playing the role of checking the outputs and assessing the criteria of functionality. In Italy, the debate on subsidiarity brought to the fore a bipartisan spirit, a consensus that transcended ideological differences between right and left and between secular and religious positions; it registered a molecular transformation of the whole society following several years of EU subsidiarity. In Ernesto Laclau's vocabulary, I would say that subsidiarity is the "equivalence" that unifies a plurality of anti-sovereign claims that are, individually taken, different and even antagonistic, such as the philosophy of individualism that inspires economic liberalism and the philosophy of social corporatism that inspires Catholicism. It is the ideology that, after the demise of traditional political ideologies, has come to dominate the public and political arena and paved the way for a doctrinaire justification of the interchangeability of the public and the private, in fact a modification of the meaning of citizenship.

Subsidiarity is thus more than a practice. It is an organic conception of society and government that proves capable of projecting a new meaning of citizenship, one that is not connected to the authorizing individual subject—the citizen as the depository of the basic legitimating power through her or his right to suffrage—but to a package of functions and rights that persons acquire when entertaining a direct relationship with the administration. This *administrative citizenship* applies to all persons who are in contact with public administrations, from the municipal up to the Member States and to the EU, for the most diverse reasons, and asks for administrative simplification, clarity of rules and procedures, and vindicates the right to know the reasons decisions have been made. Subsidiarity has achieved the goal it was supposed to achieve since it was first proposed by the Church in 1931: eroding from within the bipolar paradigm of individual citizen/state that has sustained modern democratic citizenship since the French Revolution.

## Notes

1. David Held, *Democracy and the Global Order: From the Modern State to the Cosmopolitan Governance* (Stanford, Calif.: Stanford University Press, 1995); Michelle Evans and Augusto Zimmermann, eds., *Global Perspectives on Subsidiarity* (Rotterdam: Springer Netherlands, 2014); Markus Jachtenfuchs and Nico Krisch, "Subsidiarity in Global Governance," *Law and Contemporary Problems* 79, no. 2 (2016): 1–26.
2. Among the exception is the case of South African *apartheid*, which consisted of separations into "homelands" that were justified with the argument of subsidiarity as "sovereignty in one's social circle." Patrick Baskwell, "Kuyper and Apartheid: A Revisiting," *HTS Theological Studies/Teologiese Studies* 62, no. 4 (2006): 1269–90.
3. Andreas Follesdal and Victor M. Muñis-Fraticelli, "The Principle of Subsidiarity as a Constitutional Principle in the EU and Canada," *Les ateliers de l'éthique/The Ethics Forum* 10, no. 2 (2015): 89–90, http://id.erudit.org/iderudit/1035329ar.
4. The U.S. literature on subsidiarity focuses mostly on the comparison to United States federalism. George Bermann, "Taking Subsidiarity Seriously: Federalism in the European Community and the United States," *Columbia Law Review* 94 (1994): 331–456; and Gerald L. Neuman, "Subsidiarity, Harmonization, and Their Values: Convergence and Divergence in Europe and the United States," *Columbia Journal of European Law* 2, no. 3 (1996): 573–582. Yet subsidiarity is widely practiced in many federal states from Brazil, Australia, and Germany to Switzerland, which endorsed it explicitly in its

constitution in 1999, one year before Italy, a unitary state whose society federalized through subsidiarity.

5. Jenna Bednar, "Subsidiarity and Robustness. Building the Adaptive Efficiency of Federal Systems." In *Federalism and Subsidiarity. NOMOS LV*, ed. James E. Fleming and Jacob T. Levy (New York: New York University Press, 2014), 231.

6. Victor M. Muniz-Fraticelli, *The Structure of Pluralism* (Oxford: Oxford University Press, 2014), Introduction and chap. 3; Jean L. Cohen, "The Politics and Risks of the New Legal Pluralism in the Domain of Intimacy." *International Journal of Constitutional Law* 10 (2012): 381.

7. Jachtenfuchs and Krisch, "Subsidiarity in Global Governance," 6; Andreas Follesdal, "Survey Article: Subsidiarity," *Journal of Political Philosophy* 6, no. 2 (1998): 190–218.

8. Sabino Cassese, "L'arena pubblica. Nuovi paradigmi per lo Stato," *Rivista trimestrale di diritto pubblico*, no. 3 (2001): 602.

9. Paolo G. Carozza, "Subsidiarity as a Structural Principle of International Human Rights Law," 2003, 40, http://scholarship.law.nd.edu/law_faculty_scholarship/564.

10. Follesdal, "Survey Article: Subsidiarity."

11. Pierre Rosanvallon, *Le Bon Gouvernement* (Paris: Seuil, 2015).

12. Julien Barroche, *État, libéralisme et christianisme. Critique de la subsidairité européenne* (Paris: Dalloz, 2012), 566.

13. Bermann, "Taking Subsidiarity Seriously."

14. Paolo G. Carozza, "Sussidiarietà e diritti fondamentali: un contributo europeo al diritto internazionale?," in *Esiste ancora la comunità transatlantica?*, ed. Vittorio E. Parsi, Serena Giusti, and Andrea Locatelli (Milano: Vita e Pensiero, 2006), 234.

15. Barroche, *État, libéralisme et christianisme*, 31.

16. To these criteria, some scholars add "efficiency" as it entails that "powers should be allocated to the individual or institution that can best exercise them."Michelle Evans, "The Principle of Subsidiarity as a Social and Political Principle in Catholic Social Teaching," *Solidarity: The Journal of Catholic Social Though and Secular Ethics* 3, no. 1 (2013): 54.

17. Christian Fogarty, *Christian Democracy in Western Europe, 1820–1957* (Notre Dame, Ind.: University of Notre Dame Press, 1957), 50; Mario Nuzzo, ed., *Il principio di sussidiarietà nel diritto privato: I—Potere di autoregolamentazione e sistema delle fonti. Autonomia privata e diritto di famiglia. Attività negoziale e composizione alternativa delle liti* (Torino: Giappicchelli Editore, 2015), Part II.

18. Kees van Kersbergen, *Social Capitalism: A study of Christian Democracy and the Welfare State* (London: Routledge, 1995), chap. 8.

19. Samuel Moyn, *Christian Human Rights (Intellectual History of the Modern Age)* (Philadelphia: University of Pennsylvania Press, 2015), 180.

20. Paolo G. Carozza, "Sussidiarietà e diritti fondamentali: un contributo europeo al diritto internazionale?," in *Esiste ancora la comunità transatlantica?*, ed. Vittorio E. Parsi, Serena Giusti, and Andrea Locatelli (Milano: Vita e Pensiero, 2006), 233–54.

21. Jachtenfuchs and Krisch, "Subsidiarity in Global Governance," 8.

22. Chantal Millon-Delson, *L'État subsidiaire. Ingérence et non-ingérence de l'État: le principle de subsidiarité aux fondements de l'histoire européenne* (Paris: PUF, 1992), 8.

23. Bednar, "Subsidiarity and Robustness."

24. Giovanni Cotturri, *La sinistra degli indipendenti* e *La società della politica istituzionale*, in *Militanza senza appartenenza. Schede su movimenti e associazioni della politica diffusa*, n. 6 of *Materiali e atti, Democrazia e diritto* 1 (January–February 1986).

25. Kersbergen, *Social Capitalism*, 182–83.

26. Kersbergen, *Social Capitalism*, 182.

27. Barroche, *État, libéralisme et christianisme*, part 2; Michele Battini, *Social Socialism of Fools: Capitalism and Modern Anti-Semitism* (New York: Columbia University Press, 2015.

28. Carozza, "Subsidiarity as a Structural Principle," 40–41; Steven G. Calabresi and Lucy D. Bickford, "Federalism and Subsidiarity: Perspectives from U.S. Constitutional Law," in *Federalism and Subsidiarity. Nomos LV*, ed. James E. Fleming and Jacob Levy (New York: New York University Press, 2014), 126.

29. Millon-Delson, *L'État subsidiaire*, 46.

30. Julien Barroche, "L'État contre lui-même," in *Raisons politiques* 49, no. 1 (2013): 154.

31. Barroche, *État, libéralisme et christianisme*, 35.

32. Jean L. Cohen, *Globalization and Sovereignty: Rethinking Legality, Legitimacy, and Constitutionalism* (Cambridge: Cambridge University Press, 2012), chap. 2.

33. Quentin Skinner, *The Foundations of Modern Political Thought*, 2 vols. (Cambridge: Cambridge University Press, 1978), vol. 1, part 3.

34. Yet no less relevant for the history of Europe was the French trajectory of Althusius, with Proudhon as his most revered earls. Barroche, *État, libéralisme et christianisme*, 416–20.

35. Johannes Althusius, *Politica. An Abridged Translation of Politics Methodically Set Forth and Illustrated with Sacred and Profane Examples*, ed. and trans. with an Introduction by Frederick S. Carney (Indianapolis, Ind.: Liberty Fund, 1995 [1603]), section 28.

36. Althusius, *Politica*, sections 28 and 29.

37. Althusius, *Politica*, section 17.

38. Follesdal and Muñis-Fraticelli, "The Principle of Subsidiarity," 93).

39. Gareth Davies, "Subsidiarity: The Wrong Idea, in the Wrong Place, at the Wrong Time," *Common Market Law Review* 43, no. 1 (2006): 67.

40. Barroche, *État, libéralisme et christianisme*, 24–29; Carozza, "Subsidiarity as a Structural Principle," 38.

41. Baskwell, "Kuyper and Apartheid"; Daniel Menozzi, *Chiesa e diritti umani. Legge naturale e modernità politica dalla Rivoluzione francese ai nostri giorni* (Bologna: Il Mulino, 2012); Carlo Invernizzi Accetti, *Relativism and Religion: Why Democratic Societies Do Not Need Moral Absolutes* (New York: Columbia University Press, 2015).

42. Charles Taylor, *A Secular Age* (Cambridge, Mass.: Harvard University Press, 2007), chap. 8.

43. Jacques Maritain, *Scholasticism and Politics* (Garden City, N.Y.: Image Books, 1960).

44. Jan-Werner Müller, *Contesting Democracy: Political Ideas in Twentieth-Century Europe* (New Haven, Conn.: Yale University Press, 2012).

45. Barroche, *État, libéralisme et christianisme*. 32–33.

46. As Mario Monti, then prime minister of the Italian government, declared in 2012, "if the executives [of European states] allowed their parliaments to contain their decision-making power, without keeping a free space of maneuver [spazio di manovra] . . . disintegration of Europe would be more probable than integration" (interview in *Der Spiegel*, August 5, 2012).

47. On his "gauche communautaire" based on Proudhon, Illich, and Sangnier (the thinkers who dethroned Marx and the Jacobin culture of state intervention in the Left), see the excellent analysis of Barroche, *État, libéralisme et christianisme*, 379–99.

48. Simona Piattoni and Justus Schönlau, *Shaping EU Policy from Below: EU Democracy and the Committee of the Regions* (Northampton, Mass.: Edward Elgar, 2015), 32–54.

49. Follesdal and Muñis-Fraticelli, "The Principle of Subsidiarity," 102.

50. Jachtenfuchs and Krisch, "Subsidiarity in Global Governance," 8.
51. Julien Barroche, "La subsidiarité: quelle contribution à la construction européenne?," *Revue Projet* 340 (2014): 70–72.

# Bibliography

Althusius, Johannes. *Politica. An Abridged Translation of Politics Methodically Set Forth and Illustrated with Sacred and Profane Examples.* Edited and translated with an Introduction by Frederick S. Carney. Indianapolis, Ind.: Liberty Fund, 1995 [1603].

Barroche, Julien. "La subsidiarité: quelle contribution à la construction européenne?" *Revue Projet* 340 (2014): 66–75.

——. "L'État contre lui-même," in *Raisons politiques* 49, no. 1 (2013): 153–71.

——. *État, libéralisme et christianisme. Critique de la subsidairité européenne.* Paris: Dalloz, 2012.

Baskwell, Patrick. "Kuyper and Apartheid: A Revisiting." *HTS Theological Studies/Teologiese Studies* 62, no. 4 (2006): 1269–90.

Battini, Michele. *Social Socialism of Fools: Capitalism and Modern Anti-Semitism.* New York: Columbia University Press, 2015.

Bednar, Jenna. "Subsidiarity and Robustness. Building the Adaptive Efficiency of Federal Systems." In *Federalism and Subsidiarity. NOMOS LV*, ed. James E. Fleming and Jacob T. Levy, 231–57. New York: New York University Press, 2014.

Bermann, George. "Taking Subsidiarity Seriously: Federalism in the European Community and the United States." *Columbia Law Review* 94 (1994): 331–456.

Calabresi, Steven G., and Lucy D. Bickford. "Federalism and Subsidiarity: Perspectives from U.S. Constitutional Law." In *Federalism and Subsidiarity. Nomos LV*, ed. James E. Fleming and Jacob Levy, 123–89. New York: New York University Press, 2014.

Carozza, Paolo G. "Sussidiarietà e diritti fondamentali: un contributo europeo al diritto internazionale?" In *Esiste ancora la comunità transatlantica?*, ed. Vittorio E. Parsi, Serena Giusti, and Andrea Locatelli, 233–54. Milano: Vita e Pensiero, 2006.

——. "Subsidiarity as a Structural Principle of International Human Rights Law," 2003, http://scholarship.law.nd.edu/law_faculty_scholarship/564.

Cassese, Sabino. "L'arena pubblica. Nuovi paradigmi per lo Stato." In *Rivista trimestrale di diritto pubblico*, no. 3 (2001): 601–50.

Cohen, Jean L. "Pluralism, Group Rights and Corporate Religion." *Netherlands Journal of Legal Philosophy* 44, no. 3 (2015): 264–78.

——. *Globalization and Sovereignty: Rethinking Legality, Legitimacy, and Constitutionalism.* Cambridge: Cambridge University Press, 2012.

——. "The Politics and Risks of the New Legal Pluralism in the Domain of Intimacy." *International Journal of Constitutional Law* 10 (2012): 380–397.

Cotturri, Giovanni. *La sinistra degli indipendenti* e *La società della politica istituzionale.* In *Militanza senza appartenenza. Schede su movimenti e associazioni della politica diffusa,* n. 6 of *Materiali e atti. Democrazia e diritto* 1 (January–February 1986).

Davies, Gareth. "Subsidiarity: The Wrong Idea, in the Wrong Place, at the Wrong Time." *Common Market Law Review* 43, no. 1 (2006): 63–84.

Evans, Michelle. "The Principle of Subsidiarity as a Social and Political Principle in Catholic Social Teaching." *Solidarity: The Journal of Catholic Social Though and Secular Ethics* 3, no. 1 (2013): 44–60.

Evans, Michelle, and Augusto Zimmermann, eds. *Global Perspectives on Subsidiarity.* Rotterdam: Springer Netherlands, 2014.

Fogarty, Christian. *Christian Democracy in Western Europe, 1820–1957.* Notre Dame, Ind.: University of Notre Dame Press, 1957.

Follesdal, Andreas. "Survey Article: Subsidiarity." *Journal of Political Philosophy* 6, no. 2 (1998): 190–218.

Follesdal, Andreas, and Victor M. Muñis-Fraticelli. "The Principle of Subsidiarity as a Constitutional Principle in the EU and Canada." *Les ateliers de l'éthique/The Ethics Forum* 10, no. 2 (2015): 89–106. http://id.erudit.org/iderudit/1035329ar

Held, David. *Democracy and the Global Order: From the Modern State to the Cosmopolitan Governance.* Stanford, Calif.: Stanford University Press, 1995.

Invernizzi Accetti, Carlo. *Relativism and Religion: Why Democratic Societies Do Not Need Moral Absolutes.* New York: Columbia University Press, 2015.

Jachtenfuchs, Markus, and Nico Krisch. "Subsidiarity in Global Governance." *Law and Contemporary Problems* 79, no. 2 (2016): 1–26.

Kersbergen, Kees van. *Social Capitalism: A study of Christian Democracy and the Welfare State.* London: Routledge, 1995.

Maritain, Jacques. *Scholasticism and Politics.* Garden City, N.Y.: Image Books, 1960.

Menozzi, Daniele. *Chiesa e diritti umani. Legge naturale e modernità politica dalla Rivoluzione francese ai nostri giorni.* Bologna: Il Mulino, 2012.

Millon-Delson, Chantal. *L'État subsidiaire. Ingérence et non-ingérence de l'État: le principle de subsidiarité aux fondements de l'histoire européenne.* Paris: PUF, 1992.

Moyn, Samuel. *Christian Human Rights (Intellectual History of the Modern Age).* Philadelphia: University of Pennsylvania Press, 2015.

Müller, Jan-Werner. *Contesting Democracy: Political Ideas in Twentieth-Century Europe.* New Haven, Conn.: Yale University Press, 2012.

Muniz-Fraticelli, Victor M. *The Structure of Pluralism.* Oxford: Oxford University Press, 2014.

Neuman Gerald L. "Subsidiarity, Harmonization, and Their Values: Convergence and Divergence in Europe and the United States." *Columbia Journal of European Law* 2, no. 3 (1996): 573–582.

Nuzzo, Mario. ed. *Il principio di sussidiarietà nel diritto privato: I—Potere di autoregolamentazione e sistema delle fonti. Autonomia privata e diritto di famiglia. Attività negoziale e composizione alternativa delle liti.* Torino: Giappicchelli Editore, 2015.

Piattoni, Simona, and Justus Schönlau. *Shaping EU Policy from Below: EU Democracy and the Committee of the Regions.* Northampton, Mass.: Edward Elgar, 2015.

*Quadragesimo Anno. Encyclical of Pope Pius XII on Reconstruction of The Social Order.* 1931. http://w2.vatican.va/content/pius-xi/en/encyclicals/documents/hf_p-xi_enc_19310515 _quadragesimo-anno.html.

Rosanvallon, Pierre. *Le Bon Gouvernement.* Paris: Seuil, 2015.

Skinner, Quentin. *The Foundations of Modern Political Thought.* 2 vols. Cambridge: Cambridge University Press, 1978.

Taylor, Charles. *A Secular Age.* Cambridge, Mass.: Harvard University Press, 2007.

# PART III

---

# STATUS GROUP LEGAL PLURALISM

# 9

# INDIAN SECULARISM AND ITS CHALLENGES

## CHRISTOPHE JAFFRELOT

Secularism is often defined in terms of its worldly aspect in reference to its etymology: *saeculum* in Latin refers to those who live in the world, as opposed to those who pursue an otherworldly quest, thus giving rise to the distinction between secular and regular clergy.[1] But there are several other ways to construe the relationship between religion and politics in the world. Scholars who have mostly studied secularism in the West suggest three alternative criteria: (1) a state claiming to adhere to secular principles guarantees and protects the freedom of conscience, expression, and worship of citizens who hold religious beliefs;[2] (2) religions and religious communities are all equal;[3] and (3) the state remains neutral in religious matters, which rules out the existence of a state religion or any official faith.

After India's independence in 1947, secularism became so well established there that the adjective "secular" was finally enshrined in the preamble to the Constitution in 1976. But India has developed its own version of secularism.[4] The Indianization of this "ism" coined by the West and transplanted via colonization first occurred by partially discarding the third pillar of the previous definition: neutrality. The state does not acknowledge any official religion, but it does not refrain from regulating religious practices, whether it comes to banning animal sacrifice or having temples open to untouchables.[5] This transgression of the standard definition of secularism was of little consequence—even the West has considerable trouble complying with it[6]—as long as the other two criteria were observed to the letter, and in India's own particular way. But this practice has gradually begun to suffer since the 1980s, leading to the now wide-spread idea that Indian secularism is in crisis.

## A Fine Invention

Freedom of conscience, speech, and worship was written into the Constitution of 1950 through a number of articles having convergent effects. Article 15 forbids discrimination on religious grounds (among others); Article 16 applies this rule to recruitment in the civil service; Article 29 applies this rule to admission to a public school or on receiving state aid, and especially, Article 25 states:

> Subject to public order, morality and health . . . all persons are equally entitled to freedom of conscience and the right freely to profess, practise and propagate religion.

In addition to these individual rights are collective rights that confirm the principle of equality mentioned in the three-point definition of secularism: the Indian state not only recognizes no official religion, bans religious instruction from public schools and protects citizens from having to pay religious taxes, but it also gives each religion equal consideration. Articles 26 and 30 thus stipulate:

> Subject to public order, morality and health, every religion religious denomination or any section thereof shall have the right: a) to establish and maintain institutions for religious and charitable purposes; b) to manage its own affairs in matters of religion;[7] c) to own and acquire movable and immovable property; d) to administer such property in accordance with law. All minorities, whether based on religion or language, shall have the right to establish and administer educational institutions of their choice.

In awarding aid to educational institutions, the state must in no way discriminate against those administered by a religious or linguistic minority. It is worth noting that the importance given to collective rights by Indian secularism is one of its trademarks, as is its correlative respect for the role of religions in the public space.[8]

It may be objected that the Indian Union does not entirely respect the principle of equality given that Article 30 does not pertain to religious communities but only to minorities. This substantial objection deserves to be qualified, however. The Benares Hindu University, for instance, was granted similar rights to the Aligarh Muslim University, particularly with regard to the teaching of religion. On the other hand, the government was accused of partiality in the 1950s and 1960s when it reformed only Hindu personal law, recognizing sharia and the personal law of other minorities as sources of private law.

Aside from this violation of the principle of equality, which would prove to have serious consequences,[9] India fulfills the essential criteria of a secular polity, and Taylor outlines it as follows: (1) all individuals must be free to exercise their religion; (2) there must be equality among all religions—whether majority or minority—in the public sphere;[10] and (3) "all spiritual families must be heard."[11]

This definition, which complements the previous one, is perfectly applicable to the Indian configuration, particularly because it entails an important conclusion: secularism does not imply the secularization of the society in which it occurs—all the less so as it is based on state recognition of religions. Whereas French *laïcité* involves a clear separation between public and religious spaces, Indian secularism, far from excluding religion from the public sphere, officially recognizes all faiths.[12] It is located at the crossroads of individual citizenship—freedom of conscience being recognized—and multicultural communitarianism generally associated with the Anglo-Saxons.

The main craftsman of Indian secularism, Jawaharlal Nehru, was the primary spokesperson for this "ism," which is more complex than it may at first appear. He, for instance, wrote in 1961:

> We talk about a secular state in India. It is perhaps not very easy even to find a good word in Hindi for "secular." Some people think it means something opposed to religion. That obviously is not correct. What it means is that it is a state which honours all faiths equally and gives them equal opportunities.[13]

Sarvepalli Radhakrishnan, president of India when Nehru was prime minister, expressed Nehru's vision in these eloquent terms:

> When India is said to be a secular state, it does not mean that we as a people reject the reality of an unseen spirit or the relevance of religions to life or that we exalt irreligion. It does not mean that secularism itself becomes a positive religion or that the state assumes divine prerogatives. Though faith in the supreme spirit is the basic principle of the Indian tradition, our state will not identify itself with or be controlled by any particular religion.[14]

The specificity of Indian secularism transpires clearly in these quoted passages. Far from being a-, ir-, or even antireligious, this principle is on the contrary perfectly compatible with society's lack of secularization; Indian society can virtually be said to have need of it, its primary purpose being to enable several religions to live together with respect for diversity. Rajeev Bhargava, who believes that "secularism is compatible with the view that the complete secularization of society is neither possible nor desirable,"[15] offers a definition of Indian secularism that is nourished by Nehru's practice in the 1950s and 1960s:

a) secularism is fully compatible with, indeed even dictates, a defence of differentiated citizenship and the rights of religious groups; and b) the secularity of the state does not necessitate strict intervention, non-interference or equidistance but rather any or all of these, as the case may be.[16]

These principles explain certain features of Indian secularism that might otherwise seem anomalous. Recognizing the importance of the religious phenomenon in the public space, the state intervenes successively, and even simultaneously, in favor of religious communities. It thus recognizes sharia and other personal laws as sources of law (whereas the Hindu equivalent was reformed), and the Indian government subsidizes pilgrimages. Since 1993, Indian citizens' pilgrimage to Mecca has been partly state-funded. Every year, the Haj Committee, which mainly comes under the Ministry of Foreign Affairs, decides on the number of pilgrims it will subsidize (125,000 in 2011).[17] In 2009 (the last year for which figures are available), the state provided approximately seven billion rupees to pilgrims according to an answer from ministers in charge of the issue to Hindu nationalist representatives who had put the question to them.[18] Hindu nationalists, in fact, had criticized this practice, which they believed contravened Indian secularism. They brought the matter before the courts, but the Supreme Court upheld it in 2008, arguing that the state subsidized other pilgrimages,[19] including for Sikhs (to Pakistan) and Hindus (especially the one to Amarnath Cave in Jammu and Kashmir). The state also subsidizes major religious celebrations such as the Hindu Kumbha Mela. The one in 2001 in Allahabad cost 1.2 billion rupees.[20]

Indian secularism thus allows—even implies—the presence of religions in the public sphere where the state treats them equally without committing itself to any form of equidistance, freedom of conscience, expression, and worship being individual as much as collective rights, as is evident in the state recognition of denominational schools. This is probably, at least in theory, the cleverest acclimation of an "ism" developed in the West that nevertheless has a number of affinities with the local situation.

This configuration, which some who remain trapped in the European model may find baroque, is the product of a long history. Its immediate antecedent can be found in the words and deeds of Gandhi. The Mahatma—who can certainly be held responsible for the overabundant introduction of Hindu symbols in the political register[21]—advocated the recognition of religious communities in the public space and their cohabitation as early as 1919 during the Movement for the Caliphate in which he joined forces with Muslim leaders.[22] Subsequently, he continually made the Congress Party into a "parliament" in which all denominations were represented.[23] Starting with his very first (and only!) book published in 1909, *Hind Swaraj*, he promoted a conception of the Indian nation that ruled out identifying the nation with any religion:

> If the Hindus believe that India should be peopled only by Hindu, then they are living in dreamland. The Hindus, the Mahomedans, the Parsis and the Christians who have made India their country are fellow countrymen, and they will have to live in unity, if only for their own interest. In no part of the world are one nationality and one religion synonymous terms; nor has it ever been so in India.[24]

Beyond Mahatma Gandhi's contribution, going further back in time, state policy in India clearly tended to avoid taking on a theocratic form. The British to a large extent refrained from interfering in the religious practices of the inhabitants of the Raj, and they institutionalized the diversity of the personal laws of all the religious communities.[25] When some of these were reformed, it was at the behest of leaders of the communities themselves.[26] The British Empire thus laid the foundations for religious multiculturalism, which in turn laid the groundwork for Indian secularism.

Its most direct predecessor, the Mughal Empire (sixteenth–eighteenth century), if not under Aurangzeb's rule, then at least under Akbar's and most of the other Grand Mughals and even the kings of the Sultanate of Delhi (thirteenth–seventeenth century), practiced religious tolerance. To say they were "secularists" would be an anachronism, as they had imperative religious duties to fulfill—Islamic piety, for instance, required them to build monumental mosques—but only the most zealous of them tackled places of worship of other religions, which in general were respected in the public sphere. Islam moreover only held a small place in the state apparatus, in which several communities other than the Muslims participated.

These comments also pertain to the reign of Ashoka. Although he worked for the glory of Buddhism with the fervor of a new convert, this emperor also advocated for the coexistence of religions and their mutual respect. This ancient heritage gave credence to the idea of elective affinities between Indian civilization and the (Western) idea of secularism.[27]

The Weberian notion of elective affinities should not, however, lead to a culturalist reasoning. This is one of the weaknesses of Donald Smith's otherwise pioneer attempt at interpreting Indian secularism.[28] Smith explains that Hinduism fosters secularism because it is "extremely tolerant," virtually lacking "any ecclesiastic organization," and dissociates temporal and spiritual power by virtue of the division of tasks by the caste system, which moreover is, according to Smith, the only real damper on secularism due to its strict orthopraxy.[29]

Yet the Hindu nationalists were the first to dispute Indian secularism, to such a point that Nehru viewed them as his main enemies.[30] For the members of the Hindu Mahasabha (the Great Hindu Assembly) and the Rashtriya Swayamsevak Sangh (RSS—National Volunteer Association), the Muslims and the Christians, if they wanted to remain in India, had to confine their faith to the private sphere.[31] Under the thrust of this political force that finally came to power in 1998, freedom of conscience, expression, and worship, as well as equality among religions, were gradually defeated, *de facto*, if not *de jure*. None of the clauses of the constitution that supported the secularist nature of the regime has been challenged, but the state has increasingly been identified with the majority community and with rising discrimination toward minorities.

## The Demolition of Indian Secularism—a Legal Perspective

This evolution can be surmised from a number of indicators, such as the increasing difficulty Muslims encounter on the job and housing markets, as well as the violence they are subjected to by police forces that are often biased toward the majority community.[32] I focus here on court decisions that have been handed down over the past fifteen years or so that constitute a major factor of what today is call the "crisis of Indian secularism."[33]

The Supreme Court judgment regarding the religious connotations of certain election speeches in the 1990s revealed a reorientation that some partisans of Nehru's brand of secularism labeled a dangerous drift. Section 123 of the Representation of the People Act of 1951 forbids politicians from campaigning on religious themes, and in the past the courts have penalized those who departed from this rule. In their rallies or in campaign manifestos, three Hindu nationalist candidates, including the chief minister of the Maharashtra government, Manohar Joshi, a leader of Shiv Sena (an extremist Hindu nationalist party), went so far as to pose as champion of the Ayodhya movement (see below) and stated that if their party won the elections, "the first Hindu state [would] be established in Maharashtra." Opponents took the matter to the High Court of Maharashtra, which invalidated their election. But on appeal, the Supreme Court cleared them December 11, 1995, sufficing to say: "In our opinion, a mere statement that the first Hindu State will be established in Maharashtra is by itself not an appeal for votes on the ground of religion, but the expression at best of such a hope."[34] Beyond that, the Chief Justice, in his opinion, established an equation between Hinduism and Hindutva (Hindu nationalist ideology) and stated that they merely described the typical Indian "way of life":

> The words "Hinduism" or "Hindutva" are not necessarily to be understood and construed narrowly, confined only to the strict Hindu religious practices

unrelated to the culture and ethos of the People of India depicting the way of life of the Indian people. Unless the context of a speech indicates a contrary meaning or use, in the abstract, these terms are indicative more of a way of life of the Indian people and are not confined merely to describe persons practicing the Hindu religion as a faith.[35]

This approach runs counter to Indian secularism in two respects.[36] First, the parallel established by the Supreme Court between "Hinduism" and "Hindutva" amounts to expunging the strong ideological connotations of the second term, a word introduced into India's political vocabulary by Vinayak D. Savarkar, the father of Hindu nationalism, in 1923 to distinguish his ethno-religious, exclusive, and sectarian version of nationalism from Gandhi's. Second, making Hinduism (and all the more Hindutva) out to be the Indian way of life means that none of the minorities can claim a status similar to that of the majority. In fact, the Court in this case endorsed a definition of nationality and citizenship that the Hindu nationalists had been championing for decades.

The evolution in the jurisprudence of Indian courts in fact indicates an alteration of their conception of Indian identity. The Ayodhya affair illustrates this trend better than any other. After the 1992 demolition of Babri Masjid, a sixteenth-century mosque located in Ayodhya on a site claimed by the Hindu nationalists as the birthplace of the god Ram (Ramjanmabhoomi), it took the Commission of Inquiry in charge of assigning responsibility for the event seventeen years to hand in its report. In fact, it was not submitted to parliament until November 2009, and only after it had been leaked to the press. The document, drafted by a sole member of the commission, Justice Liberhan, a former Supreme Court justice, held the leaders of the Hindu nationalist movement responsible for the act in no uncertain terms.[37] To date, however, no trial has been scheduled on the judiciary agenda.

But at the same time, the courts examined complaints from Muslims and Hindus who laid claim to the site on which the Hindus had built a small temple amid the ruins to house statues of Ram and his wife Sita just after having demolished the mosque. The Allahabad High Court had handed down a highly controversial judgment in 2010. The three justices in charge of the case were divided. One of them referred to Hindu mythology to recommend that the site be handed over entirely to the majority community. The other two judges, a Hindu and a Muslim, wrote a majority opinion based on the principle that the mosque had been built on Ram's (Ramjanmabhoomi). However, no archeological evidence has ever been submitted to substantiate this claim, and for good reason: it is a belief founded on mythological tales.

The court in Allahabad thus went against established Supreme Court jurisprudence. In December 1992, Narasimha Rao's government had petitioned

the Supreme Court to know "if a Hindu temple or any other religious structure existed prior to the construction of the Ramjanmabhoomi-Babri Masjid,
including the premises of the inner and outer courtyards of the structure."
After pondering the issue for two years, the Court finally replied that the question was "superfluous and pointless." The judges thus finally admitted they
were not equipped to decide on matters of belief. Sixteen years later, however,
lower-ranking judges felt that they were in a position to settle the issue. This
prompted a remark from the great Indian lawyer, Rajeev Dhawan, congratulat-
ing them for their "theological" expertise.

The two Allahabad justices deduced from these premises not that it was
appropriate to rebuild the demolished mosque as many Muslim organizations
were asking but to grant the Hindu contesting parties the portion of the land
that was found under the central dome of the mosque—an area that they held
to be the holiest of holy places of the temple once built, according to them, on
the Ramjanmabhoomi. Furthermore, the magistrates only awarded the Muslims one-third of the land, not enough on which to rebuild a mosque, and
awarded the other two-thirds to the two Hindu parties, the Nirmohi Akhara
and the Vishva Hindu Parishad, respectively.[38]

All three litigants appealed the verdict before the Supreme Court, which in
May 2011 deemed the verdict handed down by the Uttar Pradesh regional court
"strange," simply in virtue of the fact that it recommended a course of action
that none of the parties had asked for: partition of the land.[39] The Court was
careful not to opine as to the existence of a temple preexisting the mosque or
the notion of Ramjanmabhomi. But the fact that the Allahabad court used it as
a basis for its verdict reflects a change in mind-set in legal circles.

This evolution is also evident in comments made by observers who had
previously demonstrated greater neutrality. Pratap Mehta thus welcomed the
fact that the Muslim magistrate seemed to "recognise the existence of temple
ruins at the location" whereas the most scholarly archeologists questioned it.
Even worse, Mehta was delighted that the justices had finally admitted that
"facts about the faith [were] relevant to this dispute."[40] Although this remark
was entirely in line with the spirit of Indian secularism, what was less so was the
fact of taking the religious convictions of the Hindus more into account than
those of the Muslims for whom Mehta showed no consideration. Ashis Nandy
invited the same criticism in an editorial in which he lambasted the "secular
fanatics" who rejected the Allahabad judges' verdict because according to him
they could not accept the importance of religious sentiment in Indian society,
whereas he himself made space for Hindu sentiments but said virtually nothing
about those of the Muslims. He thus recommended building beside a mosque
a Hindu temple of reasonable size, without saying any more about the mosque
to be rebuilt on the ruins of the sixteenth-century monument demolished on a
Sunday, December 6, 1992.[41]

Whereas the Allahabad court justices showed community bias, those of the Supreme Court restored the balance in the Ayodhya affair and overturned the Allahabad High Court verdict. The same cannot be said of the judgment concerning Dara Singh. This man, a member of the Bajrang Dal, a Hindu nationalist paramilitary group, first came to public attention in Orissa by carrying out hard-line offensives in favor of sacred cows and against Christian conversions. In 1998, he had intercepted a cattle truck taking cows to the slaughterhouse and beat the driver's assistant—a Muslim—to death. The following year, accompanied by a gang, he murdered a Catholic priest in September 1999 and tortured and then killed a Muslim merchant in November. In January of the same year, he had set fire to the vehicle of a missionary, Graham Staines, burning him alive with two of his children. After a manhunt that lasted several years, the police arrested him, and in 2003 the local courts sentenced him to life in prison for the first two crimes and to capital punishment for the third. He filed an appeal with the High Court of Orissa, and in May 2005 death sentence was commuted to life imprisonment on the grounds that there was no proof of Dara Singh's direct involvement. The other side filed an appeal with the Supreme Court, whose verdict warrants a detailed analysis.

The Court upheld the decision of the Orissa High Court by virtue not only of the lack of strong evidence and the fact that the death sentence should be resorted to only in "the rarest of rare cases," but also on the basis of a surprising interpretation of Indian secularism:

> Though Graham Staines and his two minor sons were burnt to death while they were sleeping inside a station wagon at Manoharpur, the intention was to teach a lesson to Graham Staines about his religious activities, namely, converting poor tribals to Christianity. Our concept of secularism is that the State will have no religion. The State shall treat all religions and religious groups equally and with equal respect without in any manner interfering with their individual right of religion, faith and worship. . . . It is undisputed that there is no justification for interfering in someone's belief by way of 'use of force', provocation, conversion, incitement or upon a flawed premise that one religion is better than the other.[42]

This judgment sparked strong reactions among minorities and organizations defending secularism because it challenged the legality of conversion to another religion—even legitimized the murder of missionaries such as Staines. In reaction—a unique occurrence in the annals of Indian law—the disputed sentences were deleted from the judgment retroactively.[43] That move did nothing to alter the impression given by the judges that the Supreme Court was quicker to defend the Hindu majority than minorities, as prohibiting religious conversions has long been part of the Hindu nationalist agenda.[44]

## Antisecular Politics: The Hinduisation of India's Public Space

The erosion of secularism in India can first be explained by the action of Hindu nationalist political entrepreneurs who aimed to turn the majority community into a vote bank. They have been working toward this explicitly at least since 1979, a year in which the head of the RSS, Balasaheb Deoras, stated:

> Politicians think only of the next election and personal gains for themselves. Hindus must now awaken themselves to such an extent that even from the elections point of view the politicians will have to respect the Hindu sentiments and change their policies accordingly. . . . Once Hindus get united, the government would start caring for them also.[45]

The launching of the Ayodhya movement should be understood in light of this speech. It was a strategy arising from what Sudipta Kaviraj calls "Hindu majoritarism,"[46] a phenomenon in flagrant contradiction with secularism given that it is based on the promotion of a dominant group at the expense of minorities and religious freedom. This process paradoxically is indissociable from the regime's democratic nature. Shiv Visvanathan writes in this regard, on a rather provocative but appropriate note: "Electoral majorities get tired of the persistence of minorities. In fact, when minorities thrive, majorities often feel paranoid."[47]

If such remarks may seem cynical, they have been corroborated by a number of Indian statistics. In this country, communal riots, which claim their first victims among minorities, often precede electoral consultations, such as the Hindu nationalist forces seeking to gain an edge from an electorate is suddenly more polarized by the violence.[48] When elections take place after a wave of rioting, the map of Bharatiya Janata Party (BJP) victories generally coincides with the geography of Hindu/Muslim riots.

The stigmatization of Islam and Christianity have contributed to the rise to power of the BJP and the electoral success of Narendra Modi, whose government has affected India's secularism more than ever before. Even if the legal framework has remained virtually intact, the dominant discourse has taken an ethno-religious turn, with state dignitaries affirming their country's Hindu identity. Usually more moderate, External Affairs Minister Sushma Swaraj came out in favor of declaring the Bhagavad Gita (the jewel of the Mahabharata epic) the "national scripture."[49]

The culture minister, Mahesh Sharma, has made it his specialty to utter provocations more or less directed explicitly at minorities. On relabeling a street in Delhi named after Aurangzeb—the Mughal emperor despised by Hindu nationalists—he declared that the man whose patronymic henceforth designates this thoroughfare, the former president Abdul Kalam, "despite being a Muslim, was a nationalist and humanist."[50]

But Christians also have been victims of a new sort of propaganda. Thus Mother Teresa, a heretofore unanimously admired figure, was the target of bitter criticism the very year she was canonized. One of the most aggressive BJP MPs, Yogi Adityanath—the high priest of a monastery/temple in North India—accused her posthumously of wanting to Christianize all of India.[51] The RSS chief, usually very discreet, followed suit, repeating those accusations almost word for word, obliging the archbishop of Kolkata to ask for an apology—in vain.

Western Uttar Pradesh, among the areas most affected by such battles of words, has been the target of state propaganda in the truest sense. In 2013, local BJP leaders had already been involved in the Muzaffarnagar incidents, where clashes degenerated into riots leaving fifty-five dead (not counting the children who did not survive in the camps where villagers run out of their homes had taken shelter). Hukum Singh, a local elected BJP representative, was accused at the time of spreading false rumors that triggered anti-Muslim attacks. In 2016, he claimed that 346 Hindu families in his district, Kairana, with a high Muslim population, had been forced to leave their homes due to Muslim intimidation. He saw it as a "Kashmir in the making," alluding to the Hindu exodus from Srinagar valley under separatist pressure. BJP leader Amit Shah, Narendra Modi's lieutenant since the party came to power in Gujarat in the early 2000s, exploited the feeling of vulnerability the episode had created among the Hindus. The National Human Rights Commission (an official body whose composition was entirely reorganized by the BJP government) lent credence to these assertions. Finally, investigations carried out by a number of journalists and documentary filmmakers showed that among the victims of persecutions, some had been dead for a long time, long since moved away, or were even still living in their homes! Claims of a mass exodus were part of a disinformation operation that has had lasting impact despite published evidence to the contrary.[52]

In addition to words, the Hindu nationalist movement has used mobilization campaigns more or less directly targeting minorities, spearheaded by veritable militias. Since the 1980s, the RSS has formed vigilante groups to enforce what it defines as Hindu traditions. The best known of these is the Bajrang Dal, which mostly targets "deviant" artists, thus forcing a world-renowned painter, M. F. Husain, into exile in 2006.[53]

Since 2014, not a month has gone by in India without a campaign being kicked off throughout the country touting one Hindu nationalist theme or another. In the wake of the 2014 elections, Muslims were accused of seducing young Hindu women to marry them and convert them in a so-called love-jihad. To resist their evil deeds, self-defense groups have been formed and posters to warn youngsters have cropped up all over—some of them showing the actress Kareena Kapoor with her face half-covered by a black headscarf (which she never wears) because she married a Muslim.

This campaign was followed by another one, called *ghar vapsi* or "homecoming," which aimed to (re)convert Muslims and Christians as a reaction to Muslim and Christian proselytism. Subsequently, in the spring of 2016, all Indians were compelled to salute the country by shouting "Bharat Mata ki Jai!" or "Hail to Mother India!" an expression typical of the Hindu national repertoire, which represents India in the guise of a goddess or a sacred cow. Muslim organizations protested that it was not part of their tradition. The RSS chief, Mohan Bhagwat, then declared, "We want the whole world to chant Bharat Mata ki Jai."[54] A Maharashtra assembly member who refused to do so was suspended, and a student in the vicinity of Delhi was beaten up for the same reason.

Many of these campaigns have gained momentum and then declined in quick succession, but one that has remained very alive practically since the 2014 elections is the movement in defense of cows. It, of course, draws on the laws passed in Maharashtra and in Haryana, but all the other states except Kerala and West Bengal had already passed similar legislation. These laws and the atmosphere created by the speech and campaigns mentioned previously have been conducive to the development of militias determined to take the law into their own hands. So-called Gau Rakshak groups have formed throughout India within a new movement called Gau Raksha Dal (GRD—Cow Protection Party).

In Maharashtra and in Haryana the state outsourced implementation of the beef ban to these militias. The Mumbai government created a new civil service position, Honorary Animal Welfare Officer, in each district. All of the applicants for these posts whose files have been made public were *gau rakshaks* from various militias already in the habit of intercepting "traffickers" (which they were not before the law was passed) and burning their cargos.[55] In Haryana, the *gau rakshaks* do not have equally official status, but their cooperation with the police has been witnessed de facto by a number of investigative reporters. Thus Ishan Marvel, in *The Caravan*, a monthly magazine known for its journalistic inquiries, recounts how he managed to be accepted into a GRD group patrolling the highway linking Chandigarh and Delhi. Armed with field hockey sticks, *gau rakshaks* inspect trucks likely to be transporting cows. They generally belong to Hindu nationalist organizations that until 2015 were operating illegally. One of them pointed out the difference introduced by the new beef ban law: "Before the BJP brought in the new law against cow-slaughter, the vehicles were returned to the owners. So we used to get angry and burn the trucks. Now, we don't have to. The vehicles become government property. So we just hand them over to the police."[56] In Haryana, the GRD boasts five thousand activists, and ten other Indian provinces (all of them in the north and west) now have branches of the organization. Other nationalist movements, such as the Hindu Mahasabha, have formed their own cow protection militias and have been found guilty of beating Muslims who transported cows even when they were not taking them to the slaughterhouse but instead to the cattle market.[57]

The case that raised the most concern, however, was the lynching of a Muslim from Dadri (Uttar Pradesh), killed by "cow vigilantes" who suspected him of storing beef in his refrigerator. The investigation proved that the meat was mutton. Other cases include the savage hanging of two Muslims who were driving buffaloes to market in Jharkhand,[58] the rape of Muslim women accused of eating beef,[59] and several racketeering incidents in which the police closed their eyes to the butchers' activities in exchange for payoffs.

Muslims are the *gau rakshaks'* primary victims, but some Dalits also are subjected to their wrath, such as those once known as "untouchables," several castes of tanners and shoemakers who traditionally carve up animal carcasses. Some were beaten and dragged to the police station by *gau rakshaks* in Una (Gujarat) for performing this task in July 2016. The video of the humiliating treatment to which they were subjected was circulated on social media.

After months of silence and afraid of losing the support of Dalits[60]— 15 percent of the Indian population, about 20 percent of whom voted for the BJP in 2014—Narendra Modi finally claimed in early August 2016 that many *gau rakshaks* were not really cow protectors.[61] On August 20, 2016, GRD president Satish Kumar was arrested on three charges: "rioting, extortion, and unnatural sex" (following accusations of sodomy made against him). But the RSS chief, Mohan Bhagwat, used the opportunity of his big annual speech made at the yearly Dusshera Rally in the fall to praise the *gau rakshaks.*[62]

In India, Hindus are gradually becoming more equal than other citizens, a process that can be analyzed in terms of majoriatianism: the Hindu majority becomes hegemonic, whereas the Muslims and, to some extent, Christians are being sidelined. Certainly, this trend was palpable before 2014, but the rise to power of the BJP is transforming a difference of degrees into a difference of nature. In purely legal terms, few things have changed, and the Constitution remains unaffected. But in practice, minorities have been subjected to new forms of domination. Not only have the rulers of the country publicly and repeatedly paid allegiance to Hinduism—at the expense of the official, secular character of the state—but they have let militias impose a new form of cultural policing upon Muslims and Christians.

Indicators that were already dropping have seen a steepening downward trend since 2014. The percentage of Muslim MPs in the lower house of parliament was never lower (hardly more than 3.7 percent), whereas the proportion of Muslims in Indian society topped the 14 percent mark in 2011. On the other hand, the percentage of Muslims awaiting trial in prison has never been higher: 21 percent.[63] The number of Muslims sentenced—15.8 percent—is, however, nearly proportional to their population, a sign that many of those arrested by the police are cleared by the courts when they go to trial.[64]

These trends suggest that India is gradually embarking on the path of ethnic democracy, a notion introduced into the social science lexicon by specialists of Israel to refer to a regime in which liberal constitutions are in place and in which all citizens have access to the same rights in theory—but not in practice.[65] The criteria put forward by Smooha are fulfilled, for instance: the Hindu nationalists define the ethno-religious majority as heir to eternal India; reject minorities, which are divided along religious and social lines, as outsiders; perceive Pakistan as a threat spread by the "fifth column" of Muslim Indians; and are supported by a strong diaspora.

Will external pressures make any difference in the medium term? Hinduism certainly continues to enjoy a very positive international image—a religion that professes pacifism and pure spirituality—and India derives from it one of the sources of its "soft power." But the United States is taking an increasingly critical approach. In 2016 the U.S. Commission on International Religious Freedom found that India was on a negative trajectory:

> In 2015, religious tolerance deteriorated and religious freedom violations increased in India. . . . Minority communities, especially Christians, Muslims, and Sikhs, experienced numerous incidents of intimidation, harassment, and violence, largely at the hands of Hindu nationalist groups. . . . These issues, combined with long-standing problems of police bias and judicial inadequacies, have created a pervasive climate of impunity, where religious minority communities feel increasingly insecure, with no recourse when religiously-motivated crimes occur.[66]

During his official visit in January 2015, Barak Obama urged Indians to prove faithful to the secular principles of their constitution. This admonition, however, was not followed by concrete measures, and *realpolitik* will probably prevail over principles if India continues to be perceived in Washington as a counterweight to China in Asia, all the more so as, formally, India continues to fulfill the criteria of democracy. Indeed, in an ethnic democracy, the core group believes in democracy precisely because it is in a majority. Hindu nationalists have always been for democracy because this regime lent itself to their community's rule, in the garb of majoritarianism.[67] They have achieved their goal by mobilizing Hindus against so-called threatening others, in the national-populist mode, at the expense of the nondemotic side of democracy, individual and collective rights.

# Notes

1. Charles Taylor, "Modes of Secularism," in *Secularism and Its Critics*, ed. R. Bhargava (New Delhi: Oxford University Press, 1998), 32.

2. Michael Sandel, "Religious Liberty: Freedom of Choice or Freedom of Conscience," in *Democracy's Discontent* (Cambridge, Mass.: Harvard University Press, 1996), 2.

3. M. Galanter, "Secularism East and West," *Comparative Studies in Society and History* 7, no. 2 (1965): 133–59.

4. R. Bhargava, "La spécificité de la laïcité à l'indienne," *Critique internationale* 35 (April–June 2007): 121–48.

5. C. Jaffrelot and G. Tarabout, "Les transformations de l'hindouisme," in *L'Inde contemporaine de 1950 à nos jours*, ed. C. Jaffrelot, 568–93 (Paris: Fayard, 2006).

6. M. Galanter, "Hinduism, Secularism and the Indian Judiciary," *Philosophy East and West* 21, no. 4 (1971): 467–87.

7. This paragraph should be understood in light of what has been said with regard to state intervention in religious affairs.

8. Regarding this breach in liberal theory which was the crucible of the "secularist" doctrine, see the fine article by Partha Chatterjee in which he writes, "It seems to me that there is no viable way out of this problem (of adapting secularism to India) within the given contours of liberal democratic theory, which must define the relation between the relatively autonomous domains of state and civil society in terms of individual rights." Partha Chatterjee, "Secularism and Tolerance," *Economic and Political Weekly* 29 (9 July 1994): 1768–77.

9. C. Jaffrelot, "La dérive ethnique du nationalisme indien," in *Le Déchirement des nations*, ed. J. Rupnik, 213–38 (Paris: Le Seuil, 1995).

10. This means that protection of minorities is not necessarily an infringement on the principle of secularism. N. Chandoke, *Beyond Secularism: The Right of Religious Minorities* (New Delhi: Oxford University Press, 2002).

11. Charles Taylor, "The Meaning of Secularism," *The Hedgehog Review* 12, no. 3 (2010): 23.

12. Regarding the differences that can be observed between the Western and South Asian (especially Indian) versions of secularism, see Sunil Khilnani, "Secularism: Western and Indian," in *The Secular State and Islam in Europe*, ed. K. Almqvist, 41–60 (Stockholm: Axel and Margaret Axson Johnson Foundation, 2007).

13. S. Gopal, ed., *Jawaharlal Nehru: An Anthology* (New Delhi: Oxford University Press, 1980), 330.

14. Cited in S. J. Tambiah, "The Crisis of Secularism in India," in *Secularism and its Critics*, ed. R. Bhargava (New Delhi: Oxford University Press, 1998), 422–23.

15. R. Bhargava, "Giving Secularism Its Due," *Economic and Political Weekly* (9 July 1994): 1774–91.

16. R. Bhargava, "What Is Secularism For?," in *Secularism and Its Critics*, ed. R. Bhargava (New Delhi: Oxford University Press, 1998), 520.

17. "Cabinet Nod for Haj Subsidy for 1.25 Lakh Pilgrims," *The Times of India*, 8 October 2011, http://articles.timesofindia.indiatimes.com/2011-10-08/india/30257502_1_number-of-haj-pilgrims-haj-subsidy-haj-committee. In practice, only 105,000 Indian Muslims benefited from this aid according to an answer given by the Indian government during the question session of the lower house of parliament, the Lok Sabha.

18. Japan K. Pathak, "A Pilgrim Spends Rs 16,000 While Govt Spends Rs 73,000 for His Haj," *DeshGujarat*, 24 October 2011, http://deshgujarat.com/2011/10/24/you-spend-rs-16000-while-govt-spends-rs-73000-for-your-haj/.

19. "Supreme Court Clears Haj Subsidy for This Year," *The Hindu*, 22 January 2008, http://www.thehindu.com/todays-paper/Supreme-Court-clears-Haj-subsidy-for-this-year/article15148826.ece. Nevertheless, in 2010, the Minister of Minorities deemed—like other Muslims—that subsidizing the Haj contravened the principles of Islam and announced the phasing out of this financial aid by 2017. Amitav Rajan, "Haj Subsidy Cuts Start Soon," *The Indian Express*, 13 October 2010, http://www.indianexpress.com/news/haj-subsidy-cuts-start-soon/696844.

20. 12,000 faucets had to be installed to supply 50 million liters of drinking water to the pilgrims, 450 km of electric lines were laid and 15,000 streetlights were installed to light an enormous camp, 70,000 toilets were installed and 7,100 employees hired to maintain them, funding was required for 11 post offices, 3,000 telephone lines and 4,000 buses and trains. In preparation for a similar event in 2013, the government of Uttar Pradesh has already budgeted 2.66 billion rupees to ensure the pilgrims' security using helicopters, metal detectors, and 30,000 additional police officers. "Salman Rushdie and India's New Theocracy," *The Hindu*, 21 January 2012.

21. Gandhi's use of Hindu symbols (starting with the way he portrayed the ascetic in politics and his emphatic references to the Gita) helped to alienate members of certain minorities, including Muslims won over to the cause of Pakistan.

22. G. Minault, *The Khilafat Movement: Religious Symbolism and Political Mobilization in India* (New York: Columbia University Press, 1982).

23. C. Jaffrelot, *La Démocratie en Inde: Religion, caste et politique* (Paris: Fayard, 1998).

24. M. K. Gandhi, *Indian Home Rule* (Madras: Ganesh and Do., 1922).

25. D. E. Smith, *India as a Secular State* (Princeton, N.J.: Princeton University Press, 1963), 66–72.

26. This was the case of the Hindu Code Bill which has roots in colonial history. Cf. R. Som, "Jawaharlal Nehru and the Hindu Code Bill: A Victory of Symbol over Substance," *Modern Asian Studies* 28, no. 1 (1994): 165–94.

27. R. Thapar, "Is Secularism Alien to Indian Civilization?," in *The Future of Secularism*, ed. T. N. Srinivasan, 83–108 (New Delhi: Oxford University Press, 2007).

28. See also the first chapter of his book "The Political Implications of Asian Religions," in *South Asian Politics and Religion*, ed. D. E. Smith (Princeton, N.J.: Princeton University Press, 1966).

29. D. E. Smith, ed., *India as a Secular State* (Princeton, N.J.: Princeton University Press, 1963).

30. J. Nehru, *Letters to Chief Ministers 1947–1964*, ed. G. Parthasarathi, vol. 1 (New Delhi: Oxford University Press, 1985–89), 33–34 and 56–57.

31. C. Jaffrelot, *Les Nationalistes hindous* (Paris: Presses la fnsp, 1993).

32. Shabnam Hashmi, ed., *What It Means to Be a Muslim in India Today* (New Delhi: Anhad, 2011).

33. T. N. Madan also uses this phrase/expression in a different perspective. See T. N. Madan, "The Crisis of Indian Secularism," chap. 8 in *Modern Myths, Locked Minds: Secularism and Fundamentalism in India*, ed. T. N. Madan, 233–65 (New Delhi: Oxford University Press, 1998); A. D. Nedham and R. S. Rajan, eds., *The Crisis of Secularism in India* (New Delhi: Permanent Black, 2007).

34. B. Crossman and R. Kapur, *Secularism's Last Sigh? Hindutva and the (Mis)Rule of Law* (New Delhi: Oxford University Press, 1999).

35. Cited in R. Sen, *Articles of Faith: Religion, Secularism and the Indian Supreme Court* (New Delhi: Oxford University Press, 2010).

36. See V. M. Tarkunde's excellent analysis, "Supreme Court Judgment: A Blow to Secular Democracy," *PUCL Bulletin*, 19 January 1996, http://www.pucl.org/from-archives/Religion-communalism/sc-judgement.htm.

37. *Report of the Liberhan Ayodhya Commission of Inquiry*, available at http://docs .indiatimes.com/liberhan/liberhan.pdf.

38. Nivedita Menon, "The Second Demolition," *Kafila Online*, 10 February 2010, https://kafila .online/2010/10/02/the-second-demolition-ayodhya-judgement-september-30-2010 and "The Ayodhya Judgment: What Next?," *Economic and Political Weekly*, 30 July 2011, 81–89.

39. J. Venkatesan, "Supreme Court Stays Allahabad High Court Verdict on Ayodhya," *The Hindu*, 9 May 2011.

40. Pratap Mehta, "The Leap and the Faith," *The Indian Express*, 1 October 2010.

41. "I am still hoping that there will be a temple and a mosque side-by-side at Ayodhya. If that is not possible, let us have a sacred grove there. We do not have to obey Uma Bharti and turn Ayodhya into a Vatican. That will be cheap mimicry. The temple need not be grand either; it has to be sacred and inspire reverence. A bhavya temple has nothing to do with size. Nirmohi Akhada, too, has said that it will be satisfied with a modest temple. Well, it does not have to be modest either; it can be exquisite. The Akshardham temple in Delhi is grand, but it is characterless and tasteless and caters mainly to tourists from the urban middle class. Indeed, one sometimes suspects that it is meant primarily for the non-resident Indians and resident non-Indians. On the other hand, the temple at Sabarimala is small but exudes sacredness. Its pilgrims are moved rather than awed by it. Given the killings, the vandalism and the petty politics that have gone into its actualisation, any new temple will need a touch of sacredness more than a surfeit of grandeur." A. Nandy, "The Judges Have Been Injudicious Enough to Create a Space for Compassion and Humane Sentiments," *Tehelka* 7 no. 44 (6 Nov. 2010), http://www.tehelka.com/story_main47.asp?filename=Op061110The _judges.asp.

42. http://judis.nic.in/supremecourt/chejudis.asp, Rabindra Kr. Pal and Dara Singh vs. Republic of India, 21 January 2011.

43. Dibyasundar, "Unique Threat to Secularism and Freedom of Speech in India," *The New Dimension* (blog), 0 February 20, 2011, http://thenewdimension.wordpress.com/tag /dara-singh.

44. C. Jaffrelot, "L'affiliation religieuse comme fait politique en Inde: la (re)conversion à l'hindouisme des aborigènes chrétiens," *Socio-anthropologie* 25/26 (2009/2010): 19–40. Regarding the Dara Singh case, see the very insightful critique of the Commission of Inquiry, M. P. Raju, ed., *Wadhwa Commission Report. A Critique*, (New Delhi: Media House, 1999).

45. "Hindu Vishva," *The Organiser*, Special Issue on the Second World Hindu Congress (March-April 1979): 13.

46. S. Kaviraj, "Démocratie et développement en Inde," in *La greffe de l'État: Les trajectoires du politique*, ed. Jean-François Bayart, vol. 2, 147–89 (Paris: Karthala, 1996).

47. S. Visvanathan, "The Unmaking of an Investigation," *Seminar* 605 (January 2010), 107.

48. S. Wilkinson, "Froids calculs et foules déchaînées: les émeutes intercommunautaires en Inde," *Critique internationale* 6 (2000): 125–42.

49. "Sushma Pushes for Declaring Bhagavad Gita as National Scripture," *The Hindu*, 7 Dec. 2014, http://www.thehindu.com/news/national/sushma-pushes-for-declaring -bhagwad-gita-as-national-scripture/article6670252.ece.

50. Culture Minister, "Mahesh Sharma Speaks: Despite Being a Muslim, APJ Abdul Kalam Was a Nationalist," *The Indian Express*, 18 Sept. 2015, http://indianexpress.com/article /india/india-others/culture-minister-speaks-despite-being-a-muslim-kalam-was-a -nationalist.

51. Taking away the epithet of "Mother," in 2016 he claimed, "Teresa was part of a conspiracy for Christianisation of India." "Mother Teresa Part of Conspiracy for 'Christianisation' of India: BJP MP Yogi Adityanath," *The Indian Express*, 21 June 2016, http://indianexpress.com/article/india/india-news-india/mother-teres . . .-christianisation -of-india-says-bjp-mp-adityanath-2866131/99/print/.

52. Nakul Singh Sawhney, "Watch: Kairana, After the Headlines," *The Wire*, September 28, 2016 ; L. Verma, "Kairana Row: Hukum Singh—Lawyer, MP, and Now Author of Exodus in MP," *The Indian Express*, June 15, 2016; Zoya Hasan, "Kairana and the Politics of Exclusion," *The Hindu*, October 17, 2016; and Rohan Venkataramakrishnan, "BJP Refuses to Let Facts Get in the Way of the 'Hindu Exodus' Story in Kairana," *Scroll.in*, June 17, 2016.

53. C. Jaffrelot and L. Gayer, "The Militias of Hindutva: Communal Violence, Terrorism and Cultural Policing," concluding chap. in *Armed Militias of South Asia. Fundamentalist, Maoists and Separatists*, ed. L. Gayer and C. Jaffrelot, 199–236 (New Delhi: Foundation Books, 2009).

54. "Why Mohan Bhagwat Wants the Whole World to Chant 'Bharat Mata Ki Jai,'" *The Indian Express*, 28 March 2016, http://indianexpress.com/article/cities/kolkata/want -the-whole-world-to-chant-bharat-mata-ki-jai-mohan-bhagwat/.

55. Smita Nair, "Refrain in Sangh Turf: Cards Will Give Us Power," *The Indian Express*, August 23, 2016.

56. Ishan Marvel, "In the name of the mother. How the State Nurtures the Gau Rakshaks of Haryana," *The Caravan*, 1 September 2016.

57. Pragya Singh, "Four Stomachs to Fill," *Outlook*, 7 August 2016.

58. "2 Muslims Herding Buffaloes Thrashed, Hanged in Jharkhand," *The Times of India*, 19 March 2016.

59. "We Were Gangraped for 'Eating Beef', Says Mewat women," *India Today*, 11 September 2016.

60. Julio Ribeiro, "Angered by the Gau Rakshaks," *The Indian Express*, 10 August 2016.

61. Modi's reference to social cohesion in his speech against the *gau rakshaks* suggest that his anger (his own term) was sparked by anti-Dalit attacks: "The people, who are troubled by the unity of the society, are in the name of 'gau rakshaks' attempting to create friction (sic) the society. I urge my fellow countrymen to be aware of such 'gau rakshaks.' " "Crackdown on 'Cow Vigilantes': Gau Raksha Dal Chief Booked," *The Indian Express*, 8 August 2016.

62. Pavan Dahat, "RSS Chief Backs Gau Rakshaks Lauds Army," *The Hindu*, 11 October 2016.

63. Not even the Dalits are so overrepresented. Deeptiman Tiwary, "Over 55 Percent of Undertrials Muslim, Dalit or Tribal," *The Indian Express*, 1 November 2016.

64. Deeptiman Tiwary, "Share of Muslims in Jail Bigger Than in the Population, Show NCRB Data," *The Indian Express*, 3 November 2016, http://indianexpress.com/article /explained/muslims-daliots-undertrials-in-prison-ncrb-3734362/.

65. Sammy Smooha, "The Model of Ethnic Democracy: Israel as a Jewish and Democratic State," *Nations and Nationalism* 8, no. 4 (2002): 475–503; "The Model of Ethnic Democracy," in *The Fate of Ethnic Democracy in Post-Communist Europe*, ed. Sammy Smooha and Priit Järve, 4–59 (Budapest: Open Society Institute, 2005).

66. "Religious Freedom in India on 'Negative Trajectory': USCIRF," *The Indian Express*, 2 May 2016.

67. C. Jaffrelot, "Hindu Nationalism and Democracy," in *Transforming India. Social and Political Dynamics of Democracy*, ed. F. Frankel, Z. Hasan, R. Bhargava and B. Arora, 353–78 (New Delhi: Oxford University Press, 2000).

# Bibliography

Berger, Peter. *The Social Reality of Religion*. London: Allen Lane, 1973.

——. "The Desecularization of the World: A Global Overview." In *The Desecularization of the World: Resurgent Religion and World Politics*, ed. Peter Berger, 1–18. Grand Rapids, Mich.: Eerdmans, 1999.

Bhargava, Rajeev. "Giving Secularism Its Due." *Economic and Political Weekly* (July 9, 1994): 1774–91.

——. *Secularism and Its Critics*. New Delhi: Oxford University Press, 1998.

——. "What Is Secularism For?" In *Secularism and Its Critics*, ed. Rajeev Bhargava, 486–542. New Delhi: Oxford University Press, 1998.

——. "La spécificité de la laïcité à l'indienne." *Critique international* 35 (April–June 2007): 121–48.

Casanova, José. *Public Religions in the Modern World*. Chicago: University of Chicago Press, 1994.

Chandoke, Neera. *Beyond Secularism: The Right of Religious Minorities*. New Delhi: Oxford University Press, 2002.

Chatterjee, Partha. *Nationalist Thought and the Colonial World: A Derivative Discourse?* New Delhi: Oxford University Press, 1986.

——. "Secularism and Tolerance." *Economic and Political Weekly* 29 (July 9, 1994): 1768–77.

Crossman, Brenda, and Ratna Kapur. *Secularism's Last Sigh? Hindutva and the (Mis)Rule of Law*. New Delhi: Oxford University Press, 1999.

Dingwaney, Anuradha N., and Rajeswari Sunder, eds. *The Crisis of Secularism in India*. Durham, N.C.: Duke University Press, 2007.

Gaborieau, M. "Les musulmans de l'Inde: une minorité de 100 millions d'âmes." In *L'Inde contemporaine de 1950 à nos jours*, ed. C. Jaffrelot, 466–507. Paris: Fayard, 1996.

Galanter, Marc. "Secularism East and West." *Comparative Studies in Society and History* 7, no. 2 (1965): 133–59.

——. "Hinduism, Secularism and the Indian Judiciary." *Philosophy East & West* 21, no. 4 (1971): 467–87.

Gandhi, Mahatma K. *Indian Home Rule*. Madras, India: Ganesh, 1922.

Gopal, Sarvepalli, ed. *Jawaharlal Nehru: An Anthology*. New Delhi: Oxford University Press, 1980.

Hashmi, Shabnam, ed. *What It Means to Be a Muslim in India Today*. New Delhi: Anhad, 2011.

Iqtidar, Humeira. *Secularizing Islamists' Jama'at-e-Islami and Jama'at-ud-Da'wa in Urban Pakistan*. Chicago: University of Chicago Press, 2011.

Iqtidar, Humeira, and David Gilmartin. "Secularism and the State in Pakistan." *Modern Asian Studies* 45, no. 3 (April 2011): 491–99.

Jaffrelot, Christophe. "L'affiliation religieuse comme fait politique en Inde: la (re)conversion à l'hindouisme des aborigènes chrétiens." *Socio-anthropologie* 25/26 (2009/2010): 19–40.

——. *La Démocratie en Inde: Religion, caste et politique*. Paris: Fayard, 1998.

——. "La dérive ethnique du nationalisme indien." In *Le Déchirement des nations*, ed. Jacques Rupnik, 213–38. Paris: Le Seuil, 1995.

——. *The Hindu Nationalist Movement and Indian Politics, 1925 to the 1990s*. New York: Columbia University Press, 1996.

——. "Hindu Nationalism and Democracy." In *Transforming India: Social and Political Dynamics of Democracy*, ed. Francine Frankel, Zoya Hasan, Rajeev Bhargava, and Balveer Arora, 353–78. New Delhi: Oxford University Press, 2000.

——. *Les Nationalistes hindous*. Paris: Presses la fnsp, 1993.

Jaffrelot, Christophe, and Laurent Gayer. "The Militias of Hindutva: Communal Violence, Terrorism and Cultural Policing." In *Armed Militias of South Asia. Fundamentalist, Maoists and Separatists*, ed. Laurent Gayer and Christophe Jaffrelot, 199–236. New Delhi: Foundation Books, 2009.

Jaffrelot, Christophe, and Gilles Tarabout, "Les transformations de l'hindouisme." In *L'Inde contemporaine de 1950 à nos jours*, ed. Christophe Jaffrelot, 568–93. Paris: Fayard, 2006.

Jalal, Ayesha. "Exploding Communalism: The Politics of Muslim Identity in South Asia." In *Nationalism, Democracy and Development: State and Politics in India*, ed. Sugata Bose and Ayesha Jalal. New Delhi: Oxford University Press, 1998.

Kaviraj, Sudipta. "Démocratie et développement en Inde." In *La greffe de l'État: Les trajectoires du politique*, vol. 2, ed. Jean-François Bayart, 147–89. Paris: Karthala, 1996.

——. "Introduction." In *Politics in India*, ed. Sudipta Kaviraj, 1–36. New Delhi: Oxford University Press, 1997.

Khilnani, Sunil. "Secularism: Western and Indian." In *The Secular State and Islam in Europe*, ed. Kurt Almqvist, 41–60. Stockholm: Axel & Margaret Axson Johnson Foundation, 2007.

Madan, Triloki N. "The Crisis of Indian Secularism." In *Modern Myths, Locked Minds: Secularism and Fundamentalism in India*, ed. Triloki N. Madan, 233–65. New Delhi: Oxford University Press, 1998.

——. "Secularism in Its Place." *The Journal of Asian Studies* 46, no. 4 (1987): 747–59.

——. "Secularism in Its Place." In *Secularism and Its Critics*, ed. Rajeev Bhargava, 297–320. New Delhi: Oxford University Press, 1998.

Manchanda, Rita, ed. *States in Conflict with Their Minorities*. New Delhi: Sage, 2010.

Minault, Gail. *The Khilafat Movement: Religious Symbolism and Political Mobilization in India*. New York: Columbia University Press, 1982.

Nedham, Anuradha D., and Rajeswari S. Rajan, eds. *The Crisis of Secularism in India*. New Delhi: Permanent Black, 2007.

Nehru, Jawaharlal. *Letters to Chief Ministers 1947–1964: Vol. 1, 1947–1949*, ed. G. Parthasarathi. New Delhi: Oxford University Press, 1985–1989.

Pandey, G. *The Construction of Communalism in Colonial North India*. New Delhi: Oxford University Press, 1990.

Raju, M. P., ed. *Wadhwa Commission Report. A Critique*. New Delhi: Media House, 1999.

Riaz, Ali, ed. *Religion and Politics in South Asia*. New York: Routledge, 2010.

Roy, Oliver. *L'Échec de Islam politique*. Paris: Le Seuil, 1992.

Samad, Saleem. "Bangladesh Likely to Make U-Turn from Secularism to Islamic Hegemony." *Bangladesh Watchdog*, May 31, 2011.

Sandel, Michael. "Religious Liberty: Freedom of Choice or Freedom of Conscience." In *Democracy's Discontent*, 55–90. Cambridge, Mass.: Harvard University Press, 1996.

Sen, Amartya. "Threats to Indian Secularism." *New York Review of Books*, April 8, 1993, 30.

Sen, Ronojoy. *Articles of Faith: Religion, Secularism and the Indian Supreme Court*. New Delhi: Oxford University Press, 2010.

Smith, Donald E. *India as a Secular State*. Princeton, N.J.: Princeton University Press, 1963.

——. "The Political Implications of Asian Religions." In *South Asian Politics and Religion*, ed. Donald E. Smith, chap. 1. Princeton, N.J.: Princeton University Press, 1966.

——. ed. *South Asian Politics and Religion*. Princeton, N.J.: Princeton University Press, 1966.

Smooha, Sammy. "Ethnic Democracy: Israel as an Archetype." *Israel Studies* 2, no. 2 (October 1997): 198–241.

——. "The Model of Ethnic Democracy." In *The Fate of Ethnic Democracy in Post-Communist Europe*, ed. Sammy Smooha and Priit Järve, 4–59. Budapest, Hungary: Open Society Institute, 2005.

——. "The Model of Ethnic Democracy: Israel as a Jewish and Democratic State." *Nations and Nationalism* 8, no. 4 (2002): 475–503.

Som, Reba. "Jawaharlal Nehru and the Hindu Code Bill: A Victory of Symbol over Substance." *Modern Asian Studies* 28, no. 1 (1994): 165–94.

Tambiah, Stanley J. "The Crisis of Secularism in India." In *Secularism and Its Critics*, ed. Rajeev Bhargava, 422–23. New Delhi: Oxford University Press, 1998.

Taylor, Charles. "Modes of Secularism." In *Secularism and Its Critics*, ed. Rejeev Bhargava, 31–53. New Delhi: Oxford University Press, 1998.

——. *A Secular Age.* Cambridge, Mass.: Belknap Press of Harvard University Press, 2007.

——. "The Meaning of Secularism." *The Hedgehog Review* 12, no. 3 (2010): 8–23.

Thapar, Romila. "Is Secularism Alien to Indian Civilization?" In *The Future of Secularism*, ed. Thirukodikaval N. Srinivasan, 83–108. New Delhi: Oxford University Press, 2007.

Vajpayee, Atal B. "The Bane of Pseudo-secularism." In *Hindu Nationalism: A Reader*, ed. Christophe Jaffrelot, 315–17. Princeton, N.J.: Princeton University Press, 2007.

——. "Secularism, Indian Concept." In *Hindu Nationalism: A Reader*, ed. Christophe Jaffrelot, 318–41. Princeton, N.J.: Princeton University Press, 2007.

Visvanathan, Shiv. "The Unmaking of an Investigation." *Seminar* 605 (January 2010): 107–17.

Weiner, M. "Minority Identities." In *Politics in India*, ed. Sudipta Kaviraj, 241–54. New Delhi: Oxford University Press, 1997.

Wilkinson, Steven. "Froids calculs et foules déchaînées: les émeutes intercommunautaires en Inde." *Critique international* 6 (2010): 125–42.

## 10

# TAINTED LIBERALISM

*Israel's Millets*

MICHAEL KARAYANNI

The various religious communities of the Palestinian-Arab minority in Israel have adjudicative and prescriptive jurisdiction over their members in a variety of family law issues.[1] In matters of marriage and divorce, this jurisdictional authority is exclusive in nature. These members cannot opt for any institution or judicial body other than those of their respective religious communities when seeking to conduct or adjudicate their marriage and divorce.[2] In other matters of family relations, such as custody over children, maintenance allowances, alimony claims between the spouses, inheritance, and more, these religious courts possess a concurrent jurisdictional capacity. What this means is that the members of the specific religious community can seize the courts of their community on these matters instead of turning to civil courts (usually the Court of Family Affairs) upon establishing a certain precondition.[3] A common condition is that of consent; the religious court will be competent to deal with one of the listed family law matters if all parties to the action have consented to such jurisdiction. As one can imagine, what exactly is included in an action pertaining to "marriage" and "divorce," what is the exact list of family law matters subject to concurrent jurisdiction, and what forms a consent for such jurisdiction have are not all that clear and thus can be the subject of much litigation. The religious courts and the civil courts do not necessarily see eye to eye on the disputed matters nor on the procedure of adjudication, so parties naturally engage in "forum shopping" to maximize their interests. Notwithstanding these controversies, there is a general agreement in the literature dealing with law and religion in Israel that the jurisdictional authority granted to the Palestinian-Arab religious communities is a form of minority accommodation that is tolerant, pluralistic, and multicultural in nature.[4] A government publication from the 1960s, "The Arabs in Israel," sought to highlight the broad jurisdictional authority granted to the Arab religious communities as part of the freedom of religion and conscience enjoyed by that community. In this vein, the text stressed that the Muslim and Christian courts enjoy a broader jurisdictional authority than the rabbinical courts, and not long before the publication appeared the Druze community also was recognized as an independent religious community.[5] To stress the accommodating Israeli policy toward its Arab minority, the publication added: "At the same time, an entirely different process has been taking place in some of the neighboring Arab countries. In Egypt, for instance, Shari'a courts and the courts of other religious communities were abolished in 1956, and their powers transferred to civil courts."[6] At the time, Egypt was Israel's arch enemy. In writing these words, the Israeli Ministry of Foreign Affairs was not trying to praise Egypt for its tolerant approach toward its religious communities, but to condemn it. The clear implication is that Egypt's act of abolishing the various religious courts deserves condemnation, whereas Israel's maintenance of this jurisdictional authority deserves praise.[7] Similarly, terms that resonate with liberalism are common in the literature dealing with the Palestinian-Arab millets. Israeli scholars have deemed the jurisdictional authority of the Palestinian-Arab millets as a form of a "group-differentiated right,"[8] a "group right,"[9] a form of "self-government,"[10] "self-determination,"[11] and "autonomy."[12] Israel is described as "a 'state of communities' that tolerates rather than assimilates the variety of groups in society."[13] Additionally, when calls for a more accommodating policy toward the Palestinian-Arab minority are made in the name of values such as liberal multiculturalism and inclusive democracy toward an indigenous minority, these invariably include quests for greater recognition of the autonomy of Palestinian-Arab religious institutions.[14]

The liberal outlook, so dominant with respect to the Palestinian-Arab millets, stands in antithesis to the normative conception of the jurisdictional authority granted to the rabbinical courts in Israel.[15] From the start, this jurisdictional authority was depicted as illiberal and even coercive.[16] Haim Cohn, a long-time Israeli Supreme Court Justice, described the jurisdiction of the rabbinical courts in Israel as "a blot on democratic legal rule that we were not able—and in the foreseeable future will not be able—to erase."[17] In the 1950s and 1960s, a high-profile public movement against religious coercion was established in Israel, voicing public criticism of the exclusive jurisdiction of the rabbinical courts over matters of marriage and divorce[18] for two main reasons. First, many Jews in Israel oppose the exclusive authority of the rabbinical courts in matters of marriage and divorce.[19] The secular sentiment among this group prefers an optional jurisdictional authority of rabbinical courts rather than an exclusive one. Second, segments of the Jewish community object to the patriarchal nature of Jewish law (*Halakha*), whose norms governing matters of marriage and divorce are discriminatory against women.[20] When evaluated in terms of liberalism, rabbinical jurisdiction comes out as intolerant and even coercive. Israel nonetheless maintains and justifies this jurisdictional authority for the following reasons: to maintain government coalitions, prevent a legal vacuum,[21] preserve Jewish unity,[22] and manage the deep conflict among Jewish Israelis as a form of consociational politics.[23]

A Janus-headed liberalism exists when it comes to the nature of the jurisdiction accorded to the religious courts in Israel. Liberalism in matters of religion and state in the Jewish community mainly involves the individual affording it with protection *against* religious coercion;[24] in the Palestinian-Arab community, liberalism is at least as much about protecting the jurisdiction of the religious community *as a whole*, at the possible expense of the individual. Izhak Englard, a law professor and later a Justice of the Supreme Court, has explicitly admitted that issues of religion and state are fundamentally different for the Palestinian-Arab minority than for the Jewish majority. For example, if one major concern of the Jewish majority is the individual freedom to be free from religious coercion,[25] for Palestinian-Arabs the concern shifts "from individual freedom of religion to collective autonomy."[26] In Englard's view, this shift is the main reason Israel has "rigorously maintained" the jurisdiction of the Palestinian-Arab religious communities over their members.[27]

These basic distinctions pertaining to the conceived nature of the jurisdictional authority granted to each of the religious communities have been the subject of my research for more than a decade. One major implication I have explored is related to the effects of this distinction on individual members who are especially vulnerable to the encroachment of religious patriarchy: namely, women and children. I have argued that given the supposed liberal character of the Palestinian-Arab religious jurisdiction, Palestinian-Arab women, for example, have a harder battle enforcing their individual autonomy against their religious community because Israeli "liberalism" in matters of religion and state is equally attuned to the collective right of their respective religious community as such.[28] A second implication concerns the option of reforming the internal family law norms of the Palestinian-Arab religious communities. Should a reform movement crystalize within one of these communities, the same group-based liberal conception guarantees a free sail forward.[29]

A second part of this project compared this accommodating Israeli policy when it comes to the Palestinian-Arab community as separate religious communities and the far less, if not repressive, policy when it comes to the Palestinian-Arab community as one national group.[30]

A third part of this project questioned the basic characterization of the juris-dictional authority of the Palestinian-Arab religious communities as liberal and accommodational.[31] My argument in this respect rests on the proposition that what sounds liberal and accommodating might not actually be so, just as one might be speaking Arabic, or any other language for that matter, that oth-ers may understand as such, but actually not be doing so when judged by the grammar of that language. The false liberal nature of the accommodation also has some important normative implications. For example, the mere characteri-zation of a legal arrangement as liberal and accommodating creates the impres-sion that it is inherently positive and desirable when, in fact, it is repressive and backward. The labeling works as a normative laundering machine, conveying the idea that the accommodation is serving the interests of the group when, in fact, it is serving some foreign interests thereto. From an analytical point of view, it is imperative, therefore, to identify what I termed "multicultural quali-fications." Group-based arrangements need to meet certain standards to qualify as multicultural. One such standard requires that the group arrangement have the best interests of the group and group members as its principle objective when prescribed and maintained by the state. Similarly, when certain groups are not under the threat of assimilation, or happen to be overrepresented in government bodies, it is questionable whether such a group is entitled to any special accommodations beyond recognition of the group members' right of association. If, notwithstanding these conditions, the group is accorded certain rights, especially with the power to instruct members to act by certain norms, then the group-based arrangement might not qualify as multicultural. This is certainly true with respect of the Ultra-Orthodox community in Israel, whose internal norms are patriarchal in nature and thereby discriminating against women, on one hand, but enjoy substantial accommodations in terms of fund-ing, educational autonomy, exemptions, and more, on the other hand.[32]

My intention in this chapter is to look into the historical motivations behind Israel's recognition of the jurisdictional authority granted to the Palestinian-Arab religious communities. This jurisdictional authority existed from the time of the Ottoman Empire,[33] was maintained by the British when granted the Mandate over Palestine, and then was adopted by Israel. My claim is that each of these regimes had its own objectives when accepting this juris-dictional authority. Building on newly discovered archival materials as well as on international legal instruments that predate the establishment of the state of Israel, I argue that the central motivations behind the recognition accorded to the Palestinian-Arab religious communities were primarily driven by insti-tutional interests of control rather than by a concern for the well-being of the minority communities.

The study is limited mainly to Israeli policy in the first two decades after the establishment of the state (1948–1967). An Israeli sociologist has claimed that until the June 1967 Six Day War, Israel could have developed a political culture that would have transcended religious, ethnic, and national boundaries by adopting a secular concept of Israeli citizenship with substance.[34] However, things did not develop in this direction. From that point on, tensions between the civil identity of the Israeli and the primordial definitions of the Jewish collective came to dominate Israeli society. These tensions were fueled by the fact that from June 1967 onward Palestinian identity took on a more crystalized form with the weakening of Pan-Arabism and the unification of the local Palestinian population—that is, Palestinians who had been living inside Israel since 1948 and those in the territories occupied by Israel in the West Bank and the Gaza Strip from 1967.[35] Among the various options available to the Israeli polity in defining the relations between religion and state from 1948 to 1967, the decisions and actions actually taken are particularly telling.

## International Legitimacy

The first major factor that influenced Israel's policy of maintaining the Palestinian-Arab millets was its quest to gain international legitimacy. In the years following Israel's establishment in 1948, a vital foreign policy interest was to acquire international recognition and secure economic support, especially from Western democracies. At the time, Israeli policy makers believed Israel would face an existential threat without the material and normative backing of major foreign powers.[36] To promote these efforts, Israel followed the provisions of the international documents upon which its establishment was based and fashioned its policies accordingly. As it turned out, these documents linked the establishment of a Jewish state to the recognition that should be accorded to the minority religions living there. Were Israel to abolish the Palestinian-Arab millets rather than maintain them, it would have jeopardized the legitimacy of its existence. This may be called the "balancing formula."

The roots of the balancing formula can be found in the historic Balfour Declaration (1917). The document attests to the British government's stand—that it views "with favor the establishment in Palestine of a national home for the Jewish people," and balances this with the proviso "that nothing shall be done which may prejudice the civil and religious rights of the existing non-Jewish communities in Palestine." Following the 1920 San Remo Resolution, the League of Nations granted Great Britain the mandate over Palestine. The document in which the Mandate for Palestine was outlined, issued in 1922, incorporated the pledge of the Balfour Declaration and explicated the Mandate's commitment to respect "the personal status of the various peoples and communities" according to which "their religious interests shall be fully guaranteed."[37] These instruments are mentioned in Israel's Declaration of Independence of

1948[38] as documents that grant international legitimacy to the establishment of the State of Israel. Consequently, an essential relationship was established between Israel's character as a Jewish state and the recognition it needed to accord to its non-Jewish religious minorities. This relationship was conditional in nature. The Jewish nation-state structure was to be balanced against recognition accorded to non-Jewish religious institutions.

Israel's actions toward the institutions and sites of its religious minorities came under close scrutiny from the start.[39] Testament to this were the special orders issued by David Ben-Gurion himself during the 1948 war, instructing Israeli soldiers "not to loot or defile a Christian or Muslim Holy Place."[40] The possible negative repercussions on world public opinion also made Ben-Gurion revoke an order already issued by an Israeli military commander to expel the inhabitants of Nazareth.[41]

Indeed, following these measures by Ben-Gurion, local Christian leaders were asked to send out cables reporting that all is well with the Christian communities and holy places.[42] This same attitude proved to be central to Israel's foreign policy after its establishment. In other words, the recognition accorded to the local non-Jewish religious communities was considered vital in the context of Israel's relations with the international community rather than being merely a local policy beneficial to local religious communities. Accordingly, Israel was willing to recognize the international community's interests in the holy places under its territorial control, notwithstanding its sovereignty.[43] This policy surfaced again as an effort to counter the campaign to internationalize Jerusalem in the early 1950s—a proposal Israel resisted[44] and resists to this day.

The balancing formula also explains how the Shari'a and Christian courts ended up having a more enhanced capacity than the rabbinical courts regarding the list of citizens' personal status that came under the exclusive jurisdiction of the religious courts. In fact, the widest jurisdictional capacity was that of the Shari'a courts.[45] Beyond issues of marriage, divorce, and alimony, these courts had exclusive jurisdictional capacity in matters of maintenance allowances for children, custody issues, paternity declarations, and more.[46] Originally, the Shari'a courts won this preferable status during the Ottoman Empire when, for a long time, they were considered to be the official state courts of the empire.[47] During the British Mandate, the Shari'a courts no longer held this status, but they continued to have the widest jurisdictional capacity. Given Israel's effort not to disrupt the existing jurisdictional capacity of Palestinian-Arab millets, in conformity with the balancing formula, the Shari'a courts retained their expanded authority in the Jewish state as well.

The balancing formula was also evident in the way Israel treated its Christian communities.[48] These communities retained their judicial hierarchy, which for some of the communities meant recognition of the authority of appellate courts sitting outside of Israel in countries such as Lebanon—a country that

Israel considers to be an enemy state.[49] These Christian courts retained their exclusive discretion to appoint whom they saw fit to their courts, a privilege that neither the Shari'a courts nor the rabbinical courts enjoyed. When Israel was established, Western nations such as France, Italy, and the Vatican showed special interest in the well-being of the local Christian communities. In an effort to resist the pressure of these countries and the influence they (especially the Vatican) might have on the rest of the Christian West, Israeli authorities became especially sensitive to maintaining the interests of local Christian communities. Thus the local Christian communities' property was retained by these communities, as opposed to the *waqf* property (religious endowments) of the Muslim community, which was massively diluted.[50]

Intragovernmental correspondence during this period reveals the extent of Israeli sensitivity to Christian interests in particular. In a letter dated February 8, 1951, from Yaacov Herzog, Director of the Christian Department at the Ministry of Religion, to Gershon Avner, Director of the West European Department at the Ministry of Foreign Affairs, Herzog urges that "we should reconsider our relations with the Christians and in the meanwhile deal with them with special care."[51] A year earlier, on January 30, 1950, the Director General of the Israeli Ministry of Foreign Affairs, Walter Eytan, writing to the Director of the same West European Department at his Ministry, declares that "we shall be prepared to take into consideration Christianity's concern for the Christian faith in our country . . . therefore it is necessary to bring before the Christian world a detailed and defined plan that provides actual guarantees."[52] In the same memorandum, Eytan goes on to clarify that Israel's sovereignty will not be diminished or undermined if it gives appropriate guarantees for the maintenance of the religious institutions and their unhampered functioning. He concludes this point by adding: "this is a tax that we have to pay in return of the fact that our country exists in the Holy Land." It is no wonder, therefore, that cases in which there was disagreement between different government departments on how the affairs of the Christian communities should be handled, it was the Ministry of Foreign Affairs that took the more accommodating policy, and other departments, in the Ministry of Religious Affairs and in the Ministry of the Interior, took a more reserved view.[53]

Sarah Ozacky-Lazar and Yoav Gelber offer another component of this balancing formula. They mention a memorandum composed in May of 1948 by the Ministry of Minorities, titled "The Arab Problem," in which the Israeli government was called upon, inter alia, to apply its international commitments toward the Arabs that remained. The concern was about lawlessness in the country and what was deemed as disgraceful acts committed by "the best of us." Living up to these commitments was justified because it was presumed that foreign states would treat their Jewish minorities in the manner that Israel would treat its Arab minority.[54]

It should be noted that when Israel was established this balancing formula had already guided the British Mandate authorities, at least during the years immediately following its institution. The British Mandate, committed as it was under the Balfour Declaration to the establishment of a national home for the Jewish people in Palestine, was well aware of the fact that the Muslims had become the most disadvantaged group in Palestine. They had lost their majority status as well as the prominence of the Shari'a and the Shari'a courts as official state institutions during the Ottoman Empire. The Christians lost nothing by the advent of the British Mandate and gained some advantage given that the Mandate was in the hands of a Western Christian state. To balance things, the British Mandate established two official Muslim bodies. The first was the office of the Grand Mufti of Palestine, and the second was the Supreme Muslim Council.[55]

This balancing formula suggests that maintaining the Palestinian-Arab millets was done to facilitate Israel's diplomatic efforts. As such, this consideration took foreign affairs into account first, with domestic affairs coming second, if at all. Somewhat paradoxically, according to this formula, the constitutional nature of Israel as a Jewish nation-state served, and to a large extent still serves, as a guarantee for the maintenance of the jurisdiction of the Palestinian-Arab millets.

## Divide and Conquer

Ian Lustick, in his 1980 seminal book, *Arabs in the Jewish State*,[56] starts off his analysis by noting how in spite of Israel's deep divisions, especially among Arabs and Jews, Israel has not witnessed ethnic disturbances as have other countries. The cause for this, Lustick argues, is the quiescence Israeli Arabs achieved through various means of control.[57] One important instrument of control is segmentation and fragmentation.[58] In this respect, the existing religious divisions among the Palestinian-Arab community as dictated by the millet system proved to be an important resource, the exploitation of which could optimize segmentation and therefore control.[59] This policy of divide and conquer is the second factor behind Israel's policy of preserving the Palestinian-Arab millets.

The argument that the Israeli establishment sought to enforce the religious divides within the Palestinian-Arab community has occasionally surfaced in scholarly writings.[60] Sabri Jiryis, writing in 1976, claimed that by "feeding and reinforcing confessional loyalties" based on religious divisions, the Israeli government "hoped to consolidate its own political position."[61] This furnishes support for the claim that Israel maintained the millet system to effectuate its policy of control.[62] The system itself not only maintains the religious divides among the different Palestinian-Arab religious communities, and by so doing nourishes the religious identity of each, but also mandates that members of different religious communities can only marry and divorce within their own religious communities, thereby curtailing, as much as the prevention of inter-religious marriage can, the emergence of a nonsectarian national identity. One powerful circumstantial piece of evidence in this respect is the split in the Israeli establishment's attitude toward the recognition and maintenance of non-Jewish religious communities, on one hand, and the official policy regarding recognition of non-Orthodox Jewish religious streams and sects, on the other. Israel has been extremely accommodating when it comes to the non-Jewish religious communities. New communities were recognized, such as the Druze[63] and the Anglican Evangelical, and very small Christian religious communities are still officially maintained despite the fact that they number only a few thousand members.[64] Yet the quest of the Jewish Reform and Conservative movements, or the Karaites, to gain official recognition has been firmly opposed by the Israeli establishment.[65] The oft-sounded argument against recognition of these groups is that it will endanger Jewish unity.[66] But of how much interest is it for the Israeli establishment to preserve and nourish Palestinian national unity?

This divide and conquer factor can now be established by newly released documents from the Israeli State Archive. These documents are minutes and memos produced by senior Israeli government officials in the first two years following the state's establishment.

In the immediate aftermath of the 1948 war, some Israeli government officials envisioned a better future for Jewish-Arab relations in the country. These officials called for a government policy that would promote a tolerant attitude toward the Arab minority, and total equality between the Jews and Arabs living in Israel.[67] The Israeli provisional government also established a separate ministry, the Ministry of Minorities, to oversee the status and conditions of the Arab minority. The minister in charge was Bechor-Shalom Shitrit (who at the same time also served as the Minster of Police). Shitrit was seemingly keen in his efforts to promote this tolerant liberal attitude toward the Arab minority, and on August 26, 1948, he sent the Minster of Religious Affairs (Yehuda Leib Hacohen Fishman) a draft of a bill titled "Public Council Assisting the Ministry of Minorities Ordinance."[68] In the accompanying letter, Shitrit asks for comments from his colleague. In substance the bill was rather bold. It proposed establishment of a public council composed of government officials and the general public to offer advice to the Ministry of Minorities on such issues as the rehabilitation of relations with the minorities; how to seek the input of the minorities on questions relating to the national economy; and even the advancement, empowerment, and recognition of the problems of minorities. The first to respond to this initiative was Haim Hirshberg, head of the Muslim Department at the Ministry of Religious Affairs,[69] apparently at the behest of Minister Fishman.[70] Hirshberg sounded a strong reservation, questioning the "necessity and effectiveness" of such a public council. Hirshberg reasoned that issues of education and culture should be handled separately by each of the religious communities (*eidot*). Additionally, if the members of this council were to be dominated by Jewish members, then the public council would appear to be one in which Jews tell Arabs what to do. If, on the other hand, the intention is to have minority members appointed to this public council, then "a dangerous precedent is set" by which a semiparliamentary body, representing the minorities, would be established, which would be "totally undesirable for us." The Minister of Religious Affairs was evidently impressed by these arguments, and in a letter to the Minister of Minorities dated September 6, 1948, Fishman suggests that this bill be dismissed or, more accurately, be shelved. His first argument is explicit: "The bill will consolidate the different religious communities in the country into one national minority, which would be not only undesirable for us at all, but [also] . . . unnecessary and even damaging."[71] Fishman states that dealing with issues of culture and religion should be in the hands of the different religious communities. What was only implicit in Hirshberg's memo now becomes plain. Fishman states that the policies and ambitions of the different religious communities are not uniform. Muslims have different objectives from those of the different Christian communities. "It is not our job to imprint upon this culture, and to empower, the stamp of Arab nationalism." The seeds of this vision were present in a meeting that took place some weeks before. On August 17, 1948, the Minister of Minorities met with representatives from the Ministry of Religious Affairs, among them Hirshberg and the head of the Christian Department at the time, Rabbi Yaacov Herzog. In the minutes documenting this meeting, Bechor-Shalom Shitrit sought to address the problem of appointing qadis to the Shari'a courts, suggesting, among other things, that the Minister of Religious Affairs himself make the appointment and that the Muslim community have the right to elect the qadis or even establish a high Muslim council to deal with the matter. Rabbi Herzog had some reservations about the qadis being appointed by the Minster of Religious Affairs, for this would detract from their autonomy, especially when compared to that granted to the Christians. Herzog then added that caution is called for in these matters, and that in general "we are not interested in forming national minorities, and should try to handle all matters on the basis of religious communities."[72]

This explicit divide and conquer doctrine was soon to spread to other departments. In a "secret" memo written on April 19 1949, Y. L. Blum, the supervisor of Arab Education, wrote to the Minster of Education and Culture that his approach to the "Arab problem" is to eliminate or to minimize all differences "between us and them," which will diminish the differences and promote "stability and tranquility."[73] Blum then relates the discussion he had with Hirshberg, who held a completely different view. Hirshberg was of the opinion that they should retreat from the idea of an "Arab minority and that we should look at them as Israeli citizens who are members of different religions and communities, such as Muslims, Christians of different sects, Druze, Circassians, Greeks, Armenian and just Arabs. . . . In other words we do not have one problem of the Arabs but problems of different communities and nations, and we should tend to each problem separately and stress and develop the conflicts between the different sects and diminish their Arabness. Thus they will forget that they are Arabs and know that they are Israelis of different creeds." The supervisor notes that these ideas of Hirshberg are revolutionary in the political sense but are "based on facts." Blum then adds that "each one of us that is closely familiar with the Arabs and is able to have them disclose their hearts knows how great is the hatred between Muslims and Christians . . . and between all of these and the Druze." Blum ends his secret memo by speculating whether he is willing to accept Hirshberg's position or to stick to his own, suggesting that both positions should be considered.

In due course, the more accommodating outlook advocated by Shitrit was completely rejected.[74] The Ministry of Minorities was dismantled, and the Office of the Adviser to the Prime Minister on Arab Affairs became the principal government organ in charge of handling issues regarding the Arab minority.[75] Ben-Gurion "vehemently objected" to the Public Council bill and vetoed the whole idea.[76] When it was clear that the Ministry of Minorities would no longer exist, a committee was appointed by the Israeli government, headed by Yehoshua Palmon. The committee recommended that a broad autonomy in religious matters be accorded to the different religious communities that would henceforth come under the jurisdiction of the Ministry of Religious Affairs.[77] The policy of this ministry was already stated explicitly. Palmon became the adviser to the Prime Minister on Arab Affairs, in charge of policy toward the Arab minority, and he acquired the title of the "czar of Israel's Arabs."[78] This "divide and conquer" formula was then adopted by a committee of the ruling party, Mapai, established in 1957 and in charge of advising on policies toward the Arab minority. Archival documents recording the minutes of this influential committee, as revealed by Yair Bäuml, show that the course advocated by Hirshberg and his ministry became the course followed and advocated by this influential committee of the ruling party.[79]

## Nation Building

Identity is relational. This is a sociological fact.[80] A group defines itself not only by stressing its past, its culture, and its aspirations but also by stressing the divides that separate it from other groups. These divides become clearer if other groups are pushed into preserving their own identity. Preserving the millet system for the Palestinian-Arab minority was also guided by the hegemonic

Jewish majority in Israel's will to preserve its distinctiveness and identity.[81] Israel is a Jewish nation-state that prioritizes Jewish collective interests.[82] Its maintenance as such mandates the preservation of Jewish identity, which is ethnic and hereditary.[83] An essential mechanism for enforcing Jewish identity is by promoting endogamy among the Jewish majority.[84] Granting religious communities exclusive jurisdiction as prescribed by the millet system is a very efficient design to circumvent intermarriage, which the Jewish majority considered to be particularly threatening to its collective interests and to Israel's identity as a Jewish state. Sammy Smooha makes this argument when depicting the characteristics of Israel as an "ethnic democracy": "So long as Israel remains a Jewish-Zionist state, Jews will continue to have a vested interest in sustaining Arabs as an ethnic minority in order to reduce the danger of assimilation and intermarriage."[85]

The interest of preserving Jewish identity was especially intense in the first two decades after establishment of the State of Israel in 1948. When asked by a journalist which of the fundamental laws characterizes Israel as a Jewish state, Zerah Warhaftig, a long-time member of Knesset and the minister of religious affairs from 1961 to 1974, answered that these happen to be two-and-a-half laws.[86] The first is the Law of Return that guarantees Jews all over the world the right to immigrate to Israel and regard it as their homeland.[87] The second is the law on marriage and divorce.

> [This law] guarantees the physical unity of the nation [and] the stability of the Jewish family. Only by this law is the state a Jewish state. Abrogating this law, the introduction of civil marriages and divorces with the possibility of mixed marriages—can bring about the abolishing of the concept of Jewish state. This would be a democratic but not a Jewish state.[88]

The other one-half law Warhaftig mentioned is the law recognizing the Sabbath as the official day of rest in the country.

These collective Jewish sentiments about preserving the exclusive jurisdiction of religious norms and courts over matters of marriage and divorce proved to be instrumental in having the Knesset enact the Rabbinical Courts Jurisdiction (RCJ) law. This law mandates that marriages among Jews in Israel are to be conducted under the Jewish (Orthodox) *halakha*, and that rabbinical courts shall have exclusive jurisdiction over divorce proceedings (RCJ). The common perception that this law came about due to the Jewish religious parties' excessive political power is erroneous and misleading.[89] Additionally, the historic status quo agreement did not include any explicit mention of exclusive jurisdiction for the rabbinical courts in matters of marriage and divorce. On the contrary, the text is vague in this respect, with some interpretations saying that the promise as made would also sustain the prospect of having a civil marriage regime alongside the religious option.[90] However, as the Knesset discussion reveals, a strong sentiment of Jewish-Zionist nation building was pivotal in adopting the exclusive jurisdiction of rabbinical courts over marriage and divorce as well as the exclusive jurisdiction of other religious communities over these matters in their respective spheres.[91] These Jewish-Zionist sentiments centered on the Jewish unity that might be threatened by a civil marriage regime—given that such a regime would eventually lead to lesser restrictions on marriage between Jews in Israel,[92] and on the threat of mixed marriages that might lead to assimilation and from there to weakening of the Jewish identity.[93] Zerah Warhaftig, who at the time RCJ was adopted was deputy minister for religious affairs, was again explicit regarding what this would entail with respect of the religious communities in Israel in general: "Any prospect for mixed marriages will not be possible when religious marriage is obligatory."[94] This exclusive jurisdictional authority should not be condemned because mixed marriages are "disastrous" as they might make assimilation possible.[95] But once again, these remarks were made not to safeguard the collective interests of the non-Jewish community but those of the Jewish community itself as they were perceived at the time.

The centrality of endogamy to the Israeli-Jewish nation building project is evident also in the policies that encouraged assimilation and mixing when it came to marriage across cultural lines within the Jewish community. Israeli sociologists pointed out that for a number of decades after its establishment, Israel was dominated by the conception of assimilating Jews coming from different cultural backgrounds. The central tenet of Zionism is the ingathering of exiles (*kibbutz* or *mizug galuyot*).[96] Thus the State of Israel encourages the ethnic mixture of the Jewish population where mixed marriages among Jews is a legitimate "and even desirable option."[97] No wonder there is a high rate of mixed marriages among Jews of different cultural backgrounds in Israel.[98]

Historically, the process of nation building has been intertwined with regulation of the family, especially the institution of the family.[99] Perceiving the nation in terms of a certain culture, be it national, ethnic, secular, or religious, will most often translate itself into legal institutions that define the formation of family relations.[100] So the Israeli experience of maintaining the exclusive jurisdiction of the rabbinical courts and the other millets is by no means a peculiar one. However, if the regulation of marriage is a reflection of how the nation is perceived, then the divides maintained by the millet system are a testament to another important feature of Israeli society that will surface in the upcoming discussion: Israel being a nonassimilative society when it comes to the Jewish and Palestinian-Arab communities. Thus far, Israel has resisted the creation of an inclusive Israeli identity. In terms of nationality, to date, a citizen of the State of Israel cannot be registered as an "Israeli" in public records.[101] It is either under such definitions as a "Jew," an "Arab," a "Druze," or nothing. So nation building in Israel is also carried out by containing Israelis within their separate identities, and in this sense, the existing divides between the millets proved to be instrumental was well.

All in all, in the Israeli context, marriage was perceived as an instrument that was intended either to delineate or to blur the divides between different Israeli groups. When the divide was deemed inappropriate, barriers that prevented intergroup marriage were lifted; but when the divides were perceived as appropriate, the policy was to maintain the existing divides and make intergroup marriage difficult to achieve. For this latter objective, the millet system was a resource the State of Israel was set to exploit from the start.

## Internal Forces

When Israel was established, the political and religious leadership of the Palestinian-Arab community displayed a position that favored the maintenance of their millets.[102] This formed the fourth factor that worked to maintain the Palestinian-Arab millets but, as I shall argue later, a rather weak one.

First of all, the Palestinian-Arab minority, like the Jewish majority, was against assimilation and antagonistic to the creation of an all-inclusive Israeli identity.[103] In fact, this minority was interested in maintaining its separate identity, an aspiration that might be jeopardized were the state to introduce a territorial-secular regime for marriage and divorce. So endogamy was a Palestinian-Arab interest as much as it was a Jewish one.[104]

But this was not all. Other internal forces joined this common policy of opting for separateness. The non-Jewish religious leadership understandably supported the maintenance of the existing millets.[105] The system formed the power structure that sustained their authority.[106] The position of the religious leadership became evident whenever a reform was proposed that encroached on the jurisdiction of the existing Palestinian-Arab millets. Each time this happened, religious community leaders argued that the restriction will undermine the autonomy of the Palestinian community over their religious affairs or even infringe upon the freedom of religion of their group members.[107] A direct account of this was provided once again by Haim H. Cohn. In his autobiography he mentions a reform proposal advanced immediately after the establishment of the State of Israel by the first minister of justice, Pinhas Rosen, by which one secular-territorial law that applies to all Israeli citizens alike would replace the religious jurisdiction over matters of personal status, including in matters of marriage and divorce.[108] When the proposal came up for discussion before the government, it was soon seen that it had no real prospects of succeeding. In large part, this was due to the opposition of the ministers and parties that wanted to preserve rabbinical jurisdiction. But this was not all. Cohn mentions an argument made at the time by representatives of the Muslim Shari'a court who protested the initiative as an act of ungratefulness. When the Muslims were the majority in the country and the Jews were but a small minority, the Jews were accorded full autonomy and jurisdiction over their personal status; now that things were the other way around, the Jewish majority wanted to abolish the jurisdiction of the Shari'a courts.[109] In an article written by Cohn in 1998, he recalls the opposition of the Muslim religious leadership and adds that "the various Christian churches likewise insisted on retaining, in the full, the ecclesiastical jurisdiction they had enjoyed in this country for a century or more."[110]

The political leadership of the Palestinian-Arab community, too, sent a strong message that it was interested in maintaining the existing millets. Apart from the nonassimilative objective that this stand served, the traditional political representatives, that is, those based on clan leadership, preferred the jurisdiction of religious courts over matters of family law because this preserved the patriarchal order and therefore bolstered their own power base. The seemingly secular leadership, led, incidentally, by the Communist Party, concentrated its efforts on the national struggle of the Palestinian-Arab minority, leaving aside issues of religion, especially in the domain of family law.[111] Given the fact that the Palestinian-Arab minority was still heavily dependent on patriarchy as a social order,[112] this secular leadership calculated that should it raise the secular flag and push for a territorial regime of family law, it could lead to internal divisions that might weaken its national agenda.[113] Additionally, the Communist Party, with which the Palestinian-Arab community identified, is on record as calling for the establishment of institutions to teach Islam, given the lack of such institutions among Muslims in Israel, as well as working to promote the increase of salaries of Shari'a court judges (qadis) and other funds for the administration of Muslim religious endowments (waqf—singular; awqaf—plural).[114]

In comparison with the three factors stated earlier, this one seems to be the weakest. The Palestinian-Arab minority that ended up inside the borders of the State of Israel as drawn by the 1949 Armistice Agreements between Israel and its neighboring countries was relatively small, comprising about 150,000 people. This community, that only a few years earlier was part of the majority group, now lacked an elite, was politically unorganized, traumatized by internal displacement and detachment from family and friends, and had no meaningful economy of its own upon which to depend.[115] Above all, Palestinian Arabs in Israel were now under the rule of a military government, and remained so for eighteen years, until 1966. As the years went by, this minority became more politically mobilized, but when Israel was established, it seems they would have settled for a lesser jurisdictional authority than the one granted.

Looking at the jurisdictional authority of the Palestinian-Arab religious communities from a historical perspective reveals that what many regard as a form of accommodation is essentially a form of control. Defining the Palestinian-Arab community in religious terms instead of as a national minority has better served the Israeli policy of control than the interests of the Palestinian-Arab minority itself, at least in terms of its aspirations as one national unit. In a broader perspective, one needs to be cautious when characterizing group-based juridical arrangements to be a form of a multicultural accommodation. Past critical writings on multiculturalism have sought to highlight the adverse effect of accommodating religious groups on the venerable members within, especially women.[116] Given the inherently patriarchal nature of religious norms, it is inevitable that the interests of women will be subordinate to those of men when a religious group is granted juridical authority over the family law affairs of its members. Apparently, this is not all. In addition to this predicament, one needs to be aware of the external circumstances associated with the accommodation of religious groups.

## Notes

1. Yüksel Sezgin, *Human Rights Under State-Enforced Religious Family Laws in Israel, Egypt and India* (Cambridge: Cambridge University Press, 2013), 84–93.
2. Adam S. Hofri-Winogradow, "A Plurality of Discontent: Legal Pluralism, Religious Adjudication and the State," *Journal of Religion and State* 26, no.1 (2011): 62. It is true that marriages can be celebrated in a civil manner outside of Israel and then be recognized in one form or another through the rules of Israeli private international law. It is also true that parties can live together as partners and gain a status and a bundle of rights similar to that of married couples. However, these alternatives have their shortcomings and do not always prove to offer an adequate alternative. Menashe Shava, "Civil Marriages Celebrated Abroad: Validity in Israel," *Tel-Aviv Studies in Law* 9 (1989): 311–46.
3. Daphna Hacker, "Religious Tribunals in Democratic States: Lessons from the Israeli Rabbinical Courts," *Journal of Religion and State* 27, no. 1 (2012): 63.
4. Michael M. Karayanni, "The Separate Nature of Religious Accommodations for the Palestinian-Arab Minority in Israel," *Northwestern Journal of International Human Rights* 5, no.1 (2006): 41–71.
5. Israel Ministry for Foreign Affairs, *The Arabs in Israel* (Jerusalem: Information Department, Israel Ministry for Foreign Affairs, 1996), 17.
6. Israel Ministry for Foreign Affairs, *The Arabs in Israel*, 17.
7. Marc Galanter and Jayenth Kirshnan, "Personal Law and Human Rights in India and Israel," *Israel Law Review* 34, no. 1 (2000): 120–21.
8. Ilan Saban, "Minority Rights in Deeply Divided Societies: A Framework for Analysis and the Case of the Arab-Palestinian Minority in Israel," *New York University Journal of International Law and Politics* 36, no. 4 (2004): 942–48, 954–60.

9.  See David Kretzmer, *The Legal Status of the Arabs in Israel* (Boulder, Colo.: Westview Press, 1990), 163–68; Gad Barzilai, "Analysis of Israelis [Jews and Arab-Palestinians]: Exploring Law in Society and Society in Law," *International Journal of Law in Context* 11, no. 3 (2015): 365; Itzhak Zamir, "Shivyon Zekhuyuot Klapei ha-Aravim be-Yisra'el" ["Equality of Rights for Arabs in Israel"], *Mishpat u-Mimshal* 9 (2005): 26, 30 (in Hebrew).

10. Rubinstein and Medina refer to the religious organization of the Palestinian-Arab religious communities as a limited form of self-government. Amnon Rubinstein and Barak Medina, *Ha-Mishpat ha-Hukati shel Medinat Yisra'el* [*The Constitutional Law of the State of Israel*], 6th ed. (Jerusalem: Schocken, 2005), 429–35 (in Hebrew).

11. Isaac S. Shiloh, "Marriage and Divorce in Israel," *Israel Law Review* 5, no. 4 (1970): 481.

12. Jacob M. Landau, *The Arab Minority in Israel, 1967–1991: Political Aspects* (Oxford: Clarendon Press, 1993), 24; Ori Stendel, "The Rights of the Arab Minority in Israel," *Israel Yearbook on Human Rights* 1 (1971): 149.

13. Mordechai Nisan, *Minorities in the Middle East: A History of Struggle and Self-Expression* (Jefferson, N.C.: McFarland, 1991), 579.

14. See Ilan Peleg and Dov Waxman, *Israel's Palestinians: The Conflict Within* (Cambridge: Cambridge University Press, 2011), 7, 149–51; Yousef T. Jabareen, "Constitution Building and Equality in Deeply-Divided Societies: The Case of the Palestinian-Arab Minority in Israel," *Wisconsin International Law Journal* 26, no. 2 (2008–2009): 346, 357–59, 397.

15. As opposed to the Jewish community, Shifman observes that the jurisdiction of the non-Jewish communities in Israel is not conceived as a matter of coercive jurisdiction but as part of the religious and judicial autonomy of these communities. See Pinhas Shifman, *Mi Mefahed mi-Nissu'in Ezrahi'im?* [*Who Is Afraid of Civil Marriage?*] (Jerusalem: Jerusalem Institute for Israel Studies, 1995), 5 (in Hebrew).

16. Ran Hirschl, *Constitutional Theocracy* (Cambridge, Mass.: Harvard University Press, 2010), 142.

17. Haim H. Cohn, *Mevo Ishi: Otobiografiya* [*A Personal Introduction: Autobiography*] (Or-Yehuda: Dvir, 2005), 242 (in Hebrew).

18. Guy Ben-Porath, *Between State and Synagogue: The Secularization of Contemporary Israel* (Cambridge: Cambridge University Press, 2013), 35.

19. Martin Edelman, *Courts, Politics, and Culture in Israel* (Charlottesville: University Press of Virginia, 1994), 61.

20. Frances Raday, "Culture, Religion and Gender," *International Journal of Constitutional Law* 1, no. 4 (2003): 672.

21. Ron Harris, "Hizdamnuyot Historiyot ve-Hakhmatsot she-be-Hesse'ah ha-Da'at: Al Shiluvo shel ha-Mishpat ha-Ivri ba-Mishpat ha-Yisra'eli be-Reishito" ["Historical Opportunities and Absent-Minded Misses: On the Integration of Jewish Law into Israeli Law at Its Beginnings,"], in *Shnei Ivrei ha-Gesher: Dat u-Medina be-Reishit Darka shel Yisra'el* [*Both Sides of the Bridge: Religion and State in the Early Years of Israel,*] ed. Mordechai Bar-On and Zvi Zameret (Jerusalem: Yad Yizhak Ben-Zvi Institute, 2002), 21–22 (in Hebrew).

22. Gershon Shafir and Yoav Peled, *Being Israeli: The Dynamics of Multiple Citizenship* (Cambridge: Cambridge University Press, 2002), 142.

23. Reuven Hazan, "Religion and Politics in Israel: The Rise and Fall of the Consociational Model," *Israel Affairs* 6, no. 2 (1999): 109–37; Charles S. Liebman and Eliezer Don-Yehiya, *Religion and Politics in Israel* (Bloomington: Indiana University Press, 1984).

24. See Ruth Halperin-Kaddari, "Women, Religion and Multiculturalism in Israel," *UCLA Journal of International Law and Foreign Affairs* 5, no. 2 (2000): 343.

25. Izhak Englard, "Law and Religion in Israel," *American Journal of Comparative Law* 35, no. 1 (1987): 188.

26. Englard, "Law and Religion in Israel," 189.

27. Englard, "Law and Religion in Israel," 189.

28. See Michael Karayanni, "The Acute Multicultural Entrapment of the Palestinian-Arab Religious Minorities in Israel and the Feeble Measures Required to Relieve It," in *Mapping the Legal Boundaries of Belonging: Religion and Multiculturalism from Israel to Canada*, ed. René Provost (New York: Oxford University Press, 2014), 225–51.

29. See Michael Karayanni, "The Multicultural Nature of the Religious Accommodations for the Palestinian-Arab Minority in Israel: A Curse or a Blessing?," in *The Israeli Nation State: Political, Constitutional, and Cultural Challenges*, ed. Fania Oz-Salzberger and Yedidia Z. Stern (Boston: Academic Studies Press, 2014), 265–89.

30. See Michael Karayanni, "Two Concepts of Group Rights for the Palestinian-Arab Minority under Israel's Constitutional Definition as a 'Jewish and Democratic' State," *International Journal of Constitutional Law* 10, no. 2 (2012): 304–39.

31. See Michael Karayanni, "Multiculturalism as Covering: On the Accommodation of Minority Religions in Israel," *American Journal of Comparative Law* (forthcoming); Michael Karayanni, "Multiculture Me No More! On Multicultural Qualifications and the Palestinian-Arab Minority of Israel," *Diogenes* 54, no. 3 (2007): 39–58.

32. See Halperin-Kaddari, "Women, Religion and Multiculturalism," 343.

33. Kamel Abu Jaber, "The Millet System in the Nineteenth-Century Ottoman Empire," *The Muslim World* 57, no. 3 (1967): 212–23.

34. Baruch Kimmerling, "Boundaries and Frontiers of the Israeli Control System: Analytical Conclusions," in *The Israeli State and Society: Boundaries and Frontiers*, ed. Baruch Kimmerling (Albany: State University of New York Press, 1989), 265–84.

35. See, for example, Peleg and Waxman, *Israel's Palestinians*, 54; Landau, *The Arab Minority in Israel*, 2; Elie Rekhess, "The Evolvement of an Arab-Palestinian National Minority in Israel," *Israel Studies* 12, no. 3 (2007): 3–28.

36. Uri Bialer, "Top Hat, Tuxedo and Cannons: Israeli Foreign Policy from 1948 to 1956 as a Field of Study," *Israel Studies* 7, no. 1 (2002): 2–3, 14–15.

37. League of Nations, The Mandate for Palestine (1922), Article 9, http://www.mfa.gov.il /mfa/foreignpolicy/peace/guide/pages/the%20mandate%20for%20palestine.aspx.

38. Declaration of Independence 1948, OG no. 1, May 14, 1948.

39. Alisa Rubin Peled, "The Crystallization of an Israeli Policy Towards Muslim and Christian Holy Places, 1948–1955," *The Muslim World* 84, no. 1–2 (1994): 95.

40. Uri Bialer, *Cross on the Star of David: The Christian World in Israel's Foreign Policy, 1948–1967* (Bloomington: Indiana University Press, 2005), 8.

41. Bialer, *Cross on the Star of David*, 8.

42. Bialer, *Cross on the Star of David*, 8.

43. Walter Eytan, *The First Ten Years: A Diplomatic History of Israel* (New York: Simon and Schuster, 1958), 74–75.

44. Eytan, *The First Ten Years*, 74–75.

45. Edelman, *Courts, Politics, and Culture in Israel*, 77.

46. Moussa Abou Ramadan, "Judicial Activism of the Shari'a Appeals Court in Israel (1994–2001): Rise and Crises," *Fordham International Law Journal* 27, no. 1 (2003): 264 n.50.

47. Ido Shahar, "Forum Shopping Between Civil and Shari'a Courts: Maintenance Suits in Contemporary Jerusalem," in *Religion in Disputes: Pervasiveness of Religious Normativity in Disputing Processes*, ed. Franz von Benda-Beckman et al. (New York: Palgrave Macmillan, 2013), 150.

48. Laurence Louër, *To Be an Arab in Israel* (New York: Columbia University Press, 2007), 15–19.
49. Karayanni, "Two Concepts of Group Rights," 328–29.
50. Bialer, *Cross on the Star of David*, 144, 179, 180–81.
51. Israeli State Archive, MFA/2550/5 (February 8, 1951).
52. Israeli State Archive, MFA/2550/5 (January 30 1950).
53. Bialer, *Cross on the Star of David*, 104–05, 130–31, 189; Rubin Peled, "The Crystallization of an Israeli Policy," 96, 103.
54. Sarah Ozacky-Lazar, "Hitgabshut Yahasey ha-Gomlin bein Yehudim le-Aravim be-Medinat Yisra'el—Ha-Asor ha-Rishon, 1948–1958" ["The Crystallization of Mutual Relations Between Jews and Arabs in the State of Israel—The First Decade, 1948–1958"], PhD diss., University of Haifa, 1996, 57–58; Yoav Gelber, "Israel's Policy Towards Its Arab Minority, 1947–1950," *Israel Affairs* 19, no. 1 (2013): 55.
55. Daphne Tsimhoni, "The Status of the Arab Christians Under the British Mandate in Palestine," *Middle Eastern Studies* 20, no. 4 (1984): 169–70.
56. Ian Lustick, *Arabs in the Jewish State: Israel's Control of a National Minority* (Austin: University of Texas Press, 1980).
57. Lustick, *Arabs in the Jewish State*, 25–26.
58. Lustick, *Arabs in the Jewish State*, 82–83.
59. Lustick, *Arabs in the Jewish State*, 133.
60. Peleg and Waxman, *Israel's Palestinians*, 21–22; Baruch Kimmerling and Joel S. Migdal, *The Palestinian People: A History* (Cambridge, Mass.: Harvard University Press, 2003), 179–80; Kais M. Firro, *The Druzes in the Jewish State* (Leiden, Netherlands: Brill, 1999), 102–4.
61. Sabri Jiryis, *The Arabs in Israel* (New York: Monthly Review Press, 1976), 197.
62. Gad Barzilai, "Fantasies of Liberalism and Liberal Jurisprudence: State Law, Politics and Israeli Arab-Palestinian Community," *Israel Law Review* 34, no. 3 (2000): 436.
63. Druze Religious Courts Law, 5723–1962, 17 LSI 27 (1962–63).
64. Asher Maoz, "Religious Human Rights in the State of Israel," in *Religious Human Rights in Global Perspective: Legal Perspectives*, ed. D. Van der Vyvert and John Witte Jr. (The Hague: Kluwer Law International, 1996), 352–53.
65. Michael Corinaldi, "The Social, Educational and Cultural Aspects of Religious Pluralism in Israel: Discussion," in *The Status of Religious Pluralism in Israel* (Jerusalem: The American Jewish Committee, 1982), 17–18.
66. Shifman, *Mi Mefahed mi-Nissu'in Ezrahi'im?*, 10; Charles Liebman, "Religious Pluralism in the United States," in *The Status of Religious Pluralism in Israel* (Jerusalem: The American Jewish Committee, 1982), 23–25.
67. Ozacky-Lazar, "Hitgabshut Yahasey ha-Gomlin bein Yehudim le-Aravim," 57–58.
68. Israeli State Archive, RG 98/G/4778/39 (August 26, 1948).
69. Dr. Hirshberg's biography indicates that he was a trained academic in Jewish history, a rabbi, and was familiar with Arabic language and culture; see Alisa Rubin Peled, *Debating Islam in the Jewish State: The Development of Policy Toward Islamic Institutions in Israel* (Albany: State University of New York Press, 2001), 26.
70. Israeli State Archive, RG 98/G/4778/39 (August 31, 1948).
71. Israeli State Archive, RG 98/G/4778/39 (September 6, 1948).
72. Israeli State Archive, RG 98/G/4778/39 (August 17, 1948).
73. Israeli State Archive, G/1733/1 (April 19, 1949).
74. Rubin Peled, *Debating Islam in the Jewish State*, 18.
75. Rubin Peled, *Debating Islam in the Jewish State*, 18.

76. Gelber, "Israel's Policy Towards Its Arab Minority," 55.
77. Gelber, "Israel's Policy Towards Its Arab Minority," 67.
78. Gelber, "Israel's Policy Towards Its Arab Minority," 67.
79. Yair Bäuml, "Ekronot Mediniyut ha-Aflaya Klapei ha-Aravim be-Yisrael, 1948–1968" ["Principles of the Discrimination Policy Towards the Arabs in Israel, 1948–1968"], *Iyunim be-Tkumat Yisra'el* 16 (2006): 403–4 (in Hebrew).
80. Aziza Khazzoom, "The Great Chain of Orientalism: Jewish Identity, Stigma Management, and Ethnic Exclusion in Israel," *American Sociological Review* 68, no. 4 (2003): 481.
81. Sammy Smooha, "The Model of Ethnic Democracy: Israel as a Jewish and Democratic State," *Nations and Nationalism* 8, no. 4 (2002): 478, 483.
82. Mark Tessler, "The Identity of Religious Minorities in Non-Secular States: Jews in Tunisia and Morocco and Arabs in Israel," *Comparative Studies in Society and History* 20, no. 3 (1978): 359–60.
83. Uzi Rebhun and Chaim I. Waxman, "Challenges for the Twenty-First Century," in *Jews in Israel: Contemporary Social and Cultural Patterns*, ed. Uzi Rebhun and Chaim I. Waxman (Hanover, Mass.: Brandeis University Press, 2004), 469.
84. See Steven V. Mazie, *Israel's Higher Law: Religion and Liberal Democracy in the Jewish State* (Lanham, Md.: Lexington Books, 2006), 174; Simha Meron, "Freedom of Religion as Distinct from Freedom from Religion in Israel," *Israel Yearbook on Human Rights* 4 (1974): 223.
85. Sammy Smooha, "Ethnic Democracy: Israel as an Archetype," *Israel Studies* 2, no. 2 (1997): 222.
86. Zerach Warhaftig, "Medinat Yisra'el ke-Medina Yehudit" ["The State of Israel as a Jewish State"], in *Ha-Dat ve-ha-Medinah* [*Religion and the State*], ed. Matityahu Rothenburg (Tel-Aviv, National Religious Party in Israel, 1964), 72 (in Hebrew).
87. Warhaftig, "Medinat Yisra'el ke-Medina Yehudit," 74.
88. Warhaftig, "Medinat Yisra'el ke-Medina Yehudit," 75.
89. Zvi Triger, "Yesh Medina la-Ahava: Nissu'im ve-Gerushim bein Yehudim be-Medinat Yisra'el" ["There Is a State for Love: Marriage and Divorce Between Jews in the State of Israel"], in *Mishpatim al Ahava* [*Trials of Love,*], ed. Orna Ben-Naftali and Hanna Naveh (Tel-Aviv: Ramot, 2005) (in Hebrew).
90. Triger, "Yesh Medina la-Ahava: Nissu'im ve-Gerushim bein Yehudim be-Medinat Yisra'el," 193.
91. Triger, "Yesh Medina la-Ahava: Nissu'im ve-Gerushim bein Yehudim be-Medinat Yisra'el," 198.
92. Triger, "Yesh Medina la-Ahava: Nissu'im ve-Gerushim bein Yehudim be-Medinat Yisra'el," 198.
93. Triger, "Yesh Medina la-Ahava: Nissu'im ve-Gerushim bein Yehudim be-Medinat Yisra'el," 204.
94. Triger, "Yesh Medina la-Ahava: Nissu'im ve-Gerushim bein Yehudim be-Medinat Yisra'el," 204.
95. Triger, "Yesh Medina la-Ahava: Nissu'im ve-Gerushim bein Yehudim be-Medinat Yisra'el," 204.
96. Oren Yiftachel, "'Ethnocracy' and Its Discontents: Minorities, Protests, and the Israeli Polity," *Critical Inquiry* 26, no. 4 (2000): 742.
97. Sammy Smooha, "Jewish Ethnicity in Israel: Symbolic or Real," in *Jews in Israel: Contemporary Social and Cultural Patterns*, ed. Uzi Rebhun and Chaim I. Waxman (Hanover, Mass.: Brandeis University Press, 2004), 51.

98. Yochanan Peres, "Ethnic Relations in Israel," *American Journal of Sociology* 76, no. 6 (1971): 1026.

99. Philomila Tsoukala, "Marrying Family Law to the Nation," *American Journal of Comparative Law* 58, no. 4 (2010): 874.

100. Michael Karayanni, "In the Best Interests of the Group: Religious Matching Under Israeli Adoption Law," *Berkeley Journal of Middle Eastern and Islamic Law* 3, no. 1 (2010): 33–36.

101. HCJ 8140/13 Ornan v. State of Israel 2013 (December 9, 2013).

102. Yet when pressed it was not always clear that the Palestinian-Arabs were positively for the system and in fact "tried not to emphasize their interreligious and interethnic differences." Kimmerling and Migdal, *The Palestinian People*, 180.

103. Sammy Smooha, "Arab-Jewish Relations in Israel: A Deeply Divided Society," in *Israeli Identity in Transition*, ed. Anita Shapira (Westport, Conn. : Praeger, 2004), 43.

104. Karayanni, "In the Best Interests of the Group," 33–36.

105. Nadim N. Rouhana, *Palestinian Citizens in an Ethnic Jewish State: Identities in Conflict* (New Haven, Conn.: Yale University Press, 1997), 183.

106. See David M. Neuhaus, "Between Quiescence and Arousal: The Political Functions of Religion: A Case Study of the Arab Minority in Israel: 1948–1990" (PhD diss., Hebrew University of Jerusalem, 1991), 16.

107. See Robert H. Eisenman, *Islamic Law in Palestine and Israel: A History of the Survival of Tanzimat and Shari'a in the British Mandate and the Jewish State* (Leiden, Netherlands: Brill, 1978), 168–95.

108. Cohn, *Mevo Ishi*, 227.

109. Cohn, *Mevo Ishi*, 227.

110. Haim H. Cohn, "Religious Freedom and Religious Coercion in the State of Israel," in *Israel Among the Nations*, ed. Alfred E. Kellerman et al. (The Hague: Kluwer Law International, 1998), 94.

111. See Elie Rekhess, *Ha-Mi'ut ha-Aravi be-Yisra'el: Bein Komunizm ve-Le'umiyut Aravit, 1965–1991* [*The Arab Minority in Israel: Between Communism and Arab Nationalism, 1965–1991*] (Tel-Aviv: United Kibbutz, 1993) (in Hebrew).

112. Kimmerling and Migdal, *The Palestinian People*, 188–90.

113. Manar Hassan, "Ha-Politika shel ha-Kavod: Ha-Patriarkhiya, ha-Medina ve-Retsakh Nashim Beshem Kvod ha-Mishpaha" ["The Politics of Honor: The Patriarchy, the State and the Murder of Women in the Name of Family Honor"], in *Min, Migdar, Politika* [*Sex, Gender, Politics*], ed. Daphna N. Yizre'eli et al. (Tel-Aviv: United Kibbutz, 1999), 297–301 (in Hebrew).

114. Danny Rubinstein, "Ha-Shesa Ha-Dati-Hiloni Bekerev Arviyei Yisrael" ["The Religious-Secular Rift Among Israeli Arabs"], in *Shnaton Dat u-Medinah 5753–5754* [*State and Religion Yearbook 1993–1994*], ed. Avner Horwitz (Tel-Aviv: United Kibbutz, 1994), 90 (in Hebrew).

115. See Mark Tessler and Audra Grant, "Israel's Arab Citizens: The Continuing Struggle," *Annals of the American Academy of Political and Social Science* 555 (1998): 99; Peleg and Waxman, *Israel's Palestinians*, 48–50; Kimmerling and Migdal, *The Palestinian People*, 170–71, 187; Jiryis, *The Arabs in Israel*, 162.

116. See Susan Moller Okin, "Is Multiculturalism Bad for Women?," in *Is Multiculturalism Bad For Women?*, ed. Joshua Cohen et al. (Princeton, N.J.: Princeton University Press, 1999), 7–24.

# Bibliography

Abou Ramadan, Moussa. "Judicial Activism of the Shari'a Appeals Court in Israel (1994–2001): Rise and Crises." *Fordham International Law Journal* 27, no. 1 (2003): 254–98.

Abu Jaber, Kamel. "The Millet System in the Nineteenth-Century Ottoman Empire." *The Muslim World* 57, no. 3 (1967): 212–23.

Barzilai, Gad. "Analysis of Israelis [Jews and Arab-Palestinians]: Exploring Law in Society and Society in Law." *International Journal of Law in Context* 11, no. 3 (2015): 361–78.

——. "Fantasies of Liberalism and Liberal Jurisprudence: State Law, Politics and Israeli Arab-Palestinian Community." *Israel Law Review* 34, no. 3 (2000): 425–51.

Bäuml, Yair. "Ekronot Mediniyut ha-Aflaya Klapei ha-Aravim be-Yisrael, 1948–1968" ["Principles of the Discrimination Policy towards the Arabs in Israel, 1948–1968"]. *Iyunim be-Tkumat Yisra'el* 16 (2006): 391–414 (in Hebrew).

Ben-Porath, Guy. *Between State and Synagogue: The Secularization of Contemporary Israel.* Cambridge: Cambridge University Press, 2013.

Bialer, Uri. *Cross on the Star of David: The Christian World in Israel's Foreign Policy, 1948–1967.* Bloomington: Indiana University Press, 2005.

——. "Top Hat, Tuxedo and Cannons: Israeli Foreign Policy from 1948 to 1956 as a Field of Study." *Israel Studies* 7, no. 1 (2002): 1–80.

Cohn, Haim H. *Mevo Ishi: Otobiografiya* [*A Personal Introduction: Autobiography*]. Or-Yehuda: Dvir, 2005 (in Hebrew).

——. "Religious Freedom and Religious Coercion in the State of Israel." In *Israel Among the Nations*, ed. Alfred E. Kellerman et al., 79–110. The Hague: Kluwer Law International, 1998.

Corinaldi, Michael. "The Social, Educational and Cultural Aspects of Religious Pluralism in Israel: Discussion." In *The Status of Religious Pluralism in Israel*, 17–18. Jerusalem: The American Jewish Committee, 1982.

Edelman, Martin. *Courts, Politics, and Culture in Israel.* Charlottesville: University Press of Virginia, 1994.

Eisenman, Robert H. *Islamic Law in Palestine and Israel: A History of the Survival of Tanzimat and Shari'a in the British Mandate and the Jewish State.* Leiden, Netherlands: Brill, 1978.

Englard, Izhak. "Law and Religion in Israel." *American Journal of Comparative Law* 35, no. 1 (1987): 185–208.

Eytan, Walter. *The First Ten Years: A Diplomatic History of Israel.* New York: Simon and Schuster, 1958.

Firro, Kais M. *The Druzes in the Jewish State.* Leiden, Netherlands: Brill, 1999.

Galanter, Marc, and Jayenth Kirshnan. "Personal Law and Human Rights in India and Israel." *Israel Law Review* 34, no. 1 (2000): 101–133.

Gelber, Yoav. "Israel's Policy Towards Its Arab Minority, 1947–1950." *Israel Affairs* 19, no. 1 (2013): 51–81.

Hacker, Daphna. "Religious Tribunals in Democratic States: Lessons from the Israeli Rabbinical Courts." *Journal of Religion and State* 27, no. 1 (2012): 59–81.

Halperin-Kaddari, Ruth. "Women, Religion and Multiculturalism in Israel." *UCLA Journal of International Law and Foreign Affairs* 5, no. 2 (2000): 339–66.

Harris, Ron. "Hizdamnuyot Historiyot ve-Hakhmatsot she-be-Hesse'ah ha-Da'at: Al Shiluvo shel ha-Mishpat ha-Ivri ba-Mishpat ha-Yisra'eli be-Reishito" ["Historical Opportunities and Absent-Minded Misses: On the Integration of Jewish Law into Israeli Law at Its Beginnings"]. In *Shnei Ivrei ha-Gesher: Dat u-Medina be-Reishit Darka shel Yisra'el* [*Both Sides of the Bridge: Religion and State in the Early Years of Israel*], ed. Mordechai Bar-On and Zvi Zameret, 21–55. Jerusalem: Yad Yizhak Ben-Zvi Institute, 2002 (in Hebrew).

Hassan, Manar. "Ha-Politika shel ha-Kavod: Ha-Patriarkhiya, ha-Medina ve-Retsakh Nashim Beshem Kvod ha-Mishpaha" ["The Politics of Honor: The Patriarchy, the State and the Murder of Women in the Name of Family Honor"]. In *Min, Migdar, Politika* [*Sex, Gender, Politics*], ed. Daphna N. Yizre'eli et al., 267–305. Tel-Aviv: United Kibbutz, 1999 (in Hebrew).

Hazan, Reuven. "Religion and Politics in Israel: The Rise and Fall of the Consociational Model." *Israel Affairs* 6, no. 2 (1999) 109–37.

Hirschl, Ran. *Constitutional Theocracy*. Cambridge, Mass.: Harvard University Press, 2010.

Hofri-Winogradow, Adam S. "A Plurality of Discontent: Legal Pluralism, Religious Adjudication and the State." *Journal of Religion and State* 26, no.1 (2011): 57–89.

Israel Ministry for Foreign Affairs. *The Arabs in Israel*. Jerusalem: Information Department, Israel Ministry for Foreign Affairs, 1996.

Jabareen, Yousef T. "Constitution Building and Equality in Deeply-Divided Societies: The Case of the Palestinian-Arab Minority in Israel." *Wisconsin International Law Journal* 26, no. 2 (2008–2009): 345–401.

Jiryis, Sabri. *The Arabs in Israel*. New York: Monthly Review Press, 1976.

Karayanni, Michael. "The Acute Multicultural Entrapment of the Palestinian-Arab Religious Minorities in Israel and the Feeble Measures Required to Relieve It." In *Mapping the Legal Boundaries of Belonging: Religion and Multiculturalism from Israel to Canada*, ed. René Provost, 225–51. New York: Oxford University Press, 2014.

——. "In the Best Interests of the Group: Religious Matching Under Israeli Adoption Law." *Berkeley Journal of Middle Eastern and Islamic Law* 3, no. 1 (2010): 1–80.

——. "The Multicultural Nature of the Religious Accommodations for the Palestinian-Arab Minority in Israel: A Curse or a Blessing?" In *The Israeli Nation State: Political, Constitutional, and Cultural Challenges*, ed. Fania Oz-Salzberger and Yedidia Z. Stern, 265–89. Boston: Academic Studies Press, 2014.

——. "Multiculturalism as Covering: On the Accommodation of Minority Religions in Israel." *American Journal of Comparative Law* (forthcoming).

——. "Multiculture Me No More! On Multicultural Qualifications and the Palestinian-Arab Minority of Israel." *Diogenes* 54, no. 3 (2007): 39–58.

——. "The Separate Nature of Religious Accommodations for the Palestinian-Arab Minority in Israel." *Northwestern Journal of International Human Rights* 5, no.1 (2006): 41–71.

——. "Tainted Liberalism: Israel's Palestinian-Arab Millets." *Constellations* 23, no. 1 (2015): 71–83.

——. "Two Concepts of Group Rights for the Palestinian-Arab Minority under Israel's Constitutional Definition as a 'Jewish and Democratic' State." *International Journal of Constitutional Law* 10, no. 2 (2012): 304–39.

Khazzoom, Aziza. "The Great Chain of Orientalism: Jewish Identity, Stigma Management, and Ethnic Exclusion in Israel." *American Sociological Review* 68, no. 4 (2003): 481–510.

Kimmerling, Baruch. "Boundaries and Frontiers of the Israeli Control System: Analytical Conclusions." In *The Israeli State and Society: Boundaries and Frontiers*, ed. Baruch Kimmerling, 265–84. Albany: State University of New York Press, 1989.

Kimmerling, Baruch, and Joel S. Migdal. *The Palestinian People: A History*. Cambridge, Mass.: Harvard University Press, 2003.

Kretzmer, David. *The Legal Status of the Arabs in Israel*. Boulder, Colo: Westview Press, 1990.

Landau, Jacob M. *The Arab Minority in Israel, 1967–1991: Political Aspects*. Oxford: Clarendon Press, 1993.

Liebman, Charles. "Religious Pluralism in the United States." In *The Status of Religious Pluralism in Israel*, 23–25. Jerusalem: The American Jewish Committee, 1982.

Liebman Charles S., and Eliezer Don-Yehiya. *Religion and Politics in Israel*. Bloomington: Indiana University Press, 1984.

Louër, Laurence. *To Be an Arab in Israel*. New York: Columbia University Press, 2007.

Lustick, Ian. *Arabs in the Jewish State: Israel's Control of a National Minority*. Austin: University of Texas Press, 1980.

Maoz, Asher. "Religious Human Rights in the State of Israel." In *Religious Human Rights in Global Perspective: Legal Perspectives*, ed. Johan D. Van der Vyvert and John Witte Jr., 349–90. The Hague: Kluwer Law International, 1996.

Mazie, Steven V. *Israel's Higher Law: Religion and Liberal Democracy in the Jewish State*. Lanham, Md.: Lexington Books, 2006.

Meron, Simha. "Freedom of Religion as Distinct from Freedom from Religion in Israel." *Israel Yearbook on Human Rights* 4 (1974): 219–40.

Moller Okin, Susan. "Is Multiculturalism Bad for Women?" In *Is Multiculturalism Bad For Women?*, ed. Joshua Cohen et al., 7–26. Princeton, N.J.: Princeton University Press, 1999.

Neuhaus, David M. "Between Quiescence and Arousal: The Political Functions of Religion: A Case Study of the Arab Minority in Israel: 1948–1990." PhD diss., Hebrew University of Jerusalem, 1991.

Nisan, Mordechai. *Minorities in the Middle East: A History of Struggle and Self-Expression*. Jefferson, N.C.: McFarland, 1991.

Ozacky-Lazar, Sarah. "Hitgabshut Yahasey ha-Gomlin bein Yehudim le-Aravim be-Medinat Yisra'el—Ha-Asor ha-Rishon, 1948–1958" ["The Crystallization of Mutual Relations between Jews and Arabs in the State of Israel—The First Decade, 1948–1958"]. PhD diss., University of Haifa, 1996.

Peleg, Ilan, and Dov Waxman. *Israel's Palestinians: The Conflict Within*. Cambridge: Cambridge University Press, 2011.

Peres, Yochanan. "Ethnic Relations in Israel." *American Journal of Sociology* 76, no. 6 (1971): 1021–47.

Raday, Frances. "Culture, Religion and Gender." *International Journal of Constitutional Law* 1, no. 4 (2003): 663–715.

Rebhun, Uzi, and Chaim I. Waxman. "Challenges for the Twenty-First Century." In *Jews in Israel: Contemporary Social and Cultural Patterns*, ed. Uzi Rebhun and Chaim I. Waxman, 465–80. Hanover, Mass.: Brandeis University Press, 2004.

Rekhess, Elie. "The Evolvement of an Arab-Palestinian National Minority in Israel." *Israel Studies* 12, no. 3 (2007): 3–28.

——. *Ha-Mi'ut ha-Aravi be-Yisra'el: Bein Komunizm ve-Le'umiyut Aravit, 1965–1991* [*The Arab Minority in Israel: Between Communism and Arab Nationalism, 1965–1991*]. Tel-Aviv: United Kibbutz, 1993 (in Hebrew).

Rouhana, Nadim N. *Palestinian Citizens in an Ethnic Jewish State: Identities in Conflict*. New Haven, Conn.: Yale University Press, 1997.

Rubin Peled, Alisa. "The Crystallization of an Israeli Policy Towards Muslim and Christian Holy Places, 1948–1955." *The Muslim World* 84, no. 1–2 (1994): 95–121.

——. *Debating Islam in the Jewish State: The Development of Policy Toward Islamic Institutions in Israel*. Albany: State University of New York Press, 2001.

Rubinstein, Amnon, and Barak Medina. *Ha-Mishpat ha-Hukati shel Medinat Yisra'el* [*The Constitutional Law of the State of Israel*], 6th ed. Jerusalem: Schocken, 2005 (in Hebrew).

Rubinstein, Danny. "Ha-Shesa Ha-Dati-Hiloni Bekerev Arviyei Yisrael" ["The Religious-Secular Rift Among Israeli Arabs"]. In *Shnaton Dat u-Medinah 5753–5754* [*State and*

*Religion Yearbook 1993–1994*], ed. Avner Horwitz, 89–90. Tel-Aviv: United Kibbutz, 1994 (in Hebrew).

Saban, Ilan. "Minority Rights in Deeply Divided Societies: A Framework for Analysis and the Case of the Arab-Palestinian Minority in Israel." *New York University Journal of International Law and Politics* 36, no. 4 (2004): 885–1003.

Shahar, Ido. "Forum Shopping Between Civil and Shari'a Courts: Maintenance Suits in Contemporary Jerusalem." In *Religion in Disputes: Pervasiveness of Religious Normativity in Disputing Processes*, ed. Franz von Benda-Beckman et al., 47–80. New York: Palgrave Macmillan, 2013.

Sezgin, Yüksel. *Human Rights Under State-Enforced Religious Family Laws in Israel, Egypt and India*. Cambridge: Cambridge University Press, 2013.

Shafir, Gershon, and Yoav Peled. *Being Israeli: The Dynamics of Multiple Citizenship*. Cambridge: Cambridge University Press, 2002.

Shava, Menashe. "Civil Marriages Celebrated Abroad: Validity in Israel." *Tel-Aviv Studies in Law* 9 (1989): 311–46.

Shifman, Pinhas. *Mi Mefahed mi-Nissu'in Ezrahi'im?* [*Who Is Afraid of Civil Marriage?*], Jerusalem: Jerusalem Institute for Israel Studies, 1995 (in Hebrew).

Shiloh, Isaac S. "Marriage and Divorce in Israel." *Israel Law Review* 5, no. 4 (1970): 479–98.

Smooha, Sammy. "Arab-Jewish Relations in Israel: A Deeply Divided Society." In *Israeli Identity in Transition*, ed. Anita Shapira, 47–80. Westport, Conn.: Praeger, 2004.

——. "Ethnic Democracy: Israel as an Archetype." *Israel Studies* 2, no. 2 (1997): 198–241.

——. "Jewish Ethnicity in Israel: Symbolic or Real." In *Jews in Israel: Contemporary Social and Cultural Patterns*, ed. Uzi Rebhun and Chaim I. Waxman, 467–80. Hanover, Mass.: Brandeis University Press, 2004.

——. "The Model of Ethnic Democracy: Israel as a Jewish and Democratic State." *Nations and Nationalism* 8, no. 4 (2002): 475–503.

Stendel, Ori. "The Rights of the Arab Minority in Israel." *Israel Yearbook on Human Rights* 1 (1971): 134–55.

Tessler, Mark. "The Identity of Religious Minorities in Non-Secular States: Jews in Tunisia and Morocco and Arabs in Israel." *Comparative Studies in Society and History* 20, no. 3 (1978): 359–73.

Tessler, Mark, and Audra Grant. "Israel's Arab Citizens: The Continuing Struggle." *Annals of the American Academy of Political and Social Science* 555 (1998): 97–113.

Triger, Zvi. "Yesh Medina la-Ahava: Nissu'im ve-Gerushim bein Yehudim be-Medinat Yisra'el" ["There Is a State for Love: Marriage and Divorce between Jews in the State of Israel"]. In *Mishpatim al Ahava* [*Trials of Love*], ed. Orna Ben-Naftali and Hanna Naveh, 173–225. Tel-Aviv: Ramot, 2005 (in Hebrew).

Tsimhoni, Daphne. "The Status of the Arab Christians Under the British Mandate in Palestine." *Middle Eastern Studies* 20, no. 4 (1984): 166–92.

Tsoukala, Philomila. "Marrying Family Law to the Nation." *American Journal of Comparative Law* 58, no. 4 (2010): 873–910.

Warhaftig, Zerach. "Medinat Yisra'el ke-Medina Yehudit" ["The State of Israel as a Jewish State"]. In *Ha-Dat ve-ha-Medinah* [*Religion and the State*], ed. Matityahu Rothenburg, 72–76. Tel-Aviv, National Religious Party in Israel, 1964 (in Hebrew).

Yiftachel, Oren. "'Ethnocracy' and Its Discontents: Minorities, Protests, and the Israeli Polity." *Critical Inquiry* 26, no. 4 (2000): 725–56.

Zamir, Itzhak. "Shivyon Zekhuyot Klapei ha-Aravim be-Yisra'el" ["Equality of Rights for Arabs in Israel"], *Mishpat u-Mimshal* 9 (2005), 11–37 (in Hebrew).

## 11

# JURISDICTIONAL COMPETITION AND INTERNAL REFORM IN MUSLIM FAMILY LAW IN ISRAEL AND GREECE

YÜKSEL SEZGIN

Should a democratic state accommodate the demands of ethno-religious communities for legal autonomy by recognizing and formally incorporating their laws and dispute-resolution mechanisms (particularly in the field of family law) into a pluri-legal framework? Over the last decades, this question, which lies at the heart of the so-called multiculturalism debates (especially as it relates to Shari'a and Muslim communities), has drawn the attention of many scholars, activists, policy makers, and politicians.

Multicultural accommodations that bestow on minority groups positive rights to preserve their distinctive religio-legal traditions pose a challenging normative puzzle, especially when well-intended group rights clash with the rights of individuals within those communities. When that happens, whose rights should prevail—those of ethno-religious groups or those of individuals? And what should the liberal state do—sit silently on the sidelines or step in to protect individuals against the "oppressive" practices of their cultural communities? Answers to these questions form the main intellectual fault lines in the multiculturalism literature. Apart from those,[1] such as critical feminists,[2] who categorically reject pluri-legal accommodations in family law, most scholars have suggested that religion or custom-based legal orders might be tolerated if individuals were given the right to choose between religious and secular law and to exit from their cultural communities.

The list of democratic countries that recognize and formally integrate religious laws/courts within their legal systems is short. In fact, there are only four such nations: Israel, Greece, India and Ghana.[3] Policy makers in these countries have long confronted two important questions that largely have been ignored in the multiculturalism literature: (1) How should secular and religious laws and courts relate to one another in a democratic regime? and (2) What role should secular state institutions (especially civil courts) play in making sure religious courts respect fundamental rights and liberties while making their decisions?

The only scholar who has taken on these practical challenges and offered a comprehensive framework to address them is Ayelet Shachar. In a series of publications, Shachar has laid out an institutional framework to address the question of jurisdictional relations between secular and religious judiciaries and the question of reducing inter-and intracommunal inequalities. In *Multicultural Jurisdictions*, she proposes a joint governance model, called "transformative accommodation" (TA), that envisions a scheme of power sharing between religious and civil courts in matters of family law along the lines of three cumulative principles: the "submatter" allocation of authority, the "no monopoly" rule, and the establishment of clearly delineated choice options (that is, partial exit).[4] An accommodation based on these foundational principles, Shachar argues, would potentially transform the religious communities and institutions by encouraging them to reform discriminatory internal practices and rules. TA is particularly concerned with lateral power relations between religious and civil courts, which often share concurrent jurisdiction. In a later work addressing the vertical power relations between religious and secular judiciaries, Shachar has argued for the adoption of centralized *ex ante* oversight techniques over religious courts to ensure the compliance of their decisions with predefined rules and procedures (for example, basic rights and liberties).[5]

The accommodation model that Shachar has developed over the last two decades remains the most comprehensive model for addressing the practical challenges of accommodating religious laws/courts within otherwise secular and democratic regimes. Daphna Hacker, who tested the feasibility of Shachar's TA model in the context of Israeli rabbinical courts, found strong empirical evidence that under certain conditions, jurisdictional competition between religious and seculars court may bring about internal reform in religious norms and practices.[6] Both rabbinical and civil courts in Israel are controlled by members of the country's majority ethno-religious group. But what about Shari'a courts in non-Muslim democracies? Can Shachar's accommodative framework help us understand the relations between secular and Islamic courts in non-Muslim democracies such as Israel and Greece? State-enforced Muslim Family Laws (MFLs), such as those in Israel and Greece, are often reported to place certain limitations on the rights of women and children. Can civil courts in non-Muslim countries help mitigate the negative effects of MFLs by bringing about (direct or indirect) changes in Muslim laws and courts? In this chapter I aim to answer these questions and contribute to our understanding of challenges and possibilities of multicultural pluri-legal accommodations, with specific attention to Islamic law and institutions in two non-Muslim democracies: Israel and Greece.

Of the four non-Muslim-majority democracies in the world that formally integrate MFLs in their national legal systems, I focus on the first two due to their common heritage: both countries inherited their MFLs directly from the Ottoman Empire. Also, despite their many similarities, these two countries exemplify two contrasting cases: in Greece the civil-court-initiated MFL reform almost completely failed, whereas in Israel it was (modestly) successful.

Success is in the eye of the beholder. As I demonstrate through a comparative analysis of Israeli and Greek MFL systems, although both jurisdictions incorporated some of the elements of Shachar's TA model and employed some ex ante oversight techniques, there has been no "transformative" change in Muslim law or institutions in either country. This does not mean there was no change. There was change, but it was more limited than what Shachar would have predicted. The prospects for internal reform in MFL systems were better when lower and higher civil courts worked in tandem (exerting simultaneous lateral and vertical pressure, respectively, on Islamic courts), and the Shari'a system was closely integrated into the normative hierarchy of the national legal system. The direction and magnitude of change was also influenced by three other elements: (1) the availability of legal aid nongovernmental organizations (NGOs) that helped litigants take full advantage of concurrent jurisdictions, (2) the political context (that is, relations between the government and the Muslim minority, and relations between the non-Muslim government in question and foreign nations acting as "protectors" of the Muslim minority), and (3) the relative legitimacy of the civil judiciary in the eyes of the Muslim minority, which correlates with the relative absence/presence of Muslim judges on the bench in civil courts.

## Civil-Religious Court Relations and Internal Reform in Muslim Family Law

Fifty countries in the world today formally integrate MFLs into their legal systems. The manner and extent to which each country incorporates MFL into its legal system ("mode of integration") varies considerably. In some countries, religious laws are fully integrated into the national system and are applied by secularly trained judges at civil courts ("full integration mode," as in India); in some countries they are applied by specialized Shari'a courts ("confessional mode," as in Israel), and in other countries they are applied by state-recognized religious authorities without a formal court system ("traditional authority mode," as in Greece). The understanding and interpretation of MFLs in these fifty countries varies considerably—some adopt more "liberal" interpretations, some more "conservative" ones. However, despite this variation, it is often reported that different aspects of MFLs (underage marriage, polygyny, and so forth) negatively affect human rights, particularly those of women and children.[7] In other words, group-based rights accorded to Muslim communities as collectives often clash with individual rights and liberties accorded to their members under constitutional and international law. Shachar refers to this phenomenon as "the paradox of multicultural vulnerability."[8] The paradox poses its greatest challenge to MFL-applying democracies that are normatively expected to balance their constitutional obligations to individual Muslim citizens with their multicultural commitments to Muslim communities.

As Shachar notes, a comprehensive solution to this paradox requires establishing an institutional framework that would allow cultural differences to flourish while creating a catalyst for internal change to reduce intragroup inequalities and protect the rights of vulnerable group members.[9] She calls her proposed framework for this challenging task "transformative accommodation.".

With regard to family law, TA assumes that religious and secular courts will share jurisdiction by establishing their respective subject-matter jurisdiction over separate but complementary submatters. For instance, if marriage and divorce are placed under the purview of religious courts, related family matters such as custody and alimony would be placed under the jurisdiction of civil courts. Shachar calls this "joint governance," wherein neither civil nor religious courts are given monopolistic control that will have bearing on the rights of individuals as both group members and citizens. Finally, civil and religious courts have concurrent jurisdictions that allow individuals to transfer their disputes from one court system to another if they feel that one jurisdiction is systematically failing to address their concerns.

Religious courts usually interact with two types of civil courts: (1) high courts (that exercise supervisory powers over religious courts), and (2) lower courts (district or specialized family courts that share concurrent jurisdiction with religious courts). Here Shachar's TA model may be particularly helpful in analyzing the relations between lower civil and Islamic courts in Israel and Greece and identifying the direct or indirect roles civil courts may play in respect to regulation and administration of MFLs in minority contexts.

In many non-Muslim countries, religious courts share jurisdiction concurrently with lower civil courts. In some instances, Muslim litigants can take advantage of concurrent jurisdictions and forum shop between civil and religious laws/courts. As Shachar suggests, forum shopping may promote jurisdictional competition.[10] Facing competition from civil courts, religious courts may feel pressured and respond by undertaking self-reform to retain their authority and clientele.

In Shachar's conceptualization, lower civil courts are an important but indirect source of internal change in religious law and institutions. By contrast, higher civil courts, which may conduct *ex post* review of religious court rulings and repeal them, have a more equivocal role. According to Shachar, the institution of ex post judicial review conducted by superior courts places the burden of reporting alleged human rights violations on vulnerable groups (for example, women, children) who may already have been coerced into accepting the jurisdiction of religious courts. Ex post judicial review is, therefore, a problematic oversight mechanism. Instead of relying solely on ex post review, Shachar suggests, additional ex ante oversight mechanisms should be adopted. Examples of ex ante oversight include mandatory secular legal training (for example, constitutional law) for religious judges, mandatory legal counsel for individuals appearing before religious courts, permission for third parties to appear as *amicus curiae*, and mandatory a priori review of religious court decisions. Shachar argues that, over time, the continuous use of *ex ante* oversight techniques, as in the case of TA, may bring about "change from within." To avoid clashing with statutory laws, she suggests that religious judges might exercise self-restraint and voluntarily internalize certain secular norms.[11]

Shachar's reservations regarding the limitations of ex post review are particularly germane to relations between secular high courts and Shari'a courts in non-Muslim democracies. It is usually difficult for Muslim litigants to challenge the religious court decisions at majority-controlled higher civil courts, which are often viewed as alien institutions by the Muslim minority. In this respect, Shachar's suggestion to adopt complementary ex ante oversight techniques to overcome the limitations of ex post judicial review and thereby bring about internal change in religious courts is particularly welcome. In fact, some of the MFL-applying democracies have already adopted various sorts of ex ante oversight mechanisms to control the practices of Islamic courts. For instance, Israel passed an amendment law in 2002 that makes it possible to appoint Shari'a court judges (*qadis*) with secular training in law, social sciences, and humanities. Proponents of the law held the view that secularly trained qadis would be more receptive to secular ideas and norms than previous generations of qadis who had religious training exclusively.[12] Likewise, Greek law (1920/1991) requires a priori review of all *mufti* decisions for constitutional compliance before they may be declared "enforceable." In other words, some ex ante oversight measures are already in place in both Israel and Greece. But have they produced the outcomes Shachar hypothesizes they will? For instance, are religious courts now more compliant with secular law? Has the competition between civil and religious courts brought about a transformation in religious courts?

I briefly describe the MFL establishments in Israel and Greece next, and I answer these questions by analyzing the relations between religious and civil courts in both countries.

## MFL Establishment in Israel and Greece

Both Israel and Greece have sizable Muslim minorities (18 percent in Israel, 5 percent in Greece[13]) and formally integrate MFL in their legal systems—Israel since 1948 and Greece since 1881. Nearly all aspects of Shachar's TA model—albeit to varying degrees—and some ex ante oversight techniques have long been incorporated in Israeli and Greek MFL systems.

Israel inherited its MFL system from the Ottoman Empire. Under the current system, there are eight regional Shari'a courts and a Shari'a Court of Appeals (SCA) within Israel's pre–June 5, 1967 borders. The Israeli government appoints and pays the salaries of the qadis, who staff these courts, and executes Shari'a decisions.

Shari'a courts have exclusive jurisdiction over marriage and divorce and concurrent jurisdiction with civil family courts over all other matters of personal status involving Muslim citizens. Since the 2001 enactment of the Law of Family Courts (Amendment No. 5), Muslim litigants can choose between civil family and Shari'a courts for matters such as custody and maintenance. Both qadis and civil judges apply the same material law, which includes Islamic as well as relevant secular laws. The main source of MFLs applied by Israeli Shari'a courts (and civil family courts) is the Ottoman Law of Family Rights (OLFR) of 1917. Shari'a courts must also consider a body of civil legislation in making their decisions. These laws include the Marriage Age Law (1950), the Women's Equal Rights Law (1951), Penal Law Amendment (Bigamy) Law (1959), and the Law of Legal Capacity and Guardianship (1962).

The Supreme Court of Israel, sitting in its capacity as the High Court of Justice (HCJ), is authorized to hear petitions regarding the competence and jurisdiction of Shari'a courts. It reviews Shari'a courts' interpretations and applications of relevant statutory laws and overturns their decisions if found ultra vires.[14]

As a result of bilateral treaties between the Greek and Ottoman (later Turkish) governments in the late nineteenth and early twentieth centuries, Greece continues to officially recognize the jurisdiction of three Muslim muftis in the Thrace region to adjudicate family matters among Muslims in accordance with local usage and custom. Muftis are appointed and salaried by the Greek government and accorded adjudicative functions without necessarily establishing a network of Shari'a courts similar to those in Israel. The source of substantive and procedural Islamic law that mufti*s* apply is uncodified, and direct appeals are not permitted against mufti decisions.

The mufti jurisdiction has long been deemed exclusively for Thracian Muslims. However, some Greek judges and legal scholars argue that mufti jurisdiction should be considered concurrent with that of civil courts— meaning that Muslims should be able to choose between a civil court and a mufti with respect to family matters.[15] Mufti decisions cannot be implemented without an accompanying enforceability decree issued by the competent Court of First Instance (CoFI). The CoFI is required by law to review whether mufti decisions have been rendered within the bounds of mufti's jurisdiction and whether they have contravened the constitution.

Even though both Israeli and Greek governments have enacted legislation restricting the jurisdiction of MFL, regulating the appointment of qadis and muftis, and placing restrictions (through penal sanctions) on certain practices (such as polygyny), neither government has directly intervened in substantive MFL through executive or legislative means. Despite penal sanctions, polygyny (albeit limited), child marriage, and gender-unequal custody laws continue to be upheld in both countries (even recognized by religious authorities) and undermine the constitutionally/internationally protected fundamental rights of Muslim citizens (especially women and children).[16]

As Shachar puts it, when religious courts systematically violate the rights of members of the most vulnerable groups in society and fail to address their concerns, people often start shopping between competing jurisdictions and legal regimes—if "partial exit" is allowed.[17] This is the case in both Israel and Greece, where Muslims, under certain conditions, are allowed to choose between civil and religious laws and courts in personal status matters. Israeli and Greek Muslims also may ask higher civil courts to review and overturn the rulings of religious courts if they believe the religious authority overstepped its jurisdiction. As a result, in both countries, the use of civil law and courts by Muslim litigants for family matters is on the rise. For instance, the mufti of Komotini, who issued about 185 inheritance (*faraiz*) *fatwas* per year in 1964–1985, and 20 from 1985–2005, nowadays issues only about 3 to 5 fatwas per year.[18] A similar trend is reported in Israel. For instance, between 2006 and 2010, 66 percent of child custody cases, 22 percent of alimony cases, and 39 percent of child support cases filed by Kayan, a feminist legal aid organization serving Arab women in Israel, were filed at civil family courts.[19] Prior to 2001 the civil court option was not even available to Muslims.

In brief, in both countries civil courts have become more involved in daily regulation and application of MFLs, especially over the last decade. How has the rising competition and increasing involvement of civil courts (lower and higher) in the administration of MFLs affected the development of Islamic law in each country?

## Israeli Civil Courts and Muslim Family Law

### The High Court of Justice: Ex post Review of Shari'a Court Rulings

Decisions of Israeli Shari'a courts are subject to HCJ review. In cases involving Shari'a law, the court notes in almost every judgment that its intervention is limited to cases involving *ultra vires*, infringement of the principles of natural justice, and disregard for binding statutory rules that religious courts are legally bound to apply.[20] For instance, as early as 1955, in a Muslim custody case, the HCJ ruled that if a Shari'a court confines itself to the religious law alone and disregards the secular legislation that it is legally bound to apply, it will be acting *ultra vires* and its decision will, therefore, have no effect under the law.[21] In the following decades, the court continued to hold Shari'a courts responsible for the application of secular laws and reminded them that it would strike down their rulings if statutory laws were ignored.[22] The first two generations of Israeli qadis embraced a pragmatic approach toward the HCJ, often complying with secular laws to avoid any direct conflict with the civil judiciary.[23]

However, the nature of the relationship between the HCJ and Islamic courts began to change during the 1990s. In 1992, the Knesset enacted two Basic Laws dealing with fundamental rights. In a landmark ruling three years later,[24] the HCJ established its authority to conduct constitutional review of any legislation enacted by the Knesset.[25] Afterward, the court increasingly used its new powers to challenge the authority of religious courts and require them to comply with the newly enacted Basic Law of Human Dignity and Liberty (1992) to ensure that individuals appearing before religious courts continued to enjoy their basic rights.[26]

Historically, the court usually refrained from interfering with substantive aspects of Islamic law, particularly with respect to marriage and divorce.[27] In the post-1992 era, however, although largely maintaining its policy of non-interference in marriage and divorce, the court began to take a more activist stance with respect to other family matters to protect the rights of women and children. For instance, in a 1995 paternity case, the HCJ granted a Muslim child born out of wedlock civil paternity by bypassing the jurisdiction of shari'a courts, which had refused to grant the child religious paternity.[28] The HCJ reasoned that the Basic Law of Human Dignity is the supreme law of the land (that is, binding upon religious courts), and it gave the child a fundamental right to know her filiation. In another decision in 2013, the court declared that gender equality was integral to human dignity, and that Shari'a courts, like other state agencies, were obliged to abide by the principle of equality: "If there is a school of thought [e.g. Hanafi, Hanbali, etc.] that accepts the principle of [gender] equality, then religious courts should prefer it over schools of religious law that are inconsistent with this principle."[29] The HCJ's increasing secular activism provoked a strong defensive reaction from the Shari'a courts. Qadi Ahmad Natour, who served as the president of the SCA between 1994 and 2013, banned the application of all non-Shari'a-based laws (including the Basic Laws) by the Shari'a courts.[30]

On the surface, relations between the HCJ and Shari'a courts have seemed increasingly adversarial following the ban. In reality, however, the rhetoric of confrontation has gradually given way to a new phase of dialectical trans-formations at Shari'a courts and to a symbiotic relationship between civil and Islamic judiciaries. To defend the jurisdiction of the Islamic judiciary against the HCJ's increasing interventions, the SCA embraced a new defensive strategy—subtle compliance—the SCA would comply with the spirit of the secular law while publicly refusing to recognize it. In essence, the court internalized and Islamicized the concepts derived from secular legislation to prevent future HCJ interventions into Shari'a.[31] Principles such as "human dignity" are no longer treated as secular impositions but as concepts integral to the Islamic tradition.[32]

The strategy of subtle compliance has been most visible in child custody cases. The Legal Capacity and Guardianship Law of 1962 established the principle of "the best interests of the child" as the sole criterion in custody cases. Although the first two generations of qadis often based their custody decisions on the 1962 law, Qadi Natour prohibited application of that law—along with other secular laws—by the Islamic judiciary. The SCA has repeatedly indicated in its judgments that the 1962 law was inferior to the "noble" Shari'a and hence was not to be implemented by Islamic courts.[33] Despite its refusal to recognize the 1962 law, however, the court claimed that "the best interest of the child" principle "originated" in Islamic law and as such was to be considered the guiding principle in custody cases.[34] By internalizing secular frames and references such as "the best interest of the child," the court mainly aimed to restrict the HCJ's interventions into its jurisdiction.[35] This strategy proved successful to the extent that religious courts were able and willing to comply with civil procedures and the normative outcomes that the HCJ has sought to advance.[36]

Israeli Shari'a courts operate under pressure from three distinct groups and institutions: feminists and Islamists (both within the Muslim community) and the civil judiciary.[37] In response, Shari'a courts have undergone a semivoluntary process of dialectical transformation, simultaneously undertaking "Islamization" and "secularization" of their norms and procedures.[38] The indirect role that the HCJ has played in this process cannot be denied. Its constant threat of intervention has forced the Shari'a courts to internalize certain normative frames and civil law concepts, and to amend their rules and procedures.[39] Qadis are more receptive to ideas and concepts (for example, best interests of the child, human dignity) for which they can find a legitimate basis and justification in the Islamic tradition than they are to secular concepts (such as gender equality) that may be interpreted as contradictory to the religious texts. However, civil family courts, with which Shari'a courts have been in direct competition since 2001, have had an even greater impact on this reform process than the HCJ.

## Civil Family Courts: Jurisdictional Competition and Internal Reform in MFL

Since 2001 Muslim litigants have been able to choose between civil family and Shari'a courts for any personal status matter except marriage and divorce. Concurrent jurisdiction creates an environment of competition in which civil and religious court constantly vie with another for clients, discursive power, and textual authority.

Although Shari'a courts enjoy certain structural advantages, the civil courts hold the upper hand in this competition with respect to pecuniary awards. Spousal alimony and child support awards made by civil family courts are usually larger than those made by Shari'a courts. This makes civil courts an attractive option, especially for female Muslim litigants. However, my analysis of the emerging case law reveals that the competition between civil and Islamic courts has been not just over the clientele but also over the power to interpret the "divine" law.

In maintenance cases, both family and Shari'a court judges apply the same substantive law (the OLFR of 1917). In family courts, all but four judges are Jews. Jewish family court judges, who are not trained in Arabic or Islamic law, often rely on Hebrew textbooks and English commentaries on Muslim law when making their decisions.[40] Some Jewish judges argue that they "interpret [Shari'a] more liberally [than qadis do] and adjust them to modern times."[41] However, this claim does not seem to go beyond rhetoric.[42] In contrast, my analysis of recent case law suggests that family courts sustain a conservative and patriarchal rhetoric about gender roles within the Muslim family. This patriarchal outlook becomes most apparent in spousal maintenance cases.

The institution of *ihtibas* is the foundation of spousal duties and obligations in a Muslim marriage.[43] Courts often refer to ihtibas as "the duty of the wife to devote herself to her husband, and to be physically available to him."[44] Ihtibas is the quid pro quo of maintenance. A woman who leaves the marital residence without her husband's permission may be declared disobedient (*nashiza*). A disobedient wife may lose her right to maintenance. In ihtibas cases, the burden of proof is on the husband.[45] However, if the wife has already left the home, then it is her responsibility to prove that she did not violate her confinement obligation and that her departure was justified. As evinced in some family court decisions, occasional violence by the husband is not automatically considered a "just" cause because Shari'a reportedly condones certain types of violence (for example, "educational" violence to discipline the wife).[46] In one case, a woman was declared disobedient after she had left home in response to her husband's alleged verbal assault; because Shari'a already allows a husband to "discipline" his wife by lightly beating her, verbal abuse cannot be said to qualify as a ground for violating the duty of confinement.[47] A similarly conservative and patriarchal attitude by civil courts is observed in child support cases.[48]

In brief, there is little difference in the way Shari'a and civil family courts apply Islamic law. Both court systems uphold an equally conservative and patriarchal view of Shari'a. When both courts operate with similar normative assumptions, but one of them systematically awards more child support and alimony (as is the case with Israeli family courts), that court's attractiveness to potential litigants increases. This dynamic has been at the core of the competition between Shari'a and family courts over the last two decades.

The 2001 amendment that reduced the jurisdiction of Shari'a courts from exclusive to concurrent over matters of custody, maintenance, and child support was made possible by efforts of the Working Group for Equality in Personal Status Issues (WGEPSI)—a coalition of Arab and Jewish human and women's rights groups. The coalition was founded in 1995 and immediately began lobbying for an amendment law that would reduce the jurisdiction of religious courts. In the face of an intensifying legislative campaign and realizing that they would lose their jurisdiction to civil courts if they continued business as usual, Shari'a courts responded with self-reform. The SCA issued a new judicial decree that sought to increase the attractiveness of Shari'a courts (to female litigants) by raising amounts of child support and maintenance awards through procedural innovation. Following the issuance of the new judicial decree, both child support and spousal maintenance awards by Shari'a courts steadily increased. As some commentators suggest, reform has not been limited to maintenance. Substantive and procedural reforms also have been undertaken in other areas (for example, divorce) to increase the Islamic courts' appeal vis-à-vis the civil judiciary.[49]

## Greek Civil Courts and Muslim Family Law

According to Law 1920/1991, a mufti is a religious leader who is also accorded judicial functions. In order to carry legal effects, a mufti's decisions must be declared enforceable by the local CoFI after review of their constitutionality. No direct appeals are permitted against mufti decisions. The only—indirect—way to challenge them is to appeal against the enforceability decision of the civil CoFI at the court of appeals and, eventually, at the Court of Cassation

(CoC)—the court of last resort. These stages of ratification and appeal are the only two instances when Greek civil court judges—all non-Muslims—get to rule over MFL.

## Local Courts of First Instance vs. Muftis: Jurisdictional Competition and Ambiguity

Article 5, section 1 of Law 1920/1991 states that a mufti may exercise jurisdiction only over Muslim Greek citizens residing in his region. However, despite this seemingly clear formulation in the law, in practice many questions concerning a mufti's jurisdiction arise in the process of review and ratification of his decisions by local courts.[50]

There seems to be a lot of confusion among judges, especially concerning whether mufti jurisdiction is compulsory for Muslim citizens. In a recent communique, the minister of justice stated that a mufti's jurisdiction should be viewed as concurrent with that of ordinary courts because viewing it as compulsory would violate the government's constitutional and international obligations to protect individual rights.[51] However, until recently, the majority of Greek courts have treated the mufti jurisdiction as mandatory for Muslims residing within his district and have refused to hear pertinent family cases.[52]

Since the enactment of Law 1250/1982, Greek Muslims have been free to choose between civil and religious marriage. It is now widely accepted that Muslims who marry civilly can opt out of mufti jurisdiction. But what about Muslims who marry religiously? According to the CoFI in Thiva, Muslims married in a religious ceremony also can turn to civil courts for family disputes that arise later. In the event that application of the "sacred" law infringes on basic rights protected under the constitution and the European Convention on Human Rights (ECHR), the court held, the state is required to give members of the religious minority the option to choose between the mufti and civil courts.[53] In a subsequent inheritance case, the CoFI in Rodopi confirmed Muslim citizens' right to resort to civil courts in the name of gender equality and fair trial.[54]

Historically, Greek courts have been very conservative in their dealings with Islamic law. The legal autonomy of the *muftiate* was guaranteed by international treaties as part of a reciprocal minority protection regime between Turkey and Greece. Questions concerning Islamic law were not merely matters of legality but also were of diplomatic concern. In the late 1990s and early 2000s, Turkish-Greek relations entered a new phase of détente. Right around this time, as the geostrategic value of preserving of Shari'a in Thrace was diminishing, some of the local CoFI embraced a more assertive stance vis-à-vis the mufti. They adopted an increasingly restrictive approach toward mufti jurisdiction.

In many cases (inheritance, custody, property relations, and so forth), they either refused to recognize mufti jurisdiction or declared it concurrent with that of civil courts.[55]

## The Court of Cassation: Islamic "Exceptionalism" and the Entrenchment of Mufti's Jurisdiction over Thracian Muslims

This rising assertiveness of the courts at the local level sparked a backlash from the CoC in Athens. The official Greek policy on Shari'a in Thrace has been to preserve the status quo. This policy has been long been reflected on the CoC's jurisprudence. For instance, in a series of judgments, the court has repeatedly noted that the application of Islamic law in Thrace was an international treaty obligation that bestowed upon Shari'a the status of a "special law" within the domestic system.[56] Given its special status, the court argued, Shari'a cannot be said to contradict the constitution or the ECHR. By doing so, the high court signaled to lower courts that they should exempt Islamic law from constitutional review. Moreover, by consistently upholding the mufti jurisdiction as compulsory for Thracian Muslims (hence denying them access to civil law and courts— especially in inheritance cases[57]), the CoC rebuked activist lower courts and strongly discouraged them from contesting the Islamic law or the muftiate.

The CoFI in Xanthi ruled in 2012 that the application of Shari'a-based family laws violates Muslim citizens' fundamental rights and freedoms.[58] According to Article 5, section 3 of Law 1920/1991, the CoFI is required to review the constitutionality of mufti decisions and declare them "unenforceable" if they find a violation. However, despite widespread alleged violations between 1991 and 2011, three CoFIs in Thrace[59] reviewed 3,633 mufti decisions and struck down only one[60] of them as unconstitutional.[61]

Prior to the enactment of Law 1920/1991, mufti decisions were not subject to constitutional review. By the time the new law was introduced, mufti appointments had already grown into an international problem between Turkey and Greece. Against this backdrop, any challenge by lower courts to the constitutionality of mufti's rulings will have political repercussions. Such court rulings might be interpreted as symbolic support for groups who call for the abolition of the muftiate or separation of muftis' spiritual and judicial functions. The Greek government favors neither outcome because they would mean more international pressure (especially from Turkey) and trouble with the minority. Fully embracing this strategic foreign policy concern, the CoC has effectively discouraged lower courts from conducting any meaningful constitutional review of mufti decisions.

As a member of the Council of Europe, Greece recognizes the jurisdiction of the European Court of Human Rights. A Greek Muslim who alleges a violation of convention rights due to the application of Islamic law can lodge a complaint at the Strasbourg Court after exhausting domestic remedies. However, the Strasbourg option remains underutilized. To this day, only two cases concerning the implementation of Shari'a in Thrace have been lodged at the court. The first case (*Dilek Cigdem v. Greece*) was rejected as inadmissible due to a procedural error. The second case (*Chatitze Molla Sali v. Greece*) was still pending at this time of writing.[62]

If the Court finds a violation in the pending case, this may have important implications for the mufti system in Thrace. For instance, if the government responds by amending Law 1920/1991 and making mufti jurisdiction concurrent with that of civil courts, this might create pressure on muftis to self-reform to protect their jurisdiction and clientele—as Shari'a courts did in Israel. In other words, if sufficiently utilized, the Strasbourg Court might ultimately be a source of reformist pressure on the Islamic judiciary in Thrace, a role that Greek courts have long failed to play. For the time being, however, muftis continue business as usual; in the absence of any serious threat to their judicial monopoly, they have no incentive to self-reform.

## Comparison of Israeli and Greek Experiences, and Concluding Remarks

Non-Muslim-dominated civil courts cannot bring about direct changes in MFLs because they often lack necessary moral authority. Instead, their influence tends to be indirect, pressuring religious courts and judges to undertake self-reform. As demonstrated, this is happening in Israel but not in Greece. Israeli civil courts have been able to engender indirect (albeit limited) reform in Shari'a courts, whereas Greek civil courts have failed to bring about any reform in the Thracian muftiate. Why did self-reform occur in Israel but not in Greece?

Religious courts interact with two types of civil courts: high courts and lower courts. High courts exert top-down pressure on religious courts to comply with their decisions. In theory, religious courts, as part of the national system, are obliged to comply with decisions of higher civil courts by undertaking necessary changes in their substantive and procedural rules. In practice, such changes almost never happen because relations between the two court systems are often conflictual. Moreover, as Shachar notes, high courts that conduct ex post review of religious court rulings often remain inaccessible to individual litigants.[63] However, these shortcomings do not mean that high courts have no effect on the evolution of Muslim law or institutions. Religious courts may choose to comply with high court rulings and undertake self-reform by internalizing secular discourses and principles, especially when they resonate with Islamic values.

Lower civil courts apply lateral pressure on religious courts by competing for their jurisdiction and clientele. In jurisdictions in which the partial exit option is available, competition between secular and religious courts may encourage self-reform in religious courts.

Israeli Shari'a courts, despite their public opposition to HCJ's interventions into Islamic jurisdiction, have selectively and subtly complied with some HCJ rulings—especially those for which they could find an Islamic justification, such as the best interest of the child. In addition to the HCJ's top-down pressure, Shari'a courts also operate under lateral pressure from civil family courts. Although the partial exit is incomplete (in most areas litigants may opt out of Shari'a courts but not out of Islamic law, and the interpretation of Shari'a by civil courts is not necessarily more liberal), competition between the civil and religious courts spurred some internal reform at Shari'a courts in the early 2000s.

In Israel, the HCJ and civil family courts work in tandem. In Greece, this is not the case. There is neither top-down pressure from the CoC nor lateral pressure from the local CoFI. The CoC has avoided challenging mufti jurisdiction by treating Shari'a as a sui generis system and barring lower courts from conducting review of muftis rulings and from putting any meaningful lateral pressure on them to reform. In Israel, concurrent jurisdiction is guaranteed by the law. In Greece, however, it was established by judicial activism, particularly by the CoFI. The CoC has discouraged lower courts from playing such a role despite their increasing assertiveness in the early 2000s. In the absence of meaningful vertical or lateral pressure from the civil judiciary—despite the existence of strong ex ante oversight mechanisms, at least on paper—muftis have been able to defy calls for substantive and procedural reform of Islamic law because the cost of defiance is considerably lower for them than for Israeli qadis. The latter, who are civilly trained and maintain professional ties with their civil counterparts, have been more attentive to, and dependent upon, the civil judicial hierarchy. Moreover, due to their training and professional ties, Israeli qadis are also more familiar with, and receptive to, certain secular frames, than are Greek muftis.

The relative success of reform in Israel owes much to the presence of a vibrant NGO sector, particularly women's rights groups. Such groups constitute the third (bottom-up) source of pressure upon qadis to undertake reforms. Groups such as WGEPSI and Kayan were key to the legislative process between 1995 and 2001, which opened the door to jurisdictional competition between civil and Shari'a courts. After the 2001 amendment, both groups provided legal aid to Arab women so they might utilize civil courts. The increase in the number of people who opt in for civil courts has put greater pressure on Shari'a courts to self-reform. This bottom-up pressure, absent in Greece, has proved critical for reform in Israel.

Finally, the two countries' legal cultures, especially in terms of judicial attitudes toward religious law, are very different. With the enactment of Laws 1250/1982 and 1329/1983, the Greek family law system has been almost completely secularized. Greek judges, who are familiar only with secular law, often treat Shari'a as a "special" law, not as an integral part of the national system. This attitude is one of the reasons for the ineffectiveness of constitutional review of mufti decisions. In Israel, by contrast, the family law system is almost entirely religion-based. Religious laws and courts are an integral part of the national system. This makes Israeli judges, in comparison to their Greek counterparts, less biased and more receptive to MFLs. This does not mean that Israeli judges are more knowledgeable about Islamic law, but they seem more eager to treat Shari'a courts as part of the mainstream judiciary and, as a result, require them to comply with constitutional standards. Likewise, the closer integration of religious courts in the national system seems to make religious judges more sensitive to requests from the civil judiciary and more receptive to secular ideas.

This comparative analysis largely confirms the importance of allowing individuals to partially exit from or to choose between religious and secular jurisdictions—an important element of Shachar's TA model. However, the study has also shown that the right to choose between jurisdictions is not sufficient. There is also a strong need for legal aid organizations to lobby religious courts for change and to help vulnerable groups in the minority community navigate the pluri-legal system by providing pro bono services (for translation, legal counsel, and so forth). The increased accessibility of civil courts, in turn, would incentivize religious courts to self-reform.

Shachar also recommends the adoption of ex ante oversight techniques that would complement existing ex post review of religious court rulings by the civil judiciary. But, as this study has demonstrated, like ex post review, ex ante oversight has strengths and limitations. In Greece, the constitutional review of mufti decisions has failed, whereas in Israel the appointment of secularly trained qadis (another ex ante oversight technique) seems to have played a positive role in the process of self-reform at Islamic courts. One of the reasons for the shortcomings of both ex post and ex ante oversight mechanisms seems to be the civil judiciary's lack of legitimacy in the eyes of the Muslim minority. One way to overcome this hurdle may be to increase the number of Muslim judges on civil courts. Likewise, relations between Shari'a and civil courts are intimately connected to broader political issues: majority-minority relations, security issues, and the relations between non-Muslim host nations and foreign governments that act as "protectors" of Muslim minorities. In both Israel and Greece, relative peace and calm in domestic and international relations empowered liberal, pro-reform groups and increased pressure on religious judges to self-reform whereas tense relations did the opposite.

# Notes

1. Seyla Benhabib, *The Claims of Culture: Equality and Diversity in the Global Era* (Princeton, N.J.: Princeton University Press, 2002); Chandran Kukathas, *The Liberal Archipelago: A Theory of Diversity and Freedom, Oxford Political Theory* (Oxford: Oxford University Press, 2003); Will Kymlicka, *Multicultural Citizenship: A Liberal Theory of Minority Rights* (Oxford: Clarendon Press, 1995).

2. Susan Moller Okin, "Is Multiculturalism Bad for Women?," in *Is Multiculturalism Bad for Women?*, 7–26 (Princeton, N.J.: Princeton University Press, 1999).

3. Yüksel Sezgin, "Reforming Muslim Family Laws in Non-Muslim Democracies," in *Islam, Gender and Democracy in Comparative Perspective*, ed. Jocelyne Cesari and Jose Casanova (Oxford: Oxford University Press, 2017), 162–89.

4. Ayelet Shachar, *Multicultural Jurisdictions: Cultural Differences and Women's Rights* (Cambridge: Cambridge University Press, 2001).

5. Ayelet Shachar, "Privatizing Diversity: A Cautionary Tale from Religious Arbitration in Family Law," *Theoretical Inquiries in Law* 9, no. 2 (2008): 572–607.

6. Daphna Hacker, "Religious Tribunals in Democratic States: Lessons from the Israeli Rabbinical Courts," *Journal of Law and Religion* 27, no. 1 (2012): 59–81.

7. Yüksel Sezgin, *Human Rights Under State-Enforced Religious Family Laws in Israel, Egypt and India* (Cambridge: Cambridge University Press, 2013).

8. Shachar, *Multicultural Jurisdictions*.

9. Shachar, *Multicultural Jurisdictions*, 118.

10. Shachar, *Multicultural Jurisdictions*, 118.

11. Shachar, *Multicultural Jurisdictions*, 118.

12. Ido Shahar, *Legal Pluralism in the Holy City: Competing Courts, Forum Shopping, and Institutional Dynamics in Jerusalem, Cultural Diversity and Law* (Farnham, Surrey, England: Ashgate, 2015), 30–31.

13. Only about one-fifth of Greek Muslims live in Western Thrace. PEW Research Center, *The Future of the Global Muslim Population* (Washington D.C.: Pew Research Center, 2011).

14. Ahmad Natour, "The Role of the Shari`a Court of Appeals in Promoting the Status of Women in Islamic Law in a Non-Muslim State (Israel)" (JSD thesis, American University Washington College of Law, 2009); Moussa Abou Ramadan, "Islamic Legal Hybridity and Patriarchal Liberalism in the Shari'a Courts in Israel," *Journal of Levantine Studies* 4, no. 2 (2015): 39–67.

15. Kōnstantinos Tsitselikis, "Me Aphormē Tēn Apophasē 405/2000 Tou Monomelous Prōtodikeiou Thēbōn," *Nomiko Vima* 49 (2001): 583–93.

16. CEDAW, "Concluding Comments of the Committee on the Elimination of Discrimination Against Women: Greece," 2007, http://www.unhchr.ch/tbs/doc.nsf /898586b1dc7b4043c1256a450044f331/239a466c03ee0dbᴏc12572a4003ca7bf/$FILE /N0724374.pdf; Thomas Hammarberg, "Report by Commissioner for Human Rights of the Council of Europe," 2009, https://wcd.coe.int/wcd/ViewDoc.jsp?id=1409353.

17. Shachar, *Multicultural Jurisdictions*.

18. Personal interview by author with Mustafa Imamoglu, Komotini, Greece, March 2015.

19. Kayan, "Five Years of Legal Aid: Summary and Analysis," 2011, http://www.kayan.org.il /Public/ER20110101_5%20Year%20Legal%20Aid%20Report.pdf.

20. For example, see HCJ 8906/04; HCJ 1318/11; HCJ 11230/05; HCJ 5912/06; HCJ 473/09.

21. HCJ 187/54.

22. For instance, see HCJ 5227/97.
23. Yitzhak Reiter, "Qadis and the Implementation of Islamic Law in Present Day Israel," in *Islamic Law: Theory and Practice*, ed. Robert Gleave and Eugenia Kermeli (London: I. B. Tauris, 1997), 205–31.
24. HCJ C.A. 6892/93.
25. Ran Hirschl, *Towards Juristocracy: The Origins and Consequences of the New Constitutionalism* (Cambridge, Mass.: Harvard University Press, 2004).
26. For instance, see HCJ 3914/92; HCJ 1000/92.
27. Moussa Abou Ramadan, "The Shari'a in Israel: Islamization, Israelization and the Invented Islamic Law," *UCLA Journal of Islamic and Near Eastern Law* 5 (2005–6): 81–129.
28. See HCJ C.A. 3077/90.
29. HCJ 3856/11.
30. Personal interview by the author with Qadi Natour, Jerusalem, Israel, January 2005.
31. Aharon Layish, "The Transformation of the Shari'a from Jurists' Law to Statutory Law in the Contemporary Muslim World," *Die Welt des Islams* 44, no. 1 (2004): 85–113.
32. Natour, "The Role of the Shari`a Court of Appeals"; Moussa Abou Ramadan, "Recent Developments in Child Custody in Shari'a Courts: Notes on Hcj 9740/05 Plonit v. Shari'a Court of Appeals and Hcj 1129/06 Plonit and Other v. Shari'a Court of Appeals," *Mishpakha ve Mishpat* 2 (2008): 69–105 (in Hebrew); Iyad Zahalka, *Al-Murshid Fi Al-Qada' Al-Shar'i* (Tel-Aviv: Israel Bar Association, 2008).
33. For instance, see SCA 63/1994; SCA 135/1996; SCA 127/1997.
34. For instance, see SCA 63/1994; SCA 15/1998; SCA 56/1999.
35. Moussa Abou Ramadan, "The Transition From Tradition to Reform: The Shari'a Appeals Court Rulings on Child Custody (1992–2001)," *Fordham International Law Journal* 26 (2003): 595–655; Ramadan, "Recent Developments in Child Custody."
36. Ramadan, "Islamic Legal Hybridity."
37. Shahar, *Legal Pluralism in the Holy City.*
38. Ramadan, "The Shari'a in Israel."
39. Layish, "The Transformation of the Shari'a from Jurists' Law to Statutory Law."
40. 1410–06 Hadera Family Court (2007); 11310-04-11 Nazareth Family Court (2012).
41. Email correspondence with Judge Assaf Zagury, March 7, 2013 (via the Office of the President of Supreme Court of Israel).
42. For example, see 2988-06-09 Tiberias Family Court (2011).
43. 34258-07-13 Nazareth Family Court (2014).
44. 1410–06 Hadera Family Court (2007).
45. 1320/01 Hadera Family Court (2006).
46. 34258-07-13 Nazareth Family Court (2014); 1410–06 Hadera Family Court (2007).
47. 12810/06 Tel Aviv Family Court (2009).
48. For instance, see 35921-05-13 Nazareth Family Court (2015); 791–08 Krayot Family Court (2008); 1410–06 Hadera Family Court (2007).
49. Moussa Abou Ramadan, "Divorce Reform in the Shari'a Court of Appeals in Israel (1992–2003)," *Islamic Law and Society* 13, no. 2 (2005): 242–74.
50. For instance, see CoFI, Rodopi, 313/2009; Multimember CoFI, Rodopi, 18/2008; CoFI, Xanthi, 83/2004.
51. Greek Parliament Question No. 5937/16-01-2013, http://www.hellenicparliament.gr /UserFiles/67715b2c-ec81-4f0c-ad6a-476a34d732bd/7938918.pdf.
52. Kōnstantinos Tsitselikis, *Old and New Islam in Greece: From Historical Minorities to Immigrant Newcomers* (Leiden, Netherlands: Martinus Nijhoff, 2012), 398.
53. CoFI, Thiva, 405/2000; for further information see Tsitselikis, "Me Aphormē Tēn Apophasē 405/2000 Tou Monomelous Prōtodikeiou Thēbōn."

54. CoFI, Rodopi, 9/2008.
55. Appeals Court of Thrace: 7/2011, 119/2006, 439/2005, 642/2009, 392/2011, 192/2013; CoFI, Rodopi: 5/2014, 50/2010, 11/2008, 17/2008, 130/2008, 140/2008, 183/2008; and CoFI, Xanthi: 24/2011, 30/2010; 122/2002.
56. AP 1370/2014, 1862/2013, 1097/2007.
57. AP 322/1960, 2113/2009, 1497/2013, 1862/2013, 1097/2007, 2138/2013.
58. CoFI, Xanthi, 102/2012. Yannis Ktistakis, *Charia: Tribunaux Religieux Et Droit Grec* (Istanbul: Istos 2013), 109–34.
59. CoFIs in Rodopi, Xanthi and Orestiada.
60. CoFI, Rodopi, 152/1991.
61. Ktistakis, *Charia Tribanux Religieux Et Droit Grec*, 100–101.
62. Dilek Cigdem v. Greece, 2012, http://www.strasbourgconsortium.org/portal.case .php?pageId=10#caseId=1212; Chatitze Molla Sali v. Greece, 2014, http://hrwf.eu /greeceeuropean-court-application-of-shariah-law-to-an-inheritance-dispute.
63. Shacher, "Privitzing Diversity."

## Bibliography

Benhabib, Seyla. *The Claims of Culture: Equality and Diversity in the Global Era*. Princeton, N.J.: Princeton University Press, 2002.
CEDAW. "Concluding Comments of the Committee on the Elimination of Discrimination Against Women: Greece," 2007. http://www.unhchr.ch/tbs/doc.nsf/898586b1dc7b 4043c1256a450044f331/239a466c03ee0db0c12572a4003ca7bf/$FILE/N0724374.pdf.
Hacker, Daphna. "Religious Tribunals in Democratic States: Lessons from the Israeli Rabbinical Courts." *Journal of Law and Religion* 27, no. 1 (2012): 59–81.
Hammarberg, Thomas. "Report by Commissioner for Human Rights of the Council of Europe," 2009. https://wcd.coe.int/wcd/ViewDoc.jsp?id=1409353.
Hirschl, Ran. *Towards Juristocracy: The Origins and Consequences of the New Constitutionalism*. Cambridge, Mass.: Harvard University Press, 2004.
Kayan. "Five Years of Legal Aid: Summary and Analysis," 2011. http://www.kayan.org.il /Public/ER20110101_5%20Year%20Legal%20Aid%20Report.pdf.
Ktistakis, Yannis. *Charia. Tribunaux Religieux Et Droit Grec*. Istanbul: Istos, 2013.
Kukathas, Chandran. *The Liberal Archipelago: A Theory of Diversity and Freedom, Oxford Political Theory*. Oxford: Oxford University Press, 2003.
Kymlicka, Will. *Multicultural Citizenship: A Liberal Theory of Minority Rights*. Oxford: Clarendon Press, 1995.
Layish, Aharon. "The Transformation of the Shari'a from Jurists' Law to Statutory Law in the Contemporary Muslim World." *Die Welt des Islams* 44, no. 1 (2004): 85–113.
Moller Okin, Susan. "Is Multiculturalism Bad for Women?" In *Is Multiculturalism Bad for Women?*, 7–26. Princeton, N.J.: Princeton University Press, 1999.
Natour, Ahmad. "The Role of the Shari`a Court of Appeals in Promoting the Status of Women in Islamic Law in a Non-Muslim State (Israel)." JSD thesis, American University Washington College of Law, 2009.
PEW Research Center. *The Future of the Global Muslim Population*. Washington D.C.: Pew Research Center, 2011.
Ramadan, Moussa Abou. "Divorce Reform in the Shari'a Court of Appeals in Israel (1992–2003)." *Islamic Law and Society* 13, no. 2 (2005): 242–74.
——. "Islamic Legal Hybridity and Patriarchal Liberalism in the Shari'a Courts in Israel." *Journal of Levantine Studies* 4, no. 2 (2015): 39–67.

——. "Recent Developments in Child Custody in Shari'a Courts: Notes on Hcj 9740/05 Plonit v. Shari'a Court of Appeals and Hcj 1129/06 Plonit and Other v. Shari'a Court of Appeals." *Mishpakha ve Mishpat* 2 (2008): 69–105 (in Hebrew).

——. "The Shari'a in Israel: Islamization, Israelization and the Invented Islamic Law." *UCLA Journal of Islamic and Near Eastern Law* 5 (2005–6): 81–129.

——. "The Transition Form Tradition to Reform: The Shari'a Appeals Court Rulings on Child Custody (1992–2001)." *Fordham International Law Journal* 26 (2003): 595–655.

Reiter, Yitzhak. "Qadis and the Implementation of Islamic Law in Present Day Israel." In *Islamic Law: Theory and Practice*, ed. R. Gleave and E. Kermeli, 205–31. London: I. B. Tauris, 1997.

Sezgin, Yüksel. *Human Rights Under State-Enforced Religious Family Laws in Israel, Egypt and India*. Cambridge: Cambridge University Press, 2013.

——. "Reforming Muslim Family Laws in Non-Muslim Democracies." In *Islam, Gender and Democracy in Comparative Perspective*, ed. Jocelyne Cesari and Jose Casanova, 162–89. Oxford: Oxford University Press, 2017.

Shachar, Ayelet. *Multicultural Jurisdictions: Cultural Differences and Women's Rights*. Cambridge: Cambridge University Press, 2001.

——. "Privatizing Diversity: A Cautionary Tale from Religious Arbitration in Family Law." *Theoretical Inquiries in Law* 9, no. 2 (2008): 572–607.

Shahar, Ido. *Legal Pluralism in the Holy City: Competing Courts, Forum Shopping, and Institutional Dynamics in Jerusalem, Cultural Diversity and Law*. Farnham, Surrey, England: Ashgate, 2015.

Tsitselikis, Kōnstantinos. "Me Aphormē Tēn Apophasē 405/2000 Tou Monomelous Prōtodikeiou Thēbōn." *Nomiko Vima* 49 (2001): 583–93.

——. *Old and New Islam in Greece: From Historical Minorities to Immigrant Newcomers*. Leiden, Netherlands: Martinus Nijhoff, 2012.

Zahalka, Iyad. *Al-Murshid Fi Al-Qada' Al-Shar'i*. Tel-Aviv: Israel Bar Association, 2008.

# PART IV

**———**

# THE CHALLENGE OF CORPORATE POWER

# 12

# CORPORATE LEGAL PARTICULARISM

KATHARINA PISTOR

Max Weber claimed that one of the conditions for capitalism to flourish is a "rational" legal system[1]. But he also noted that the primary beneficiaries of rationality—entrepreneurs—were seeking exemptions and autonomy from that very legal order. Instead, they craved a "particularistic" legal order of their own.[2] His foresight would prove prescient. Over the following century, the scale and scope of particularistic legal orders has greatly increased well beyond what Weber possibly could have imagined.

In this chapter, I explore the rise of what I call "corporate legal particularism." The term *particularism* as used here refers to a self-contained legal order that serves special interests. *Corporate* legal particularism is an order designed by and serving the interests of single or multiple corporations. Legal particularism needs to be distinguished from legal pluralism. Both exemplify the coexistence of multiple legal orders, a phenomenon Breton et al. have labeled "multijuralism."[3] But they stand for radically different ways of ordering the relation of these orders to one another. Particularism segregates; pluralism bridges differences.

Legal pluralism can take different forms. The term was first coined in the area of colonization. Colonial powers brought their home law with them, which applied to colonizers and, on a more select basis, to the colonized.[4] It often coincided with indigenous laws. Under colonialism, legal pluralism connoted hierarchy, if not supremacy. The formal law of the colonizers was deemed superior and prevailed in conflicts. As late as the 1950s, British jurists called for the indigenous law of the colonized to be voided, if they deemed it "'repugnant.'"[5]

The term *legal pluralism*, however, has meaning beyond the colonial context. It can be used normatively as a commitment to mutual respect and conflict resolution based on mutual recognition. Federal states are prominent examples for pluralist legal orders thus defined. They are bound by a common federal order, most important, by a federal constitution. Each unit within the federation can have its own constitutional order, but it must be compatible with core principles of the federal order. Jurisdiction over different areas of the law can be divided, or exercised jointly. The federal constitution typically specifies the allocation of jurisdiction over different matters. Conflicts between legal orders also can arise horizontally, such as between two states of a federation. This is where the so-called conflict of law rules come in, which are local laws that determine under what conditions local courts will respect and enforce foreign law.

A truly pluralist system of laws is more than a simple hierarchy in which one dominates and others are tolerated, or perhaps suppressed. A functioning pluralist order does require some common principles (the constitutional order of the federation) that serve as an anchor, but there is also mutual accommodation and tolerance for differences. States can recognize each other's laws to the point that they offer their enforcement apparatus to enforce foreign law. States also can harmonize their laws, or explicitly endorse variety. The subsidiarity principle in European Treaty Law exemplifies the latter.

*Legal particularism*, in contrast, stands for legal segregation. Particularistic legal orders can be formed by explicit or implicit carve-outs. In some countries, religious organizations exercise authority over family and inheritance law. In Israel, civil marriage is unavailable and common law families have become a regularity. Other examples for opt outs are the "free economic zones" several countries have created to attract foreign investors. These zones typically exercise delegated lawmaking powers in matters relevant for foreign investors, including tax, custom, company, and labor law granted to them by the sovereign. Legal particularism, however, does not require delegation. The key ingredients are access to some legal order that accommodates the relevant interests, liberal conflict of law rules in other jurisdictions, and sophisticated lawyering.

## The Rise of the Corporation

Corporations are creatures of the law. Only law can confer on business entities full legal personality, enabling them to own their assets, contract over them, sue, and be sued in their own name. As legal creatures, corporations need natural persons to act on their behalf; but the corporation itself is the principal in this relation, the humans are its agents.

Other business organizations can be created in contract, but the defining features of the corporation are impossible without top-down, state ordering. One such feature is the partitioning of assets between the corporation and its shareholders and the shielding of the corporation's assets from the creditors of its shareholders.[6] Asset shielding is the mirror image of limited liability, which protects shareholders from the corporation's creditors. It is possible to contract for limited liability. The corporation could, for example, include a provision in all of its contracts that its shareholders are not liable for the debts of the corporation. Such a contractual solution would not include tort creditors and may therefore be deemed incomplete, but substantial protection could be achieved in this way.

Asset partitioning is more complicated. It implies that the shareholders' creditors cannot put their hands on the assets of the corporation. Replicating this in contract would be next to impossible. It would require each and every *shareholder* to put their personal creditors on notice that they have access only to their personal wealth, including any shares they hold in a corporation, but not to the assets of the corporation. Partitioning shareholder and corporate assets in a way that is binding on everyone requires top-down coordination and enforcement.

Early examples of business organizations that used the corporate form are the chartered trading companies, including the English and the Dutch East Indian Companies, which were established in 1600 and 1602, respectively.[7] They combined business and government purposes; they were chartered by the state to secure the trading routes to the far East, by armed force if necessary. They received monopoly rights over the trading route[8] and the power to exercise delegated state power over territories and people brought under their control.

In the Netherlands, the "General States" also played a critical role in a far-reaching legal innovation: the capital lock-in. In 1612, the Dutch East Indian Company (VOC according to its Dutch acronym) became the first corporation to lock in shareholder capital in perpetuity.[9] The 1602 charter had required the company's shareholders to commit capital for a period of ten years. This ten-year commitment was already a marked change from privately chartered companies, which were unwound after each trading venture or renewed for another term.

The ten-year lock-in had enhanced investor confidence and fostered a vibrant secondary market in VOC shares. This made it far easier to take the next step and disallow shareholders to take out their capital. After all, shareholders who needed cash could sell their shares on the secondary market. Locking in share capital increased secondary trading and helped raise fresh capital. It created a comparative advantage over its English competitor, the English East Indian Company, which took much longer to impose capital lock-in.[10]

The two East India companies and other major trading companies were government chartered. They were in essence public-private partnerships. Private businesses that wished to obtain the privileges that come with incorporating a legal entity had to apply for explicit legislative or executive authorization. In England, the Bubble Act of 1719 explicitly confirmed this requirement. Still, private entrepreneurs frequently sidestepped the legal constraints by acquiring moribund corporate forms and giving them a new business purpose, or by contracting for features of the corporation in partnership agreements.[11] Courts not infrequently vindicated such practices. As a result, entry barriers for the corporate form eroded and eventually gave way to "free incorporation." The UK repealed the Bubble Act in 1825 and in 1844 became the first country to move to a regime whereby a corporation could be established without ex ante state approval. Any business organization that complied with the provisions of the new company law could obtain the status of a corporate legal entity. France and Germany followed suit much later, only in 1867 and 1870, respectively.[12]

In the United States, where corporate law falls within the jurisdiction of states, the first quasi-free incorporation statute was enacted by the state of New York. This statute, however, restricted free incorporation to manufacturing businesses, excluding riskier ventures, such as mining and banking. Moreover, the statute provided for a sunset provision (twenty years) and a ceiling for how much capital a corporation could raise (USD 100,000).[13] It almost seems as if the legislature anticipated the rise of unrestricted corporate power and the threat it would pose to democratic self-governance. Yet these restrictions did not last long, mostly because other states offered better terms, attracting more incorporations. The stage was set for states to compete for corporations by offering them the law their incorporators, managers, or owners favored.

Even after free incorporation had been firmly established, corporations remained subject to a number of important constraints, most of which were relaxed or abolished over time.[14] For example, a corporation had to define its business purpose in its founding charter. Any change in purpose over time required a charter change, requiring a supermajority vote of the corporation's shareholders. Actions managers took beyond the circumscribed business purpose were deemed "ultra vires" and thus void, exposing corporations to the risk that their contracts would be unenforceable.

An important application of the ultra vires doctrine were company groups. For most of the nineteenth century, holding shares in other corporations was deemed ultra vires in the United States. This stood in contrast to Europe, where the notion that corporations could establish and hold shares in other corporations was accepted much earlier.[15] Without this doctrine, it never would have been possible to establish complex business groups of pyramid structures that disguise ultimate owners and control structures.[16] There were many ways to sidestep the prohibition of corporations owning shares in other corporations. They formed trusts, not corporations, and got away with this until the Sherman Act, the antitrust statute enacted at the federal level in 1890 that was used to bust the trusts. This time, state law came to the rescue. In 1896, New Jersey amended its corporate law to allow corporations to acquire shares in other corporations.[17] The busted trusts could be re-created in the form of holding companies.

The ultra vires doctrine lost its teeth when registrars and courts accepted "any lawful purpose" as a sufficient definition of corporate power. The demise of the ultra vires doctrine went hand in hand with the rise of the business judgment rule. Corporations could do anything lawful, and their management had the power to act on their behalf without fearing liability, unless they acted unlawfully or with the intent to harm the corporation or its shareholders.[18]

The examples could be multiplied, but these few fulfill the purpose of this brief summary. Core characteristics of the corporation, which are taken for granted today, even viewed as an entitlement, evolved over time. They had to be fought for and approved by courts and legislatures. The long-term trend has been toward ever-greater powers given to the corporation and its sponsors. In Delaware, the favorite state for incorporation in the United States, and perhaps globally, corporate law has become largely a menu of options from which to choose.

## Legal Pluralism and Corporate Autonomy

When corporations face only a single state that exercises legal monopoly, they are beholden to that state. They may try to influence lawmakers, but future law might take away what has been given earlier. Corporations can greatly enhance their autonomy when they can choose from among different legal orders. States, in turn, can make it easier for corporations to pick and choose by recognizing legal entities created under foreign law and by offering themselves as attractive incorporation places. Recognizing the laws of other states is a sign of legal tolerance and can foster legal pluralism. But it also can expose the state that recognizes foreign law to the dangers of legal particularism because it enables corporations to pick and choose the law that best suits their interests. If and when other corporations follow suit, the diversity of multiple orders can give rise to the dominance of one.

The United States is the classic example for regulatory competition giving rise to legal particularism. Many core competencies rest with the states of the federation, including the power over contract, property, tort, and corporate law. Further, the federal constitution includes the "commerce clause," which grants the federation the power to regulate trade with foreign nations and among states. This clause has been interpreted to imply that states cannot deny corporate status to entities created by other states, even if they did no business in their home state at all. Attempts to impose at least some aspects of "domestic" law have been struck down for the most part as incompatible with the commerce clause.[19]

In theory, the multiplicity of corporate laws at the state level could have given rise to a great diversity of such laws, and of corporations each choosing a different law. In practice, the landscape is more monochrome. Most of the largest, publicly traded corporations in the United States are incorporated in the state of Delaware.[20] Smaller corporations are typically incorporated in the home state of their founders, but they are likely to switch to Delaware before a public offering. The outcome of free choice from among multiple legal orders has not been pluralism but the dominance of a single order that serves corporate interests—but hardly any other constituencies.

The literature is divided about how to explain this outcome. Some argue that regulatory competition forces states to create corporate law that finds willing takers. The state that produces the law in greatest demand will have the largest number of corporations.[21] Others suggest that regulatory competition is a thing of the past and has been replaced by a network effect. Yet others argue that convergence is not necessarily the result of superior law but of legal advice. Attorneys trained at national law schools learn local law and the corporate law of Delaware, and they recommend either of these two jurisdictions to their clients.[22]

Whatever the right answer, regulatory competition has resulted in a greater convergence of corporate law in the United States than the attempt to harmonize corporate law within the European Union.[23] Even though corporate law has been a major focus of legal harmonization since the founding of the European communities, it remains a patchwork of a dozen or so directives.[24] Several draft directives never became law. And nowhere do the normative issues related to corporate law diverge more clearly than in the statute for a European company, a kind of federal corporate law for Europe that was in the planning since the 1950s.[25] When the regulation finally came into effect, it offered only a bare bones corporate law. For the remaining gaps, it deferred to the law of the place of incorporation.

Nonetheless, there is a process of de facto convergence of corporate law on its way in Europe as well. Just as in the United Sates, it takes the form of "regulatory competition"—a shift from states exercising their prerogative to set the ground rules for corporate law to giving private parties, the founders, shareholders, or managers of the corporation the right to choose the corporate law they prefer. Just as in the United States, the judiciary, not the legislature, paved the way toward convergence.

38. Indian Law Resource Center, "Request for Consultation."
39. Indian Law Resource Center, "Request for Consultation."
40. Indian Law Resource Center, "Request for Consultation."
41. Indian Law Resource Center, "Request for Consultation."
42. Victoria Márquez-Mees, "Compliance Review Report: Mareña Renovables Wind Project," Inter-American Development Bank, 2016, http://indianlaw.org/sites/default /files/ME-MICI002-2012__COMPLIANCE_REVIEW_REPORT_FOR_MARE%C3 %91A_RENOVABLES_WIND_ENERGY_PROJECT__ENGLISH_WEB__.pdf.
43. Márquez-Mees, "Compliance Review Report."
44. Inter-American Development Bank, "Operational Policy on Indigenous Peoples and Strategy for Indigenous Development," 2006, http://idbdocs.iadb.org/wsdocs /getdocument.aspx?docnum=2032081.
45. "Oaxaca: Confrontation Over Supposed "Approval" of Wind-Energy Park in San Dionisio del Mar," (SIPAZ Blog, January 8, 2013), https://sipazen.wordpress.com.
46. "PGGM Embroiled in Conflict with Mexican Wind Farm," *Dutch News*, July 26, 2013, *HYPERLINK "http://www.dutchnews.nl/news/archives/2013/07/pggm_embroiled_in _conflict_wit/"* http://www.dutchnews.nl/news/archives/2013/07/pggm_embroiled_in _conflict_wit.
47. Rojas, "No instalará Mareña Renovable."
48. "Oaxaca: Mareña Renewables to Cancel Wind-Energy Project in San Dionisio del Mar" (SIPAZ Blog, January 15, 2014), https://sipazen.wordpress.com.
49. M. Posada, "Autoriza comunidad de Juchitán construcción de empresa eólica," *La Jornada*, August 4, 2015, www.jornada.unam.mx.
50. S. James Anaya, "Observaciones del Profesor S. Anaya sobre la consulta en el context del pryecto Energia Eolica del Sur en Juchitan de Zaragoza" (unpublished manuscript, February 23, 2015), http://fundar.org.mx/wp-content/uploads/2015/03/Juchitan -observaciones-Anaya.pdf.
51. "Resurrected Wind Farm Has Foes in Juchitán," *Mexico Daily News*, April 7, 2015, http://mexiconewsdaily.com/news/resurrected-wind-farm-foes-juchitan.
52. James Anaya, interviewed by author, May 2016.
53. "Piden mantener suspension del Proyecto Eólica del Sur en Oaxaca," *Centro Mexicano de Noticias Ambiental, Noticias*, June 21, 2016, http://www.cemda.org.mx/piden-mantener -suspension-del-proyecto-eolica-del-sur-en-oaxaca.
54. Allyson Benton, *The Origins of Mexico's Municipal Usos y Costumbres Regimes: Supporting Local Political Participation or Local Authoritarian Control?*, CIDE Working Paper 226, February 2011, http://libreriacide.com/librospdf/DTEP-226.pdf.
55. Eisenstadt and Rios, "Multicultural Institutions."

# Bibliography

Anaya, S. James. "Observaciones del Profesor S. James Anaya sobre la consulta en el context del pryecto Energia Eolica del Sur en Juchitan de Zaragoza." Unpublished manuscript, February 23, 2015. http://fundar.org.mx/wp-content/uploads/2015/03/Juchitan-observa-ciones-Anaya.pdf.
Benton, Allyson L. "Bottom-Up Challenges to National Democracy: Mexico's (legal) Subnational Authoritarian Enclaves," *Comparative Politics* 44, no. 3 (April 2012): 253–71
——. *The Origins of Mexico's Municipal Usos y Costumbres Regimes: Supporting Local Political Participation or Local Authoritarian Control?* CIDE Working Paper 226. February 2011. http://libreriacide.com/librospdf/DTEP-226.pdf.

Brown, James. *Ejidos and Comunidades in Oaxaca, Mexico: Impact of the 1992 Reforms*. Reports on Foreign and Development. No. 120. February 2004. http://www.landesa.org /wp-content/uploads/2011/01/RDI_120.pdf.

Centro Mexicano de Derecho Ambiental. "Noticias: Piden Mantener Suspensión del Proyecto Eólica del Sur en Oaxaca." June 21, 2016. http://www.cemda.org.mx/piden -mantener-suspension-del-proyecto-eolica-del-sur-en-oaxaca/.

Chirhart, Paul. "Macquairie Mexican Infrastructure Fund Announces Completion of Financing for 396MW Wind Energy Project in Oaxaca." *Macquarie*, February 24, 2012. http://www.macquarie.com/mgl/com/us/about/news/2012/20120224.

Cleary, Matthew R. "Electoral Competition and Democracy in Mexico." PhD. diss., University of Chicago, 2004.

Climate Nexus. "Country Climate Pledges." March 27, 2015, http://climatenexus.org/about-us /negotiation-issues/country-climate-pledges.

Crippa, Leonardo. *Request for Consultation and Compliance Review: Mareña Renovables Wind Project*. Indian Law Resource Center, 2012. https://idblegacy.iadb.org/en/mici /me-micio02-2012-marena-renovables-wind-project-mexico-compliance-review-report -published-after-consideration,20488.html.

Critchley, Adam. "Oaxaca Leads the Way in Mexico Wind." *20 BN Americas*, September 24, 2015. http://www.bnamericas.com/en/news/electricpower/oaxaca-leads -the-way-in-mexico-clean-energy.

Dezem, Vanessa, and Adam Williams. "Mexico Planning $46 Billion Coast-to-Coast Wind Energy Push." *Bloomberg*, October 21, 2015. http://www.bloomberg.com/news /articles/2015-10-21/mexico-planning-46-billion-coast-to-coast-wind-energy-push.

Diaz Cayeros, Alberto, Beatriz Magaloni, and Alexander Ruiz-Euler. "Traditional Governance, Citizen Engagement and Local Public Goods: Evidence from Mexico" *World Development* 53 (January 2014): 80–93. http://web.stanford.edu/~magaloni/dox /2012traditionalgovernance.pdf.

Eisenstadt, Todd. "Usos y Costumbres and Postelectoral Conflicts in Oaxaca, Mexico, 1995–2004: An Empirical and Normative Assessment." *Latin American Research Review* 42, no. 1 (2007): 52–77.

Eisenstadt, Todd, and Viridiana Rios. "Multicultural Institutions, Distributional Politics, and Post-Electoral Mobilization in Indigenous Mexico." *Latin American Politics and Society* 56, no. 2 (2014): 70–92.

Hristova, Diana. "Mexico: Oaxaca Wants to Boost Wind Power to 5.5GW by 2024." *SeeNews*, September 9, 2015. http://renewables.seenews.com/news/mexico-oaxaca-wants -to-boost-wind-power-to-5-5-gw-by-2024-492186.

Indian Law Resource Center. "Request for Consultation and Compliance Review: Mareña Renovables Wind Project ME-L1107." December 26, 2012. https://idbdocs.iadb.org /wsdocs/getdocument.aspx?docnum=37520692.

Indian Law Resource Center. "Submission to the 1st Session of the Open-Ended Intergovern-mental Working Group on Transnational Corporations and Other Business Enterprises with Respect to Human Rights." July 2015. http://indianlaw.org/sites/default/files/2015 -07-24%20Submission%20to%20OEIWG%20_%20letterhead_.pdf.

Inter-American Development Bank. "Independent Consultation and Investigation Mechanism." 2012. http://www.hc-sc.gc.ca/ewh-semt/alt_formats/hecs-sesc/pdf/pubs/air /formaldehyde-eng.pdf.

Inter-American Development Bank. "Operational Policy on Indigenous Peoples and Strategy for Indigenous Development." 2006. http://idbdocs.iadb.org/wsdocs/getdocument .aspx?docnum=2032081.

Márquez-Mees, Victoria. "Compliance Review Report: Mareña Renovables Wind Project." Inter-American Development Bank. 2016. http://indianlaw.org/sites/default/files/ME -MICI002-2012__COMPLIANCE_REVIEW_REPORT_FOR_MAREÑA_RENOVABLES _WIND_ENERGY_PROJECT__ENGLISH_WEB__.pdf.

National Wind Watch. "FAQ—Size." Accessed April 2016. https://www.wind-watch.org/faq -size.php.

Perez, Jorge A. "Emerging Mexican Wind Farm Mecca Produces Clean Power—and Problems." *Thomson Reuters Foundation News*. June 6, 2014. http://news.trust.org //slideshow/?id=eb7bb216-1a71-471b-8245-92803dc19268.

Perramond, Eric P. "The Rise, Fall and Reconfiguration of the Mexican Ejido." *Geographical Review* 98, no. 3 (2014): 356–71.

"Piden acatar fallo contra plan eólico." *El Universal*, December 10, 2012. http://archivo .eluniversal.com.mx/estados/89021.html.

Posada, M. "Autoriza comunidad de Juchitán construcción de empresa eólica." *La Jornada*, August 4, 2015. www.jornada.unam.mx.

"PGGM Embroiled in Conflict with Mexican Wind Farm." *Dutch News*, July 26, 2013. http:// www.dutchnews.nl/news/archives/2013/07/pggm_embroiled_in_conflict_wit/.

"Resurrected Wind Farm Has Foes in Juchitán." *Mexico Daily News*, April 7, 2015. http:// mexiconewsdaily.com/news/resurrected-wind-farm-foes-juchitan/.

Rojas, Rosa. "No instalará Mareña Renovables parque eólico en Dionisio del Mar." *La Jornada*, February 18, 2013. http://www.jornada.unam.mx/2013/02/18/sociedad/039n1soc.

Schaefer, Isabelle. *Supporting the Reform Agenda for Inclusive Growth in Oaxaca, Mexico*. The World Bank, September 4, 2013. http://www.worldbank.org/en/results/2013/09/04 /oaxaca-inclusive-growth.

SIPAZ Blog. "Oaxaca: Confrontation Over Supposed "Approval" of Wind-Energy Park in San Dionisio del Mar."January 8, 2013. https://sipazen.wordpress.com/.

——. "Oaxaca: Judge Concedes Motion Against Wind-Energy Project in San Dionisio de Mar." December 21, 2012. https://sipazen.wordpress.com/.

——. "Oaxaca: Mareña Renewables to Cancel Wind-Energy Project in San Dionisio del Mar." January 15, 2014. https://sipazen.wordpress.com/.

Smith, Jennifer. *Indigenous Communities in Mexico Fight Corporate Wind Farms*. November 1, 2012. http://upsidedownworld.org/archives/mexico/indigenous-communities -in-mexico-fight-corporate-wind-farms/.

"33 New Turbines for Tehuantepec." *Mexico Daily News*, September 6, 2014. http://mexiconews daily.com/news/33-new-turbines-planned-tehuantepec/.

Vance, Erik. "The Wind Rush: Green Energy Blows Trouble into Mexico." *Christian Science Monitor*, January 26, 2012.

Vélez Ascencio, O. "Oaxaca: huaves rechazan creación de parque eólico en la isla Pueblo Viejo." *La Jornada*, August 23, 2012. http://www.jornada.unam.mx/.

——. "Parque eólico; 'un suicidio.'" *Noticias de Oaxaca*. August 2012, http://old.nvinoticias .com/oaxaca/general/ambientales/112524-parque-eolico-"un-suicidio."

# CONCLUSION

*Territorial Pluralism and Language Communities*

ASTRID VON BUSEKIST

Two prominent lawyers, Hersch Lauterpacht and Raphael Lemkin, both born before WWI in Lemberg (Lvov, Lviv), a small town in Ukraine today, worked for the Allies' prosecution teams at the Nurnberg trial. Lauterpacht officially counseled the British, and Lemkin tried to convince Jackson and the American lawyers of his ideas. Lauterpacht conceptualized the notion of "crimes against humanity," one of the four counts of indictment at the International Military Tribunal. Lemkin invented the term *genocide*, which was quoted in court by the French and the Soviets but only made its way into international law in 1948 with the Genocide Convention.[1]

At stake was a profound divergence between two visions of international law: the protection of groups, on one hand (genocide), and the protection of the individual, on the other (crimes against humanity). The Allies had many reservations against using the term genocide, a neologism they mistrusted. The colonial powers, in particular, feared that this new crime would have serious implications for them and for their own guilty practices on their own soil.

It may, however, not be a matter of chance that genocide took precedence over crimes against humanity in the postwar period; genocide has become the "crime of crimes"—groups (or communities in the contemporary wording) ought to be protected. The question is how and with which consequences for the international and domestic order. As early as the 1930s, when sovereign states weren't yet accountable to any international instance and did to their citizens—or subjects—more or less what they wanted, Lauterpacht understood that groups and individuals cannot be treated alike, that the rights of individuals always take precedence over those of a group.

The Nurnberg trial, and the international law the tribunal generated, was the consequence of tragic crimes and traumatic events. But the debate between Lauterpacht and Lemkin raises important questions relevant to the topic of this volume: the *summa divisio* between securing and protecting the rights of individuals and accommodating the collective identities of groups. The contributors of this volume all address this question from different historical, legal, and political perspectives: they question the legitimacy of (and the justifications for) alternative versions to the "monist" sovereign nation-state—most prominently, and promisingly, federal forms of government (including one of its organizing principles: subsidiarity); status group legal pluralism; and various forms of new, private or corporate jurisgenerative practices—against the background of protecting and promoting equality, liberty, participation, nondomination, and self-government.

One of the implicit and ongoing dilemmas in theory as well as in practice is whether democratic polities should grant groups the same kinds of protections, rights, and liberties individuals enjoy. For a communitarian—I use the generic term—the answer is obvious. In France, she would argue, Muslims should have the same rights as Catholics, Protestants, or Jews. Fine, this is indeed one of the founding principles of the French *laïcité*: equality among religious groups. But she would also argue that they should have the same liberties in the public as well as in the private sphere: wear a headscarf to school, or the burka outside of their homes. In the United States, Canada, and Belgium, the legislation and the *mores* are less constraining than in the very secular French Republic. In the communitarian perspective, individuals are social beings, defined by their belonging to religious, cultural, and linguistic groups: what we owe one group, we should give to the others in the same way, regardless of the specific, performative, sometimes alienating meaning of religious signs of belonging for its members.

The defining principles of modern democratic politics are indeed liberty and equality. But these categories apply to individuals, not to collective entities. Even for holistic scholars such as Durkheim, despite the binding moral principles of the whole as a *sui generis* entity (society, the state, communities), in modern societies the supreme value is that of the individual. As it happens, however, *nomos* groups claim that it is legitimate to be treated in the same way as individuals, that we grant communities the same rights (to liberty, equality, coauthorship of the law) as individuals. Theoretically, this is quite an epistemological leap.

The debate opposing Lauterpacht and Lemkin goes beyond the dialectic of individual/group, and it illustrates how careful one should be when applying individual principles to collective entities and vice versa. The terms of the debate have not dramatically changed over the years: Should we recognize groups to protect individuals? or Should we protect individuals, disregarding their belonging to communities?

The general *normative* response to the claims of jurisdictional autonomy and sovereignty of (religious, ethnic, linguistic) nomos groups should be unconditional respect for individual rights and liberties, democratic accountability, self-government, and parity of participation. But there does not seem to be a universal *empirical* recipe to democratically accommodate demands of communities within given polities. The authors of this volume examine a variety of cases and suggest context-specific answers.

Group rights and individual rights can either be compatible or antagonistic, balanced within a general democratic framework guaranteeing rights and liberties for all, fair access to office, nondomination, and so forth or incompatible because granting group rights (in the form of jurisdictional autonomy, territorial rights, internal sovereignty on matters that may undermine equal recognition of individual rights) runs against the values and principles of liberal democratic polities. To find out whether democracies should make a place for community rights (including changes to the constitution by creating new federal entities, ceding territory, or granting jurisdictional rights to status groups), we should ask two questions. The first pertains to *threshold*; the second interrogates the contribution to the *democratic quality* of the polity.

The former draws boundaries between compatible and legitimate community demands for autonomy, whereas the latter asks whether granting group rights is a *plus* for liberal democratic principles, a genuine addition to the rights and liberties of individuals, on one hand, or a contribution to the democratic quality of the polity at large, on the other. Posing these questions allows us to bridge the gap between individual and collective rights and takes up the debate from another angle: instead of asking what we owe communities (in terms of respect for their culture, language, beliefs), we ask how far granting rights contributes to the democratic quality of political entities in general and, at the same time, enhances the rights of individual members of these groups.

Here I consider an example not yet addressed in this volume that pertains to territoriality, the ultimate attribute of sovereignty; it is a counterintuitive example that sheds a different light on collective rights and the normative autonomy of groups as language communities. Communities of speakers are not nomos groups, but they occasionally act as such because languages are "club goods"[2] and precious identifiers of collective belonging. Examining linguistic solidarity and territoriality illustrates how threshold and context matter, and it allows us to test the robustness of democratic constitutionalism.

## Territorializing Language Communities

Territorial language claims seem to be an entirely different story than the claims for territorial religious exemption with which we are familiar (*Kirias Joel*[3] or the debates around Eruvin, for example[4]). Although collective language claims have sometimes been compared to religious claims,[5] many battles have been fought over linguistic rights and self-government of language communities.[6]

*Caeteris paribus*, the rationality for linguistic territoriality (for example, linguistic autonomy and sovereignty in a given territory), challenges democratic constitutionalism in comparable ways to status group legal pluralism: granting collective language rights may constrain individual rights,[7] and, in some cases, undermine the exercise of statewide democratic citizenship. Language policies are a good example of political and institutional arrangements that in principle foster pluralism but empirically sometimes hinder democratic citizenship.[8]

The reason for addressing language policies is to take the important feature of language diversity and subsequent management of linguistic pluralism into account. Language communities are not status groups, but the a priori legitimacy derived from a shared tongue—often equated with a shared culture[9]— in claiming opposable rights[10] is a major challenge and a democratic test for (national, multinational, and federal) states. It also conceals important problems for policy makers: Should language diversity trump mobility and employability? Democratic deliberation and participation? How are we to manage political problems that cut across different language communities while enhancing participation, applying democratic procedures, and protecting individual rights?

Institutionalizing modes of protection, power sharing, and granting subsidiary rights to language communities are generally justified by a commitment to democratic and multicultural pluralism. What is there to be learned from the way states treat language diversity, equally protecting the (general and linguistic) rights of individual speakers while at the same time protecting (vulnerable) speech communities? What does an analysis of language policies[11] add to our understanding of forms of pluralism, federalization, and subsidiarity?

The difference between religious claims and language claims is the following: linguistic disenfranchisement is impossible. Communication between institutions and their members (or would-be members, immigrants[12]) always occurs through specific languages: institutions regulate linguistic public rights and duties; therefore, linguistic hands-off policies cannot exist.[13] Language is a specific collective good: states cannot distribute language the same way they distribute health care, social security, or housing[14] despite the fact that languages are important primary social goods. But states can and should distribute "access rights" and services related to (minority) language issues (via instrumental or accommodationist policies).[15]

Most important, language rights are the substructure of a variety of important democratic requirements: without language skills, access to various spheres, political as well as socioeconomic, is hindered.[16] Without access to these spheres of citizenship, no political, social, and economic rights and duties can be properly exercised, and no rights claims can be properly voiced. Language skills are therefore politically *enabling*.[17]

From a fairness point of view, language disadvantages are detrimental to democratic equality and therefore to democratic participation. The argument for "parity of participation"[18] is usually made in support of official common languages to foster a healthy "talkcentric"[19] participatory territorial or national democracy; but parity of participation thanks to a common tongue is also supported by *lingua franca* proposals for "Europe and for the world."[20] For most scholars, language territoriality seems to be the fairest choice, for individuals and for groups:[21] protecting languages in their territory is justified pragmatically (offering "a full societal culture" to its members[22]) and as a compensation for disparity of esteem felt by speakers of minority languages.[23]

But if language skills are to be enabling for individuals, and if we agree that states have a moral duty to accommodate (vulnerable) speech communities,[24] we should also ask about the political consequences of collective language rights in autonomous spheres for individual members, and in how far language arrangements are the outcome of democratic debate.[25]

What are the "technical" choices for the legislator vis-à-vis language policies? In multilingual states, two principles are at hand: *territoriality* and *personality*. The first and most widespread principle (Belgium, Switzerland, Cameroon, in its simplest form) is based on territorial rights: it legally recognizes the X-speaking territory on the basis of a majority of X-speaking individuals.[26] Territoriality is usually associated with administrative bilingualism (civil servants, for example, master all or part of the official languages); it provides language stability and language security (small languages are protected on their territory[27]), and the public space functions in the given official language (schools, public services, and so on). Territoriality often leads to juxtaposed unilingualisms and may disrupt intercommunity communication such as in Belgium (see below).

The *personality* principle, on the other hand, is best described by institutional multilingualism where the state acknowledges and recognizes *individual* language choices (within the limits of legally recognized languages): regardless of where I am on the territory, civil administration has a duty to respect my language rights. Canada was ruled by this principle but has abandoned it, in part because of Quebec's battle to protect French and the subsequent legislations making French the sole official language in the province.[28] Political choices associated with language governance are a consequence of specific historical and political contexts.

In line with what I asked earlier (Are group rights a *plus* for liberal democratic principles, an addition to the rights and liberties of individuals, and a
contribution to the democratic quality of the polity?), I would like to comment
on an example in which collective language claims indeed led to constitutional
revisions and internal federalization, but this new constitutional architecture—
meant to recognize, accommodate, and pacify ethno-linguistic tensions—has
achieved quite the opposite. A fine constitutional architecture, as in Belgium,
may also be a political failure.

## Divisive Federalism

The four Belgian constitutional revisions (1970–1993/94) were tailored to accommodate the two main communities and to pacify the tensions between the Flemish
northern part of the country and the Walloon southern part. Shifting from a unitarian state to a federation met the legitimate demands of both sides: Flemings and
Walloons claimed that an autonomous administration of their national, cultural,
and linguistic community would solve most of the problems the unitarian state had
encountered in the one hundred or so previous years. Paradoxically, the federal
institutions not only created unknown frictions but also contributed to deeply
dividing the two communities. Once a consociational democracy, Belgium has
become a divided society in which two communities coexist in almost two different political regimes. The federal institutions partitioned the linguistic communities instead of fostering intercommunitarian dialogue within the federation.[29]
Pluralism management has led to a form of juxtaposed monisms.

Belgium was created in 1830 as a French-speaking, liberal, constitutional
monarchy. Some fifteen years later, a Flemish national movement, patriotic
in its essence, demanded equal recognition of Flemish language and culture.
The movement obtained official bilingualism in Flanders at the end of the
nineteenth century, official unilingualism in Flanders in 1932, and the constitutional recognition of Flemish as a second official language in 1935.

The recognition of language was intrinsically linked to the recognition of
a distinct, specific, and autonomous cultural community and resulted in language territorialization along a frontier definitively fixed in 1963. Language disputes progressively became the core (and the alibi) of most political conflicts. In
1988 Belgium abandoned compulsory training in the other country's language
for high school students. On the Walloon French-speaking side, a regional
movement was established much later as a reaction to Flemish nationalism.[30]
Cleavages, unlike Switzerland or Canada, overlap in Belgium: a rich, Catholic,
agricultural, traditional north, represented by the Christian democrats (today
the Flemish nationalists), faces a socialist, industrial, relatively poorer south,
mainly represented by the socialist party and strong unions.

How did these transformations come about? How did Belgium shift from free individual language choice to constraining territorial unilingualism with two strong nationalisms facing each other and preventing democratic *vivre ensemble*, social justice, and interregional economic solidarity? Belgium is home to three distinctive communities (the European capital, Brussels, an enclave in Flemish territory, remains officially bilingual), each of which is a microdemocracy on its own. The political culture and the citizen's allegiances are mapped by linguistic boundaries. There is very little interregional or inter-community communication or solidarity between Flanders and Wallonia, and the agendas of the Region Brussels-Capital and the rest of the francophone region in the south of the country do not overlap.

On the federal level, the 1994 Constitution explicitly states that "Belgium contains three communities: the French, Dutch, and the German-speaking community" (Article 3, *ter*). These communities were instituted on purely linguistic criteria, proving that language took precedence over other political and democratic criteria. The simultaneous creation of the Regions in the Constitution, "the French language region, the Dutch language region, the Brussels-capital bilingual region, and the German language region" (Article 3, *bis*), even reinforces the role of language: legislators recognized the predominance of language in administrative divisions. The Communities and Regions have autonomous parliaments and governments and may pursue diverging policies. Belgium has become a plurilegislative federation in which the federal entities and the central state are strictly equal,[31] but in which the "law is not the same for all" anymore.[32]

The Communities and Regions have been assigned more and more autonomous competences through subsidiarity; political agendas do not overlap, and a far richer north faces an impoverished south and refuses to foot the bill of the Walloon industrial decline. Belgian party politics have become a multilevel game in which there is no congruence between the political identity of the federal government and the regional or community governments: electoral cycles are dissociated, electoral sequences with changing coalitions follow each other very closely, and compromise has become almost impossible.[33]

## From Holding Together Federalism to Divided Constituencies

Territorial federalism is geographic and collective; personal federalism considers individual rights regardless of geographical location. Belgium combines the two types: regional matters such as country planning and zoning laws belong to territorial federalism, but communities are competent in linguistic matters. Only in the Brussels-Capital area does personal federalism prevail (culture and education).[34] With regard to the European Union, Belgium is represented both by a Flemish and a Walloon representative, alternatively, in the European Commission. But the true problem is *application* of the European laws: the central state does not have the prerogatives to implement the correct application of the European law within the federal entities, although it is the Belgian state that is liable (environment, for instance, is a regional competence).[35] Belgium, in a way, resembles a "plural society"[36] with sharp ethnic, linguistic, and religious distinctions; little common will; and a profound potential for instability.

The electoral system and the organization of party politics is a fair illustration. The political parties split in the late 1960s and reformed with linguistic branches in the 1970s. Once elected, parties have to compromise with the members of the other community at the federal level. However, MPs are never elected by a federal constituency, only by their own communities, and can be sanctioned only by their community.

Since the schism of the political parties along linguistic lines, four novelties have appeared (not all are specific to Belgian federalism): (1) there are no dominant parties (until the 1970s or 1980s there was one dominant party in each region[37]); (2) the governments at the federal and the regional level are not congruent; (3) there is an ongoing electoral campaign and all parties behave as if they were opposition parties; and (4) there is a growing electoral mobility. Paradoxically, the urgency (and hence the will) to find a compromise is much less important in the federal setting: the state can "function" with or without a reduced federal government. There are very few federal competences, and the important ones (social security, justice) are huge bureaucracies that routinely work without the intervention of the government. Public transportation, education, culture, environment, energy, and many aspects of international affairs are regional competences and continue to work normally even without a central federal government. In short, in case of failure to constitute a government coalition, the price to pay is not very high. Belgium managed to survive 540 days without a government in 2012.

In its project, Belgium was a consensual "holding together" federalism; it is today a bipolar, asymmetrical, dissociation federalism, despite the guarantees the constitution offers against the legal domination of one community over the other.[38] Interestingly, the linguistic and territorial subsidiarity principle has replaced the "pillars" (Catholic, Socialist, Liberal), which were forms of religious, political, and partisan subsidiarities[39] that transcended the linguistic cleavages.

The Belgian pillars were forms of social and corporate units of subsidiarity within the framework of the unitarian state.[40] The linguistic form of subsidiarity, paradoxically, is a new form of antisovereign legal pluralism within the federal state. But unlike the pillars, this form of linguistic and communitarian pluralism seems almost more problematic from a democratic perspective than the old corporate bodies. Instead of strengthening the federation through

autonomous administration of language communities, it has fragmented constituencies and tied members to language communities without any means of
escaping territoriality. Local interests and local goals have achieved a centrifugal system with very few counterbalancing mechanisms.

In short, the new institutional architecture has generated more problems
than it has solved. Federalization and linguistic territoriality may have been the
political and contextual answer to a long-lasting struggle, but practically, the
consequence is a failure:

> The country's other community is practically a foreign people. It is rather diffi-
> cult for a political system to keep functioning with such mutual ignorance and
> hence such lack of mutual understanding of the two halves of the country.[41]

On September 23, 2012, the *New York Times* published an opinion piece
predicting the end of Belgium in the very near future, arguing that "national
borders will become less important than cultural and ethnic lines."[42] Maybe.
There are, however, solutions to prevent the fatality of divorce: a change in the
electoral law would be a simple intermediary solution to achieve constitutional
patriotism *and* a renewed overlapping consensus.[43] Even if one-third of the
electoral body were transregional and transcommunitarian within a single federal circumscription, both linguistic wings of the different parties would have
to agree on explicit common programs.

The Belgian state has already made important concessions to its linguistic communities. However, in the name of laudable principles—pluralism and
self-government—the process of federalization has in reality created two polities, a "sphere sovereignty" accountable only to one specific linguistic constituency. Belgium's federalism is neither the result of restorative justice nor
a liberation from forced assimilation or the desire to save a culture. Linguistic territoriality in Belgium is the result of a certain blindness: language has
become a practical alibi to lead nationalist policies and avoid redistribution,
especially on the Flemish side. Shared rule between ethno-national groups, as
in the consociational model, is played down to a very minimum, and self-rule
has become decisive.

Linguistic pluralism, in the case I have presented, questions the notion of
territoriality in relation to pluralism management. Territoriality is perhaps the
most difficult challenge for the contemporary sovereign state. The control of
boundaries, physical or imaginary, is an integral and indivisible attribute of
state sovereignty. Shared control over boundaries and hybridity of space are, as
I have shown, met with skepticism by citizens, parties, and governments.

I have argued that context matters and that we should look at threshold
cases to find out whether group claims and their accommodation threaten
or, on the contrary, contribute to enhance individual rights and democratic

constitutionalism. In many cases, they obviously undermine liberal democratic or republican values, some of them discussed in this volume.

The debate about territoriality and (new) internal boundaries should be led in the light of two principles: those affected by a law must participate in elaborating it (and must be able to approve it[44]), and democracy must justify coercion (coercion through the law is legitimate only if those subjected to the law also view themselves as its authors). They can only do so if they enjoy the full bundle of political rights and opportunities of participation and representation.[45] These principles are good measures to test the democratic legitimacy of accommodation in pluralist polities.

Because it questions the notion of territoriality, the case I have presented is particularly suggestive. It highlights the difficulty of sharing space or territory among linguistic communities without undermining democratic sovereignty. Tensions and undesirable side effects are unavoidable, but success depends on the respect of the three conditions I have spelled out: respect for individual rights, recognition of groups, and democratic constitutionalism.

The first two conditions do not necessarily occur together. Enhancing the rights of the community does not *ipso facto* respect or augment the rights of individuals. Communities expect the liberal state to grant them the same rights as individual citizens: to be treated in the same way as other groups, benefit from the same liberties as individuals, and participate in the making of the law. Sui generis entities such as communities are not, however, a simple addition of their composing elements: they may affirm their identity against their members, they may favor some and wrong others, or they may believe they count more than the individuals they comprise. But who exactly do they stand for, whom do they represent? A religious community—to take up the comparison I began with anew—speaks in the name of those who recognize themselves as its members, but how far reaching is their hold? Holistic religious communities rarely engage in conflicts with their members. Convictions or feelings of individual discomfort of fellow believers of the wider circle may arise, but they do not, *stricto sensu*, belong to the community. The judge or the legislator has to appreciate his or her burden compared to the benefit of the inner circle and test whether laws *obliges* individual dissenters or *enables* members to enjoy new forms of liberty.

In large individualistic communities, on the other hand, there is no difference between inner circle and outer circle members: language ispo facto identifies speakers with their community, and linguistic territoriality obliges them. The francophone and the Flemish of Belgium are indeed obliged by the territorial option of the Belgian federalization. As opposed to nonjurisdictional spaces (think of Castro, for example, or ethnic neighborhoods), the territorial jurisdiction of the Belgian language communities is imposed on all individuals, regardless of the language community to which they belong. The multiple benefits the linguistic majority derives from the constitutional architecture comes with a heavy cost for the minorities within the territory. Their burden may well outweigh the benefits of the majority.[46] Belgian federalism and its subsidiarity principle protect language groups but at the same time disavow minority speakers within majoritarian language territories. Territorial group rights have taken precedence over individual rights.

As I have argued here, the simple principle I have sketched around the triangle of individual rights, recognition of communities, and democratic integrity is difficult to apply without further precaution in diverse contexts and different historical situations. Optimal arrangements are difficult to achieve empirically. The legacy of the Ottoman Empire in the Middle East and in Greece, for example[47]—jurisdictional competition between religious tribunals and civil courts—is a fact with long-lasting consequences for the communities and their members, as well as a problem for constitutionalists and egalitarians, but adequate responses may not be the same as in other (postcolonial) contexts. International and domestic environment matter, and political contexts are more or less conducive to institutional change and constitutional revisions. Sweeping normative solutions are of little help in the context of deeply divided societies with a long history of adversity.

Lacking an adequate general normative proposal, it is safer to reason in terms of more or less. The rights of all individuals, even the most marginal ones, should be protected under all circumstances, but this *petitio principis* holds only where the interests of individuals and groups never conflict.

So where should democracies place the threshold or the trade-off between competing interests? The challenges status groups pose to democratic integrity differ. Status group claims for normative autonomy and jurisdictional sovereignty sheltered from the state (yet operating within the boundaries of the state and reclaiming the social or educational benefits of the state as in the *Kiryas Joel* case addressed earlier), and cultural claims for recognition, restorative justice or accommodation, do not defy democratic integrity in the same way. The former may seriously endanger individual rights, democratic and civic values, especially those of the most vulnerable members of such groups. Their hubris— our norms are incompatible with the general law (and therefore we deserve exemptions from the general law), on equal footing or superior to the general law (our commands identify us as a community, and the source of our norms are extraneous to the legal sources of the polity, therefore our autonomous rules ought to be respected as intrinsically valuable[48])—is obviously incompatible with the defining principles of well-ordered democracies.

This is not to say that I am unsympathetic to community claims, quite the opposite. Multiculturalism and accommodation policies have done the job as "agents of love," in Rorty's terms.[49] But the contextual approach I am advocating is sensitive to threshold,[50] on one hand, and to political and legislative contributions to democracy, on the other. Depending on the degree to which instituted communities challenge or, on the contrary, enhance democratic integrity, institutional and political answers should differ.

An empirical and contextual evaluation will deceive categorical spirits, liberals, and communitarians alike, but it is closer to reality and better reflects the inspiration of this volume.

## Notes

1. The story of these two men is recounted in Philippe Sands, *East West Street: On the Origins of Genocide and Crimes Against Humanity* (London: Weidenfeld and Nicholson, 2016).
2. Club goods are excludable although not necessarily rivalrous goods. Languages are, *in principle*, nonexcludable goods with positive network externalities (as argued by Abram de Swaan, *Words of the World* [London: Polity Press, 2001]), but citizens, members of political communities, may view their (national, official) language as excludable "club goods," that is, restricted to a specific constituency or accessible only via cost-sharing. James Buchanan, "An Economic Theory of Clubs," *Economica* 32, no. 125 (February 1965): 1–14; Joseph Carens, *The Ethics of Immigration* (Oxford: Oxford University Press, 2013).
3. A good example is the *Kiryas Joel* case in the Monroe-Woodbury district. See Jeffrey Rosen, "Village People," *The New Republic*, November 4, 1994; Ira Lupu, "Uncovering the Village of Kiryas Joel," *Columbia Law Review* 96, no. 1 (1996): 104–20; Judith Failer, "The Draw and Drawbacks of Religious Enclaves in Constitutional Democracy: Hasidic Public Schools in Kiryas Joel," *Indiana Law Review* 72, no. 2 (1997): 382–402; *contra* Abner S. Greene, "Kiryas Joel and Two Mistakes About Equality," *Columbia Law Review* 96, no. 1 (1996): 1–104.
4. An eruv is a Jewish boundary, an almost immaterial wall that bounds an area and transforms a public space into a private area (usually by attaching wire, strings, or fishing lines to public poles). It allows observant Jews to do things otherwise prohibited on the Sabbath: carrying keys, books, bringing food to a friend's home, pushing a baby carriage or wheelchair. As it is forbidden to transfer objects from private to public and vice versa on the Sabbath, the eruv allows rabbinical Jews to move within the bounded zone while considering it as an extension of their homes. It mixes spaces, public and private, and creates a third, hybrid entity of which the immaterial boundary is the eruv. The area remains public for non-Jews or simply nonbelievers; it becomes private for observant Jews. The court cases involving rabbinical communities and opponents to the eruv were disputes about territorial takeover by orthodox Jews, colonization of public land versus sharing of public space, and allowing women, in particular, to leave their homes on the Sabbath. "The eruv literally attaches normative weight to jurisdictional lines; it represents the rare situation in which the normative community is coextensive with the descriptive neighborhood (as defined by the limits of the eruv)." Rich C. Schragger, "The Limits of Localism," *Michigan Law Review* 100, no. 2 (2001): 440. I have argued this in Astrid von Busekist, *Portes et Murs. Des frontières en démocratie* (Paris: Albin Michel, 2016).
5. The analogy between language and religion is heuristic to some. Allan Patten, for instance, argues in favor of a non-outcome-oriented policy designed to establish "fair background conditions in which speakers of different languages can strive for the success and survival of their own language communities." AlanPatten, "Liberal Neutrality

and Language Policy," *Philosophy and Public Affairs* 31, no. 4 (2003): 366. Rogers Bru-baker compares language claims to religious claims and argues that religious claims have replaced language claims in Western democracies: "religion has tended to displace language as the cutting edge of contestation over the political accommodation of cul-tural difference—a striking reversal of the longer-term historical process through which language had previously displaced religion as the primary focus of contention." Rogers Brubaker, "Language, Religion and the Politics of Difference," *Nations and Nationalism* 19, no. 1 (2013): 1.

6. These battles have resulted either in secession and creation of new monolingual states (current attempts in Catalonia), federalization and power sharing (Canada, Switzer-land, Belgium), or recognition of the relative autonomy of ethno-linguistic groups (South Africa, India).

7. In the sense that people do not want to be territorially coerced into using only one language.

8. I will not address the long history of language rationalization in Western democra-cies as a key condition not only for nationalism and state building but most impor-tant for nationwide literacy, politization, and inclusion into the demos. See David Laitin, "What Is a Language Community?", *American Journal of Political Science* 44, no. 1 (2000): 142–55; building on Ernest Gellner, *Nations and Nationalism* (Oxford: B. Blackwell, 1983).

9. Scholars dealing with language issues are quite divided about the way we should publicly recognize language groups, communities, and individual speakers. They advise we either value *identity-related* claims or *utility-related* claims. For the former, language is intrinsically linked to something precious, worth being publicly defended and protected—our personal and political identity—and the state has a moral duty to accommodate this quest for (collective) recognition. See, for example, Denise Réaume, "Official Language Rights: Intrinsic Value and the Protection of Difference," in *Citizenship in Diverse Societies*, ed. Will Kymlicka and Wayne Norman (Oxford: Oxford University Press, 2000); Stephen May, *Language and Minority Rights. Ethnicity, Nationalism and the Politics of Language*, 2nd ed. (New York: Routledge, 2012). Regard-ing collective rights, the idea is that one cannot remedy or rectify linguistic injustice (which is often a result of socioeconomic inequalities, large power structures), without granting collective rights. Restorative justice mechanisms would typically compensate forceful assimilation into the majority (often colonial) language.

Scholars committed to utility and efficiency believe that languages are foremost tools to connect people, and often defend *lingua franca* policies to achieve efficient integrated political practices reaching constituencies beyond specific linguistic repertoires, in the EU, for example). The most radical consequentialists argue that language communities engage in—or should engage in—a cost-benefit analysis with compensations, trade-offs, and "side payments" to evaluate what they are ready to give up in exchange for being able to communicate with a larger group than their native community. See, for example, de Swaan, *Words of the World*; Reinhard Selten and Jonathan Pool, "The Distribution of Foreign Language Skills as a Game Equilibrium," in *Game Equilibrium Models*, vol. 4, ed. Reinhard Selten (Berlin: Springer, 1991), 64–87; Victor Ginsburg and Shlomo Weber, *How Many Languages Do We Need? The Economics of Linguistic Diversity* (Princeton, N.J.: Princeton University Press, 2011).

10. Will Kymlicka, *Politics in the Vernacular: Nationalism, Multiculturalism and Citizenship* (Oxford: Oxford University Press, 2001); Will Kymlicka, *Multicultural Odysseys: Navigating the New International Politics of Diversity* (Oxford: Oxford University Press, 2007).

11.  *Language policy* or *political linguistics* examines the ways in which governments attempt to shape the linguistic structure of the society or the claims issued by linguistic groups to change existing language arrangements or legislations. Language policy is an attempt to weigh on collective language choices by institutional means, to prescribe the public use of one (or more) language(s), and to adopt language legislation.

12.  Benjanim Boudou and Astrid von Busekist, "Language Proficiency and Migration: An Argument Against Testing," in *Language Policy and Linguistic Justice: Economics, Philosophical and Sociolinguistics Approaches*, ed. Michele Gazzola, Torsten Templin, and Bengt-Arne Wickström (Berlin: Springer, 2018).

13.  States or institutions impose official language(s), manage language diversity in multi-lingual settings, and legislate on international linguistic rules (such as in the EU).

14.  Yael Peled, "Language, Rights and the Language of Language Rights: The Need for a Conceptual Framework in the Political Theory of Language Policy," *Journal of Language and Politics* 10, no. 3 (2011): 445.

15.  See, for example, Reine Meylaerts, "Translational Justice in a Multilingual World," *Meta* 56, no. 4 (2011): 743–57; Gabriel González Núñez, "Translation Policy in a Linguistically Diverse World," *Journal on Ethnopolitics and Minority Issues in Europe* 15, no. 1 (2016): 1–18.

16.  Astrid von Busekist, "The Ethics of Language Policies," *The Routledge Handbook of Ethics and Public Policy*, ed. Annabelle Lever and Andrei Poama (New York: Taylor and Francis, 2017).

17.  We argue this is a systematic way applied to immigrants in Boudou and von Busekist, "Language Proficiency and Migration."

18.  Nancy Fraser and Axel Honneth, *Redistribution or Recognition?* (London: Verso, 2003); Philippe Van Parijs, *Linguistic Justice for Europe and for the World* (New York: Oxford University Press, 2011).

19.  John Dryzec, *Discursive Democracy* (Cambridge: Cambridge University Press, 1990).

20.  Van Parijs, *Linguistic Justice for Europe and the World*.

21.  There is an ongoing debate about the fairness of the territoriality principle. One of the most vocal opponents to territoriality is Helder de Schutter, "The Linguistic Territoriality Principle—A Critique," *Journal of Applied Philosophy* 25, no. 2 (May 2008): 105–20.

22.  In contrast to Will Kymlicka, *Politics in the Vernacular: Nationalism, Multiculturalism and Citizenship* (Oxford: Oxford University Press, 2001), see Brian Barry, who believes that Welsh is not fit to offer such a societal culture. Brian Barry, *Culture and Equality: An Egalitarian Critique of Multiculturalism* (Cambridge: Polity Press, 2001).

23.  Van Parijs, *Linguistic Justice for Europe and for the World*.

24.  Kymicka distinguishes multinationality, being concerned with historical minorities or nations, from polyethnicity of immigrant groups. The rationality regarding historical nations is to provide them with specific and quite far-reaching collective rights, whereas the rationality regarding immigrant groups is to facilitate integration while offering transitional preferential treatment. Kymlicka, *Politics in the Vernacular*.

25.  Laitin and Reich argue for a "non-outcome" oriented language policy in which citizens decide on their language regime. David Laitin and Rob Reich, "A Liberal Democratic Approach to Language Justice," in *Language Rights and Political Theory*, ed. Alan Patten and Will Kymlicka (Oxford: Oxford University Press, 2003), 80–104.

      We owe a more sophisticated account regarding democracy to Rainer Bauböck: instead of supporting territoriality and coercive language policies within given boundaries, he rightly notes that languages are tools for self-government. Establishing a particular language in a given polity is hence "the legitimate outcome of democratic procedures that have been suitably constrained by linguistic freedoms and minority rights" and not an *a priori* requirement for linguistic justice. He endorses an instrumental account of languages framed in egalitarian terms (identity claims are morally relevant but constrained by the rules of democratic self-government). He rejects the fact that *individual* language rights are the building blocks of coercive territorial language regimes: it is rather that a language regime is a democratic choice "constrained by, but not derived from individual language rights." Languages are tools to build self-governing policies. We hence ought to test the legitimacy of language laws by "asking whether they are the result of legitimate exercise of self-government powers." Rainer Bauböck, "The Political Value of Language," *Critical Review of International Social and Political Philosophy* 18, no. 2 (2015): 214, 222, 221.

26. Variants are territorialized individual rights (Catalonia, South Tyrol), sectorial policies for minorities (Australia, United States, Germany, Hungary) and territorial bilingualism for minorities (Estonia, Bosnia, Pakistan). Astrid von Busekist, "Language and Politics," in *International Encyclopedia of Political Science*, ed. Bertrand Badie, Dirk Bergschlosser, and Leonardo Morlino, 8 vols. (London: Sage, 2011), 2070–72.

27. "Every language should be a 'queen in its own territory,'" according to Van Parijs, *Linguistic Justice for Europe and for the World*.

28. José Woehrling, "La protection des minorités nationales dans le système fédéral canadien," in *Le fédéralisme en Belgique et au Canada* (Brussels: De Boeck, 2009); Michel Seymour and Alain-G. Gagnon, eds., *Multinational Federalism: Problems and Prospects* (Basingstoke, UK: Palgrave and Macmillan, 2012).

29. Astrid v. Busekist, ed., *Singulière Belgique* (Paris: Fayard, 2012).

30. Astrd v. Busekist, *La Belgique, Politiques de la langue et construction de l'État: De 1780 à nos jours* (Louvain-la-Neuve, Belgium: De Boeck-Duculot, 1997).

31. Francis Delpérée, "Territorialité ou personnalité linguistique?," in *Langues et Constitutions*, ed. Anne Marie Le Pourhiet (Paris: Economica, 2004).

32. Francis Delpérée, *Le Droit constitutionnel de la Belgique* (Brussels, Belgium: Bruylant, 2000), 394. To settle conflicts between different policies pursued by the two communities and the ensuing inequalities among citizens, Belgium created an arbitration court in 1984 (*cour d'arbitrage*) that became the Belgian "constitutional court" (*cour constitutionnelle*) in the 1990s.

33. The Flemish parliament (Flemish Community parliament) and the Flemish Region are one and the same institution: the Flemish parliament carries out all the competences of the Flemings. The French speakers from Brussels and Wallonia, on the other hand, are administered by three different parliaments and governments, partially overlapping and competent only for francophone matters: the "Commission communautaire française," the Parliament and the government of the Walloon region (all public policies, transportation, economy, and so on), and the government of the French-speaking Community (education, culture, research, health). The three regions (including the German one) have different attributions.

34. Brussels has an independent sociology, a different economy—mainly because of the presence of the European Union—and has suffered less from the severe economic decline that struck Wallonia. In 1968, the University of Leuven/Louvain split during important riots. The Belgian solution to divide the universities equally was to also divide the books in the university libraries with such a wonderful sense of equality that even the reviews were divided: the odd numbered years went to the Flemish side (KUL), and the even ones to the Walloons (UCL).

35. Hugues Dumont, "Le partage des compétences relatives à l'élaboration des normes européennes entre l'Etat belge et ses composantes fédérées," *Revue des Affaires européennes—Law and European Affairs*, no. 1 (2013): 37–53.

36. "The typical plural society is a business partnership in which, to many partners, bankruptcy signifies release rather than disaster." John S. Furnivall, *Colonial Policy and Practice: A Comparative Study of Burma and Netherlands India* (Cambridge: Cambridge University Press, 1948), 307.

37. Until 1999, the parties included the Christian-Democrats in Flanders, the Liberals from 1999 on, and in 2004 the Christian-Democrats anew in an alliance with the N-VA (Nieuwe Vlaamse Alliantie). On the Walloon side, until 2000, the largest francophone Walloon party was the Socialist party (for a long time the biggest socialist party in Europe). In 2007, the Liberals came to power, and in 2009 the Socialists rose anew. Since 1999, at every election there is double alternation.

38. Parity within the federal government is the rule: equal numbers of Flemish and Walloon members renders political decision making more difficult, but this requires representatives of the different communities to negotiate. A sufficient number of issues must mobilize the majority within both communities before any agreement is possible. A number of "special laws" can only pass with two-thirds of the expressed votes and a simple majority in each linguistic assembly (MPs and Senators). To protect the rights of the communities, and if three-fourths of the community representatives feel threatened by a bill, they may engage in a recourse procedure that requires a new discussion over the bill, and the bill can only pass if a two-thirds majority within each community agrees to it. This procedure is called the "alarm bell" (Article 38), and it has only been used once since 1970.

39. Hugues Dumont, "La 'pilarisation' dans la société multiculturelle belge," *La Revue nouvelle* (March 1999): 46–75.

40. Hugues Dumont, "La subsidiarité et le fédéralisme belge: un principe discret ou dangereux," in *Le principe de subsidiarité*, ed. Francis Delpérée (Brussels, Belgium: Bruylant, 2002), 471–493; Hugues Dumont, "Au-delà du principe de territorialité: fédéralisme, intégration et subsidiarité," in *Administration publique: Revue du droit public et des sciences administratives*, vol. 1 (1999), 64–73.

41. Wilfried Dewachter, "La Belgique d'aujourd'hui comme société politique," in *La Belgique, la force de la désunion*, ed. Alain Dieckhoff (Complexe, 1996), 105–42.

42. "Belgium (finally) splits up. Divided along linguistic lines between French and Flemish speakers, the once-unified, French-dominated country has been drifting toward a split for decades. Observers point out that if it weren't for Brussels, a separate, officially bilingual but mainly Francophone enclave inside the Flemish-speaking north, Belgium would have split up long ago. Strangely, it is "Brussels"—in its role as shorthand for the European Union—that could facilitate a divorce. As Europe integrates, national borders will become less important than cultural and ethnic lines." Frank Jacobs and Parag Khanna, "The New World," *New York Times*, September 22, 2012.

43. Philippe Van Parijs, *La Libre Belgique*, February 4, 2005.

44. Laborde argues that citizens should also feel represented (and not alienated) by their institutions. Cécile Laborde, "Political Liberalism and Religion: On Separation and Establishment," *The Journal of Political Philosophy* 21, no. 1 (2013): 67–86. In the case of the eruv debates, this would apply to the rabbinical communities.

45. Robert Goodin, "Enfranchising All Affected Interests, and Its Alternatives," *Philosophy and Public Affairs* 35, no. 1 (Winter 2007): 40–68; Arash Abizadeh, "On the Demos and Its Kin: Nationalism, Democracy, and the Boundary Problem," *American Political Science Review* 106, no. 4 (2012): 867–82.

46. The leader of the Flemish nationalist Right, Bart de Wever, declared in 2008 that "there is no Francophone minority in Flanders, there are only immigrants who need to adapt.". "Les francophones en Flandre sont des 'immigrants qui doivent s'adapter." Bart de Wever, *7SUR7*, August 1, 2008, http://www.7sur7.be/7s7/fr/1861/Crise-politique/article /detail/366175/2008/08/01/Les-francophones-en-Flandre-sont-des-immigrants-qui -doivent-s-adapter.dhtml.
47. See chapter 10 by Michael Karayanni and chapter 11 by Yüksel Sezgin in this volume.
48. Cohen discusses the flawed theoretical defenses of these arguments, namely, by Abner S. Greene and Victor M. Muniz-Fraticelli. Jean L. Cohen, "Sovereignty, the Corporate Religious, and Jurisdictional/Political Pluralism," *Theoretical Inquiries in Law* 18, no. 2 (2017): 547–75.
49. "The moral tasks of liberal democracies are shared between agents of love and agents of justice." Our moral progress has been obtained by agents of love, connoisseurs of diversity, rather than agents of justice, guardians of universality. "The former (agents of love, connoisseurs of diversity) insist that there are people out there whom society has failed to notice. They make these candidates for admission visible by showing how to explain their odd behavior in terms of a coherent, if unfamiliar, set of beliefs and desires—as opposed to explaining this behavior with terms like stupidity, madness, baseness or sin. . . . The latter, the guardians of universality, make sure that once these people are admitted as citizens, once they have been shepherded into the light by the connoisseurs of diversity, they are treated just like all the rest of us." Richard Rorty, *Objectivity, Relativism and Truth, Philosophical Papers*, vol. 1 (Cambridge: Cambridge University Press, 1991), 206.
50. One may argue that threshold thinking is unsatisfactory for many good reasons. What is the threshold between "supreme emergency" and emergency tout court, for example? When should we take action, if any? Michael Walzer, "Emergency Ethics," in *Arguing About War* (New Haven. Conn.: Yale University Press, 2004), 33–50.

# Bibliography

Abizadeh, Arash. "On the Demos and Its Kin: Nationalism, Democracy, and the Boundary Problem." *American Political Science Review* 106, no. 4 (2012): 867–82.
Barry, Brian. *Culture and Equality: An Egalitarian Critique of Multiculturalism*. Cambridge: Polity Press, 2001.
Bauböck, Rainer. "The Political Value of Language." *Critical Review of International Social and Political Philosophy* 18, no. 2 (2015): 212–23.
Boudou, Benjamin, and Astrid von Busekist. "Language Proficiency and Migration: An Argument Against Testing." In *Language Policy and Linguistic Justice: Economics, Philosophical and Sociolinguistics Approaches*, ed. Michele Gazzola, Torsten Templin, and Bengt-Arne Wickström. Berlin: Springer, 2018.
Brubaker, Rogers. "Language, Religion and the Politics of Difference." *Nations and Nationalism* 19, no. 1 (2013): 1–20.
Buchanan, James. "An Economic Theory of Clubs." *Economica* 32, no. 125 (February 1965): 1–14.
Busekist, Astrid von. *La Belgique, Politiques de la langue et construction de l'État: De 1780 à nos jours*. Louvain-la-Neuve, Belgium: De Boeck-Duculot, 1997.
——. "The Ethics of Language Policies." In *The Routledge Handbook of Ethics and Public Policy*, ed. Annabelle Lever and Andrei Poama. New York: Taylor and Francis, 2017.

——. "Language and Politics." In *International Encyclopedia of Political Science*, 8 vols., ed. Bertrand Badie, Dirk Bergschlosser, and Leonardo Morlino, 2070–72. London: Sage, 2011.

——. *Portes et Murs. Des frontières en démocratie*. Paris: Albin Michel, 2016.

——. ed. *Singulière Belgique*. Paris: Fayard, 2012.

Carens, Joseph. *The Ethics of Immigration*. Oxford: Oxford University Press, 2013.

Cohen, Jean L. "Sovereignty, the Corporate Religious, and Jurisdictional/Political Pluralism." *Theoretical Inquiries in Law* 18, no. 2 (2017): 547–75.

Delpérée, Francis, *Le Droit constitutionnel de la Belgique*. Brussels, Belgium: Bruylant, 2000.

——. "Territorialité ou personnalité linguistique?" In *Langues et Constitutions*, ed. Anne Marie Le Pourhiet. Paris: Economica, 2004.

Dewachter, Wilfried. "La Belgique d'aujourd'hui comme société politique." In *La Belgique, la force de la désunion*, ed. Alain Dieckhoff, 105–42. Complexe, 1996.

Dryzec, John. *Discursive Democracy*. Cambridge: Cambridge University Press, 1990.

Dumont, Hugues. "Au-delà du principe de territorialité: fédéralisme, intégration et subsidiarité." In *Administration publique: Revue du droit public et des sciences administratives*, vol. 1, 64–73. 1999.

——. "Le partage des compétences relatives à l'élaboration des normes européennes entre l'Etat belge et ses composantes fédérées," *Revue des Affaires européennes—Law and European Affairs*, no. 1 (2013): 37–53.

——. "La 'pilarisation' dans la société multiculturelle belge." *La Revue nouvelle* (March 1999): 46–75.

——. "La subsidiarité et le fédéralisme belge: un principe discret ou dangereux." In *Le principe de subsidiarité*, ed. F. Delpérée. Brussels, Belgium: Bruylant, 2002.

Failer, Judith."The Draw and Drawbacks of Religious Enclaves in Constitutional Democracy: Hasidic Public Schools in Kiryas Joel." *Indiana Law Review* 72, no. 2 (1997): 382–402.

Fraser, Nancy, and Axel Honneth, *Redistribution or Recognition?* London: Verso, 2003.

Furnivall, John S. *Colonial Policy and Practice: A Comparative Study of Burma and Netherlands India*. Cambridge: Cambridge University Press, 1948.

Gellner, Ernest. *Nations and Nationalism*. Oxford: B. Blackwell, 1983.

Ginsburg, Victor, and Shlomo Weber. *How Many Languages Do We Need? The Economics of Linguistic Diversity*. Princeton, N.J.: Princeton University Press, 2011.

González Núñez, Gabriel. "Translation Policy in a Linguistically Diverse World," *Journal on Ethnopolitics and Minority Issues in Europe* 15, no. 1 (2016): 1–18.

Goodin, Robert. "Enfranchising All Affected Interests, and Its Alternatives." *Philosophy and Public Affairs* 35, no. 1 (Winter 2007): 40–68.

Greene, Abner S. "Kiryas Joel and Two Mistakes About Equality." *Columbia Law Review* 96, no. 1 (1996): 1–104.

Jacobs, Frank, and Parag Khanna, "The New World." *New York Times*, September 22, 2012.

Kymlicka, Will. *Multicultural Odysseys: Navigating the New International Politics of Diversity*. Oxford: Oxford University Press, 2007.

——. *Politics in the Vernacular: Nationalism, Multiculturalism and Citizenship*. Oxford: Oxford University Press, 2001.

Laborde, Cécile. "Political Liberalism and Religion: On Separation and Establishment." *Journal of Political Philosophy* 21, no. 1 (2013): 67–86.

Laitin, David. "What Is a Language Community?" *American Journal of Political Science* 44, no. 1 (2000): 142–55.

Laitin, David, and Rob Reich. "A Liberal Democratic Approach to Language Justice." In *Language Rights and Political Theory*, ed. Alan Patten and Will Kymlicka, 80–104. Oxford: Oxford University Press, 2003.

Lupu, Ira. "Uncovering the Village of Kiryas Joel." *Columbia Law Review* 96, no. 1 (1996): 104–20.

May, Stephen. *Language and Minority Rights: Ethnicity, Nationalism and the Politics of Language.* 2nd ed. New York: Routledge, 2012.

Meylaerts, Reine. "Translational Justice in a Multilingual World." *Meta* 56, no. 4 (2011): 743–57.

Patten, Alan. "Liberal Neutrality and Language Policy." *Philosophy and Public Affairs* 31, no. 4 (2003): 356–86.

Peled, Yael. "Language, Rights and the Language of Language Rights: The Need for a Conceptual Framework in the Political Theory of Language Policy." *Journal of Language and Politics* 10, no. 3 (2011): 436–456.

Réaume, Denise. "Official Language Rights: Intrinsic Value and the Protection of Difference." In *Citizenship in Diverse Societies*, ed. Will Kymlicka and Wayne Norman. Oxford: Oxford University Press, 2000.

Rorty, Richard. *Objectivity, Relativism and Truth, Philosophical Papers.* vol. 1. Cambridge: Cambridge University Press, 1991.

Rosen, Jeffery. "Village People." *The New Republic*, November 4, 1994.

Sands, Phillipe. *East West Street: On the Origins of Genocide and Crimes Against Humanity.* London: Weidenfeld and Nicholson, 2016.

Schragger, Rich C. "The Limits of Localism." *Michigan Law Review* 100, no. 2 (2001): 371–472.

de Schutter, Helder. "The Linguistic Territoriality Principle—A Critique." *Journal of Applied Philosophy* 25, no. 2 (May 2008): 105–20.

Seymour, Michel, and Alain-G. Gagnon, eds. *Multinational Federalism: Problems and Prospects.* Basingstoke, UK: Palgrave and Macmillan, 2012.

Selten, Reinhard, and Jonathan Pool. "The Distribution of Foreign Language Skills as a Game Equilibrium." In *Game Equilibrium Models*, vol. 4, ed. Reinhard Selten, 64–87. Berlin: Springer, 1991.

de Swaan, Abram. *Words of the World.* London: Polity Press, 2001.

Van Parijs, Philippe. *Linguistic Justice for Europe and the World.* Oxford: Oxford University Press, 2011.

Walzer, Michael. "Emergency Ethics." In *Arguing About War*, 33–50. New Haven. Conn.: Yale University Press, 2004.

Woehrling, José. "La protection des minorités nationales dans le système fédéral canadien." In *Le fédéralisme en Belgique et au Canada.* Brussels: De Boeck, 2009.

# CONTRIBUTORS

**Frederick Cooper** is professor of history at New York University. He is the author most
recently of *Colonialism in Question: Theory, Knowledge, History* (2005), *Empires
in World History: Power and the Politics of Difference* (with Jane Burbank, 2010),
*Citizenship Between Empire and Nation: Remaking France and French Africa,
1945–1960* (2014), *Africa in the World: Capitalism, Empire, Nation-State* (2014), and
*Citizenship, Inequality, and Difference: Historical Perspectives* (2018).

**Tsilly Dagan** is a professor of law at Bar-Ilan University. Her book, *International
Tax Policy: Between Competition and Cooperation* was recently published by
Cambridge University Press. Professor Dagan is also the author of numerous
articles, including "International Tax and Global Justice" (2017), "The Currency of
Taxation" (2016), and "The Tax Treaties Myth" (2000).

**Robert Howse** is Lloyd C. Nelson Professor of International Law at New York University
Law School. Among his books are *The Federal Vision: Legitimacy and Levels of
Governance in the United States and the European Union* (coedited with Kalypso
Nicolaidis); *Alexandre Kojève: Outline for a Phenomenology of Right*, translation
with notes and an introductory essay (with Bryan-Paul Frost); and most recently,
*Leo Strauss, Man of Peace*. He is at work on a new manuscript, which is a defense
of populism.

**Christophe Jaffrelot** is senior research fellow at CERI-Sciences Po/CNRS, professor
of Indian politics and sociology at the King's India Institute (London), and
nonresident scholar at the Carnegie Endowment for International Peace. Among
his publications are *The Hindu Nationalist Movement and Indian Politics, 1925
to 1990s* (Columbia University Press, 1996), *India's Silent Revolution* (Columbia
University Press, 2003), and *The Pakistan Paradox. Instability and Resilience* (2015).

**Courtney Jung** is a professor of political science at the University of Toronto. Her work intersects critical theory and identity politics in contemporary political theory and comparative politics. She has received various awards and fellowships in Canada and the United States and is the author of three books and many articles.

**Michael Karayanni** is the Bruce W. Wayne Professor of Law and Dean of the Faculty of Law, Hebrew University of Jerusalem. He was the founding director of the Center of the Study of Multiculturalism and Diversity. He held visiting positions at Georgetown Law Center, Melbourne Law School, Stanford Law School, Yale Law School, and the Institute for Advanced Study in Princeton. His research interests are in private international law and interreligious law, multiculturalism, and civil procedure. Among his most recent publications is *Conflicts in Conflict, a Conflict of Laws Case Study of Israel and the Palestinian Territories* (2014).

**Patrick Macklem** is the William C. Graham Professor of Law at the University of Toronto Faculty of Law. He holds law degrees from Harvard and Toronto, and an undergraduate degree in political science and philosophy from McGill. Professor Macklem's teaching interests include constitutional law, public international law, international human rights law, indigenous peoples, ethnic and cultural minorities, and labor law and policy. He is the author of *The Sovereignty of Human Rights* (2015) and *Indigenous Difference and the Constitution of Canada* (2001); coeditor of *From Recognition to Reconciliation: Essays on the Constitutional Entrenchment of Aboriginal and Treaty Rights* (2016), *Canadian Constitutional Law* (2010), *The Security of Freedom: Essays on Canada's Anti-Terrorism Bill* (2001), and *Labour and Employment Law* (2004); and has published numerous articles on constitutional law, labor law, indigenous peoples and the law, and international human rights law. He is a Fellow of the Royal Society of Canada.

**Jeff Miley** is a lecturer of political sociology at the University of Cambridge. His research focuses on nationalism and empirical democratic theory. He has published widely on dynamics of nationalist conflict and accommodation in Spain and Turkey. He is currently working on a project on comparative struggles for self-determination in the twenty-first century. His most recent publications include "Austerity Politics and Constitutional Crisis in Spain" (2017), "The Nation as Hegemonic Project" (2018), and *Your Freedom and Mine: Abdullah Öcalan and the Kurdish Question in Erdogan's Turkey* (with Federico Venturini, 2018).

**Katharina Pistor** is the Michael I. Sovern Professor of Law at Columbia Law School and director of the Law School's Center on Global Legal Transformation. Her research and teaching spans corporate law, corporate governance, money and finance, property rights, comparative law, and law and development. She has published widely in legal and interdisciplinary journals and is the author coauthor of several books. Her most recent coedited volume is *Governing Access to Essential Resources* (Columbia University Press, 2015). In 2012 she received the Max Planck Research Award on International Financial Regulation, and in 2015 she was elected member of the Berlin-Brandenburg Academy of Sciences. She is also the recipient of research grants by the Institute for New Economic Thinking and the National Science Foundation.

**Emmanuelle Saada** teaches in the Departments of French and History at Columbia University. Her main fields of research are the history of French imperialism and the sociology of immigration to France, with a specific interest in law. Her first book, *Empire's Children: Race, Filiation, and Citizenship in the French Colonies,* was published in English in 2012. Her forthcoming book on the historiography of French colonization is titled *La Colonisation: Une Histoire du Présent.* She is currently working on a project on legality in Algeria and France in the nineteenth century.

**Yüksel Sezgin** is the director of the Middle Eastern Studies program and an associate professor of political science at Syracuse University. He is the author of *Human Rights Under State-Enforced Religious Family Laws in Israel, Egypt and India* (2013). He is currently writing a new book, *Making "Sharia" and Democracy Work: The Regulation and Application of Muslim Family Laws in Non-Muslim Democracies,* which looks at formal integration and administration of Muslim family laws by four non-Muslim democracies: Israel, India, Greece, and Ghana.

**Joshua Simon** is assistant professor of political science at Columbia University. He is the author of *The Ideology of Creole Revolution: Imperialism and Independence in American and Latin American Political Thought* (2017).

**Alfred Stepan** served as the Wallace Sayre Professor of Government at Columbia University. Among his many books are *Democracies in Danger: Problems of Democratic Transition and Consolidation, The Breakdown of Democratic Regimes* (both with Juan J. Linz), and *Crafting State-Nations: India and Other Multinational Democracies* (with Juan J. Linz and Yogendra Yadav). Professor Stepan died as this volume was in press.

**Nadia Urbinati** is Kyriakos Tsakopoulos professor of political theory at the Department of Political Science, Columbia University. She is the author of several books in Italian and English, and more recently of *Democracy Disfigured: Opinion, Truth and the People* (2014) and *Democrazia in diretta* (2013). She is completing a book manuscript on *The Populist Turn* for Harvard University Press.

**Gary Wilder** is a professor in the PdD programs of anthropology, history, and French and director of the Committee on Globalization and Social Change at the Graduate Center of the City University of New York. He is the author of *Freedom Time: Negritude, Decolonization, and the Future of the World* (2015) and *The French Imperial Nation-State: Negritude and Colonial Humanism Between the World Wars* (2005), and coeditor (with Jini Kim Watson) of *The Postcolonial Contemporary: Political Imaginaries for the Global Present* (2018).

## About the Editors

**Andrew Arato** is the Dorothy Hart Hirshon Professor in Political and Social Theory at the New School for Social Research. He is the author of many books, most recently *Post-Sovereign Constitution Making: Learning and Legitimacy* (2016) and *The Adventures of the Constituent Power: Beyond Revolutions?* (2017). He has held Fulbright, Humboldt, and NEH Fellowships and is a former editor of the joeurnal *Constellations*. He is currently researching the role of external forms of intervention in domestic constitution making.

**Jean L. Cohen** is Nell and Herbert Singer Professor of Political Theory in the Department of Political Science at Columbia University. She is the author of many books and articles, including *Globalization and Sovereignty: Rethinking Legality, Legitimacy, and Constitutionalism* (2012) and *Religion, Secularism, and Constitutional Democracy* (with Cecile Laborde, Columbia University Press, 2016). She is currently coeditor of the journal *Constellations* and is researching the issues of solidarity, pluralism, and democratic legitimacy.

**Astrid von Busekist** is professor of political theory at Sciences Po in Paris. She has published on language policy, nationalism, and boundaries. Her latest books include *Ponts et portes: Essai sur la frontière* (2016), *Singulière Belgique* (2012), and *Penser la politique* (2010). She is currently chief editor of *Raisons Politiques*. *Justes Frontières* will be published in 2018.

# INDEX

Abbas, Ferhat, 37
Abi-Mershed, Osama, 100
aboriginal rights, indigenous peoples, in
Canada, and, 129–31
aboriginal title: constitutional pluralism
and, 126–29; indigenous peoples, in
Canada, and, 122–23, 126–29, 139*nn*19–
20, 139*nn*22–26, 140*n*45, 140*nn*25–26
Aceh, Indonesia: Aland Islands and, 160;
federacy and, 159–61; GAM and, 159–61;
MoU and, 160–61; self-government and,
160–61
Adams, John Quincy, 82, 85–86
Adityanath (Yogi), 223, 230*n*51
administrative rationality, subsidiarity and,
19–20
AEF. *See* French Equatorial Africa
Agamben, Giorgio, 170, 174
Agrarian Law, energy development and, 325
Ahtisaari, Martti, 160, 165*n*12
Aland Autonomy Act, federacy and, 151–52
Aland Islands: Aceh and, 160; federacy and,
149–52, 160; Finland and, 150; France
and, 150–51; League of Nations and, 151;
Russia, Imperial, and, 150; sovereignty
and, 149–52; Sweden and, 150; UK and,
150–51; US and, 150–51; USSR and, 151

Alexandrowicz, Charles, 100
Algeria: citizenship and, 37; 1830 convention
and, 102–5; federalism and, 37–38; French
Constitution, 1848, and, 107–8; French
Empire conquest of, 96, 101–9; nationality
and, 105; religious law and, 105–6; rule of
difference and, 96, 107–9; status group
legal pluralism in, 13–14; Tocqueville and,
102; universal suffrage and, 107
Algiers, Regency of, capitulation of, 102–4
Althusius, Johannes, 197–98
American independence movement, as
revolution, 72–73
American political identity: Europe,
defined against, 76–77; Hamilton and,
76–77; imperialism and, 76–77; Western
hemisphere idea and, 78
American System: Anglo-Saxon
supremacism and, 73, 83–88; Clay on,
79–80; Hamilton on, 77; imperialism
and, 86–87, 91*n*34; Monroe Doctrine
and, 80–85; Panama Congress and,
82–85; racism and, 83–88; slavery and,
82–83, 86; Spanish America and, 78–86;
Troppau Protocol and, 80–81
*ampáro*, indigenous peoples, in Mexico,
using, 327, 330, 332